THE COPPER SCROLL DECODED

THE COPPER SCROLL DECODED

One Man's Search for the Fabulous
Treasures of Ancient Egypt

Robert Feather

Thorsons

Thorsons
An Imprint of HarperCollins*Publishers*
77–85 Fulham Palace Road,
Hammersmith, London W6 8JB
The Thorsons website address is: www.thorsons.com

First published in hardback 1999
First published in paperback 2000
10 9 8 7 6 5 4 3 2 1

A catalogue record for this book
is available from the British Library

ISBN 0 7225 3941 X

Printed and bound in Great Britain by
Omnia Books Limited, Glasgow

To Vivien, Adam, Sarah, Jasmine, and Oxyrynchus

CONTENTS

ACKNOWLEDGEMENTS

A large number of people have been hugely generous in giving of their time, consideration and expert opinion during the preparation of this book. I do not list them in any particular order of appreciation. Each and every one has contributed a vital element in the completion of the book.

Thanks are due to the many librarians, archivists and museum personnel who have helped me in the gathering of information from so many different disciplines. Without the works of the authors from whom I quote I could not even have begun to write this book.

There are two people whose initial encouragement, ongoing support and friendship have been invaluable: Caroline Davidson, of The Caroline Davidson Literary Agency; and Professor George J. Brooke, Rylands Professor of Biblical Criticism and Exegesis, The University of Manchester. Co-director, The Manchester–Sheffield Centre for Dead Sea Scrolls Research.

To the many others my gratitude and thanks:

- Dr Rosalie David, Reader and Keeper of Egyptology, The Manchester Museum
- Rabbi William Wolff, Wimbledon and District Synagogue
- Graham Young, Penciuk, Scotland
- Jozef Milik, previously leader of the Dead Sea Scroll translation team at the École Biblique, Jerusalem
- Henri de Contenson, Directeur de Recherche Honoraire au CNRS, France
- Professor John Tait, University College London
- Irene Morley, University College London
- Csaba La'da, Hamburg University, Germany

- Brian Norman, Editorial consultant
- Barry Weitz, Cartographic and textual consultant
- Alice Hunt, The Caroline Davidson Literary Agency
- Donald W. Parry, Brigham Young University, Utah, USA
- Jonathan Stoppi, Qualum computer consultants, London
- Mark Vidler, author of *The Star Mirror*
- Miriam Blank Sachs, West Newton, Massachusetts, USA, for permission to quote a poem from her mother's book, *The Spoken Choice*
- Chris Elston, Chief Executive, London Bullion Market Association
- Lesley Fitton, Department of Greek and Roman Antiquities, The British Museum
- Dr Paul Roberts, Department of Greek and Roman Antiquities, The British Museum
- Paul Craddock, Research Laboratory, The British Museum
- Michelle Pilley, Senior Editor, Thorsons, HarperCollins Publishers
- Belinda Budge, Editorial Director, Thorsons, HarperCollins Publishers
- Paul Redhead, Managing Editor, Thorsons, HarperCollins Publishers
- Suzanne Collins, Picture Editor, HarperCollins Publishers
- Samantha Grant, Editorial Assistant, Thorsons, HarperCollins Publishers
- Aislinn McCormick, Editorial Assistant, Thorsons, HarperCollins Publishers
- Charlotte Ridings, Editor, Thorsons, HarperCollins Publishers
- Adrian Morris, Designer, HarperCollins Publishers
- Elizabeth Hutchins, Freelance Editor
- Christopher O'Hare, Producer/Director, Convergence Productions Ltd
- Lesley-Ann Liddiard, Department of History and Applied Art, National Museums of Scotland
- Andrea Davis, Egyptology Department, Liverpool Museum, Merseyside
- Carol Andrews, Assistant Keeper, Department of Egyptian Antiquities, The British Museum
- Dalia Tracz, Assistant Librarian, Library Services, University College London
- Professor Stefan Reif, Director of the Taylor-Schechter Genizah Research Unit, Cambridge University Library. Professor of Medieval Hebrew Studies, Cambridge University
- Gwil Owen, Faculty of Archaeology and Anthropology, Cambridge University
- Dott Carla Gallorini, Librarian, The Egypt Exploration Society, London
- P.W. Van Boxel, Librarian, Leo Baeck College, London
- Lionel Bochurberg, Avocat au Barreau de Paris, France
- Martin Stammers, The Institute of Materials, London
- Dr Jack Harris, Consultant metallurgist and lecturer
- Jonathan Williams, Curator, Department of Coins and Medals, British Museum, London
- Robert Shrager, Consultant Historian, Chairman, House of Fraser plc

FOREWORD

The Dead Sea Scrolls have played a part in popular imagination for over fifty years. Their public appeal stems from a distinct combination of factors. Reflecting some of the highest human aspirations, they were found in caves near the lowest place on earth, in an area where it was thought no ancient manuscripts could have survived. Against the odds the scrolls speak to us from 2,000 years ago. They tell us of the time when the Pharisees established their dominance and formed the religion which was the immediate predecessor of the Rabbinic Judaism, which in many ways is still with us. They describe for us much of the background of Christianity, in their portrayal of views of the end times and their expressions of messianic hope. They fill a void which historians and theologians of many generations have tried to sketch in vain.

Of all the Dead Sea Scrolls, however, none is more fascinating than the famous Copper Scroll. Here is what seems to be a list of buried treasure, perhaps in quantities that would impress even the richest person today, engraved peculiarly on copper pieces, written in a Hebrew which is difficult to decipher, with several coded elements in Greek. After over a generation of study by some of the best modern detectives of the ancient world it still refuses to yield all its secrets.

Robert Feather's study represents the best work of the English amateur, a tradition of research which is based on asking common-sense questions from a variety of angles, and then pursuing the answers doggedly so as to take the discussion forward. The great enthusiasm with which the work is written may result in more being said than the sceptic might allow, but there are some nuggets of insight here which even the authors of the Copper Scroll might well have recognized.

From the outset the debate about the meaning of the Copper Scroll was focused on whether the treasure was real or fantastic. To begin with, those on the side of realism were few and far between. They were argued against vociferously by some experts whose principal evidence was that the weights of the gold and silver mentioned in the scroll were simply incredible – producing a total of precious metal which exceeded all that had been smelted in the world until then. The realists could only argue back that to inscribe a fantasy on expensive copper plates with such care and with elements of code seemed to be playing a game too far.

Nevertheless, in recent years the reality of the treasure has become increasingly accepted by the experts, but always with qualified remarks about the quantities. Now Robert Feather, from his own background expertise as a metallurgist, offers us a very intriguing interpretation of the troublesome signs for weights, by reading them in light of Egyptian systems of a somewhat earlier time. The results may not convince everybody, but as far as understanding the system of weights and measures in use by the authors of the scroll is concerned, they are a valuable contribution to the ongoing, weighty debate.

Significantly too, Robert Feather recognizes almost instinctively that the Dead Sea Scrolls deserve to be set in a broader context than that of the desolate desert domicile of the Qumran-Essenes. The scrolls can no longer be marginalized by historians and theologians alike. More than any other evidence, the biblical manuscripts from Qumran tell us about the transmission of what were to become the official canonical books of the Hebrew Bible in the three centuries before the Romans destroyed the Jerusalem Temple in 70 CE. Furthermore, the manuscripts which describe the life of what most take to be the Essene sect, show them not to be a narrow-minded group of bigots, but sharing much in common with their Jewish neighbours and thoroughly involved in the arguments and debates of the period.

Most significantly, however, over half of the manuscripts found in the caves near Qumran describe Judaism more broadly than their sectarian traditors may have supposed: here to be rediscovered by us today are the wisdom texts, the prayers and the poems, the biblical interpretations, the astronomical calculations, and the best-loved stories of a golden age of Jewish literature. The comparable flourishing of Jewish literature in Egypt in the late Second Temple period is an obvious, but seldom recognized, place to start looking for evidence which might help in the better appreciation of the Dead Sea Scrolls themselves.

Robert Feather's work is also stimulating for the way it raises acutely a major historiographical problem. Put simply, the issue is about how two apparently similar phenomena should be related. Some scholars naturally tend to split all the evidence into minute pieces and, in so doing, to stress the differences between things; however similar things may seem, they can rarely be directly associated with one another. Other readers of the same evidence will tend to put things together and in so doing emphasize the similarities; differences are explained away through acknowledging that the evidence comes from alternative times and contexts, but the similarities remain and often suggest a direct causal relationship between the two phenomena. Those who read this book will be faced with placing themselves in one school of thought or the other.

This same historiographical issue has bedevilled Qumran scholarship of late. Some voices have shouted loudly that the scrolls found in the caves have nothing to do with the people who lived at Qumran, but were placed there by others from another place. Others have highlighted the differences between the classical descriptions of the Essenes in the writings of Philo, Pliny and Josephus and the descriptions in the scrolls of the community and the wider movement of which it was a part. All the evidence is split up and emphasis put upon how little can be known. Other scholars have argued forcefully that what the site of Qumran, the manuscripts in the caves and the descriptions of the Essenes in the classical sources have in common, far outweighs some few discrepancies which can be accounted for relatively simply. Neither side has yet won the argument.

Here is a book that spans times and places in its own challenging, historiographical way. We are forced to ask many questions. Was the treasure real? Has some of it been found? Is there still some located in the places suggested? Are the scrolls pointing us to temples and priests further away from Qumran in time and place than previously imagined? Should we view not only the Judaism of the late Second Temple differently, but even the very origins of Israelite monotheism? Is this synthetic reading of such varied evidence more fabulous than the enigmatic Copper Scroll itself? Let the reader decide.

George J. Brooke
Rylands Professor of Biblical Criticism and Exegesis
The University of Manchester

CHAPTER ONE

THE COPPER SCROLL
– TWO THOUSAND YEARS
IN HIDING

Three-and-a-half hours of bumping across the rolling sandy hills of the Judaean Desert is not the easiest way to approach Qumran from Jerusalem. Passing picture-book monasteries in a bleak landscape dotted with rock-strewn mounds and occasional makeshift shelters, you see scenery that has not changed for thousands of years. Stopping on a high point of Mount Muntar to view the pastel shades of Mar Saba Monastery, you turn to find two small, dusky, Arab children and a donkey, who have appeared from nowhere to beg alms and stare wide-eyed at these invaders of their lonely land. When your open truck finally shudders to a halt, perched high on a cliff overlooking the Dead Sea, the heat is oppressive, your back is aching, and you wonder if it was really all worthwhile. The breath-taking view that meets your eyes soon dispels all doubts! *(see Plate 1.)*

Below lies a vast beige-hued, flat coastal plain, cut by a dark strip of road, and patched by green rectangles of cultivation, sparse outcrops of boulders and scraggy trees. Beyond, in the far distance, you can almost taste the salty indigo thickness of the Dead Sea as it merges from violets and mauves into soft blue skies.

Here is where my story begins, and where I saw for the first time the ruins left by a mysterious lost 'community' of pious, frugal, religious ascetics – the 'Qumran-Essenes' – who lived on the shores of the Dead Sea in the Biblical land of Judaea. The famous Dead Sea Scrolls, concealed in caves overlooking the Dead Sea, comprise the oldest collection of Biblical documents ever discovered.[1] Documents of immense importance to biblical scholars, and with profound implications for all the major western religions.

It was the start of a journey of enquiry that would take me back to the time when the Scrolls were written down and copied out – the era of Jesus. Back a further 1,500 years to the time of Abraham and Sarah and their encounter with an Egyptian pharaoh, to the time of Jacob and Joseph and their meeting with the most enigmatic of pharaohs, and to the time of Moses, Prince of Egypt, as he led his people to the promised land of Canaan.

As I scrambled about the rock-strewn wadis and rolling foothills behind Qumran, my guide, Avner Goren, pointed out two low-lying caves, one of which he referred to as 'Cave 3', where the Copper Scroll of the Essenes had been found back in 1952. I had read about this strange artefact, but now saw for the first time the place where the Qumran-Essenes had hidden perhaps their most precious of scrolls, some 2,000 years earlier.

As a metallurgist, with a Jewish background and knowledge of Hebrew, I found the Copper Scroll of special interest and was, quite naturally, intrigued by the unusual use of this material as a means of record. Even more tantalizing was the fact that this scroll contains a list of hidden treasure, none of which had previously been found. Conventional translations of the Copper Scroll seemed to me to give totally unrealistic numerical values and weights relating to the treasure, contrary to all my knowledge of metallurgy and experience in the refining of precious metals. So I began to question these traditional interpretations.

I had studied metallurgy at university, almost as a random choice. Several of us at Marylebone Grammar School had decided to go to London University simply because we were friends, and I spent many happy hours in the warm basement of Sir John Cass College trying to extract metals from their ores, or purifying gold by scorification.[2] I eventually qualified as a professional metallurgist and subsequently became a Chartered Engineer, working initially on the refining and assaying of precious metals, and later for the then British Iron and Steel Corporation. When the call of clattering typewriter keys called me to journalism, I joined *Steel Times* as Assistant Editor, and then edited *The British Foundryman*. Later I launched a journal for the Institution of Metallurgists, and a magazine on metrology.[3]

COINCIDENCE OR MIRACLE?

There are conflicting accounts of the finding of the first of the Dead Sea Scrolls, but what we can be certain about is that they were found by Arab Bedouin,[4] and that the date was early 1947.

The story of how the original seven major scrolls* found by Mohammed edh-Dhib and his brother in what became known as Cave 1 were bought on behalf of the State of Israel, prior to 1967, is strange in itself. After passing through the hands of various intermediaries, three of the scrolls found by the Bedouin were finally acquired by Professor E.L. Sukenik, of the Hebrew University of West Jerusalem, on the very day the United Nations voted for the re-creation of the State of Israel – 29 November 1947. The recovery into Jewish hands of this first 'treasury' of lost documents has about it an almost miraculous co-incidentality after they had lain hidden for almost 2,000 years in a dusty cave. It is almost as if God said, 'Let's start again and here is a reminder of My words and some of My words that you have never seen. Also I will give you back your Promised Land this very same day!' The other four major scrolls from Cave 1 were recovered by Professor Sukenik's son, Yigael Yadin, in 1954.

At the time of the finding of Cave 1 the territory was part of the British Mandate of Palestine, but after Israel's War of Independence in 1948–49, it became part of the Hashemite Kingdom of Jordan. Between 1949 and 1967, Bedouin and archaeologists under the jurisdiction of the Jordanian Antiquities Department (led by Father Roland de Vaux, Head of the Dominican École Biblique et Archéologique Française, in Jerusalem), between them recovered all the known contents of the remaining 10 caves, except for one major scroll from Cave 11. This latter 'Temple Scroll' was recovered by the Israelis during the 1967 Six-Day War.

DATING THE DEAD SEA SCROLLS

The general consensus of opinion amongst historians is that the Dead Sea Scrolls from Qumran were written or copied between 350 BCE** and 68 CE. These conclusions are based on archaeological studies of associated artefacts, palaeological comparisons of ancient writing, and scientific analysis using radiocarbon dating and Accelerator Mass Spectroscopy (AMS).[5]

Radiocarbon analysis is a particularly useful tool in dating carbonaceous materials and, with modern techniques, can provide dates

---

* The seven scrolls comprise two almost complete versions of the Old Testament Book of Isaiah, a War Scroll and a Manual of Discipline for the Qumran-Essenes, a commentary on Habakkuk, a Genesis Apocryphon and a scroll of Thanksgiving Psalms.

** Before Common (or Christian) Era – i.e., before 1 BC. CE or Common (Christian) Era corresponds to AD 1 and after.

accurate to within tens of years. The principle on which it works is based on the presence of the Carbon 14 isotope in all organic materials, such as parchment, papyrus, leather, or linen. When a living organism dies it stops taking in Carbon 14 from the atmosphere; the radioactivity bound in the isotope decays at a precisely measurable rate, with a predictable half-life of 5730 years. (*See Glossary – Carbon Dating.*) Given this predictable rate of decay, scientists are thus able to calculate the age of the material being tested.

Until the early 1990s radiocarbon dating required several grams of organic material for a measurement, but AMS has reduced the sample requirement to under 2mg, and much more use is now being made of the technique. A recent sample test, for example, at the AMS facility of the Institute für Mittelenergiephysik, Zurich, Switzerland,[6] dated the Isaiah Scroll to 205–200 BCE. Other tests done in 1994 at the Arizona AMS Laboratory, University of Arizona, in Tucson,[7] gave results of between 400–200 BCE for the Testament of Kohath Scroll, 100–0 BCE for the Temple Scroll, 80–0 BCE for the Genesis Apochryphon Scroll and 75 BCE–60 CE for the Thanksgiving Psalms Scroll.

In theory, radiocarbon dating is more accurate than any other form of dating (with its accuracy being confirmed by correlation with palaeographic studies, which are, to some extent, subjective). The Standard Deviation (SD) for radiocarbon dating for the period of the Scrolls is ±40 years, with a best achievable result of ±25 years. Radiocarbon dating's main weakness is that it does not determine when the *text* was actually written, but only the earliest date the writing base material was made. Analyses of ink media can, however, give additional information, and this is a subject we will return to later.

In their entirety, the Dead Sea Scroll collection comprises many almost complete scrolls, together with some 80,000 individual scroll fragments, that form part of about 830 different documents. They are generally attributed as being part of a library kept by a small, secretive, monastic sect, the Qumran-Essenes, who are known from archaeological evidence and historical records to have inhabited the area between 150 BCE and 68 CE. Many of these documents are now thought to have been copied, or originally written, by the Essenes.

THE CONTENTS OF THE SCROLLS

The scrolls include extracts of writings from all the Books of the Old Testament (except the Book of Esther), apocryphal and pseudepigraphic texts, Biblical commentaries and expansions, and sectarian writings of the Qumran-Essenes describing activities peculiar to them – such as descriptions of their ritual immersion in water and initiation ceremonies. (*See Glossary – Dead Sea Scrolls.*)

The scrolls constitute a definitive record of early Jewish life and religious beliefs, untrammelled by the subsequent editing and mistranslations of later copied documents. Nor have the contents of the scrolls been subjected to the Rabbinic and Christian censorship of later mediaeval documents. They have, however, been subjected to modern partisan interpretation and delays in publication, mainly for reasons of personal aggrandizement, which means that half of the texts still await official publication.[8] I am not going to open that particular cupboard of 'skeletons' at the moment, but we will look in later on, when it is germane to the story.

From what has been published, it is clear that the scrolls throw new light on the early days of Judaism and Christianity, on the surrounding culture, and on the strange activities that took place at Qumran.

The excitement these finds generated, both in the public and in academic circles, was unprecedented and, if anything, has increased with the passing of time. As the oldest known collection of Biblical texts ever discovered, they pre-date all previous Hebrew written texts by almost 900 years.

There are very different views as to the origins of those of the Dead Sea Scrolls that are thought to be original works of the Qumran-Essenes, like the War Scroll. Some scholars take the view that they are rooted in the post-First Temple* period of the prophets Ezekiel and Habakkuk, around 600 BCE. Others consider the texts to have been based on 2nd or 1st century BCE experience. All are convinced that they are of immense importance in evaluating the early beliefs of the Jewish and Christian faiths and, subsequently, the Muslim faith.

WHO WERE THE QUMRAN-ESSENES?

Although the affiliations of the people that lived at Qumran are mentioned by contemporary commentators, such as Josephus, Pliny the Elder and Philo,[9] their 'eye-witness' reports vary in important details and are quite sketchy. These commentators are assumed to be talking about a sect of the Essene movement which existed in Judaea at the

---

* The First Jerusalem Temple, built around 930 BCE, was destroyed in 586 BCE by the Babylonians.

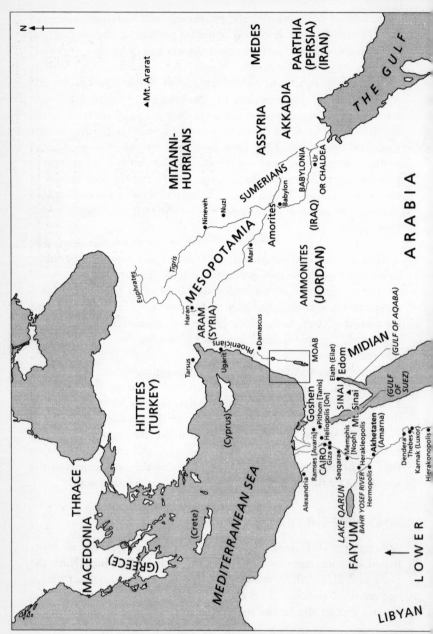

Figure 1: Relational map of the Ancient Middle East.

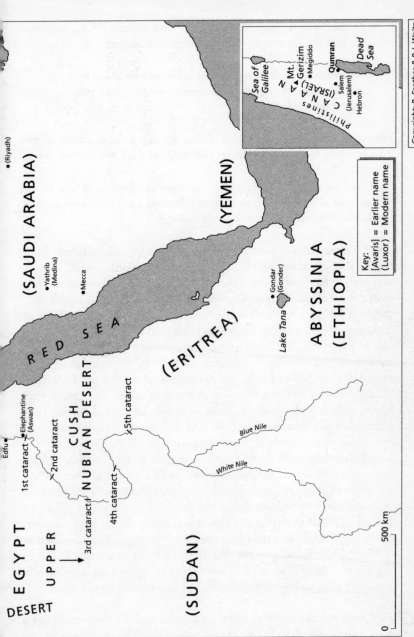

EGYPT

DESERT

UPPER

Edfu •

1st cataract •Elephantine (Aswan)

2nd cataract

CUSH

3rd cataract NUBIAN DESERT

4th cataract

×5th cataract

RED SEA

(SUDAN)

White Nile

Blue Nile

•Gondar (Gonder)

Lake Tana

(ERITREA)

ABYSSINIA (ETHIOPIA)

(SAUDI ARABIA)

•(Riyadh)

•Yathrib (Medina)

•Mecca

(YEMEN)

Sea of Galilee

N Mt. ▲ Gerizim •Megiddo

C A N A A N (ISRAEL)

•Qumran

Salem (Jerusalem)

Dead Sea

Hebron

Philistines

Key: [Avaris] = Earlier name (Luxor) = Modern name

0   500 km

Copyright: R. Feather & B.J. Weitz

time of the Second Temple, around the 2nd century BCE, and who survived into the 1st century CE. As Josephus describes:

> They assemble themselves together again into one place; and when they have clothed themselves in white veils, they then bathe their bodies in cold water.[10]

Pliny the Elder has the 'Esseni' living in the Judaean desert above En-Gedi and following a celibate lifestyle,[11] whilst Philo says of them:

> They have shown themselves especially devout in the service of God, not by sacrificing living animals, but by deeming it proper to prepare their own minds as befits their sacred calling.[12]

The Qumran-Essenes practised a form of Judaism quite different from that of the rest of the people. They eschewed personal wealth, living a very simple life, and devoted themselves to religious observance. They disapproved of the Temple in Jerusalem – the very heart of Jewish worship – believing it to be wrongly constructed, its priests to be 'sons of darkness' and the festivals the priests celebrated to be held at the wrong times of the year! This last point was based on the fact that the Essenes used their own solar-based calendar, rather than the more usual lunar calendar. They believed in a final apocalypse when two good Messiahs would come to save the world at the end of time. Their dead were buried naked, without adornments, in simple unmarked graves. They believed in the immortality of the soul and in some form of afterlife, but not in their own physical resurrection.

Modern historians disagree on the origins of the Qumran-Essenes and aren't even sure as to what they were really doing at Qumran. Their arrival and departure are shrouded in mystery. Archaeological evidence indicates that they were settled on the shores of the Dead Sea at least by 150 BCE. Their tranquil way of life was abruptly shattered by an earthquake in 31 BCE, and they temporarily left the area. They returned in 4 BCE[13] – interestingly, in the year accepted by most scholars as that of the birth of Jesus – or am I just letting my fondness for coincidences run away with me! By 68 CE they were gone, no-one knows where.

As I explored the ruins of Qumran I could still see the remains of a large room with low ledges around the walls. This is known as the 'scriptorium', where 20 or so scribes must have laboured at their work of copying and writing the Dead Sea Scrolls.[14] The materials they wrote on were parchment, papyrus, leather and clay. However, on 20 March 1952,[15] a very strange scroll was unearthed, one which was engraved on almost pure copper – the so-called Copper Scroll.

The Copper Scroll was discovered in a cave, some 2km north of Qumran, by an archaeological group led by Henri de Contenson working for the American School of Oriental Research, the École Biblique et Archéologique Française de Jerusalem and the Palestine Archaeological Museum. The roof of the 10m-deep cave had collapsed, sealing it with a large boulder. Within the 3m-deep chamber that remained, lying against the northern wall, were two pieces of copper scroll – one on top of the other *(see Plate 2.)*

Why on earth would the Qumran-Essenes have had a scroll of copper?

Its contents and nature have never been fully explained and, to this day, nearly 50 years after its discovery, they remain an enigma. Experts in the field do not agree about the scroll's origins, its dating, its translation, or even its reason for existing, and they remain baffled by its confusing contents. As I set about unravelling its mysteries it became increasingly clear that this apparently incongruous scroll is not only a catalogue of fabulous ancient treasures, but also an historical document with momentous implications for our understanding of modern religions and beliefs.

CHAPTER TWO

BULLION
BY THE BILLION

My increasing interest in the Dead Sea Scrolls was further sparked in 1996, when I visited the 'Genizah' collection of arcane texts held at the University of Cambridge, and heard that some of these manuscripts, found in Cairo at the end of the 19th century, were common to the much earlier texts of the Qumran-Essenes. I also learned that a three-day international conference, specifically devoted to the Copper Scroll, was due to be held at Manchester in September. I could not resist attending as my metallurgical curiosity was aroused by the idea that copper was used as a writing medium 2,000 years ago.

I was soon to discover that many thousands of researchers, scholars, academics, historians and theologians were beavering away around the world, deciphering and analysing the voluminous contents of the Dead Sea Scrolls. Most of these people were also interested in the Copper Scroll.

When the Copper Scroll was discovered it was in an highly oxidized condition, and had broken into two separate rolled up sections. In its original state it measured 0.3m in width, 2.4m in length, and was about 1mm thick. No-one knew quite how to open it up without damaging the text. One lunatic suggestion was to try to reduce the copper oxides with hydrogen, or even electrolysis, to recover the copper! After considerable preparatory research, John Allegro of Oxford University, a member of the original international translation team working on the Dead Sea Scrolls in Jerusalem,[1] persuaded Lankester Harding, Director of the Department of Antiquities of Jordan, and Father Roland de Vaux, Head of the École Biblique in Jerusalem, to let him take one of the copper pieces to England. There the first piece of scroll was finally 'opened' by Professor H. Wright Baker at Manchester College of Technology (now UMIST) in 1955, followed by the second piece in 1956. The technique Wright Baker used was to coat the outside of the scroll with Araldite adhesive and then slice the scroll, using a 4,000th/inch-thick saw, into 23 separate sections *(see Plate 2 (bottom))*. (Ever since that time Manchester has retained a special interest in the Copper Scroll.)

THE LANGUAGE OF THE COPPER SCROLL

In academic circles the Copper Scroll is known, rather prosaically, as 3Q15, the 3Q indicating that it was found in Cave 3 at Qumran. The scroll was written in an early form of Hebrew – a square-form script – and has been shown to have linguistic affinities to pre-Mishnaic Hebrew and Aramaic *(see Glossary)*, with some terms only comprehensible through study of Arabic and Akkadian cognates.[2] Other Dead Sea Scrolls were written in square-form Aramaic script, or the so-called 'Paleo-Hebrew' script, derived from 'Proto-Canaanite' – itself an evolution from 'Ugarit', Egyptian hieroglyphs and 'Phoenician'.[3]

There are many unusual things about the Copper Scroll, but the language in which it is engraved is one of the major puzzles for scholars. The Hebrew palaeography (style of script) and orthography (spelling) in the Copper Scroll is quite unlike anything found in other texts of the time, from Qumran or from elsewhere. Palaeographic analysis shows the style of writing to be relatively crude, partly because the artisans working on the scroll had to tap the shapes out with fairly primitive tools, and partly because they appear to have had difficulty in reading some of the material they seemed to be copying from.

The scroll doesn't fall into the category of being a religious or literary document, unlike other Dead Sea Scrolls. It contains words, particularly architectural terms, which are not found in any other of the scrolls. The Copper Scroll is truly a 'one off', totally unlike any of the other Qumran scrolls. It has, nevertheless, been almost unanimously classified as one of the Dead Sea Scrolls, and now resides in the Archaeological Museum of Amman, in Jordan.

I knew from my experience in handling non-ferrous metals that engraving on copper, at the period before 68 CE (the *terminus ante quem* for its production[4]), would have been an extremely expensive and laborious process. Its use indicates the importance the Qumran-Essenes attached to this text and their determination that it should not deteriorate easily – unlike parchment or papyrus.

The next step, obviously, after its opening was to decipher and translate the scroll's contents. Not such an easy task in view of the 'odd' nature of the writing, style and language. So difficult, in fact, that different versions are still coming out to this day, and scholars argue relentlessly about how best to read individual letters![5]

It was because of these differences in scholarly interpretations that I felt I had something to contribute to the debate, by bringing a scientist's view to the problem. Virtually all those currently working in the field of Dead Sea Scroll research are linguistic scholars, historians, theologians or archaeologists attached to learned institutions. They tend not to be highly numerate; there are almost no engineers and, to my knowledge, no metallurgists studying the problem. Little did I know then that metallurgy would provide the lever to prise open the secrets of the Copper Scroll.

DECIPHERING THE COPPER SCROLL

In essence the Copper Scroll contains a list of 64 locations,* spread over a wide geographical area, where large quantities of gold, silver, jewellery, precious perfumes, ritual clothing and other scrolls were said to be buried. Because of their relative rarity, all these materials would have been of considerable value in the ancient world. Perfumes, oils and unguents, for example, were sought after items that could have come from distant lands, whilst ritual clothing would have been heavily embroidered with gold and silver thread.

The first translation of the Copper Scroll was done by John Allegro in Manchester, and the first published translation (in French) was by Father J.T. Milik, in 1959.[6] John Allegro, a member of the original translation team, strongly disagreed with the content of this published translation, but his superiors in Jerusalem would not permit him to publish his version. They liked to keep a tight control on everything in their possession and make sure that their official stamp was on all related publications.

The mixture of frustration and excitement soon became too much for John Allegro as he began to realize that there were other – more

---

* Most translators agree that there are 64 treasure locations listed in the Copper Scroll, although John Allegro only lists 61 items in his *The Treasure of the Copper Scroll*, published in 1960 by Routledge & Kegan Paul.

sinister – reasons for the strictures that were being put on him. In particular, the Copper Scroll contents tended to undermine the official line that the Qumran-Essenes were not interested in worldly goods. He relieved his frustration by mounting two archaeological expeditions to Jordan hoping to find some of the treasure mentioned in the Copper Scroll, in December 1959 and again in March 1960. Like many who get lost in the desert, he wandered around in a circle, eventually coming back to where he started from, having found absolutely nothing.

John Allegro's frustration with the École Biblique team in Jerusalem was only vented when he disregarded his 'masters' orders' and published an English version of the translation in 1960, under the title *The Treasure of the Copper Scroll*.[7] The reasons put about after his book came out for trying to delay its publication, and for not allowing him to use photographs of the scroll text, were that the Jerusalem 'team' feared an invasion of treasure hunters storming down to the area of Qumran and interfering with their serious work. A more probable explanation was that the Copper Scroll's listing of vast treasures conflicted with the already committed view that the Qumran-Essenes were an impoverished, spiritual community that eschewed wealth of any kind.

Scholars, notably Father Roland de Vaux, Head of the École Biblique et Archéologique Française de Jerusalem, and Father Jozef Milik, a member of the original Dead Sea Scrolls translation team, denounced John Allegro's translation as defective, and even cast doubts on the authenticity of the Copper Scroll's contents, assigning them to folklore. Others were not so sure.

The Jerusalem team's translation finally came out in 1962, entitled 'Les "Petites Grottes" de Qumran'[8] in the *Discoveries in the Judaean Desert* series. Although this is the 'official' version, there is no accepted 'definitive' translation of the Copper Scroll to date, and all of the numerous editions that have been published have many significant variations.

Most scholars, however, are now convinced that the Copper Scroll was engraved by the Qumran-Essenes and that it forms part of the Dead Sea Scrolls.[9] Nevertheless, opinion still differs as to whether the Copper Scroll was an original piece of work by the Qumran-Essenes. Some scholars suggest that it was copied, possibly from an earlier document. I tend towards this latter view and, later on, I will put forward my own arguments as to the origins of the Copper Scroll.

In conventional translations of the Copper Scroll[10] the weight of gold mentioned in the various locations is generally given as adding up to a staggering 26 tonnes, with 65 tonnes of silver,[11] although different understandings of the terms for gold and silver allow totals of approximately 44 tonnes of gold and 23 tonnes of silver to be arrived at.

When the weights of the treasures itemized in the Copper Scroll are added up, we reach the following:

Gold	1285 Talents
Silver	666 Talents
Gold and silver	17 Talents
Gold and silver vessels	600 Talents
Mixed precious metals	2,088 Talents, 21 Minas, 4 Staters

Items with unspecified weights are as follows:

Gold ingots	165
Silver bars	7
Gold and silver vessels	609

In Biblical Talent terms, the sheer weight of the gold and silver is enormous. One Talent is estimated to have weighed about 76lb or 34.47kg, a Mina about 0.5kg, whilst a Stater was a coin (equivalent to a half Shekel) weighing about 5g.[12]

Where weights are given of the listed treasures, the approximate amounts of precious metals, using a Biblical Talent weight of 34.47kg, are as follows:

Gold	44.3 tonnes	today worth approx. £414 million
Silver	22.9 tonnes	today worth approx. £3 million
Mixed precious metals	93.2 tonnes	today worth approx. £583 million

In addition, there are lists where no weights are given but enormous quantities of precious materials are mentioned. These lists are divided into 12 columns, and itemize the location and type of treasure hidden.

The Copper Scroll seems to be referring to precious metals worth around £1 billion at current prices, but whose intrinsic historic value would be many, many times this figure!

Measuring some 2.4m (8 feet) in length, the Copper Scroll was engraved in 12 vertical columns, each of between 13 and 17 lines of right-to-left reading text, some 30cm deep.

Table 1: Indication of where valuable items are mentioned in the textual columns of the Copper Scroll

	Col.1	Col.2	Col.3	Col.4	Col.5	Col.6	Col.7	Col.8	Col.9	Col.10	Col.11	Col.12
Gold Bars	100	65										
Silver Bars								*	*			
Precious Metals	*	*	*	*	*	*	*	*	*	*	*	*
Money Chests	*									*	*	
Vessels			*		*					*		*
Ritual Clothing	*		*									
Pitchers/Jugs		600		*			*	*			*	
Scrolls						*		*				*
Unguents/Oils											*	
Pine/Resins										*	*	

Where numerical amounts of precious materials are given in the text of the Copper Scroll these are indicated in the Table. The asterisks indicate where only a more general description of precious materials is mentioned in particular columns of the text.

WHOSE TREASURES WERE THEY?

The scroll does not reveal by whom, or when, the treasures were buried, let alone why. But from some of the recognizable place-names mentioned, the treasures are generally assumed to have been hidden within Judaea or near to Mount Gerizim in Samaria (both parts of modern Israel), and to relate to treasures of the Second, or possibly First, Temple of Jerusalem. Both temples were known to be places where considerable wealth was accumulated through donations of sacrificial gifts and tithes.

The First Temple of Jerusalem was built by King Solomon, around 930 BCE, to house the Ark of the Covenant containing the Ten Commandments, and to be the central place of worship for the Israelites. After its destruction by the Babylonians in 586 BCE, it was partly rebuilt some 50 years later and became known as the Second Temple. Its reconstruction continued until a final reconstitution was undertaken by Herod the Great around 30 BCE. It was subsequently destroyed by the Romans in 70 CE.

The Copper Scroll makes no mention of the Qumran-Essenes, nor does it contain any of their sectarian style of terminology.[13] Controversy over the origins of the treasures listed in the Copper Scroll has led to the proposition of almost as many conspiracy theories as those put forward for President Kennedy's assasination. There are, however, five main theories held by modern scholars.

These are that the treasures were:

a) hidden by the Qumran-Essenes and came from the Second Temple in Jerusalem *just prior* to its destruction by the Romans in 70 CE

b) hidden by predecessors of the Qumran-Essenes and came from the First Temple in Jerusalem *at the time* of its destruction by the Babylonians under Nebuchadnezzar

c) hidden by the Qumran-Essenes before 68 CE and belonged to them

d) not real, and that the Scroll was a hoax perpetrated by the Qumran-Essenes[14]

e) from the Second Temple, but were hidden by priests or others coming out of Jerusalem, and that the Qumran-Essenes did not write the Dead Sea Scrolls.[15]

(There is another theory, that the treasures were collected and hidden in Jerusalem, after the destruction of the Second Temple, suggested some 35 years ago by Manfred Lehmann and some others,[16] but there is little following for that idea today.)

There are counter-arguments to all these theories; the main elements of these are listed below in the same order:

a) the Qumran-Essenes held the priests and those attending the Second Temple unworthy and even contemptible (a theme taken up by Jesus in his ministry). Relations would hardly have been consistent with the Second Temple priests entrusting the Qumran-Essenes with any treasures. The testimony of Josephus[17] on the antipathy between Jerusalem and the Qumran-Essenes also conflicts with this possibility

b) the intervening period is too long; the Qumran-Essenes were not established at Qumran for another 300 years

c) an impoverished small community would not have been able to acquire such priceless treasures

d) engraving on copper was an expensive and difficult business – the scroll was obviously intended to have some permanency. The 'realism' in the style and content of writing, so unlike any other ancient legends, and the lack of any sensible explanation of why the Qumran-Essenes would invent such information tends to refute this idea. Who would they be trying to fool? The Qumran-Essenes were the people of righteousness and truth. Elaborate and expensive frauds were not their style

e) the close connection between the Copper Scroll and the Qumran-Essenes, and the difficulty in imagining how or why vast Temple treasures were hidden prior to 68 CE, before the Temple came under threat.

The majority of scholars, such as John Allegro, Kyle McCarter, Judah Lefkovits, Michael Wise, David Wilmot and Al Wolters,[18] now favour the theory that the treasures came from the Second Temple, and were hidden by the Essenes (or others), just before its destruction. Part of their justification for this theory is that the Triumphal Arch of Titus in Rome, depicts items of treasure, such as trumpets and the seven-branched candlestick, carried off by the Romans when they captured Jerusalem. Whilst the Copper Scroll describes other items of Temple treasure, it makes no mention of any of the items depicted on the Arch of Titus, so there is a sort of logic *in absentia*.

Most scholars discount the theory of the First Temple as being the source of the listed treasures. There are two protagonists of the theory, however, Conklin and Andrea,[19] who have expounded a curious idea known as 'Jeremiah's Wheelbarrow', which has the Prophet Jeremiah wheeling the treasures of the First Temple around the countryside to hide them, before fleeing to Egypt having confided their locations to 'caretakers' in the Qumran hills. Some 70 years after the destruction of the Temple, Ezra,[20] a relative of Jeremiah, and Nehemiah return from forced exile in Babylon but are not given the information about the locations of the treasure by its guardians. Personally, I find this theory extremely seductive as an explanation of where part of the treasures described in the Copper Scroll may have come from.

Some French scholars and others,[21] tend toward the view that the treasures came from the wealth of the Qumran Community itself, on the basis that new members gave all their worldly goods to the Community on joining.

Arguments that the contents of the Copper Scroll are fiction were initially propounded by Father de Vaux and his Polish colleague, Father Jozef Milik. They met bitter opposition from John Allegro and, increasingly, other scholars have come round to the view that they were wrong.

The remaining theory, that the treasures came from and were hidden by Second Temple personnel, and that the Qumran-Essenes had nothing to do with it, is a pet theory of Dr Norman Golb of the University of Chicago. It finds limited support.

However, there are over-riding problems with all of these theories which, until now, have not been resolved. Scholars have all puzzled over how so much gold could have come from either the First, or the Second, Temple of Jerusalem, let alone could have come into the ownership of an ascetic, relatively impoverished sect like the Qumran-Essenes.

Another major stumbling block for all of the current theories is that not one of them has led to the discovery of any of the treasures listed in the Copper Scroll.

Well, that last statement is open to challenge by a certain Mr Vendyl Jones, who is sometimes portrayed as the role model for Indiana Jones in Steven Spielberg's *Raiders of the Lost Ark*. I will briefly digress to deal with his claims. He was born on 29 May 1930 and grew up in the State of Texas. By the age of 16, Vendyl knew that his life was to be dedicated to doing God's work, and he eventually founded the Institute of Judaic-Christian Research (now known as the Vendyl Jones Research Institute, based in Arlington, Texas).

I first met Vendyl in September 1996 at the Conference on the Copper Scroll held in Manchester. He appeared a friendly, larger-than-life Dead Sea Scroll enthusiast, with a fierce white Mormonesque beard, who asked rather too many awkward questions. When I met him again, in July 1997 at a Conference in Jerusalem, we had a long chat about his 'discoveries'. Vendyl had done a lot of digging in Israel, and from 1967 onwards had concentrated his efforts on the area around Qumran. He claimed that in April 1988 he found the anointing oil from the Second Temple of Jerusalem, and in 1992, the spices mentioned in the Copper Scroll. I was suitably impressed, especially as I had never heard of, or seen any report on anything being found from information given in the Copper Scroll. As we talked another Conference delegate walked by and, *en passant,* delivered a verbal assault on Vendyl.

Not surprisingly I was a bit non-plussed, but subsequently learned that Vendyl was banned from digging in Israel by the Antiquities Authority. No-one in scientific circles takes his claims seriously, and no learned journal has confirmed the authenticity of his claims.

I returned from the Jerusalem Conference in July 1997, reinvigorat-ed with some of the information I had learned and by the people I had talked to, and excited with the theory that was beginning to form in my mind – of how the puzzle of the Copper Scroll might be solved, and where the treasures might have originally come from.

My own view is rather different from other scholars. I do not believe the treasures came from the Second Jerusalem Temple, as the Qumran-Essenes were violently opposed to this Temple and its priestly activities. Whilst part of the treasures may possibly have come from the First Temple at Jerusalem, as descriptions in the Copper Scroll certainly refer to Temple-associated objects, when we have unravelled the secrets of the Copper Scroll it will become patently clear that *another* Temple is described – and that the Qumran-Essenes were guardians, not just of treasure, but also of secrets that belonged to a much earlier time and a very distant place.

The scroll had been engraved on a thin copper sheet in an unusual form of 'cursive' ancient Hebrew script. Although (from palaeographic studies) it is now thought to have been copied at a date between 150 BCE and 70 CE, a number of scholars, notably John Elwolde[22] (who is working on a Hebrew Dictionary Project at the University of Sheffield), have pointed out that there are enigmatic passages in the Copper Scroll which correspond to early Biblical Hebrew – which dates back to 800 or 700 BCE – and that the scroll contains many unique word constructions not in use in mainstream Judaism at the time of its copying.

The presence of Greek letters interspersed at the end of sections of the text had aroused my interest. Their meaning was not understood and they appeared to be some kind of cryptic code.* Although Greek influences were pervasive at the time of the engraving of the Copper Scroll, the only texts of the Dead Sea Scrolls written in Greek are of Biblical passages relating to the Old Testament. Greek does not appear in Qumran-Essene sectarian texts, so why should Greek letters be included in the Copper Scroll?

Many theories have been put forward to explain these apparently random letters. They are variously considered to be made by scribes as reference marks of some sort, initials of place-names, entry dates, or location directions, but none of these explanations is accepted as conclusive, and they remain a puzzle.

The numbering units given in the text, which relate to the amounts of treasure, are also not clearly understood by modern translators. The

---

* The full text of the Copper Scroll in its original script form, including the position of the Greek letters, can be seen in the Appendix at the back of the book.

numerals are in an unsophisticated long-hand form, involving apparently unnecessary duplication.[23]

There were other 'anomalies' for which there appeared to be no satisfactory answers. My metallurgical experience kept on bringing me back to these unanswered questions: Why should a non-materialistic community go to such trouble to preserve this information on a copper scroll? Where did they get the copper from? How could they afford its very high cost? No other Dead Sea Scroll was engraved on copper, nor were any known Hebrew texts from anywhere else, prior to this period.

The questions were beginning to mount and I started looking for scientific, rather than scriptural, ways of analysing the content and material of the scroll. I decided to concentrate first on the metallurgy, the technique of fabrication and the metrology of the Copper Scroll.

CHAPTER THREE

METALLURGY
AND
METROLOGY

The first thing I decided to do was to look more closely at the listings of treasure in the Copper Scroll, and the various translations of the text, and to try and bring an inter-disciplinary, or lateral-thinking type of approach to the unresolved problems.

For each of the 64 locations* listed in the Copper Scroll, the description of each item of treasure follows a set pattern: a geographical and, sometimes, a directional clue; an instruction to dig; a measurement in cubits;[1] a weight amount, invariably translated as Talents; and the type of treasure.

The unit of weight, given in the Copper Scroll as a 'K', is assumed by modern scholars to refer to the Biblical Talent. This is known to be equivalent to about 76lb or 35kg – a huge unit of weight to use when dealing with small items such as gold earrings, weighing 30–40g. Remember that the *tonnages* of precious metals given in the conventional translations are 26 tonnes (26,000kg) of gold and 65 tonnes (65,000kg) of silver!

All my metallurgical and scientific experience told me that, with the relatively primitive metal refining techniques that would have been available over 2,000 years ago,[2] the units of weight in use for precious metals would have to have been many orders of magnitude less than those assumed by modern translators.

* This is the generally accepted number, although John Allegro gives only 61.

GOLD AND SILVER

I started looking at historical references relating to precious metals and found, from a 1993 NATO Conference on 'Prehistoric Gold' and various other references,[3] that the list of treasures in the Copper Scroll, based on the conventionally translated units of weight, would have accounted for more than 25 per cent of the world's entire supply of gold at that time, and the 65 tonnes of silver would have accounted for the stock of the entire world!

The graph in Figure 2 shows that even at the time of Jesus, the total tonnage of gold existing in the world was no more than about 150 tonnes, and silver was, prior to about 900 BCE, rarer than gold.[4] The big surge in gold production came between 1850 and 1900 (with the Californian gold rush), when more gold was mined in 50 years than in the previous 5,000. Up to 1850 no more than 10,000 tonnes of gold had ever been mined. Even today, the total gold mined throughout history only totals about 130,000 tonnes.

This last figure may seem rather surprising when one thinks of today's widespread use of gold in jewellery, industry, dentistry, decorative furnishings, space vehicles, electronics, or just held as bullion and coinage. But gold is one of the most malleable and ductile of all metals.

Figure 2: Graph showing the cumulative amounts of gold mined throughout the world between 4000 BCE and 68 CE.

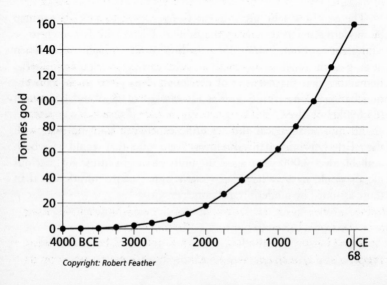

Copyright: Robert Feather

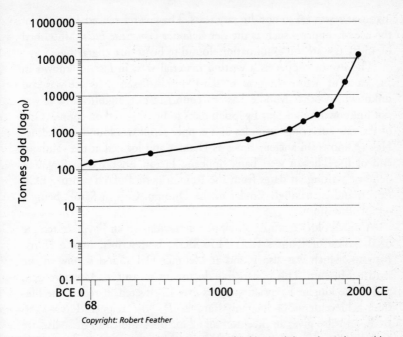

Copyright: Robert Feather

Figure 3: Graph showing cumulative amounts of gold mined throughout the world between 68 and 1998 CE.

One ounce can be beaten into an area covering 100sq. feet – so thin (5 millionths/inch or 0.0000127cm) that it can transmit green light – or be drawn into wire 80km in length!

For a quarter of the world's supply of gold to have been in either the First or Second Temples at Jerusalem, let alone to have survived after their sacking, seems extremely unlikely. Similarly, it is hard, if not impossible to believe that an isolated ascetic sect like the Qumran-Essenes could have, on their own account, acquired such vast resources.

Something was seriously wrong with the conventional translations of the weights given in the Copper Scroll!

PROVENANCE OF THE COPPER SCROLL

I decided to investigate the background of the scroll in detail, focusing first on the aspect I knew about most – the metal itself.

It is well known that the Romans and Greeks used bronze (an alloy of copper and tin) as an engraving medium, but the use of copper on its own was restricted to non-literary texts. The few referenced examples of the use of copper – such as the *Lex Coloniae Genetivae Juliae*,[5] inscribed in 43 BCE – are, on examination, found to be bronze engravings.

The use of copper as a writing material was, in fact, unknown in Judaea at or before the time of the Qumran-Essenes. Its use was also unknown in other Middle Eastern countries but, significantly, it was not unknown for ancient Egyptian texts to be engraved on copper. One of the rare surviving examples of a copper scroll was found at Medinet Habu,[6] known in ancient times as Djamet and located at the southern end of the Theban west bank opposite Luxor. Engraved in Egyptian demotic writing,* it dates from the Roman period of 1st century-BCE Egypt, and is strikingly similar to the Qumran Copper Scroll, being a temple inventory.

A much older example of copper engraving, on an Egyptian temple of the time of Ramses III, *c.*1156 BCE, is described in the Harris Papyrus, which was also found at Medinet Habu, and is now in the British Museum. This remarkable document measures 133ft in length, and is the longest Egyptian papyrus ever discovered. It recites the lifetime achievements of Pharaoh Ramses III, who reigned 1189–1156 BCE, and also gives an inventory of all his possessions. In these lists we find mention of stocks of copper being used for engraving.[7]

> I made for thee great tablets of silver, in beaten work, engraved with
> the great name of thy majesty, carved with the graver's tool, bearing
> the decrees and the inventories of the houses and temples which I
> made in Egypt, during my reign on earth; in order to administer them
> in thy name forever and ever. Thou are their protector answering for
> them. I made for thee *other tablets of copper in beaten work,* of a
> mixture of six [parts], of the colour of gold, engraved and carved with
> the graver's tool with the great name of thy majesty, with the house
> regulations of the temples; likewise the many praises and adorations,
> which I made for thy name. Thy heart was glad at hearing them,
> O lord of gods.[8]

This is the only known reference to copper tablets or plaques being used for engraving in Egypt. The Egyptians of this period were well able

---

* Demotic was a script form of writing which came into use in Egypt as a replacement for the earlier hieratic script (except for religious and funereal subjects) around 670 BCE. It remained in use, alongside Greek, through to the 2nd century CE.

to distinguish between copper and bronze, as the two metals are referred to quite separately in the Harris Papyrus.[9]

These two early Egyptian examples, and the lack of any other known examples of engraving on copper outside Egypt before the time of the Qumran-Essenes, make it even more surprising that this strange, isolated sect were able to make use of such a rare and expensive metal. The only place in the Middle East where copper was used, albeit rarely, was in Egypt. There is clear evidence that engraving lists on copper was being practised as early as 1200 BCE, and relatively pure copper was available from the bronze age onwards, 1550–1300 BCE (18th Dynasty).

Where did the Qumran-Essenes get the copper from then? Why did they use it in the first place? It was not used in Judaea at the time of the Qumran-Essenes, and would have been very difficult to obtain, not to mention extremely expensive. How did they learn the engraving skills and rivetting techniques that were applied to the Copper Scroll?

The logical place for learning such skills would be Egypt, as the Egyptians had an established tradition of advanced metallurgical knowledge. There had been a long association between the Hebrew tribes and Egypt. Could it be possible that the expertise and copper materials were brought out of Egypt with the Hebrews when Moses led them out of slavery?

ASPECTS OF ANCIENT COPPER TECHNOLOGY

It is quite reasonable to assume that the format of copper tablet production in the time of Ramses III had changed little with time, and was similar in the period of Ramses II – the pharaoh generally assumed to be ruling at the time of the Hebrew Exodus. In fact it would be quite usual for a pharaoh's son to inherit his father's possessions. If the raw material for the Copper Scroll came out of Egypt, it would almost certainly have been in the flat, beaten copper format described in the Harris Papyrus.[10]

Three separate pieces of flat copper were joined together to form the Copper Scroll. The equal sizes of the pieces indicates that this joining was done after its engraving, to produce one long scroll, rather than as a repair to breaks in the material. By the turn of the millennium brazing, welding and soldering were still not common techniques available to the metal fabricator.[11] So it is not surprising that the Copper Scroll was joined by rivetting, but it is the use of copper rivets, the neatness, hole size and straight-line nature of the rivetting that is of interest. It is identical to the type of rivetting in use at the time of the Egyptian 18th Dynasty.[12] The significance of this will become clear later.

Apart from the scroll's mechanical form, the other two main characteristics which I considered might enable a comparison to be made of the copper materials from Egypt and those from Qumran, are its chemical composition and weight.

Chemical composition

The ancient Egyptians were highly skilled in metalwork, and their expertise in smelting and working copper can be traced back to at least 3000 BCE. For me, as a metallurgist, there is a certain thrill in looking into the face of the 'oldest known metallurgist in the world', preserved in all his long-bearded solemnity for over 3,000 years on a cartonnage* above a 'mummy' in the Museum of Cairo.[13]

The cupriferrous ores** available to the Egyptians came from the Eastern Desert, Nubia and Sinai and were readily reducible from their combined states, enabling very pure and easily workable copper to be produced. A typical analysis of an early Dynasty copper dagger, shows it contained 99.5 per cent copper, 0.39 per cent arsenic, 0.08 per cent iron, and a trace of lead.[14] By the time of the New Kingdom and the 18th Dynasty (c.1350 BCE), the technique of smelting using crucibles and reed blow-pipes had been refined, and leather-enclosed clay vessels with an inserted blow-pipe were being utilized. This technique enabled very pure copper – of the order of 99.9 per cent pure – to be produced.

Chemical analysis of the Copper Scroll has shown it too to have originally been made from very pure copper (99.9 per cent), with traces of arsenic, tin and iron – almost identical in chemical composition to the copper being produced in the 18th Dynasty![15]

Weight

I then started to think about what the actual weight of the Copper Scroll might have been in its original state. In its present form the scroll is heavily corroded – during its 2,000-year sojourn in a dank, warm cave near to the salty environment of the Dead Sea, it had become almost fully converted from copper into copper oxides. The original uncorroded copper material is estimated to have been 1mm thick, and

---

* A representational carving.
** Copper-bearing ores. Sometimes found in metallic form, copper usually occurs as an oxide (cuprite) or, combined with iron, as a sulphide (pyrite).

each of the three sections it was made from measured 30cm x 80cm.[16] The total weight of the pure copper on which the scroll was originally engraved would therefore have been:

$3 \times (30 \times 80) \times 0.1 \times 8.93 = 6,429.6g$

where 8.93 is the density of copper in g/cc

So where did this large chunk of extremely pure copper come from? Can it possibly be from a batch of copper described in the Harris Papyrus?

The weight of each of the copper tablets described in the Harris Papyrus as being part of the 'stock' held by Pharaoh Ramses III, is given as 205.5 Deben, and there were four tablets in all.

The *British Museum Dictionary of Ancient Egypt*[17] gives the Deben as a unit of weight, used for weighing metals such as copper, as 93.3g. From this we can calculate that each of the copper tablets weighed:

$205.5 \times 93.3g = 19,173.15g$, or 42.3lb

Weighing around 42lb, when it came to actually engraving a copper tablet and carrying it around, it would almost certainly have been reduced into more convenient smaller, equal weights. A more convenient size would have been 1/10 or 1/9 of the original – typical divisors known to have been used by the Egyptians when dealing with the weighing of copper. If the original tablet weight was, in fact, divided into nine equal sections, each section would weigh:

$19,173.15/9 = 2,130.35g$

If three of these smaller sections were then rivetted together (comfortably accommodating the text needed to describe the 64 locations of treasure mentioned in the Copper Scroll), the final weight would be:

$2,130.35 \times 3 = 6,391.05g$

This is remarkably close to the estimated weight of the Copper Scroll in its original state, of 6,429.6g.

To summarize, the correspondences between the Copper Scroll and copper material available in Egypt at the time of the Hebrew Exodus, are as follows:

	Egyptian Copper *c.*1200 BCE	The Copper Scroll *c.*100 BCE
Mechanical Format	Flat, beaten	Flat, beaten
Method of joining	Rivetting, straight-line	Rivetting, straight-line
Chemical composition	99.9% Copper, traces of Arsenic and Iron	99.9% Copper, traces of Arsenic and Iron
Unit Weight	6,391g	6,429g

The closeness in weight of the Copper Scroll to exact sections of the copper tablets described in the Harris Papyrus would not seem to be just coincidence. It is within 0.6 per cent, indicating we can be 99.4 per cent certain, in terms of weight correlation alone, that the Copper Scroll came from a piece of ancient Egyptian copper, similar to those once in the possession of Ramses III.[18] When other factors – relating to physical and chemical characteristics of the materials – are compared, the connection becomes irresistible.

NUMBERING AND WEIGHING SYSTEMS

What about the form of writing and units of measurement used in the Copper Scroll – do *they* have any comparable Egyptian overtones, particularly the numbering units of Talents, Minas and Staters mentioned previously? I began comparing the contents of the Copper Scroll with Egyptian texts, dating back from 500 BCE, and came to another startling conclusion. The numbering units and weights used in the scroll were not of Canaanite or Judaean origin, where the Qumran-Essenes resided, but Egyptian! Indeed, the numbering system in the Copper Scroll is typical of that in use in Egypt around 1300 BCE. The Egyptian system used repetitive single vertical strokes, up to the number 9, combined with repetitive decimal units for larger numbers. A good example of this can be seen in Column 6 of the Copper Scroll *(see Plate 3)*, where repeated single down strokes are used to represent the number 7. *(See also Appendix, column 6, line 13.)*

I returned again to the problem of the weights generally ascribed to the treasures by modern translators of the Copper Scroll. This time I applied an Egyptian perspective.

The ancient Egyptians had developed a system of weights specifically designed for weighing precious metals. This system was based on the 'Kite', a unit weighing approximately 10g, but sometimes used as a double unit (KK) of 20.4g. I believe that it is no coincidence that the 'hard ch' sound of the weight term used in the Copper Scroll text equates to the Egyptian 'K' in 'Kite'! When I used these ancient Egyptian weight units, typical of the period prior to 1000 BCE, to calculate the quantities of gold, silver and jewellery mentioned in the scroll, I obtained rather more realistic weights than those given earlier. The approximate totals of precious metals mentioned in the scroll now became:

Gold	26kg
Silver	13.6kg
Mixed precious metals	55.2kg

(There are also hundreds of gold and silver bars, and pitchers of precious metals, where weights are not specified.)

We are now looking at weights which are a fraction of those given in modern translations of the Copper Scroll, but they are at least plausible values, quite consistent with the amounts of gold and silver in circulation for the period. For example, if we look again at the Harris Papyrus it gives the total gold holdings accumulated over a 31-year period by Egypt (by far the most wealthy country in the ancient Middle East), as 387kg. The downside is that the value of our treasure has diminished somewhat! However, we are still talking about hundreds of millions of pounds in real terms.

So what can we make of all these calculations? The logical conclusion is that the weighing and numbering systems used in the Copper Scroll are based on ancient Egyptian systems.

When I applied this conclusion to calculations of precious metals and locations described in the Copper Scroll, they started to point in the direction the treasure hunt should begin to take and, perhaps, the location of where much of the treasure can be found.

A SECOND OPINION

I sought a second opinion on the ancient Egyptian numbering and weighing systems from Dr Rosalie David, Keeper of Egyptology at The Manchester Museum. She confirmed that, although the type of numbering system used in the Copper Scroll might have persisted in Egyptian temple writing for some time after the Greek conquest of Egypt (in 330 BCE), its use 'was always specific to Egypt and it was not in use outside Egypt, except in the period of Egypt's campaigns in Canaan from 1400 to 1100 BCE'.[19]

According to Dr David, the use of the ancient Egyptian system for weighing metals 'died out around 500 BCE and had previously always been specific to Egypt'.

Dr David's views raised yet more questions for me. Why would a document, ostensibly written by a devout, unorthodox Jewish community living near the Dead Sea in Judaea around the time of Jesus, have so many Egyptian characteristics? And why would the writing material, numbering system and system of weights used be typical of Egyptian usage from a period at least 1,000 years earlier?

A first answer would seem to be that, although the Copper Scroll may have been copied in the 1st century BCE, some of its contents originated from a period perhaps as many as 1,200 or 1,300 years earlier.

As my researches continued, I became convinced that this conjecture was right, and that at least part of the Copper Scroll was not originally written by the Qumran-Essenes, but was copied by them from something much more ancient: something written in Egyptian, something written perhaps as early as 1300 BCE.

As far as I know, no-one has tried to trace a direct connection between the ancient Egyptians of the 13th and 12th centuries BCE and the Qumran-Essenes of the 2nd and 1st centuries BCE. The Copper Scroll was undoubtedly a document of enormous importance to the Qumran-Essenes, considering the trouble and expense they must have gone to to produce it.[20] If its contents do have a connection to Egypt, that connection would have to have been extremely noteworthy to the Qumran-Essenes... and might be a key to other secrets.

If the pre–1000 BCE Egyptian period had left its technological mark on the Copper Scroll, why not other influences? What cultural or religious parallels could there be between this period and that existing in Judaea around the time of Jesus and, more specifically, with the practices of the Qumran-Essenes as authors of the Copper Scroll?

The next step, therefore, in my journey of detection was to examine what other relevant connections there might be between Egypt and Israel. To do that I needed to focus on Ancient Egypt, and to see how its culture and religion might have interacted with early Judaism.

CHAPTER FOUR

THE
HEBREW TRIBES
AND EGYPT

Having established that the Copper Scroll had so many key connections with Egypt, I began to wonder why this relatively isolated community of abstemious, devout Jews living at Qumran might possibly have come to have this scroll in their possession. What conceivable links might they have had to ancient Egypt? Indeed, could there be any connection between the treasures the Qumran-Essenes were writing about in the Copper Scroll and Egypt? The Qumran-Essenes had always been thought to have come from pure Hebrew stock,[1] but even this assumption had to be called into question.

I started looking back at the connections between the Hebrew tribes and the adjacent land of Egypt, and was surprised to discover the sheer extent of interaction between the two peoples. (It may be helpful to look back at Figure 1, the relational map of the Middle East).

From as early as 3000 BCE, right up to 1200 BCE, Egypt had maintained an armed presence in Canaan, often using it as a stepping stone to further conquests to the east. Trade routes along the Mediterranean coast were well established and commercial interaction brought people and goods to the northern parts of Egypt. The Hebrews, as a semi-nomadic tribe with herds to feed, were drawn to Egypt, particularly at times of drought and famine. Egypt was, after all, a country whose advanced irrigation systems and grain storage facilities put them in a better position to deal with natural disasters than any other country in the Middle East.

All the major characters of the Bible, from Abraham and Sarah to Jesus and Mary, had strong links to Egypt. Jacob, Joseph, Joseph's brothers – the founders of the twelve tribes of Israel, as well as Moses,

Aaron and Miriam, Joshua, Jeremiah and Baruch, all lived for long periods in Egypt and were influenced by its culture and religions.

When we look at the Biblical references to Egypt, it is quite apparent that the authors are unable to avoid frequent and detailed references to Egypt. In fact, as they are chronicled, it can be seen that both the Old and the New Testaments have an ongoing 'hate–love' relationship with Egypt.[2] Throughout the Bible, Egypt is a place for the Hebrews to flee to, a place of sanctuary – for Abraham, Jacob, Jeroboam, Jeremiah and Baruch, Onias IV and Jesus. Or it is a place to flee from, in the case of Moses and the Exodus. The following few verses from Isaiah illustrate the enmity and reverence exhibited in the Bible towards Egypt:

> And the land of Judah shall be a terror unto Egypt; every one that
> maketh mention thereof shall be afraid in himself; because of the
> counsel of the Lord of hosts, which he hath determined against it. In
> that day shall five cities in the land of Egypt speak the language of
> Canaan, and swear to the Lord of hosts: one shall be called the city of
> destruction. In that day shall there be *an altar to the Lord in the midst
> of the land of Egypt,* and a pillar at the border thereof to the Lord…
>
> Whom the Lord of hosts shall bless, saying, *'Blessed be Egypt my people,*
> and Assyria the work of my hand, and Israel mine inheritance.'
>
> [Isaiah 19: 17–19, 25]

In delving into the histories of these Biblical characters, from both Biblical and historical sources, I continually asked myself how their stories and supposed motivations might give a clue to the provenance and location of the treasures of the Copper Scroll. I was looking for any characters in the Old Testament who might have had access to enormous amounts of wealth. Here is a summary of my findings from the Biblical accounts. (More detail can be found in the notes.)

ABRAHAM

Abraham was the first of the Hebrew Patriarchs (Fathers) and the generally accepted founder of monotheism (the belief in one God to the exclusion of all others). Leaving the city of Ur in Chaldea (southern Babylonia), he travelled to Canaan and visited Egypt with his wife Sarah around 1500 BCE. Although he was a tribal chief, his wealth was mainly in livestock – but he did come away from Egypt 'rich in cattle, in silver, and in gold'.[3]

So Abraham is a possible candidate, with access to modest amounts of ancient treasure.

JACOB

The third of the Hebrew Patriarchs and the father of Joseph, Jacob returned from Canaan to his uncle's home in Haran, in Mesopotamia (northern Syria), to find a wife, coming away with two – Leah and Rachel. Together with them (and their two handmaidens) he fathered twelve sons and one daughter. Later in his life he took the name 'Israel'. He was encouraged to come to Egypt with all his family, by Joseph, and settled in the most favourable part of the land.

Jacob became a highly respected friend of Pharaoh, who gave him a state funeral on his death. His wealth could well have gone to his two favourite grandsons, Ephraim and Manasseh, the sons of Joseph.

JOSEPH

The great-grandson of Abraham, and eleventh son of Jacob, Joseph was sold by his brothers into slavery in Egypt.[4] His reputation as an interpreter of dreams came to the attention of Pharaoh, who had been suffering strange dreams about seven lean cows devouring seven fat ones, and seven full ears of corn being devoured by seven thin ears of corn. Joseph, relating God's words, told Pharaoh that the dreams meant there would be seven good years of harvest in Egypt, followed by seven bad years, and that measures should be taken to store the seventh-year produce. So impressed with Joseph was Pharaoh, a Pharaoh that I identify as Amenhotep IV, that he appointed him Vizier – the second most powerful figure in the land.

As Joseph kept his privileged position for at least 14 years, he could well have become one of the richest men in Egypt, especially as Pharaoh Amenhotep IV is known to have been prone to lavish collars of gold on those he favoured.

Here, clearly, was the first Biblical character to have access to enormous amounts of wealth and treasure.

THE LEADERS OF THE TWELVE TRIBES OF ISRAEL

The leaders of the twelve tribes of Israel were the sons of both Jacob and Joseph, who eventually founded the twelve regions of Canaan that formed the Hebrew Kingdom of Israel. They all lived in Egypt for a prolonged period of time, and their descendants finally left with Moses when he led the Hebrews out of Egypt to the Promised Land.

MOSES

The central figure of the Old Testament, being the architect of the Hebrew religion, Moses was born in Egypt, around 1250 BCE, as were his supposed brother Aaron and sister Miriam. After being abandoned in a reed basket in the River Nile as a baby, Moses was brought up by an Egyptian Princess until, as an adult, he took on the cause of the Hebrew slaves. Moses obtained the release of the Hebrews from slavery in Egypt and began the process of welding them into one nation, with one monotheistic religion, giving them the Ten Commandments, or laws, to live by.

Moses the Egyptian?

Detailed analyses of the Torah (the Hebrew Bible) and other texts, such as the Talmud (commentaries on Jewish law and customs) and Midrash (interpretations of Hebrew scriptures – *see Glossary*), led me to the conclusion that Moses was not only born and raised as an Egyptian, but was, in fact, a Prince of Egypt – a son of the Royal House of Pharaohs. This is not a conclusion that any religious writer would openly care to admit, but it has been suggested by others, and much earlier in history.[5]

It would have been anathema for the early Hebrew compilers of the Old Testament to have had to acknowledge that their most important leader and law-giver was not a Hebrew. Nevertheless, controversy has continued through the ages, in Christian and Jewish theology and, to a lesser extent, in Muslim theology. Debate was particularly lively in the so-called 'period of enlightenment' in Germany, in the late 19th and early 20th centuries.

The idea that Moses was an Egyptian, and that his teachings on monotheism had close Egyptian affinities, is therefore not particularly new. It was a theme of both Popper-Linkeus,[6] in 1899, and Sigmund Freud, the father of psychoanalysis, writing in 1931.[7] New studies, especially those coming from the work on the Dead Sea Scrolls over the last few years, and my own research, have dramatically added to the available evidence, warranting a re-assessment of the idea.[8]

Moses was, according to the Old Testament, discovered by Pharaoh's daughter floating in an ark made of bulrushes in a river. He had been abandoned by a Levi family* fearing Pharaoh's decree of death to new-born Hebrews. Unusually the names of his father and mother are not given when Moses is first mentioned in the Bible. Only later on, in Exodus 6:20, do we learn that Moses's father was named Amram and that his mother, Jochebed, was his father's aunt. Moses was apparently wet-nursed by a Hebrew, but then brought up from early childhood as the son of Pharaoh's daughter in the Egyptian Court. Under these circumstances it would have been inevitable that he absorbed Egyptian customs and learning and spoke the language. Of his youth we know little, but we are told that at some stage in his early maturity he apparently rebelled and was forced to flee the Court.

A description of the upbringing of Moses must have presented considerable problems for the chroniclers of the Old Testament. The nature of the story that describes his upbringing has fairy-tale qualities and, it would seem, would only have been required if Moses was born an Egyptian from a non-Semitic stock. Not only had it to be shown that he was born a Hebrew, but there needed to be a plausible explanation as to why he grew up and spent most of his early life in the Court of Pharaoh – living the life of a Prince of Egypt. This was not an easy problem to overcome, and called for all the ingenuity of the writers' imaginations. What to do? Simple: create a story linking Moses to the ancestry of the Hebrews.

Rather than dream up an original story, the writers cast around for a suitable myth or fable of the times that might suit the bill. There was the ancient Mesopotamian myth of Sargon, dating back to 2800 BCE:

> I am Sargon, the mighty king, king of Agade…my mother, the Vestal, conceived me. Secretly she bore me. She laid me in a basket of sedge, closed the opening with pitch and lowered me into the river. The stream did not drown me, but carried me to Akki, the drawer of water…as his own son he brought me up…When I was a gardener Ishtar fell in love with me. I became king and for forty-five years I ruled as king.[9]

However, the Egyptian story of the birth of Horus fits the bill more closely. This myth relates how the baby Horus was placed in a reed boat by his mother, Isis, and concealed in the Delta marshland to save him

---

* Descendants of this Levi family were later designated as priests and guardians of the Temple in Jerusalem.

from his enemy Seth.[10] A neat little story, easily transformed to allow Moses to be born a Hebrew but live as an Egyptian.

There was another reason why the latter story was to be preferred. A fundamental difference existed between Sumerian and Mesopotamian – as distinct from Egyptian – mythology. The former tended towards long plots involving complicated relationships, whereas Egyptian myths were shorter stories that were integrated into and formed part of the living language. As such they were more malleable and could be changed and updated, like words and ideas in any living language, without any self-conscious reproach.[11]

This divergence from Mesopotamian mythology made Egyptian mythology much more adaptable and attractive to another culture, or religion.[12] This is another reason why adoption of ideas from Egyptian mythology into Hebrew thinking was easier than those of Sumeria and Mesopotamia, apart from the ready availability of those ideas.

Whilst religious tradition and a number of historians testify to the upbringing and education of Moses, their versions, not surprisingly, differ in detail. Nevertheless the general thread is that he received his formative education from priests – either Egyptian or Midianite.* Manetho, a 3rd century BCE Egyptian author, and High Priest at Heliopolis, reports that Moses discharged priestly functions in the temple of Heliopolis.[13]

Manetho goes on to relate that Moses's original name was Osarsiph, and that he was named after Osiris, a patron god of Heliopolis. Justin Martyr, an early Church Father, refers to the education of Moses in the following passage:

> Moses also is depicted as a very ancient and venerable leader of the Jews by such writers of Athenian history as Hellanicus, Philochoros, Castor, Thallus and Alexander Polyhistor, as well as by the learned Jewish historians Philo and Josephus…
>
> These writers, who do not belong to our religion [Christianity], affirmed that their information was gathered from Egyptian priests, among whom Moses was born and educated; in fact, he was given a very thorough Egyptian education, since he was adopted son of a king's daughter.[14]

To quote Paul Goodman, 'the historical Moses who was to become the

---

* A nomadic tribe of Bedouin based in north-west Arabia.

leader and teacher of the Children of Israel, appears to have been brought up as an Egyptian and to have taken little interest or share in the servitude of his people'.[15]

Some historians find difficulty in locating a 'real' individual Moses in the ancient texts. Others find more than one Moses with a different emphasis in their concepts of God. Textual research, primarily by scholars such as Julius Wellhausen,[16] is based on the name applied to God in different sections of the Pentateuch.* The analyses demonstrate that there are at least four or five dominant authors behind the writings of the five books of Moses. This can be explained by relating the Mosaic period authors, or later authors, to influences from differing regional sources. This multi-author conclusion is strengthened by the different Biblical versions of where Moses fled to when he first left Egypt, and by conflicts in the names given for his father-in-law, who is variously Jethro, Reuel, Raguel or Hobab.[17]

The interesting (and at least consistent) thing is that Moses is said to have married into a priestly family, when he married 'Zipporah', and to have dwelt with the Midianites for some period. However, I find it unlikely that a wandering tribe of Bedouin, such as the Midianites, had priests with a highly developed religious philosophy from which Moses could learn anything useful. Moreover, the god that the Midianites worshipped was the idolatrous Baal. Nor does it seem in character for a 'Prince of Egypt', someone brought up in the luxuries of Court as the son of Pharaoh's daughter, to voluntarily serve as a shepherd for his father-in-law. Especially as amongst the Bedouin it is still the custom for the women to tend the flocks.[18]

In fact, in Numbers 31 the Bible relates how Moses later exacted an incredibly cruel vengeance on the Midianite tribe of his putative father-in-law. He instructed 12,000 armed men to go against the Midianites and 'they slew all the males', and all five kings of Midian, and all the male children, and all the women who were not virgins, and distributed all their captured goods and livestock amongst the twelve tribes of Israel. Hardly the way to treat the tribe of one's wife!

Why would Moses have fled to Midian, and married into a family of priests who worshipped the contaminating, idolatrous god Baal? The cumulative evidence, in my view, is that he didn't, and that this proposition was not the complete story.

---

* The Pentateuch comprises the first five Books of the Old Testament: Genesis, Exodus, Leviticus, Numbers and Deuteronomy.

Could it be that Moses actually fled South, and married into a 'priestly family' of another religious following?

An alternative destination is relayed to us in the Midrash,* where we are told Moses takes a wife from the land of Cush, a land to the South of Egypt, beginning in the region of Elephantine Island, and equating to Nubia and the Northern part of modern day Ethiopia. The Bible, in Numbers 12:1, confirms the story: '...and Moses took a "kush" (Ethiopian) woman for his wife.'

Josephus, the authoritative Jewish/Roman historian, writing shortly after the time of Jesus, is even more specific about Moses' presence in Ethiopia, and his marriage to 'Tharbis, daughter of the King of Ethiopia.'

> The Ethiopians pursued their advantage so closely, that they over-ran the whole country as far as Memphis, and from thence to the sea.[19]

Themuthis (the Greek name for Ramses), the King persuades Moses to lead a force of Hebrews against the Ethiopians. Josephus continues:

> The joy of the Egyptians [priests] arose, first, from the hopes of subduing their enemies under his conduct; and, next, from the prospect of being able, after having obtained the ends for which he was advanced to the above post, to effect the destruction of Moses. The Hebrews, on the other hand, were happy in the idea, that, under the direction of so expert a leader, they might probably, in a course of time, be enabled to throw off the yoke of the Egyptians.[20]

Josephus cannot find confirmation in the 'sacred records' of Moses being appointed to the post as a military leader, nor do we have any record of a substantial Ethiopian invasion during this period. The only definite record of an Ethiopian invasion is on a stele fragment (an inscribed stone slab) at the British Museum, which dates an invasion back to *c.*1680 BCE. Whilst the timing of the military aspects are there-fore suspect, the substance of Josephus is that Moses is forced by hostil-ity from the priests of Amun-Ra to flee to Cush, accompanied by a number of Hebrews, where he takes a Nubian wife. The Hebrew word for Nubia (Ethiopia) is 'Cush', which is sometimes spelled as 'Kush',

---

* The Midrash is the explanation, teachings and commentary of the rabbis on the Old Testament scrolls, while Mishna is the Oral Law of Moses, written down about 200 CE, and held by Orthodox Jews as equivalent in authority to the Torah.

and significantly this is the same word as used in the Egyptian. The office of 'Prince of Cush'[21] is first mentioned in the reign of Tutmoses I, son of Amenhotep I. It is quite feasible to consider that Moses was banished to the furthest limits of the Kingdom, as Manetho's evidence implies, and given the title of 'Prince of Cush' to keep him quiet and out of the way.

The works of Josephus are probably one of the best sources we have to compare historical evidence with the Old Testament and the events surroundings its evolution. He also gives us a wealth of background fabric to the New Testament. Undoubtedly he wrote with a bias towards the authenticity of Judaism and, although he seems to have got some of the timing of events he wrote about out of phase, the content of the events he discusses appear to be relatively secure. Josephus had access to unique sources. As a Roman citizen he was a confidant of Titus Caesar, the son of the Emperor Vespasian, and from his own writings it is apparent that he witnessed the destruction of the Second Temple in Jerusalem in 70 CE. From his statement that Titus gave him the opportunity to remove whatever he wanted from the doomed city, and his claim: 'I also had the holy books by his [Titus'] concession', it can be deduced that Josephus may have had direct access to the Holy Scrolls of the Temple. He also appears to have visited Nehemiah's 5th century BCE library of documents held in the Herodian Temple.

There is another 'physical' skein of evidence which indicates that Moses was not a Hebrew, and therefore might play a part in linking pharaonic Egypt to the Hebrews.

Circumcision

The first mention of circumcision in the Torah occurs in Genesis 17:9–27, as part of God's covenant with Abraham. The ceremony was to be performed on the eighth day after the birth of every Hebrew boy – and is still the custom today.

The Old Testament is ambiguous as to whether Moses was circumcised. In Exodus 4, we are told that Gershom, his first-born son, was circumcised as a matter of urgency.[22]

Some commentators have taken this passage on circumcision to refer to Moses, citing later references to his 'uncircumcised lips'; these references, however, occur after the event, in Exodus 6:12, 30. The verses immediately preceding give more of a clue. They are about Moses's warning to Pharaoh that God will slay the first-born of Egypt if he does not free the Hebrews. The immediate need for Gershom,

Moses's first-born, to be circumcised so that he will be 'passed over' on that fateful day, seems more to indicate that the passage refers to Moses's son. But most commentators, for various other reasons, conclude that Moses was not at this stage circumcised.[23]

This conclusion, from the Biblical evidence, seems to support the case that Moses was an Egyptian.

So, how does the practice of circumcision relate Moses to Egypt? The practice of circumcision had long been customary in Egypt, but not mandatory – a fact confirmed by examination of relics and tomb inscriptions.[24] Amongst objects found at the Royal Tomb of El-Amarna is a clay model of a circumcised penis,[25] and inscriptions (see Plate 4) on the tombs of Nefer-Seshem-Ptah and Ankh-Ma-Hor, at Saqqara, show circumcised Egyptians at work.[26] Other Middle Eastern peoples, such as the Semites, Babylonians, Philistines and Sumerians, did not practise circumcision.

It is likely that many of the Hebrews were circumcised, through assimilation of the Egyptian custom and, later on, compulsorily as slaves – a common practice. Whether Moses, after the Children of Israel left Egypt, decided to adopt the practice for everyone, including himself, to distinguish his people from the surrounding idolaters, is conjecture.

The Bible relates, in Joshua 5:2–8, that all the male Hebrews who came out of Egypt were circumcised, but that those born during the wanderings were not. A mass circumcision was therefore performed on all the males at Gilgal, in the plains of Jericho.

A further clue comes from the passage describing events after the mass circumcision had been performed:

> And the Lord said unto Joshua. 'This day have I rolled away the
> reproach of Egypt from off you. Wherefore the name of the place is
> called Gilgal to this day.'
>
> [Joshua 5:9]

Now, in a snub to Egypt and as free men, circumcision was entered into voluntarily, and any stigma previously attached to it was henceforth negated.

The Biblical account supports the case that Moses was a Prince of Egypt when it, apparently, says that for much of his life Moses was uncircumcised: in Biblical terms this would indicate he was not a Hebrew. However as the Hebrews were supposed to have been circumcised, the Biblical writers would have wanted to equate Moses with the

Hebrews, rather than as an Egyptian – especially as circumcision was later taken as a unique sign of the Covenant.

There is, to put it mildly, a wealth of circumstantial exegetic detail derived from the Bible, together with numerous cogent 'handed-down' historical anecdotes, which suggest that Moses was a high-born 'Prince of Egypt'. Here is a summary of the evidence so far:

a) the testimony of four historical authorities – Manetho, Philo, Josephus and Justin Martyr

b) the tenuous story of his being cast into the Nile as an infant – which I relate to a story closely paralleling an Egyptian fable about the Egyptian god Horus, who was placed in a reed basket and set adrift in the River Nile by his mother Isis to save him from his enemies

c) his Egyptian name – probably meaning 'child of Amon' – which alludes to an Egyptian god known as 'the hidden one'. 'Mose' was a known suffix to pharaonic names, such as Ahmose and Tutmoses

d) the Egyptian names of his 'parents', Amram and Jochebed

e) the Bible's claim that he was raised by an un-named Egyptian princess in the Court of Pharaoh

f) his marrying a non-Hebrew named Zipporah, daughter of a Midianite priest (the Talmud also records Moses marrying a second, un-named, Kushite wife he acquired from lands to the south of Egypt)

g) his apparent speech impediment, which the Bible explains as the reason he needed a spokesman when talking to others. I take this as an 'excuse' for Moses needing an interpreter to talk to the Hebrews, whose language he would not have been familiar with

h) evidence that he was uncircumcised, unlike the Hebrews.

As a Prince of Egypt, Moses was a second Biblical character, in addition to Joseph, who would have had access to great wealth and valuable possessions.

OTHER POSSIBLE INFLUENCES ON THE HEBREWS

Mesopotamia, Babylonia and Canaan

What about Mesopotamia and Babylonia and all those other countries mentioned in the Bible that surrounded Canaan? What were their influences?

There were, of course, connections between Canaan and Mesopotamia and Babylonia to the north, but these were relatively minor compared to those with Egypt, and largely reflect the very earliest Biblical experience of the Hebrews.

Received wisdom does indeed assign an expected larger background influence on the roots of the three great world religions to Mesopotamia and Sumerian cultures. If one looks at relatively recent treatises, for example the *Atlas of the Jewish World* by Nicholas de Lange,[27] *The Oxford Companion to the Bible*, edited by Metzger and Coogan,[28] *The Lion Encyclopedia of the Bible* by Pat Alexander,[29] or *Ancient Judaism* by Irving Zeitlin,[30] the army of scholars represented in these works barely consider Egyptian influences, and talk largely of Babylonian and Mesopotamian antecedents. (I give more detail on the effects of Mesopotamia and Babylonia, or relative lack of it, on the Hebrews in the Glossary.)

Yes, there are many similarities in the biblical 'lifestyles' of the Patriarchs to those of the region bounded by the rivers Euphrates and Tigris, but very little connection to their *religious* innovations. There are few references to Northern Mesopotamia (Assyria), and little to indicate the writers of the Old Testament had much knowledge of its geography. As John Rogerson, Emeritus Professor of Biblical Studies at Sheffield University, points out:

> This is all the more surprising in view of the traditions that indicate
> that the forebears of the Hebrews came from Northern
> Mesopotamia.
>
> [Genesis 11:27–30][31]

Siegfried Morenz, Director of the Institute of Egyptology at the University of Leipzig, Germany, in his study on Egyptian religion, is more convinced and even amazed:

> hardly any consideration has been given to the fact that the religious
> forms of the land of the Nile also had an effect upon the New
> Testament (in addition to the Old Testament) and so upon early
> Christianity…scholars have failed to appreciate the influence which
> Egypt has exerted upon the entire Hellenistic world in which
> Christianity was destined to take shape.[32]

What about Canaan itself? Weren't the Canaanites just as influential as Egypt? What do other scholars say on the subject? The influence of Canaan on the Hebrews only starts to become apparent well after their entry from Egypt in about 1200–1180 BCE, and even then it is remarkably limited in its effects. Irving Zeitlin, Professor of Sociology at the University of Toronto, succinctly analyses the position and concludes: '…the Israelite cult was her own, and shows no signs of having been acquired in Canaan.'[33] Two other eminent historians, Yehezkel Kaufman and John Gray, reiterate Zeitlin's findings.[34]

Orthodox religions and their 'spin doctrinaires' are the main reasons why conventional Hebrew, and, by induction, Christian and Muslim philosophies downgrade, or even ignore, early Egyptian influences. But by reading 'on the lines' and 'between the lines' of the holy scriptures, a multiplicity of parallels can be found. When we look at ritual and religious practices there are numerous commonalities. When we examine the early evolutionary development of the 'core' religions, we find remarkable linkages to Egypt. (Some of these Egyptian influences have also found their way into fundamental Vedic, Hindu and Buddhist ideas.)

However, no self-respecting Rabbi, or Priest, or Imam wishes to examine in any detail an era which is instinctively considered idolatrous. Few Jewish scholars would be seen dead reading the *Book of the Dead* (*see Glossary*).

Let me tread here on rather contentious ground. For orthodox/fundamentalist Jews, Christians and Muslims, the Torah – the Five Books of Moses – were handed down by God to Moses on Mount Sinai in the same Hebrew version we have today. It is immutable, right down to each single 792,077 of the letters. It is 'Torah min Hashamayim' – 'Torah from Heaven'. The same rigidity does not apply for progressive Jews, Christians or Muslims. For them the Bible is divinely *inspired* by God, but it is not to be taken literally word-for-word.

Not surprisingly the barriers that fundamentalist religions have erected and maintained have increasingly marginalized them from academic institutions and biblical research. I quote one example from an acquaintance of mine, who specializes in book translations. At the first lecture she attended for a degree course in Jewish Studies at the University of London, the lecturer commenced with words to the effect that, anyone on the course who believed in 'Torah min Hashamayim' might as well leave then, as they would fail their degree.

A similar attitude to Old Testament studies can be seen at almost every academic university throughout the world. From Wellhausen to Friedman[35] there is a pile of evidence as high as Mount Sinai demonstrating that, whilst the Bible may have been 'inspired' by God, it was written by numerous different hands at different periods in history. To their credit, Progressive Judaism, founded in the mid-19th century, some 'enlightened' sectors of orthodoxy, and the Catholic Church, following Pope Pius XII's encyclical *Divinio Afflante Spiritu* of 1943,[36] have taken on board this 'truth'.

For 'un-enlightened' Biblical research, much of which was, in earlier times, dominated by devout religious expertise, I describe this phenomenon, which still pervades beyond the walls of academia as follows: All religions have a vested interest in minimizing, and in some instances distorting, the acknowledgeable influences of their antecedents and surrounding cultures, in order to preserve and maximize the uniqueness of the particular religion and the divine nature of its revelation.

I do not want to get bogged down here in a morass of examples of scholarly bickering that support the above statement. Two examples will suffice.

For nearly 50 years after the discovery of the Dead Sea Scrolls in 1947, religious personalities and historians continued scandalously to suppress their content (and probably still do). People like Father Roland de Vaux, Father Jozef Milik, Frank Moore Cross and others at the École Biblique et Archéologique Française in Jerusalem, as well as trustees of some of the scrolls at the Rockefeller Museum, Jerusalem, eked out the results of their researches in an agonizingly slow process, as they sought to maximize their own international kudos and support their in-built prejudices.

In another example I have already mentioned, John Allegro, one of the foremost historians working in the field, who was instrumental in bringing the Copper Scroll to Manchester College of Technology and deciphering the engraved text, was literally shunned by his so-called authoritative colleagues because his ideas did not comply with their beliefs.

As part of the original team that worked on the Dead Sea Scrolls at the École Biblique in Jerusalem, a Dominican Institution, he found himself the only agnostic amongst four Catholics, one Anglican, one Presbyterian, and one other Protestant. Frustrated by the delays in publishing an English translation of the Copper Scroll he went ahead and published his own version.[37] He soon became embittered as his senior colleagues attacked him for jumping the gun, maintaining that the contents of the Copper Scroll were a 'fairy-tale'. Disillusioned and depressed Allegro eventually withdrew from academia and, in a gesture of defiance, wrote a best-selling book to the effect that the early Christians had come to their faith through eating *Amanita Muscaria* – hallucinatory mushrooms![38]

As I proceed it will become abundantly clear that my maxim, that religions tend to distance themselves from their origins, is no more apparent for the 'core' religions than in their relationship with early Egyptian culture. However, the really interesting questions are why should ancient Egyptian religion/philosophy feature so strongly as the basis of Western equivalents, as I claim, and how?

Having identified two Biblical Hebrews, Joseph – as second-in-command to a Pharaoh, and Moses – as a Prince of Egypt, who had obtained or inherited enormous wealth from Egypt, and one character, Abraham, who had been rich in silver and gold, I now looked to see if there was any link between their wealth and the treasures of the Copper Scroll of the Qumran-Essenes.

A simple piece of detective work. Just find a connection between one of the three suspects and the Qumran-Essenes and…'case solved'! Not so easy, of course. I was dealing with events that took place, at the outside, 3,500 years ago. Even the very existence of Abraham as a person has never been historically proven. And there were surprising twists in the trail ahead, which I could never have foreseen.

The first step was to examine in detail the nature of Egyptian religion, particularly that existing at the times of Joseph and Moses, to see if its influence could be traced down through the ages to the Qumran-Essenes.

CHAPTER FIVE

THE COCOONED
CAULDRON OF EGYPT
– HOTBED OF CIVILIZATION

The story of Egypt starts back in the grey mists of time in the baking glare of a hostile sun. A sun that, for many months of the year, beats down everything in its path, parches the land, withers the plants and turns the land into an arid desert. At the same time, without the sun nothing grows, nothing ripens, nothing lives.

What a strange dichotomy for the ancient mind to grapple with – a creator sun and yet a destroyer sun. A powerful force to be revered and loved, and yet to be both feared and dreaded. Throughout the Bible this conflict of qualities is reflected in its stories, and in our present day concept of a loving yet vengeful God.

Of course, the other great impelling icon for the ancient Egyptian mind was the Nile River, and it too meanders its way through several Biblical stories. Suffice it to say, the river also presented and reinforced the same dichotomous imagery. It nourished the crops, bringing food and vital sustenance, but it could also bring disastrous floods, death and destruction.

Both the sun and the Nile, as the two most powerful natural forces known to the ancient Egyptians, understandably became the main bases of spiritual interest and the sources for the Egyptians' ideas on the origins of creation and life itself.

EGYPT AND CREATION

Before getting to *why* Egypt should be so influential on formative Western religions and subsequent attitudes about morality, as I claim, it is necessary to examine in some detail the *what*, to see if the fundamental ideas, which might relate to Western religious concepts, actually existed.

I started my search with some early Egyptian mythology in relation to the creation, to see what interesting correlations were discernable. To understand the mythological background we need to examine a bit more closely the early history and legends of Egypt.

The conventional view of Egyptian religion is one of multifarious deities, with an overbearing emphasis on death and exotic half-human creature-like gods exemplified by Horus – the falcon-headed human-bodied god of war, the sky and divine kingship; or Anubis – the canine god of the dead.

These conceptions are not in themselves incorrect, but underlying the diverse religious beliefs of the ancient Egyptians there was also a deep comprehension that one Supreme Being lay behind this panoply of gods.

The idea of a single God, in fact, dated back a thousand years *before* the time of Abraham. Even by the beginning of the Old Kingdom period, in 2700 BCE, there was recognition that one source of authority on earth (Pharaoh) was paralleled by one single creator and originator of divine power. By the height of the Old Kingdom, *c.*2500 BCE, the High God of Heliopolis was envisaged as a spiritual and intellectual force that controlled time and motion, morality and natural order.[1]

Until about 1760 BCE, with the invasion of the Hyksos[2] tribes from Asia, Egypt remained remarkably unaffected by outside cultural influences. Cut off by the sea to the north, by desert to the south-west and north-east, and by impassable cataracts downstream of the Nile, it developed its own unique social, scientific and religious environment, and its own hieroglyphic (pictorial imagery) form of writing. This cultural isolation allowed a distinct religious and philosophical framework to evolve, which, although continually modified by re-evaluation, remained essentially the same for 1,250 years, from 3000 BCE. The main religious icons were, as I have already mentioned, the Sun and the Nile, together with a third, the natural sequel to Creation – Death.

Our view of the events in this period has largely been deduced from ancient inscriptions found inside the tombs of the 5th- and 6th-Dynasty pharaohs, queens and officials, dating from 2350 to 2250 BCE. Other sources of information come from the Coffin Texts of the 7th to the 10th Dynasties, dating from 2250 to 2050 BCE, and the *Book of the Dead*, which dates from immediately before 2000 BCE (*see Glossary*).

Table 2: The main historical periods of Egypt from 3100 BCE to 1070 BCE

Period	Dynasty	BCE	Event	Texts
		3100	Kingdom united by Menes MEMPHIS Capital	
ARCHAIC PERIOD	0 – 2nd Dynasty	3000	Horus dominant god	
		2686		
OLD KINGDOM	3rd – 6th Dynasty	2500		Pyramid Inscription Texts*
			Power of Sun god Re rises at HELIOPOLIS	
FIRST INTERMEDIATE PERIOD	7th – 11th Dynasty	2180	HERAKLEOPOLIS becomes Capital	Coffin and Sarcophagi Inscription Texts**
		2040 2000	THEBES becomes Capital	Tombs/Coffins in Theban Hills
MIDDLE KINGDOM	12th – 14th Dynasty			
SECOND INTERMEDIATE PERIOD	15th – 17th Dynasty	1782	Hyksos invaders from the East Capital AVARIS	
		1570	(Nubian invaders from the South)	
		1500	THEBES reinstated as Capital	Coffin Papyrus Texts***
NEW KINGDOM	18th – 20th Dynasty	1350 1331	AKHETATEN made Capital THEBES reinstated as Capital	
		1070 1000		

* Inscription of spells and rituals for interment and safe attainment of the afterlife.

** Inscriptions on Coffins and Sarcophagi.

*** Coffin Text Spells on papyrus as Book of the Dead (largely incorporated in The Papyrus of Ani) essentially contained formulae for spells, sacrificial rituals, hymns, and details of supplies needed to ward off evil and reach immortality. Later compiled in Book of Breathings, Rhind Mortuary Papyrus, Book of Traversing Eternity. The Guides to the Beyond include the Book of the Two Ways, certain spells from Book of Dead, Fields of Rushes, Amduat (Book of that which is in the underworld), Book of Gates, Book of Caverns.

These sources show that the Egyptians, some 4,000 years before our time, were amazingly intellectually and religiously inquisitive. Their ways of conceptualizing, often in highly sexual terms, were through myths and stories which related to a complex structure of gods and their creativity.

In many respects their ideas, recognized by such historians as the American Professor James Breasted,[3] and E. Wallis Budge,[4] Curator at the British Museum, were well in advance of Greek and Christian philosophy. Early Egyptian ideas were compounded by an almost surrealistic concept of a single divine creator, who could, nevertheless, without any conflict of understanding, take numerous forms – vengeful, destructive, combative, as well as loving, creative and assistive.

INSTABILITY BRINGS NEW IDEAS

At the end of the Middle Kingdom period (2055–1780 BCE), asiatic invaders began to overturn the status quo of Egyptian customs, and wrought havoc on the religious structures. The invaders adopted many Egyptian ways, but brought with them Syro-Palestinian influences. The catharsis of chaos spawned a new philosophical examination of the role of man's own will, his relationship with God, good and evil, and man's soul. The idea of God as the shepherd and His children as the flock, an analogy later borrowed in modified form by the Christian Gospels, could no longer be maintained.

After the upheavals of the Second Intermediate Period, from 1650 to 1550 BCE, the Hyksos invaders left a legacy of doubt in the Egyptians' minds about the supreme God's desire to protect them from outside disaster. An Egyptian poet of the period, Ipu, touchingly calls on the 'director of the universe' to awake from his slumbers and, as a 'loving shepherd', protect his people:

> It used to be said that He was everyman's shepherd, that there was no
> evil in his heart, that however insignificant his flock he would spend
> the whole day in caring for them...[6]

R.T. Rundle Clark, Lecturer in Ancient History at Birmingham University, described Ipu's poem:

> it reveals the underlying monotheism of the Egyptian mind and the

Table 3: Egyptian Pharaoh-Ruler Chronology and Probable Scheme of Dates for the Hebrew Patriarchs[5]

	Dynasties	Pharaohs (Rulers)	BCE	Biblical Figures (Historical Events)
Early Period	I–II		2996–2688	
Old Kingdom	III–VI		2688–2180	
First Intermediate Period	VII–XI		2180–2011	
Middle Kingdom	XII–XIV		2011–1640	
Second Intermediate Period	XV–XVII	(The Hyksos)	1640–1538	
New Kingdom	XVIII	Ahmose	1538–1517	
		Amenhotep I	1517–1496	Abraham and Sarah in Egypt
		Tutmoses I	1496–1485	
		Tutmoses II	1485–1476	
		Hatshepsut	1476–1455	
		Tutmoses III	1476–1422	
		Amenhotep II	1424–1396	
		Tutmoses IV	1396–1387	
		Amenhotep III	1387–1349	
		Amenhotep IV (Akhenaten)	1349–1332	Joseph sold into Egypt Jacob and Hebrews arrive in Egypt
		Smenkhkara	1332–1328	
		Tutankhamun	1328–1319	
		Ay	1319–1315	
		Haremhab	1315–1296	
	XIX	Ramses I	1296–1295	
		Seti I	1295–1281	
		Ramses II	1281–1215	
		Merneptah	1215–1206	

- -

Period of anarchy and upheaval by foreigners		Setnakhte		Moses and Aaron lead Exodus from Egypt

- -

	XX	Ramses III–XI	1187–1072	
Third Intermediate Period	XXI–XXIV		1072–713	King David (1000 BCE) makes Jerusalem capital of Israel. King Solomon (970 BCE) builds Temple in Jerusalem
1st Late Period	XXV	(Kushites)	713–655	
	XXVI	Psamtek I	664–610	
		Neko II	610–595	King Josiah
Saite Period Kushite and Assyrian dominance shaken off. Egyptian rule from Sais in the Delta region		Psamtek II	595–589	
		Apries	589–570	1st Temple destroyed (586 BCE) by Nebuchadnezzar. Northern Israelites exiled to Babylon and other areas
		Amasis	570–526	
	XXVII	(Persians)	525–404	
	XXVIII		404–399	
	XXIX		399–380	
	XXX	Nektanebo I	380–362	
		Nektanebo II	360–343	
		(Persians)	343–332	

tragic situation that results when this imposing conception has been shaken to the very roots.[7]

Where was God now? Could man stand on his own judgements? Who would care for his soul?

Around this period we find a clear acknowledgement that man has been granted the free-will to do good or evil, and injunctions to take care of others – particularly dead parents and their resting places – become apparent. With the accession of the Pharaohs of the New Kingdom, and the Amenhotep family (beginning with Ahmose in 1538 BCE), the concept of free-will was consolidated into the idea of a unifying God.

The few examples given below show how this 'evolving' early monotheism left its mark on the Old and the New Testaments, and underline the power of Egyptian ideas and their influence on the Hebrew mind.

EGYPTIAN TEXTS AND THE BIBLE

The *Book of the Dead*, chapter 85, records the Supreme Creator as saying:

'I came into being of myself in the midst of the Primeval Waters in this my name Khopri.'[8]

Atum was the ultimate God in invisible form, Re was God as the sun in the heavens, Khopri was God in visible form.

The initiator of light from the utter darkness of the all-enveloping waters, which were conceived as filling the universe, brought morning. The emergence of Atum to create the light was marked by the appearance of a 'Light-bird', or 'Phoenix'. In the Pyramid Texts, composed largely by the priests of Heliopolis, Utterance 600 is a prayer for the protection of the pyramid:

O Atum! When you came into being you rose up as a High Hill, You shone as the Benben Stone in the Temple of the Phoenix in Heliopolis.[9]

We can see this 'Phoenix-like bird' today, appearing in numerous guises in Hebrew as well as Christian mythology. It has an early

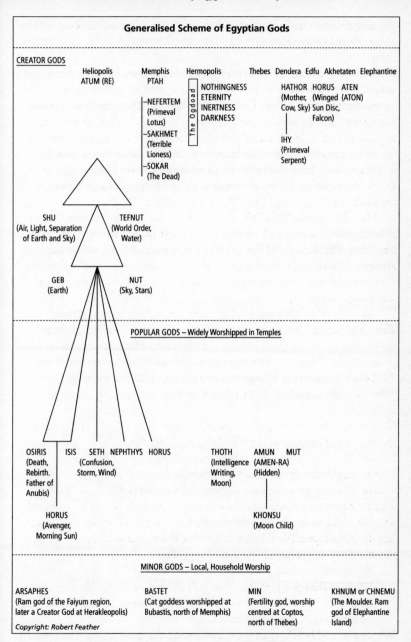

Figure 4: A generalized scheme of the Egyptian gods.

colourful depiction in the Catacombs of Priscilla, outside Rome, where the earliest known depiction of Mary, the Mother of Jesus, can also be seen.

Before creation, in Egyptian mythology, there was nothing but water everywhere. Darkness was upon the face of the deep. The first manifestation of the High God is in the form of Light. Sounds familiar? Compare Genesis 1:1–3:

> In the beginning God created the heaven and the earth. Now the earth was without form, and void; and darkness was upon the face of the deep; and the spirit of God moved upon the face of the waters. And God said: 'Let there be light.' And there was light.

The Egyptian myths of how the 'word' of Ptah and the 'eye' of Atum, the creator gods, became the vehicles of creation and the seeing element of light, are directly analogous to the Old Testament creation stories. The parallel role of mythological creatures, such as the snake, can also be clearly identified.[10]

The order of creation in Egyptian cosmology varies through the dynastic periods, as well as according to the perspectives at the different centres of religious culture – Heliopolis, Hermopolis, Memphis, Thebes, Herakleopolis – so it is not easy to establish a standard format. Usually all the core elements are present, but interpretations vary. The prevailing pattern as presented in later dynasties is, generally, as follows:

1) The Supreme Being exists and nothing else.
2) Primeval waters encompass everything.
3) Light and space (Shu and Tefnut).
4) Heaven and earth are separated (Nut and Geb).
5) Light creates the first dawn.
6) Land emerges from the waters.
7) Vegetation (flowers), spring from the pure earth.
8) Creatures emerge from mud and slime.
9) Primeval geese, birds, and animals.
10) Man is created.[11]

Compare the contents of Genesis 1:1–31.

1) There is God and nothing else.

2) Formless heaven and earth are covered by endless water and darkness.
3) There was light.
4) Earth and heaven are separated.
5) Land and sea are separated.
6) Vegetation appears.
7) Day is separated from night.
8) Birds, creatures and animals are created.
9) Man is created.

The Biblical version encompasses all the elements of the Egyptian cycle, and perpetuates the anomalies and confusions which become apparent in the light of modern science and cosmology.

In both versions there is a clear concept of earth and sky being connected and, therefore, having a need to be separated. One could, of course, argue that this was a profound understanding of the 20th-century idea of 'Big Bang', where everything in the Universe started from one concentration of matter about 15 billion years ago. In Biblical and Egyptian terms, original light is conceived as being independent of the sun and the stars and darkness as separate from light, whereas darkness is purely an absence of light.[12]

The ancient Egyptians, however, had a deeper understanding of the universe. The mistaken concept that early Egyptian deism was centred on the Sun is absolutely dispelled by Pyramid Text 449:

I know his name, Eternity is his name,
'Eternity, the master of years' is his name,
exalted over the vaults of the sky,
bringing the sun to life every day.[13]

To the early Egyptians the pivotal movements of the stars around the Pole Star were an obsessive wonder, more so than to any other contemporary civilization. Here was the centre of celestial movement and what better place for the Great God, the protector of mankind, to reside than on the very axis of the universe?*

Central to the early creation concept was the idea that order should come out of chaos. This striving for order was taken as the justification

* Nikolas Copernicus (1473–1543 CE), correctly deduced that the planets circle the sun, but wrongly thought that the sun was the centre of the universe.

for the development of an ordered State, as well as for the conquest of neighbouring states whose houses needed putting in order, as the gods would have desired. The early Egyptians also held that at the end of time chaos and disorder would return. Strange that these early minds had, in a sense, formulated the Second Law of Thermodynamics – 'Entropy of a closed system increases with time'!* Later I will show that this understanding of the process of chaos–order–chaos was echoed by the Qumran-Essenes, who also envisaged chaos reigning at the end of time.

Establishing order on behalf of the gods was a prime earthly motivator, originating from the earliest conception of Egyptian religion. The motivation inevitably spread to a desire for a more ordered theism. By the time the Old Kingdom is centred at Memphis, around 2600 BCE, the High God is worshipped in the name of Ptah. Ptah subordinates all the previous gods and mythical figures to one supreme spirit. The previous Sun God, Horus, purveyor of intelligence and spoken authority, and the Moon God, Thoth, the god of insight and learning, are replaced by a God of mind and will.[14]

The tone now is of thoughts, rather than personalities, as being the force behind creation. Here we begin to see Vedic and even Buddhist ideas being previewed. Karma for the Buddhists is the 'Ka' (a kind of vital power transferred from the gods to man) of the Egyptians – the power to become divine and eternal.

Although the New Testament and the Koran were both written at a much later date than the Torah, one can still find Egyptian influences that have 'jumped' the Old Testament. One example is the Christian belief that God is present in three forms as a 'Trinity' – the Father, Son and Holy Ghost. Implicit in the early development of Egyptian belief was this idea that the Supreme God could manifest Himself in three forms. The grouping of gods into a 'trinity' was not evident in other religions, such as those in Syria. Thus when Syrian goddesses were adopted into Egyptian theology, they were combined as a 'trinity' of Kadesh, Astarte and Anath.[15]

Initially, these groupings were apparently designed to enhance the power of the unit, but later there evolved a definite pattern of spiritual unity. This can be seen in the Leyden Hymns to Amon, which appeared after the Amarna period (*c.*1350 BCE), and was almost certainly a consequence of that period's monotheistic ideas.

---

* Entropy is the measure of a system's disorder. The higher the entropy the greater the disorder. In other words a closed system, which the universe can be considered to be, tends towards chaos with the passing of time.

> All gods are three: Amon, Re and Ptah...'Hidden' is His name as
> Amon, He is Re in face, and His body is Ptah.[16]

There were also groupings of gods, like Ptah – a national god, Osiris –
power god of the dead, and Sokaris – a local god of Memphis – into a
'trinity' that was also looked on as a 'unity'.

In the Coffin Texts we find a vibrant expression of the 'Trinity':

> 'I am "life", the lord of years, alive until infinity, a lord of eternity, I am
> he whom Atum, the eldest, has brought forth through his might when
> he brought forth Shu and Tefnut at Heliopolis, when he was One,
> when he became Three.'[17]

DEATH AND THE AFTERLIFE

Lurking behind in this 'competition of the gods' we have a dark horse.
Dating back to at least 3000 BCE, he is Osiris. His appearance is more
formalized in the Pyramid Texts, written between 2400 and 2200
BCE.[18] A figure of fertility, rebirth, life and death, his popularity ebbs
and flows over the years, at times even rivalling Re, the Sun God of the
Pharaohs.

The myths surrounding Osiris are many and varied, but from the
Coffin Texts, and sources such as Plutarch (*see Glossary*), the general
theme is that Osiris is eventually incapacitated by his rival, and brother,
Seth. It is worth looking at this story in a bit more detail, as it relates to
a number of issues that will arise later on.

A real blood-thirsty character is Seth; not content with killing
Osiris, he tears his brother into pieces and scatters the bits around
Egypt for good measure. Isis (Osiris' wife-sister), aided by her sister
Nephthys, gathers all the pieces of their brother together, but can't find
his penis. Undeterred, she still manages to impregnate herself from
Osiris's reconstructed parts, and gives birth secretly to his son Horus.
When Horus grows up he seeks out his father's tormentor, and in the
ensuing ferocious fight tears out Seth's testicles – vengeance is sweet! –
although at the expense of his left eye – not so sweet! – which is gouged
out by Seth. The High God rules that the feuding must cease, and
Horus is made the successor–ruler to Osiris as the Sun King, whilst
Seth is reduced to the role of a carrier or boat transporter, perhaps as
controller of the wind, or the bringer of death.

Meanwhile, poor Osiris has descended into the underworld and lies in a state of limbo. He perks up, however, on learning from Horus of his success in defeating the dreaded Seth. Osiris is resurrected, becoming the spirit of renewed life and rebirth, Lord of the Dead, with a soul that is again free.

This myth largely reflects the fear that the early Egyptians had for the safety of the soul of the recently dead. The vulnerable time for evil spirits to attack the soul was while the dead body awaited, in a state of limbo, the coming of Horus to 'free the soul'. To prevent any mischief priests would stand watch through the night to guard the mummified body.[19] The myth also manifests itself in modern cultures in many guises – the wake, tomb vigils, the urgency of burial, the need for an intact cadaver.

By the time of Ramses II, around 1200 BCE, traditionally believed to be the Pharaoh ruling at the time of the Exodus of the Hebrews from Egypt, Re and Osiris have merged and act as one god. In a piece of jewellery of Osorkon II we have an image of Osiris' wife and son, Isis and Horus, ministering to the needs of the unified God (*see Plate 5*).

After 1000 BCE, Osiris gains ascendancy in the Egyptian pantheon, and is still going strong when the Romans reach Egypt in 30 BCE.

PUBESCENT MONOTHEISM

I think I have now given sufficient evidence to justify the conclusion that monotheism was a developing force in Egypt from quite early on its history. There is a possibility, therefore, that Moses, as an Egyptian Prince, was an heir to this belief, and might have brought with him strong Egyptian influences on the Hebrew religion and its texts – perhaps to be reflected in some of the Dead Sea Scrolls and, as I believe I have already established, in the Copper Scroll of the Qumran-Essenes.

As far back as 2250 BCE, pubescent monotheism was a central belief. For the Egyptians – intelligentsia and peasants alike – there was a single Creator and a single supreme God standing behind all the other gods. Yes, their concept of God was different from ours in peripheral understanding, worship, and interpretation, but it was nevertheless basically the same monotheism that we understand today.

Thus an intense religious philosophy was being built up against a background of cultural, artistic, scientific and medical knowledge and ability far superior to that existing anywhere else in the world. Pioneering developments in writing and numbering systems, astronomical mapping, surgical operations, the processing of iron and bronze, metal polishing, the construction of vast buildings, complex geometry and mathematics were but a few of the fruits of these intellectual activities. Moreover, the driving forces for all these disciplines were religious considerations and demands.

These ideas of monotheism were unique to the Egyptians. No other Middle Eastern, or, for that matter, any civilization anywhere in the world at that time, had conceived of monotheism – belief in one God, to the exclusion of all others.

Through the generations, the supreme God took many forms and was known by different names, but at each changing perception came a deeper and more sophisticated interpretation of the moral and ethical standards required by the Creator. Around the Supreme God were a paraphernalia of other gods, vying for attention, meeting local and class needs, and attending to different aspects of the life-cycle. The names of these gods invariably had a descriptive meaning, but there is some evidence that some of these descriptive names hid a 'taboo' name which was unique, and that 'taboo' names carried an element of danger if referred to lightly.[20] The Sun God Re's secret name is only revealed once, to his daughter Isis. There are also examples of secret texts, only to be recited by an authorized priest in the hidden chamber of an Egyptian temple of worship.

Hide it, hide it, do not let anyone read it.[21]

This extreme reverence for God's name is reflected in Judaism and other religions to this day, and is emphasized in the Hebrew Third Commandment ('You shall not take the name of the Lord your God in vain'). In the time of the Jewish Temples only the High Priest was allowed to intone God's name, and then only on one occasion in the year, in the innermost sanctuary of the Temple – 'The Holy of Holies'.

The Old Testament says of this sacred place, in the Temple in Jerusalem built by Solomon:

Then spake Solomon, 'The Lord said that He would dwell in the thick darkness. I have surely built thee an house to dwell in, a settled place for thee to abide in forever.'

[I Kings 8:12–13]

The corresponding example from Egypt is markedly similar. The innermost chamber in the Egyptian temple of worship is structured so that it is in pitch darkness, and only the faintest light can enter the ante-chamber.[22] No-one, except the chief priest, was allowed to enter the sanctuary of the Egyptian temples. For example, at the Temple of Edfu:

> No man may ascend to it except he who is 'the great priest' and who is
> to perform the divine ritual.[23]

Another characteristic which appears to have been adopted into later Hebrew prayer ritual, relates to the reciting of a separate explanation of a prayer text after it had been read. This practice was evident at ritual services held at Thebes and Edfu,[24] and appears similar to the practice in Canaan where a priestly assistant translated, and sometimes inter-preted, the sacred Hebrew texts into colloquial Hebrew or Aramaic, in the form of what are called 'Targums'.[*]

THE NEW KINGDOM AND RELIGION

After the Hyksos tribes – conquerors from the north-east – were oust-ed from the country, Egyptian rule was re-established in 1520 BCE. Relative normality ensued until, at around 1350 BCE, something quite extraordinary happened in Egyptian society. There was a 'hiccup' in the religious continuity, when the entire pantheon of gods was swept away by one of the Amenhotep Pharaohs. After this brief episode, a modi-fied traditional multi-deity worship is re-instated in the time of Tutankhamun (*c.*1320 BCE) (and continued its influence right through to 300 BCE and, in an adapted form, beyond the conquest of Egypt by the Romans).

However, by the 12th century BCE, the priests of Karnak had become so powerful that they effectively controlled a third of the coun-try; some 80,000 people were in their direct employ and their wealth was enormous.

Not surprisingly, the Pharaohs became more concerned with reliev-ing the priests of their gold and treasures than in defending the country. The whole ethos that had motivated an enlarged Egyptian Empire and the building of architectural wonders was lost. Before this period, the enforcement of order on the foreigners outside Egypt was a duty to the gods to impose order over chaos – just as the gods had done in the crea-tion stories. The building of monumental structures was a gift to the

---

[*] Oral translations of the Bible given during public readings, explaining and adding legal and ethical details.

gods, expressing Pharaoh's loyalty, as were material and financial payments to the temples and the priests. Now things were changed. The priests had appropriated so much power, possessions and land that the process itself became a real threat to the king's authority.

In addition to this debilitating factor, by the 10th and 9th centuries BCE, the sense of national identity and national gods had begun to wane and local deities were gaining power. The ritual and practice of Egyptian religion and social life had become so wrapped around by magic and mythology, and the bodily wearing of protective amulets and charms so onerous, that its followers were both mentally and physically weighed down. No less than 275 main categories of amulets, some to be worn permanently, others for emergency situations, have been identified.[25] The air was thick with 'hi ti ti bi ti' – the equivalent of the Kabbalistic magic spell which has come down to us today as 'abra-ca-dabra'.

It became virtually impossible to perform any routine task without some ritualistic incantation or magic formula, which helped to contribute to the progressive intellectual and military decline of the Empire. The debilitating degeneration brought about by moral, spiritual and religious corruption, was not long in becoming fatal. When the corporeal body becomes so pre-occupied with its own internal illnesses, outside bacteria and viruses soon start to sense an easy target.

Egypt lost its grip on its vassal states to the north, eventually withdrawing from Canaan, its immediate neighbour. Invaders from Nubia to the south and Persia to the east, conquered parts of Egypt around 700 BCE and 525 BCE respectively, and in 332 BCE Alexander the Great completed the downfall of the Pharaonic period.

It is, however, the hiccup in religious and social life that occurred between 1349 and 1332 BCE that will now become the focus of our attention – the most intriguing period of religious life in Egypt.

Often referred to as the 'heretic' period, it was far from that. Only 'heretic' in the sense of overturning the traditional religion, it was during this brief period that monotheism was at its purest form in Egypt.

CHAPTER SIX

THE
AMENHOTEP FAMILY
CONTINUUM

The philosophical build-up to the period of 'purest monotheism' in Egypt began with the founder of the Egyptian family that finally drove out the Hyksos, in 1538 BCE. This was the family which, more than any other, developed and brought to fruition the fundamentals of monotheism.

Pharaoh Ahmose was the 'strong arm' that expelled the Hyksos and re-established Egyptian rule in the land. When his successor, Amenhotep I, died in *c*.1496 BCE, he in turn was followed by a succession of three Pharaohs with the names of Tutmoses, and a Queen – Hatshepsut. Tutmoses III had come to the throne as a child, and his power-hungry aunt, Hatshepsut, effectively seized control of the upper and lower Kingdoms of Egypt, ruling from Thebes for about 15 years. When, in 1455 BCE, the young 'Pharaoh-in-waiting' assumed the throne, his pent-up energies found release in military activity. He embarked on a series of conquests across Canaan and on northward into Mesopotamia and Anatolia (modern Turkey) that laid the foundations for Egypt's future domination of these regions for the next century.

The first beneficiary of Tutmoses III's exploits was his successor, Amenhotep II, a man of immense physical stature, who continued the military campaigns and extended Egypt's empire further southwards than any previous ruler.

In attempting to visualize the actions and understand the motivations of the Amenhotep pharaohs, I have tried to follow the thought processes they might have gone through. Thinking, for the ancient Egyptians, did not take place in the head but in the heart. The kind of scene and conversation, based on what is known about the participating characters, might have gone something like this:

A gentle breeze rustles through the huddle of mottled-white tents like a giant fluttering egret. Across the sparse desert nightscape, variegated speckled lights of camp fires flicker and illuminate tents glowing from oil lamps within.

At the centre of the encampment stands a large white pennanted tent. Inside, a powerfully built man, four cubits tall, perfumed unguent glistening on his bronzed physique, reclines on a couch. Between his gold-sandalled feet a small boy, almost a miniature replica in features and dress, gazes up at his grandfather in wonderment. The older man wears the pleated Nemes *headcloth – the sign of royalty – clasped by a central* Uraeus, *with* Lappets* *draped over his chest and back towards his bare torso and short, ornately clasped kilt.*

'Today my little one, we have ventured South, further than any of my fathers, to beyond the first cataract of our beloved Mother Nile. Tomorrow I will take you to a hidden place near to the Isle of Yeb, and we will explore the land to the West.

'Mark my words well, son of my son. Our Empire has grown as never before, not because the lesser gods have fought with us, but because Aten has been at our side. For it is to Him only that I pray. I have long pondered, if there is but one Great God, as we believe, and the others are subservient to Him and often interfere with His will, what need is there of them in any form?'

'Oh, my mighty Pharaoh, if this is so why do you not destroy the other gods?'

'A great question indeed, my child of destiny. But the time is not now. The priests are too strong. The people are not ready. Osiris and Re and Seth, Isis and Nephthys, and Horus, Hathor, Shu and Tefnut, Geb and Nut…are in their thinking hearts and moving tongues.'

The Egyptian Pharaoh Amenhotep II and the 'Pharaoh-to-be' that are talking here are members of this close-knit interrelated family of the 18th Dynasty *(see Plate 8)*. The evolutionary moral development of this

---

* The Nemes headcloth was a striped piece of cloth pulled tight across the forehead and tied into a tail at the back, with two strands or Lappets hanging down at either side of the face. The Uraeus was an insignia decoration worn at the centre of the forehead.

clan is fundamental to the links that will be made between Egypt and our real world.

Amenhotep II's son, Amenhotep III, came to the throne in 1387 BCE and ruled for 38 years. From his actions during this period it can reasonably be assumed that we had more of a thinker than a warrior on the throne. The advances that are made are more on the spiritual front rather than the battle field and construction rather than destruction is more important to the new Pharaoh.

From the beginning of the New Kingdom, through the 18th Dynasty, which lasted from 1539–1296 BCE, we see a shift in the standing of the Pharaoh from being God – or Horus incarnate, to that of Pharaoh being a human son of God. Thus by the time of Tutmoses III (1476–1422 BCE), a father–son relationship between God and Pharaoh has already begun to evolve,[1] and Tutmoses undertakes his campaigns 'at the command of the divine father – Amon-Re'.

This key change is emphasized in a flowering of literature and science, and in the architecture of buildings. In the 4th Dynasty, huge monuments, exemplified by the Great Pyramid at Giza, were built in honour of the pharaoh and to house his mortal remains. But by the 18th Dynasty these are replaced by huge temples of worship in honour of the divine father, whilst the royal tombs were more modest.

For Ramses III (*c.*1190 BCE) his principal temple, at Medinet Habu, in the Valley of the Kings opposite Luxor, is built in honour of the god Khonsu: '…of fine sandstone, red quartzite and black granite. I overlaid its doorposts and doors with gold, with inlay figures of electrum* like the horizon of heaven.'[2]

Coupled with the increasing power of the priesthood of Karnak comes moves to make the gods more approachable to ordinary people. Priests develop the role of mediating on the people's behalf. Individuals are encouraged to make supplication at the temple, as can be seen from inscriptions on statues erected in the reign of Amenhotep III at the Temple of Thebes, and on Pylon X at the Temple of Karnak. The exploits of his father, Amenhotep II, in conquering most of Nubia (Ethiopia) to the south, also led to the construction of temples in honour of Amenhotep III's name in that region.

The scene is set for the coming of the most revolutionary Pharaoh of all – Amenhotep IV. He inherits the Amenhotep and Tutmoses family

---

* Electrum derived from naturally occurring ores containing approximately 80 per cent gold and 20 per cent silver. It was pale amber in appearance.

traits of skilled strategic battle thinking and palace guile, along with the mantle of intellectual radicalism exhibited by his great-grandfather, cultivated by his grandfather and emboldened by his father.

Just when we arrive at the period when Amenhotep IV takes the throne, in 1349 BCE, a number of 'emerging enlightenments' reach their culmination.

It is a golden period of literature, art, and design. New materials, in the form of sparkling glass, shining bronze and brightly coloured glazed earthenware, open up wider creative horizons for craftsmen. Developments in dyes allow the 'cat-walk' of fashion to strut in new, highly-coloured directions, encouraging sensual designs in female dress accoutred with gold and faience jewellery.

Canaan was still firmly under Egyptian domination, as was the northern 'empire', although marauding tribes were always trying to carve out land for themselves away at the weaker spots. Vassal rulers or their emissaries came in a continuous stream, bringing tributes to Pharaoh; it was these tributes flowing into the burgeoning coffers of Egypt that helped make it the richest country in the Middle East, and probably in the world.

On the military front, Egypt had 'upgraded' its forces with the latest advance in technological warfare – the horse-drawn chariot – supplemented by the composite bow, spear, and heavy bronze sword. The watchful eye of a well-disciplined army, fiercely loyal to its rulers, had little to do in maintaining social order. Members of the families of the military commanders frequently married into the pharaonic families, cementing an 'axis' of power that underpinned the ordered life of the country.

So well-structured was the chain of command, which led on down through the army, civil service and regional governors to individual administrators that, whoever stepped into the golden sandals of pharaoh automatically inherited a dictatorial authority which was almost unchallengeable. This 'mechanism of successive power' helps to explain why Amenhotep IV was so easily able to implement his innovative ideas on religion and philosophy. Pharaoh, as 'father and mother of mankind alone, without peer',[3] had the bowed sanction of his priests as well as the bronze fist of his army to support his diktat.

|| cf Wilbur Smith : 'River God'

THE RELIGIOUS REVOLUTION

As well as the marked changes in cultural, artistic and philosophical thinking, there is an ongoing revolution in religious thought. In practical terms this can be seen in the altered relationship of Pharaoh with God. From Pharaoh being a god, and then 'son of the Father', he now becomes *useful* to God: still divinely inspired, however, and with a special contractual relationship.

Heliopolis (near modern Cairo) – the centre of theological thought – was largely instrumental in re-inventing the old ideas of pharaoh as a god, and replacing them with the idea of a Supreme God who did not dwell on earth. The priests carried the new messages to the people and set about re-writing the traditional texts to reflect the change.

The changing concept of 'fate', which now begins to carry the force of pre-destination, is important in this philosophical journey towards an enlightened religion. This concept of fate was painfully slow in its development, taking some 2,000 years. Early on, *c*.2500 BCE, in the instructions of Ptah-hotep, an Old Kingdom sage, we see the idea of ordained events beginning:

'He cannot escape from him who pre-determined him.'[4]
'The forces of fate were seen in the Seven Hathors.'[5]

By the early 18th Dynasty, we find the rebel Ahmose El-Kab, being spoken of in these terms:

His fate made his death draw near.[6]

Then, almost with explosive force, the concept of determination becomes clarified in the Amarna period (1346–1332 BCE). Aten (sometimes referred to as Aton), the God of the reforming Pharaoh Amenhotep IV, is referred to as:

'The Fate that gives life.'[7]

In other words, now there is a chance to escape from pre-destination, through God's beneficence. We have to go 150 years beyond the Amarna period, as the new ideas become solidified, to the time of Ramses III to get a clearer view of what was understood by the term 'fate' during the Amarna period. Here, in the Leyden Hymns to Amon we find Amon saying:

'He gives more than that which is fated to him whom he loves.'[8]

Or, on an inscription in the Temple of Ramses III at Karnak, we find Amon telling the king:

'Thy enemy is smitten in his time...'[9]

It now becomes clear that 'fate' is seen as a predetermined 'lifespan' but, significantly, the love of God cultivated by prayer and righteousness can, if not avert death, prolong life and enhance its quality. Here then is the template for a revised religious philosophy.

Some of the earlier Egyptian ideas on 'fate' nevertheless still found their way into the Old Testament, as we see in the Book of Ecclesiastes. Probably written around the 3rd century BCE, it advises on social behaviour and ethics, based on the assumption that all human existence is pre-ordained, and that man must accept that there will be suffering and injustice in life. Whilst these ideas are recognizable and accepted in Buddhist belief, and may have found their way there from Egypt, they were anathema to some post-Second Temple rabbinic thinkers who tried to suppress the book.

However, because of Ecclesiastes' attribution to 'Kohelet' – the son of King David, i.e., King Solomon, it has remained as part of the holy scriptures, and is read in synagogues during the Feast of Tabernacles.

All these philosophical-religious evolutions, which had been bubbling away for hundreds of years, culminated in the Amarna period, and created the pre-conditions necessary for the emergence of a 'New Religion'.

CHAPTER SEVEN

ABRAHAM
– FATHER OF THREE RELIGIONS,
FOUNDER OF NONE

The stage is now set for the entrance of a youthful character whose encounter with Pharaoh will echo down through the ages. However, before I introduce him, I must look at a previous meeting between a famous Hebrew and another, earlier, Pharaoh belonging to the Amenhotep line, because it is this that establishes the thread of continuity that runs between the ancient Hebrew tribes and the Egyptian pharaohs. He is also the first of the three major players in the Hebrew–Egyptian encounter that had access to considerable amounts of wealth. This was where I hoped to find a clue to the whereabouts of the treasures of the Copper Scroll.

All three of these major players – Abraham, Joseph and Moses – had one common biblical denominator that distinguished them from other Hebrews in Egypt. According to the Bible, they all met pharaohs.

Abraham was the first of the Hebrew Patriarchs to enter Egypt and to come away with substantial riches from that country. His story starts when he and his father, Terah, journey from Ur in Chaldea to Haran, in Northern Mesopotamia. They cross the River Euphrates, and Abraham takes on the style of a 'Hebrew', a person from the other side of the river.

Little is known of Terah's occupation (although he is referred to as a maker of idols by some sources[1]) but Abraham, following in his footsteps, is a 'wanderer', a semi-nomad with many cattle and sheep. His lifestyle is dictated by the demands of his livestock, necessitating continuous travelling between the tilled and steppe lands, following routes that can sustain the flocks' feeding. Abraham's lifestyle contrasts with the Midianite Bedouin, whose main assets are their stubborn but adaptable camels, and who are truly nomadic.

Under divine command, Abraham migrated once again, to the land of Canaan – a land later to be known as Israel, Judaea, Palestine, and finally, the modern State of Israel.

When famine engulfed the country, Abraham and his family are forced south to Egypt, to seek food for themselves and their livestock. Here Abraham meets one of the pharaohs. But which one? There was also a more fundamental question that I had to answer – did Abraham, as a person, even exist?

The earliest references to Abraham are found in Genesis 11:26 and, according to most historical authorities,[2] were probably written as many as 1,000 years after his time, although some of the texts may have been compiled only a few hundred years after he might have lived.[3]

From what we are told in the Torah, Abraham was undoubtedly a man of considerable wealth, in terms of livestock and possessions, and influence and power, in terms of the size of his family clan. His ancestors also probably lived part of their lives in an ambiance of civilization in Mesopotamia.

Around 1800 BCE, areas in Mesopotamia were invaded by Semitic tribes (sometimes referred to as Amorites), centred at a place called Mari in northern Mesopotamia and not far from Haran, from where, as Genesis 12:4, records, Abraham journeyed to Canaan. *(See Figure 1: Relational Map of The Ancient Middle East.)*

Many of Abraham's relatives have names that echo the names of cities in the region, and many of the patriarchal names correspond to Amorite tribal names mentioned in texts found at Mari (modern Tel Hariri), near the Euphrates. These texts were deciphered from the many thousands of clay tablets excavated from the area over the past 70 years, and include references to a marauding tribe of Banu-yamina (Benjamites).[4]

Other texts, known as the 'Nuzu' found near the River Tigris in Mesopotamia, give a graphic overview of contemporary life in a town in Mitanni some 300 years later (around 1500 BCE). Comprising a ruling class of Indo-Aryans, the main population were Hurrians – a non-Semitic people referred to in the Bible as 'Horites'. Certain of their legal and social practices bear similarities to patriarchal references and injunctions in the Torah:

a) the adoption of an heir by a childless couple
b) the reversion, in the above event, of the right of inheritance to a subsequently born son

c) the provision by a barren wife of a concubine for her husband

d) a law against the expulsion of such a concubine and her children

e) the adoption of a son-in-law where there were no sons in a family

f) possession of the household gods constituted title to inheritance.[5]

It seems reasonable to conclude, therefore, that memories of Mesopotamian life and society were 'built in' to Abraham's personal story when it came to be written down in the 5th century BCE. G.W. Anderson, formerly Professor of Hebrew and Old Testament Studies at the University of Edinburgh, puts it like this:

> It is, therefore, evident that the Patriarchal narratives do not merely reflect conditions, practices, and beliefs in Israel in the period of the Judges and the monarchy, but have preserved faithfully the traditions of a much earlier age.[6]

There can be little doubt that the 'persona' of Abraham existed, and that the biblical descriptions of his character are essentially correct. The Biblical Abraham who finally arrives in Egypt embodies all the characteristics and experiences of his predecessors.

How is it, however, that Abraham, a semi-nomad, is accepted by Judaism, Christianity and Islam as the Founding Father of their faiths? A man whose apparent genius and insight enabled him to fashion a radical new philosophy virtually single-handed, and found a 'monotheistic religion' that was to transform the entire world's outlook on religion?

The simple answer is: 'I don't think he did.'

To understand why later scribes found such inspiration from Abraham's story, it seems reasonable to conclude that there was some truth in the main elements, as handed down from generation to generation by word of mouth, and as described in the Old Testament.

However, Abraham does not come across as a 'messianic' leader who publicly preached a new creed. It even seems unlikely that monotheism was Abraham's original idea.

How could Abraham, on his own, have evolved the biblical sophistications ascribed to him?

In an attempt to help find the answer to this question, I turned to one of the most articulate and perceptive thinkers of the 20th century, and his views in relation to Abraham and the manner of lifestyle that he followed.

THE ASCENT OF MAN

In his book *The Ascent of Man,* and the BBC Television series of the same title, Dr J. Bronowski traced the evolution of man from the dawn of civilization, along what the poet W.B. Yeats called the 'monuments of unageing intellect', up to the 1970s.[7]

Around 10,000 years ago man, who had battled through the Ice Ages and wandered for a million years, found conditions at last suitable for it to be possible to settle in one place and still survive. He was thus presented with a crucial decision: whether or not he would cease to be a nomad and become a villager. As Dr Bronowski put it:

> We have an anthropological record of the struggle of the conscience of
> a people who make this decision: the record is the Bible, the Old
> Testament. I believe that civilization rests on that decision.[8]

He continues:

> There are some nomad tribes who still go through these vast
> transhumance journeys from one grazing ground to another: the
> Bakhtiari in Persia, for example. And you have actually to travel with
> them and live with them to understand that civilization can never grow
> up on the move.

Dr Bronowski's conclusion is that everything in nomad life is immemorial.

He notes a remarkable parallel between the life of the Bakhtiari, who, like other nomads, think of themselves as a private family, the sons of a single founding father – exactly as the Jews referred to themselves as the children of Israel, of Jacob. As with the children of Israel, the flocks are all important in dictating the mode of lifestyle and wanderings of the tribe. The story that the Bakhtiari relate of their founding father tells of a legendary herdsman, Bakhtyar, whose origins echo time and time again the biblical story of the Patriarchs – Abraham, his son Isaac, and his son Jacob.

The women of the Bakhtiari bake bread – in the same biblical manner of unleavened cake on hot stones, which we now know as 'Matzoh'. Their simple technologies for making yogurt, spinning wool or making repairs, is light and easily transportable and suitable only for immediate use on their journeying – and of no permanency. Anything of more substantial nature is bought by barter and trading. There is no capacity for innovation or to develop new ideas.

As Dr Bronowski puts it: 'The only habits that survive are the old habits. The only ambition of the son is to be like the father ... Nothing is memorable. Nomads have no memorials, even to the dead. (Where is Bakhtyar, where was Jacob buried?)'[9]

Although the Patriarchs are traditionally associated with various resting places – Abraham with Hebron 30km south of Jerusalem, Isaac with Beersheba in southern Israel, and Jacob with Bethel some 15km north of Jerusalem – there is no archaeological certainty to these locations.

It is no surprise, therefore, that Chaldea, whence Abraham's tribe started their wanderings, was in the region that was influenced by the culture and mythology of what is now Iran (and was previously Persia) – the land of the ancient Bakhtiari. Could someone leading a semi-nomadic life be the founder of three great religions? Dr Bronowski's views strongly mitigate against this possibility.

Human progress is, in general, a process of slow methodical endeavour, each advance building on previous extant understanding and slowly edging back the frontiers of knowledge. Occasionally a blip of acceleration occurs when geniuses like Archimedes, Leonardo da Vinci or Einstein make a giant leap of imagination, but even they need to be immersed almost to the point of obsessive abstraction in their work, and nurtured by the stimulation of like-minded colleagues. As Professor Hans Eysenck, the IQ guru, puts it: 'Einstein would not have prospered in an igloo, or Mozart in a kraal, or Shakespeare in a wigwam!'[10]

The same is true, I believe, of religious progress. All religious 'geniuses' have, at a formative period of their lives, found themselves in an intellectually stimulating environment operating at or near to the frontiers of man's experience.

Another 'essence' of a religious founder is the need to stand apart from their contemporaries and to take the opportunity to evolve, through reflection and perhaps divine inspiration, the structure of their own innovative religious philosophy.

There appears to be no reference to a time when Abraham isolated himself from his clan and worldly responsibilities.

Self-evident, also, for the founder of any religion, is the need to communicate his ideas and inspire others to follow and believe. In the Old Testament, Abraham does not exhibit the characteristics of someone who preaches to a wide, or even select audience. You cannot found a religion unless you go out and preach the new gospel.

In fact we see that by the time of the writing of Isaiah, Abraham has been repositioned as a friend, rather than the chosen founder. In Isaiah 41:8 we find:

> *But you Israel, My servant,*
> *Jacob, whom I have chosen,*
> *Seed of Abraham My friend.*

Nevertheless, encountering 'fixed' idols and shrines to many gods on his sojourns in centres of population, the very inability to carry them on the wanderings of a caravan may have moved Abraham's mind to the contemplation of a more easily 'transportable' god. Gazing heavenward at the wondrous stars in the desert night sky, perhaps the embryo of inspiration came to him.

My overall conclusion is that, whilst Abraham may have been the initiator or progenitor of Judaism, he shows few if any of the characteristics of a founder or architect capable of laying down a blueprint of its basic beliefs.

So where did the depth of monotheism that apparently bound the Hebrews together come from if not from Abraham? If Abraham is an unlikely candidate as founder of the Israelite religion, who was?

The most likely answer to the first question is that Abraham, or his grandson Jacob, obtained much of their religious sophistication from elsewhere – and that that elsewhere was Egypt.

DATES OF THE PATRIARCHS

We cannot determine which pharaoh Abraham, or subsequently Joseph, met without a reasonably accurate assessment of the dates that they lived through. The chronologies of the pharaohs are fairly well agreed,[11] but those for the Patriarchs differ from source to source, and religious sources, particularly, tend to push them well back into the Middle Bronze Age (2100–1600 BCE).

The dates of Abraham's life that can be gleaned from the Bible are none too certain. Some parts of the Old Testament associate Abraham with the Babylonian period of 1900 BCE, others with the Hurrian period of 1500 BCE, and yet others with the Amarna period of 1400 BCE.

The Biblical span of 400 years which covers the historically accepted probable times of the Patriarchs – Abraham to his grandson Jacob – indicates that the lineage between the first and last Patriarch, although a direct tribal descent, was 'stretched' out by intermediate descendants other than just Abraham, Isaac and Jacob. It also helps to explain the great longevities given in the Old Testament for each of the Patriarchs.

By working back from the time Egyptian control of Canaan started to loosen sufficiently to allow the Hebrews the chance of conquering the land, it is possible to get an idea of when Abraham first entered Egypt.

The Egyptians, after driving out the Hyksos rulers, conquered Canaan and retained a strong presence there from 1550 to 1200 BCE. Many of the military campaigns of the 18th and 19th Dynasties that were pursued against the Mitannis of Northern Mesopotamia and Syria, and later against the Hittites in Anatolia, took the Egyptians through Canaan. There are well-chronicled records of, for example, the drive by Tutmoses III to Megiddo in 1482 BCE. An archive of clay tablets discovered at El-Amarna, site of the capital of Egypt in the time of Amenhotep IV, refers to exchanges between Egyptian rulers and vassal kings in Canaan. Local fortified city states such as Lachish, Gezer, Megiddo and Hazor were charged with protecting Egyptian interests in Canaan. These exchanges were written in the first half of the 14th century BCE in Akkadian – the *lingua franca* of the Middle East in that period.

In the 13th and 12th centuries BCE Egypt still had a strong military presence in Canaan, but around 1170–1150 BCE the Egyptians were gone, leaving a power vacuum soon to be filled by the Philistines and the Israelites. This vacuum gives us the likely earliest dates for the Israelites to have entered Canaan. Prior to that time, the Egyptian grip on the country was still too strong to allow any substantial infiltration by outsiders.

However, there is almost no archaeological evidence between 1250–950 BCE to indicate that the Israelites had arrived in Canaan. The only tangible evidence is from a 'Hymn of Victory' stele found at Thebes, set up by the Egyptian King Merneptah, which records:

Israel is laid waste, his seed is not.[12]

The stele places the date at *c*.1210 BCE, but the reference to Israel is written in the sense of 'Israel' being a people, rather than a land. The interpretation is, therefore, that the Israelites had suffered a military defeat but that they were not yet in 'Israel'.

The date of the departure of the Egyptians from Canaan indicates that the date of the Exodus of the Israelites from Egypt cannot have allowed them to have arrived in Canaan until around 1170–1150 BCE. Paul Goodman[13] gives the Exodus as 1220 BCE, the *Encyclopaedia of the Bible*[14] and G.W. Anderson[15] both date it to 1250 BCE. In terms of consistency with the Bible, Paul Goodman's 1220 BCE becomes more convincing. If we assume the Bible is correct in saying that the Israelites wandered in the desert for 40 years, they would have arrived in Canaan around 1180–1170 BCE, just about the time the Egyptian presence was ending.

A COOKE'S TOUR OF MIDDLE EASTERN TIME*

We can now begin to work back from the date of the Israelites' arrival in Canaan to the date of Abraham's arrival in Egypt.

According to the Old Testament:

- Abraham is 100 when Isaac is born
- Abraham spends 100 years in Canaan
- Abraham dies at the age of 175
- Isaac, his son, dies aged 180
- Jacob, Isaac's son, dies aged 147.

The problem of the ages of biblical characters is one of considerable difficulty for scholars and orthodox believers. The extreme example is Methuselah, whose age is given as 969 years! – the longest living person mentioned in the Bible.[16]

It could be that a much shorter year was in use. This seems very unlikely, however. The cycle of easily observable heavenly bodies provided a ready-made 'clock' for early civilizations.[17]

The more interesting, and more plausible, explanation that I now

---

*Alistair Cooke's 'Letter from America' radio broadcasts to Great Britain often take several diversions before coming back to the original point!

propose relates to the integers, the numbers themselves. It appears that the chroniclers of the story of Abraham made up the ages of the Patriarchs as a means of indicating the thread of continuity between them, and because of the significance of the numbers themselves. If we look at the ages of Abraham, Isaac and Jacob we find the Bible gives their ages as 175, 180 and 147 respectively, each of which has a precise mathematical relationship, being summations of squared numbers.

Abraham: $175 = 2^2 + 3^2 + 4^2 + 5^2 + 11^2$
Isaac: $180 = 6^2 + 12^2$
Jacob: $147 = 3^2 + 5^2 + 7^2 + 8^2$

The chroniclers appear to have had an ongoing fascination with squared numbers, as did the Egyptians. The mathematical relationship of these three numbers is too precise to be accidental. In fact, all the main early characters of the Old Testament have ages which conform to squared number relationships.[18]

In further mathematical investigations, I also discovered that two of the most important characters in the Old Testament, Joseph and Moses, were allocated very special mathematical ages.

Joseph (Jacob's son): $110 = 2^2 + 3^2 + 4^2 + 9^2$

Joseph's Biblical age of 110 is not only mathematically consistent with the schemes of square numbers, but also has a highly meaningful significance in Egyptian mythological terms.[*] It is the precise figure mentioned in Coffin Text 228 (Spell 170), as being allowed to a person completing the magic spell.

We know that a generation for Egyptians in Biblical times was about 30 years, and anyone living over 100 years was considered exceptional. In the 12th Dynasty (2000 BCE), Egyptian scribes wrote:

> If anyone learns this spell[**] he will complete one hundred and ten
> years of life, of which the last ten will be without weakness and

---

[*]Joshua (Moses' appointee as leader of the Israelites after his own death) died at the same age as Joseph: $110 = 2^2 + 3^2 + 4^2 + 9^2$
[**] The spell referred to is from Coffin Text 228.

impurity, without transgression or lies, and he will finally consume
meals beside that helpful god [Osiris], every day.[19]

The lifespan of Moses is recorded as 120 years. Again, this is another
precise mathematical figure, but, because of his importance, the number is assigned with two rather unique properties:

Moses: 　　$120 = 5!$
where 　　$5! = 1 \times 2 \times 3 \times 4 \times 5$　*or*
　　　　　$120 = 2^2 + 4^2 + 10^2$

Any doubts about the ability of the ancient Egyptians to cope with
squared numbers is quickly dispelled by an examination of the accura-
cies of measurement achieved in the building of the pyramids over
5,000 years ago, or of the Egyptians' understanding of *pi*, which they
calculated to a greater degree of accuracy than any other contemporary
civilization.[20]

The inevitable conclusion is that the ages of the early Biblical characters, and timespans quoted in years (at least up to Joshua), are artificial-
ly large, and cannot be used as an accurate basis for chronological
extrapolations.

BACK ON COURSE

After my slight digression, I can now return to the problem of when
Abraham might have visited Egypt, and will approach it from the other
end, in a 'pincer' movement!

Assuming, that the Hebrews arrived in Canaan in about 1180 BCE,
they would have been led out of Egypt around 1220 BCE. The Bible
gives the time of the stay of the Hebrews in Egypt as 440 years, which
would mean Jacob and the twelve tribes came down to Egypt in 1660
BCE. However, this was the time of the Hyksos, of chaos and turmoil,
which is inconsistent with the settled conditions described for Joseph's
lifetime and an unlikely time for the Hebrew tribes to come seeking
food, sustenance and shelter. Also, as we have already seen, in the earlier
Bible tracts there was a tendency for the authors to grossly exaggerate
the numbers of elapsed years.
　　Some authorities give the period of the stay of the Hebrews, from

Jacob to the Exodus, as around 300 years, but there is no historical evidence for this. There is indeed a remarkable lack of any reference to Hebrew tribes or slaves as being a significant factor in Egyptian consciousness in this period, especially in view of the Biblical claim that their numbers amounted to a significantly huge number of 600,000 at the time of the Exodus. The longer the period of stay is assumed to be, the more strange it becomes that there were no Egyptian records on the existence or activities of the Hebrews.

It is not unreasonable, therefore, to assume, as a number of authorities do, that the sojourn of the Hebrews in Egypt could have been a relatively short period – perhaps 130 to 160 years from the time of Jacob's move into Egypt and the Exodus.

This would date Jacob's arrival in Egypt to 1350–1380 BCE.

This date is also the preferred date for Jacob's 'Descent into Egypt' given by Professor G.W. Anderson. He produces a strong case for the move into Egypt being in the first half of the 14th century, i.e., 1350 BCE, 'possibly in the reign of the heretic king Ikhanaton'.[21] He discounts references to Hammurabi* as equating to the Biblical Amraphel as being generally rejected, and also works back from the Exodus to confirm his date. The Hebrews' 'Sojourn in Egypt', was, he maintains, not the 400 years of Genesis 15:13, or the 430 years of Exodus 12:40, but more like 140–150 years. For Professor Anderson, the Mari and Nuzi texts of Mesopotamia (*see above*) give a background to the early wanderings of the Hebrews 300 years before the descent, and this accounts for the vagueness of their descriptiveness – bearing in mind that the texts were not written until perhaps 200 or 300 years further on past the events of the descent.

If we now extrapolate back from Jacob to Abraham, to complete our 'pincer movement', we find that in real and Biblical terms a period of 150 years is not unreasonable for the span of three long-lived successive generations. However, as we have seen, Biblical ages in this part of the Bible are problematic; it is likely that the period of real elapsed time is approximately correct, but that the ages of individual Patriarchs listed is not, as they have been extended back to encompass the ancestral remembrances of Abraham's forebears in Ur, perhaps some 200 years before his arrival in Egypt.

All this puts the date of Abraham's arrival in Egypt at around 1500 BCE.

---

* A Babylonian king, who ruled from 1728–1686 BCE.

I consider that I have now established a Scheme of Probable Dates, consistent to within ± 30 years of those given by many modern, authoritative Egyptologists and writers on the subject. (*See Table 3 in Chapter 5 – Egyptian Pharaoh-Ruler Chronology and Scheme of Probable Dates for the Hebrew Patriarchs.*)

I had now also established the name of the Pharaoh that Abraham met. No doubt you have already worked it out.

CHAPTER EIGHT

ABRAHAM
AT
PHARAOH'S PALACE

So who was reigning in Egypt when Abraham arrived with Sarah?

The first confrontational 'taste' that Abraham had of the most highly developed culture in his contemporary world probably came around 1520–1510 BCE, and the Pharaoh he encountered was, I believe, Amenhotep I.

The year is 1520 BCE and times are hard. Drought has devastated the traditional pasturelands, food supplies are running low and Abraham's family seek fresh pastures to the south. The Bible records that Abraham and his followers enter Egypt and, because he feared that the astounding beauty of his wife Sarai* could be a threat to his life, Abraham passes her off as his sister. Her beauty does, nevertheless, bring her to the attention of Pharaoh and he takes her into his palace.

On the face of it, the Biblical story in Genesis 12 and 13 is curious, and appears to cast Abraham as, at the very least, exploiting the loveliness of Sarai – especially as we are told Abraham leaves Egypt well rewarded for Pharaoh's dalliance with Sarai: 'rich in cattle, in silver, and in gold', and with a handmaiden named Hagar. One might give Abraham the benefit of the doubt, were this the only occasion where he apparently 'exploits' Sarah – but it isn't. In Genesis 20 Abraham again passes Sarah off as his sister, and appears to sell her to King Abimelech.[1]

However, when I establish my version of the outcome of the meeting between Abraham and Pharaoh, another, more plausible, reason for

---

* Abraham's wife is called Sarai until after they leave Egypt, when her name changes to Sarah after God makes a Covenant with Abraham (Genesis 17:15).

Abraham coming away from Egypt laden with wealth becomes apparent – a reason which completely exonerates Abraham and gives to Sarah a vital role as a catalyst in bringing together two mighty figures of history.

ABRAHAM MEETS PHARAOH

Sarai is brought to the royal palace at Thebes at the request of Amenhotep I. This pharaoh is a member of a family of pharaohs of the New Kingdom period that, as I have shown, held rather different views from the mainstream multi-deity cults that generally prevailed. We already have an insight into the distinct monotheism that Amenhotep I might have espoused, and have looked forward through his familial successors to see how each of them edged ever-closer to the new religion, which came to final fruition in the reign of Amenhotep IV.

The encounter between Pharaoh and Sarai recorded by the Bible raises an interesting possibility. It is not inconceivable, to excuse the pun, that Sarai produced a child for Amenhotep I and that Semitic genes entered the Amenhotep family line. There are certainly records of Amenhotep's descendant, Amenhotep IV, being ridiculed for his 'foreign look', thick lips and Semitic features *(see Plate 6)*.

Through Sarai, Abraham meets Amenhotep. One can only imagine at the outcome of the coming-together of the two critical masses of intellect represented by Amenhotep I and Abraham. What nuclear explosion of ideas must have resulted! On the one hand, Amenhotep I: an intellectual by-product of 3,000 years of prolific human endeavour distilled into one lifetime. A law unto himself, unchallenged by other mortals, surrounded by luxury and with all the trappings of power. On the other, a sharp-witted merchant adventurer, whose heritage of ancestral travellers had given him an insight into something more than a one-dimensional view of worship. A tribal chief of wealth, and yet still living close to the forces of nature.

Perhaps Abraham's first impression was one of awe and trepidation. Here was a ruler whose power over his subjects was, in contemporary terms, almost unimaginable. The mere flick of his regal flail could mean the summary death of thousands of people. And yet, and yet...with the passage of time a tentative familiarity, bred of arrogant curiosity on the part of Amenhotep, and fearful wondering on the part of Abraham, developed. So too came a slow mutual respect and recognition that each, though on different paths, was groping towards a new religious realization.

Each had much to give to the other. The youthful Abraham brought stories of Gilgamesh from Mesopotamia, of King Uruk's search for eternal life, of ancient floods and naked priests bringing offerings to Inanna – goddess of fertility, a magical ram. For him, God was a reality of simple uncluttered nature, who was always with him in the desert when he looked to the stars or towards the sun. For Amenhotep there was a dream of sweeping away the ever-advancing throng of complex gods and ritual rigmarole in a new morality, which this wandering Semite could crystallize for him with his simple, straightforward way of talking and thinking.[2]

Thus Abraham, his family and his retainers departed from Egypt laden down with precious gifts and cattle showered upon them by Amenhotep I, because he and Pharaoh had become friends and not necessarily because Sarai had slept with Amenhotep. Abraham also took with him something much more valuable than material things – a new depth of understanding in God, supplicative prayer, and a pattern of ritual behaviour towards the Almighty. He left behind him an inspired Pharaoh, keener than ever to pursue the goal of purifying his country's beliefs – if not in his own lifetime, in the lifetime of his children.

THE AFTERGLOW OF EGYPT

Traditional religious commentators, as has been indicated before, are reticent to the point of negativity when admitting anything of theological value came out of Egypt – let alone an original conceptualization and belief in one God. When it came to the writing of the Old Testament the association was downgraded – conforming to the initial axiom in Chapter 4: that innovations came largely as a result of original developments from within the faith.

There are many writers, such as Ernst Sellin[3] and Sigmund Freud[4] – all of German extraction, and all writing in the first half of the 20th century – who have noted the many parallels between Judaism and Egyptian ideologies. These authors tend to the view (as I do) that previous historical encounters are much more significant for the development of Judaism than is generally recognized.

For my money the balance is quite convincingly tipped against the conventional view. If the weight of evidence is placed on the 'scales of truth', it is clear that when the 'pan' containing 1,500 years of leading-edge knowledge from the world's most advanced civilization, concentrated into the intelligentsia surrounding Amenhotep I, is balanced against the 'pan' of a wandering merchant adventurer, there could only be one result. As Dr Bronowski reminds us: 'Everything in nomad life is immemorial…There is no capacity for innovation, to develop a new device, a new idea – not even a new tune.'[5] That Abraham took away from Egypt a defined monotheism is, indeed, indicated by the order of Abraham's story in the Old Testament. Significantly Abraham's stay in Egypt is recounted as taking place at the beginning of the very first chapter (in Genesis 12) that describes his life – when he was relatively young and therefore most impressionable. The only previous encounter he has had with God is an instruction to leave his homeland. It is only after Abraham's departure from Egypt and his encounter with Amenhotep I, that there are more detailed accounts of bipartisan involvement with God, the promise of a homeland, a defined covenant with God, and the foretelling of a future return of his descendants to Egypt. The first time Abraham encounters God (Genesis 18:2, 6), God appears in the form of three men – the typical triad formulation of God current in Egypt at that time (*see Glossary – Triad*).

Also of considerable relevance in these post-Pharaoh encounters, is the story of Abraham and Melchizedek, the King of Salem. In Genesis 14, we find Abraham demonstrating his mettle as a warrior chief and his loyalty to his family. His nephew, Lot, has been captured by a group of five warring kings led by Chedorlaomer, who overthrew four kings led by the kings of Sodom and Gomorrah. Abraham recruits help from friendly tribes of Mamre the Amorite, and his brothers Eshkol and Aner. Together with 318 of his own followers they pursue the enemy to Hobah, near to Damascus, kill Chedorlaomer and manage to rescue Lot, his family, their chattels and the other captives.

So pleased is the King of Sodom that he comes out to welcome the returning warriors and, together with Melchizedek, he fetes Abraham. This latter passage is particularly intriguing. At this time much of Canaan was under the control of Egypt. Salem, which is identified with Jerusalem, would have been an important administrative centre and its ruler, 'Melchizedek' (whose name indicates he was a combination of King and High Priest), would not have been appointed had he not had an adherence to Amenhotep I's beliefs. This conclusion is further confirmed by the greeting that Melchizedek gives to Abraham:

> And Melchizedek, King of Salem, brought out bread and wine; he was a priest of *the Most High God*. He blessed him, saying, 'Blessed be Abram of *the Most High God*, Creator of heaven and earth. And blessed

be *the Most High God,* who has delivered your foes into your hand.'
And [Abram] gave him a tenth of everything.

Then the King of Sodom said to Abram, 'Give me the persons, and
take the possessions for yourself.' But Abram said to the king of
Sodom, 'I swear to the Lord, *the God Most High,* Creator of heaven and
earth: I will not take so much as a thread or a sandal strap of what is
yours, you shall not say, "It is I who made Abram rich." For me,
nothing but what my servants have used up; as for the share of the men
with me – Aner, Eshkol, and Mamre – let them take their share.'

[Genesis 14:18–24 (my italics)]

However the Hebrew words *El Elyon* ('God Most High') are translated,
both Abram and Melchizedek use exactly the same phrase when referring to God. For religious scholars the duality of expression used by
such an important 'Biblical Hebrew' and an apparently pagan king has
been hard to digest. Numerous explanations have been devised, but
they all leave an undercurrent of implausibility. If the religious basis of
the two key players in this scenario is, as I have postulated, the same,
then the question is readily resolved.

Abram and Melchizedek's phraseology is, in fact, typical of that used
in Egypt for the Supreme Deity. In addition, Abram readily gives up a
tenth of his spoils (a tithe) – a usual custom in Egypt – acknowledging
his duty to the King-Priest.* The only logical conclusion is that, as they
both referred to the same God, they both believed in the same God.
Clearly Melchizedek, a vassal king appointed by Egypt, must have been
aware of Abram's relationship with Pharaoh and counted him as being
loyal to Egypt.

Analysis of the Old Testament confirms that the Patriarchs did not
know God by the name or characteristics that were later revealed to
Moses.[6]

So Abraham, or Abram as he is at this stage referred to in the Old
Testament (like Sarah, Abraham is referred to in the Old Testament
as Abram, prior to God making a Covenant with him and his
descendants[7]), journeyed forth from Egypt with his family, servants,
attendants and livestock heading back to the land of Canaan – the land
designated for him in a vision from God. He entered Egypt with a flick-
ering candle of monotheism, and now headed off into the bleak desert

---

* A custom in use long before the First Temple in Jerusalem was built.

night with a brightly burning torch, lit by a Pharaoh of inspiration.

After the story of Abraham's audience with Amenhotep I, it subsequently transpires that he leaves Egypt with much gold and silver, but where that treasure disappeared to cannot be discerned. It certainly didn't accrue to his grandson Jacob, because he was virtually penniless, and had to work like a slave for his uncle for 14 years to make his way in life.

There is no feasible link to the treasures of the Copper Scroll. The trail, as far as Abraham is concerned, has gone cold.

However, there are still two more Biblical candidates, who had vastly more wealth at their disposal than Abraham – Joseph and Moses – and both of their lives were intimately involved with Egypt. Joseph is next on my list for investigation, although first I will introduce the Pharaoh whom, I believe, had such an important influence on all subsequent links between the Hebrews and the Egyptians.

CHAPTER NINE

PHARAOH AKHENATEN
– THE KING WHO DISCOVERED
GOD

As the power, wealth and land of the priests of Amun waxed during the 18th Dynasty, so their challenge to pharaonic authority increased. Amenhotep III's choice of a foreigner as his second wife, Princess Gilukhepa of Mitanni, did little to endear him to the people.

When Amenhotep IV came to power in 1349 BCE, his response to the threat was both dramatic and drastic. While still in control of the army and the civil service, the Amenhotep inheritance of 'secret monotheism' was now to be his tool to neutralize the power of the cult priests. The torch that Amenhotep I had set smouldering 175 years earlier now burst forth in a blaze of light, which would shine down through history.

The new Pharaoh began systematically to destroy the cults and replace the gods of Thebes with one God known as 'Aten', symbolized by a solar disc. It was Amenhotep IV who was the iconoclast, the destroyer of idols.[1] *(See Figure 5.)*

Whether he conceived of replacing all the other gods with one sole God, without any associated imagery, is difficult to determine. Perhaps he did, but realized that the minds of his subjects would not be capable of adjusting to the complete loss of their indigenous idols, as well as accepting a single, spiritual God who needed no mental crutches of visual representation.

What is clear, from the inscriptions we have from El-Amarna, is that Amenhotep IV conceived of God as 'un-imaginable'. In the representation of God as the sun, he did not envisage the solar disc of 'Aten' as an image or an idol to worship in itself. The depiction of outstretched fingers as the rays of the sun were indicative that it was merely a guide to a

Figure 5: Akhenaten and his wife Nefertiti bringing offerings to 'Aten'. The Queen appears to have equal status in worship to the King. From an inscription found at the entrance to the Tomb of Apy, at El-Amarna.

greater Supreme Being that must be sought elsewhere.

Nor did Amenhotep see himself as on a par with 'Aten', as previous pharaohs had seen themselves in relation to their gods. "'You are my heart," says the King, "There is no other who knows you except for your son, Neferkhepure Waenre,* for you have made him aware of your plans and your strength.'"[2]

Bit by bit, continuing the process of his father, Amenhotep IV placed disciples of the new religion into key positions in the army and the administration and wherever royal patronage ran. He boldly opened up worship to the populace, where previously only the priests had had private access to the main gods. This unaccustomed freedom to worship, the refreshing lack of ritual and mythological baggage, and the promise of equality for all men, obtainable through the King of Heaven and the King of the Earth, made the new religion extremely attractive

---

* Neferkhepure Waenre was the throne name of Amenhotep IV.

to the common people. Temples to Aten were built in every region of Egypt as persuasion and example were used to wean worshippers away from the gods of the old cults.

For the priests of Thebes and Memphis, not only could they see the 'writing on the wall', they could, quite literally, see the 'writing falling off the walls' as Amenhotep's administrators set about hacking their gods from statues across the land. The priests fought back, resisting wherever and whenever they could, and not without some success. Entrenched beliefs and traditions nurtured over thousands of years could not be eradicated overnight.

Amenhotep decided to move his capital from Thebes north to a greenfield site, and to build a mighty temple in honour of Aten. The place he chose he called 'Akhetaten' – 'the Horizon of Aten', in an area on the banks of the River Nile now known as El-Amarna. At the same time the Pharaoh added to his name the title 'Akhenaten' – 'he who serves on Aten's behalf', further disassociating himself from Amun, the pre-eminent god of Thebes, and severing any links with the traditional deities.

The move to Akhetaten was not only symbolic, it removed the power-base of Egyptian government and military command from an environment where three main gods – Amun, Mut, and Khons – were worshipped, with their associated powerful priesthoods and hangers-on. From Akhetaten, his new 'Holy City', Pharaoh set about removing the images of all the other gods throughout Egypt (as evidenced by archaeological research), enforcing a complete break from multi-deity worship.

In vigorously destroying all previous mentions of a plurality of gods, Akhenaten reversed many of the main characteristics of the previous religions and instituted his own new teachings:

1. Only one God could be worshipped
The worship of Amon-re and all the current gods was forbidden. Akhenaten set about removing the gods' inscriptions and closing their Temples.

> Oh, Thou only God!
> There is no other God than Thou.[3]

2. Graven images were banned

> The true God, said the King, had no form;
> and he held to this opinion throughout his life.[4]

No personal representation of Aten has ever been found from the Amarna period.

3. The cult of death worship and idea of immortality was abandoned completely

No other culture had been so obsessed with death and provisions for immortality than the Egyptian. Akhenaten banished inscriptions or hymns on tombs, and made no mention of immortality.

> Osiris [the death god] is completely ignored. He is never mentioned in any record of Ikhnaton [Akhenaten] or in any of the tombs of Amarna.[5]

In the tombs of El-Amarna there are no carvings showing the deceased or the usual Osiris figures for the protection of the dead. The scenes are of graceful figures dominated by illustrations of Akhenaten, who is the human 'link' for salvation from 'Aten'.

4. Ritual animal sacrifice was not practised

Akhenaten counted it sinful to shed blood or to take away the life which Aten gave.

> No sacrifices were offered up in his temple; the fruits of the earth alone were laid on the altars.[6]

5. Universality of worship

Akhenaten opened up religious worship of the Supreme Deity to the common people rather than just the privileged few. He preached the gospel of equality and universal brotherhood.[7]

Archaeological excavations of the remains of the gigantic Temple to 'Aten' at El-Amarna show that its precinct courtyards were well provided with open-air altars for worship by ordinary citizens, in sharp contrast to the secretive, closed cult chambers of other Egyptian temples. Pictures of everyday life in Akhetaten are beautifully preserved in the reconstructed wall of a temple to Akhenaten at Thebes, in the Luxor Museum. Here, bathed in a stream of sunlight, we see Aten's priests and Pharaoh in acts of worship in the temple, whilst further out in the town the citizens go about their daily tasks – obtaining grain from the storehouses, metalworking, woodworking, brewing, baking and cleaning.

6. Burial without worldly goods

No manifestations of daily life pandering to wealth, such as statues of servants or ostentatious possessions, are evident in the tombs at El-Amarna. Walls are generally devoid of sculpture, apart from prayers and pictures of Aten being worshipped, or representations of the royal family.[8]

7. Magic and myth were confined to the bin

Akhenaten flung all these formulae into the fire. Djins, bogies, spirits, monsters, demigods and Osiris himself with all his court, were swept into the blaze and reduced to ashes.[9]

8. Monogamy

Monogamy was demonstrated by the example of his own life. Akhenaten remained faithful and loving towards his wife, Nefertiti, during her lifetime. She produced six daughters for him, and despite the pressure to sire a son, he stayed loyal to her. Akhenaten appears not to have had any mistresses.*

INTERPRETATIONS OF AKHENATEN'S ACTIONS

The relationship between God and ruler, as we have seen, had undergone subtle, in mathematical terms 'differential', changes over the millennia, culminating in the thinking of Akhenaten. Now we find the feeling 'the pharaoh who is useful to [God], who is useful to Him',[10] and inscribed on a stone memorial in the Temple to Ptah, at Karnak:

He has made great the victories of my majesty above [those of] any king who has been before. My majesty commanded that his altar should be supplied with everything good.[11]

The Pharaoh, rather than being a contemporary, or incarnate representative, now expresses joy and thankfulness to God and offers sacrifices in gratitude, not in placation.

I believe it is at this point in history that there was a true moving over from the earlier 'cult' type religion, where ritual practices and magical

---

* There is evidence that Akhenaten had a secondary, diplomatic wife, Kiya, but she appears to have played no part in his family or religious life.

spells are undertaken for what is desired, and if they don't work there is pique and even menaces.[12] The necessity of sacrifice, as a means of appeasement, can also be seen to be weakening. By jumping back in time the antecedents of this pivotal change in attitudes can be clearly detected.

In the *Instructions* on sacrifices and worship of the 10th Dynasty, King Merikare (*c.*2000 BCE) is told:

> More acceptable to God is the virtue of one that is just of heart than the ox [of sacrifice] of him that doeth iniquity.[13]

We see this fundamental religious tenet clearly echoed in the Old Testament in Hosea 6:6:

> For I desired mercy, and not sacrifice; and the knowledge of God more than burnt offerings.

Akhenaten's strength of purpose in resisting ritual animal sacrifice, against a background of the relatively primitive and violent cultural society, marks him out as one of the greatest humanitarians of history. It took Hebrew society a further 1,400 years – and then only by *force majeure*, with the destruction of the Second Temple in 70 CE – to abandon animal sacrifice. Even by today's standards Akhenaten was 3,300 years ahead of his time, as animal sacrifices still continue in certain parts of the world.

Nevertheless, Akhenaten has often been labelled as an 'heretic' and dismissed as a worshipper of the sun, particularly by religious writers both Jewish and Christian. This is a complete misrepresentation of his much deeper spiritual beliefs. 'Aten' is, indeed, figuratively represented by the sun, with out-stretched hands giving the power of life and goodness to the world. But Akhenaten's prayers and texts, of which we have numerous examples, make it quite clear that the God he believed in was not the sun, but an unknowable Supreme Force that had power over everything in the universe.[14]

A number of modern scholars, described eloquently by Cyril Aldred, who wrote the classic *Akhenaten King of Egypt*, have tried, and it seems in some ways, succeeded in submerging Akhenaten's reputation in a sea of character assassination. His pacifism and internationalism have been attacked, his features ridiculed, his social and political innovations denied him, even his relationship with his daughters postulated as incestuous. Whenever religious writers mention Akhenaten, and that is generally very seldom, he is often labelled an 'heretic', with all the overtones that word implies.

Earlier Egyptologists, however, took a different line. W.M. Flinders Petrie, one of the foremost archaeologists of the 19th century, was rapturous in his view of Akhenaten as philosopher, moralist, religious reformer, innovator and idealist. His views were particularly influential on James Henry Breasted, Professor of Egyptology and Oriental History at the University of Chicago. Breasted was a fascinating man in his own right and has been described as the American 'bridge between the old world of indoor scholarship and the new one of excavation'.[15] (*See the Glossary for more information on Professor Breasted.*) Having made an intense study of hymns composed for Aten, probably partly by Akhenaten, Breasted wrote:

> ...there died with him such a spirit as the world had never seen before – a brave soul, undauntedly facing the momentum of immemorial tradition, and thereby stepping out from the long line of conventional and colourless Pharaohs, that he might disseminate ideas far beyond and above the capacity of his age to understand...[16]

Akhenaten took the revolutionary step that previous rulers had moved towards and possibly contemplated, but had not dared to take. To quote Cyril Aldred, Keeper of Archaeology at the Royal Scottish Museum at Edinburgh:

> In essence his [Akhenaten's] doctrine rejected the universal concept of idolatry. He taught that the graven images in which Egyptian gods revealed themselves had been invented by man and made by the skill of artisans. He proclaimed a new God, unique, mysterious, whose forms could not be known and which were not fashioned by human hands.[17]

What Akhenaten attempted was incredibly brave. He tried to turn back, in 17 short years, the tide of several thousand years of history and, in mainstream Egyptian society after his death, he failed. Some historians still argue that Akhenaten's religion was of little consequence in overall history, as it was 'ephemeral'. To judge it on its survival only in Egypt is to misjudge completely its significance. In its purest form it may have faded quite rapidly in mainstream Egypt, but its core ideas, underscored by the progressive wisdom of past dynasties, lived on, and were far from ephemeral for the Jews, or, subsequently, for the rest of the world's main religions.

As N. de G. Davies, one of the most eminent archaeologists of Akhenaten's capital city put it:

> It is astonishing that Akhenaten had not only reached monotheism,
> but had carried worship to a height which required no nearer symbol
> or other outward embodiment than the mysterious and intangible sun
> in the heavens, which to the ancients was far from being, as it is to us,
> clearly a material body, explained, analysed and weighed.[18]

I believe that Akhenaten's legacy of monotheism had a much more profound influence on the Hebrews than has previously been admitted or realized.

LINKS WITH JUDAISM

It is significant to note that the main fundamental tenets of Judaism are identical with those of Akhenatenism, namely:

a) worship of only one God
b) forbidding of graven images and rejection of all idolatry
c) abandonment of death worship and ideas of imminent physical resurrection
d) burial without any worldly goods or protective ornaments
e) abandonment of holocaust sacrifices
f) universality of worship – it is not just for the privileged few
g) monogamy
h) rejection of magic, sorcery and charms[19]
i) worship centred on a temple.

All these principles, except (i), were also complete denunciations of traditional Egyptian religious practices, emphasizing the stark immiscibility of Akhenaten's new religion with the old.

The nine main characteristics of Akhenaten's monotheism listed above, closely follow the fundamental tenets of the Jewish faith as it is practised today.[20]

The early Israelite religion entirely abandoned ideas of immortality and existence after death was never mentioned. The Pentateuch makes no mention of any kind of separate world or afterlife, and has no terminology for such a state.[21] The idea of a 'life to come' was a much later concept, introduced by prophets such as Isaiah, Daniel and Ezekiel. It was probably developed as a requirement to encompass God's judgement and to explain how sinners in this life would get their just desserts in the next, and why the faithful person's reward is not always in this life. When this 'idea' was re-accepted, it also let in ideas of pre- and post-Akhenaten Egyptian after-life.

When Akhenaten swept away the worship of the dead, the cult of Osiris, funereal incantations and provisions for the dead the implication was that there would be no corporeal after-life. There was, nevertheless, a concept of a redeemable immortal soul, which would continue on if the dead person had led a sufficiently pure life.

As the centuries passed, mainstream Judaism in its new homeland drifted away from these original beliefs and, after the destruction of the First Temple, the weakened convictions of the priests accelerated the drift. The old Egyptian ideas on death, foreign to Akhenaten's period, crept back into usage – amulets, anti-evil magic, superstitions and Kabbalah.

The wearing of amulets and ornaments to ward off the evil-eye, can be reliably traced back to at least the 7th century BCE, when the earliest example of religious engraving on metal in the Israelite Kingdom came to light. In 1980, during the excavation of an Iron Age cemetery at Ketef Hinnom, just outside Jerusalem, two small sheets of silver, measuring 27.5mm by 11.5mm, were found tied around the necks of two children, almost certainly as protective amulets for the dark journey ahead.[22] The amulets contain the oldest-known Bible text and are now in the Israel Museum, Jerusalem. Their inscription reads:

The Lord bless you, and keep you:
The Lord make His face to shine upon you, and be gracious unto you:
The Lord lift up his countenance upon you, and give you peace.

The words are echoed in the Book of Numbers, 6:24–26, recording the Priestly Benediction still used today by rabbis and priests alike, and originally made in the Temple by the High Priest as he held both hands outward with the fingers in a special position.*

---

* The fifth and fourth fingers held together, spaced from the third and second fingers (also held together) and spaced from the thumb. A position since copied by Mr Spock in the *Star Trek* series!

The allusion to a sun that illumines the face of the worshipper is central to the blessing, and is reminiscent of the theme espoused by Akhenaten. Perhaps he too stood in prayer and made the same blessing. The three themes by which the God of Akhenaten communicated with his creatures closely equate, in number and sense, to the Hebrew Priestly Benediction. They were spoken of as:

- the Beams (*setut*) that give health and sustains all that is created
- the Beauty (*neferu*) of the light giving the power to see and enjoy life
- the Love (*merut*) from the warmth giving beneficial qualities of well-being.[23]

The reverberations of Akhenaten's 'new thinking' were not just to affect temporarily contemporary Hebrews who came into contact with it. The effects were ongoing.

Many of Akhenaten's teachings and ideas can be identified in the Old Testament and in Jewish beliefs and practices and, to a lesser extent, in Christian, Muslim and other world religions. There is a chronological lineal linkage which ties the three great religions of the world together. Both of the so-called 'daughter religions' of Judaism believe in the basics of the Old Testament. The Old Testament has also influenced the New Testament and the Koran, and, in its turn, the Koran has also been influenced by the New Testament.

I have shown how Abraham and his family made contact with the Amenhotep pharaohs, but that there were no clues to the treasures of the Copper Scroll. The next candidate for consideration is Joseph, a much more promising character, as he amassed vast wealth and power in Egypt.

CHAPTER TEN

JOSEPH
– PROPHET OF DESTINY

When we left Abraham and his entourage, he was journeying north away from Egypt towards Canaan. He settled initially between Beth-el and Hai, soon moving on to the plain of Mamre, near modern-day Hebron.

Before Abraham died, his son Isaac married Rebekah, who bore him twins – Esau and Jacob. When the time came for Isaac to die he was deceived into giving his final blessing to Jacob, rather than to his first-born son. Not surprisingly Esau was none too pleased and threatened to kill his brother, who fled to Haran in Mesopotamia (modern Syria). There Jacob worked hard and married two daughters of Laban, his uncle, Leah and Rachel. Jacob sired twelve sons, including Joseph, and one daughter.

The more Jacob prospered the more Laban's sons became envious. Seeing approaching danger, Jacob decided to flee with his family towards Canaan. Here in the story there is an interesting passage in Genesis, illustrating how fragile the Patriarch's grasp of monotheism was, and how lax his attitude, even within his own family, towards the possession of idols.

> And Laban [when he had caught up with him] said to Jacob...
> '...but the God of your father spoke to me last night...And now you
> have gone away because you longed greatly for your father's house,
> but why did you steal my gods?'...Now Rachel had taken the
> household gods and put them in the camel's saddle, and sat upon
> them.
>
> [Genesis 31:26, 29–30, 34]

Although in each of the Biblical stories of Abraham's descendants – Isaac and Jacob – there is a renewal of God's covenant, none of the Patriarchs show any missionary fervour towards others, or even their own family. Jacob spent 20 years in Laban's household, but he had not converted Laban, who still worships idols. Even within Jacob's own family, Rachel hankers after idols and takes Laban's gods with her when they leave.

The conclusion must be that the form of monotheism that the Patriarchs followed has not yet freed itself from the co-acceptance of idolatry, and that old or neighbouring cult influences were still very effective. Nor had monotheism and a rejection of idols spread among the Semitic tribes.

This attitude begins to change late in the time of Jacob, as can be seen from Genesis 35:2 and 4:

> So Jacob said to his household and to all who were with him, 'Rid yourselves of the alien gods in your midst, purify yourselves, and change your clothes.'... They gave to Jacob all the alien gods that they had, and the rings that were in their ears, and Jacob buried them under the terebinth* that was near Shechem.

After many adventures, including making peace with his brother Esau and losing Rachel giving birth to his twelfth son Benjamin, Jacob eventually returns to his father Isaac at Mamre in the vale of Hebron, shortly before Isaac's death.

Of all Jacob's sons, Joseph is his favourite. The other brothers become envious of this 'dreamer' who predicts that one day they will all do homage to him. The opportunity for retaliation comes when Joseph is sent out to where his brothers are tending their flocks, at Dothan. Reuben, the oldest, convinces his other brothers not to kill Joseph, but to throw him into a pit and to leave him in the wilderness. Fortunately for Joseph, a company of Midianite merchants pass by on their way to Egypt and, at Judah's suggestion, the brothers sell Joseph to the merchants for 20 pieces of silver. Reuben, who was unaware of the sale, finds the blood-stained, distinctive 'coat of many colours' that Joseph was given by his father, and is convinced Joseph is dead.

When Jacob sees the blood-stained coat, which the brothers had prepared, he too believes Joseph has been killed by a wild animal and

---

* A type of tree from which turpentine is derived.

'rent his clothes and put sackcloth upon his loins and mourned for his son many days' (Genesis 37:34).

Meanwhile Joseph is on his way to fulfilling his 'dream', and has been re-sold to Potiphar, captain of the Egyptian pharaoh's guard. Joseph prospers in the household and earns the trust of Potiphar. The story of Joseph's attempted seduction by Potiphar's wife, described in Genesis 39:7–20, initially follows the well-known Egyptian story of the 'Two Brothers'.[1] Joseph resists all advances, but 'Heav'n has no rage, like love to hatred turn'd, Nor Hell a fury like a woman scorned'.[2] She denounces him to her husband who has Joseph promptly imprisoned.

Even in prison, Joseph's winning ways gain him the confidence of the prison governor; he is made a trustee or overseer of all the other prisoners, two of whom are Pharaoh's head butler and head baker. Both had dreams which Joseph correctly interpreted as meaning that the former would be restored to his old position in the Palace, whilst the latter would be hanged.

Two years pass; Joseph is still in prison; whilst at the palace Pharaoh, who is a thinker and visionary, is having vivid, disturbing dreams. None of his wise counsellors or magicians can explain the dreams – of seven fat cows being eaten by seven lean cows, or seven healthy ears of corn being devoured by seven scraggy ears. Remembering Joseph, the head butler relates to Pharaoh how a Hebrew resolved his own mysterious dream. And so Joseph is summoned before Pharaoh.

JOSEPH AND PHARAOH

Previously I have provided a considerable amount of evidence which suggests that the likely dates of Joseph and the descent of Jacob and the Hebrews into Egypt was *c.*1350 BCE – the period when Pharaoh Amenhotep IV (Akhenaten) is on the throne – and it is this Pharaoh that, I believe, Joseph meets. There is corroborative evidence from Manetho,[3] and the name associations of Joseph to Akhenaten's capital, which back up this view (*see below*).

The first encounter of Joseph with Pharaoh Akhenaten is given in Genesis 41:14–44. Although the pharaoh Joseph meets is not named, I visualize the scene as follows:

'Newly washed, shaved, and in clean clothes Joseph, a handsome dark-haired young man of 30, is led into the throne room of Pharaoh Akhenaten. He is held by two guards and accompanied by

an interpreter. The glistening white marble floor of the new palace echoes as his footsteps approach the throne. He is made to bow low before Pharaoh, and the courtiers that surround him.

"'Have you learned of my dreams?" asks Pharaoh, in the clipped tones of the hieratic language, addressing the interpreter.

'To his surprise Joseph, who has spent two years of prison life mixing with the lower and higher strains of the language, answers in perfect dialect: "I know of your dreams, O Pharaoh."

"'Then what do you say is their meaning, my bright young Hebrew?", says Pharaoh, this time looking straight at Joseph.

"'Not I! God will see to Pharaoh's welfare", replies Joseph. "Immediately ahead are seven years of great abundance in all the land of Egypt. After them will come seven years of famine, and all the abundance in the land of Egypt will be forgotten. The land will be ravaged by famine. As for Pharaoh having had the same dream twice, it means that the matter has been determined by God, and that God will soon carry it out."

'Pharaoh rises from his throne, hands raised with his palms faced inward. "It is as if you have lifted a great weight from my head. Your words ring true, and you speak of the God that I recognize. What does God say must be done?"

"'Accordingly, let Pharaoh find a man of discernment and wisdom, and set him over the land of Egypt. And let Pharaoh take steps to appoint overseers over the land, and organize the land of Egypt in the seven years of plenty. Let all the food of these good years that are coming be gathered, and let the grain be collected under Pharaoh's authority as food to be stored in the cities. Let the food be a reserve for the land for the seven years of famine which will come upon the land of Egypt, so that the land may not perish in the famine."'

So taken was Pharaoh with Joseph's astuteness and winning ways that he appointed him Vizier, in charge of administration over all Egypt, second only to himself.

Joseph, his father's favourite, would have sat at Jacob's feet and for 17 years learned of the ideas that his ancestor Abraham had carried out of Egypt and passed to Isaac, and those ideas would have immediately been recognizable to him in the beliefs of Akhenaten.

It is during this period, of probably about 14 years when Joseph was Vizier, that he must have become fully conversant with the God that

Akhenaten worshipped, and immersed himself in the rituals and traditions that stood behind their evolution. He took the name of 'Zaphenath-paneah' (God speaks, He lives) and Pharaoh gave him Asenath as his wife, the daughter of Poti-phera, a priest of On (near modern Cairo). Asenath bore him two children, Manasseh and Ephraim.[4]

Joseph was now wealthy and, according to the Bible, the second most powerful person in the land. The sequence of events in his interpretation of Pharaoh's dreams followed the script, and when the second tranche of seven years heralded a famine that spread well beyond Egypt, his wisdom and standing were confirmed.

One can imagine that Joseph was rewarded with a position of immense power and, as part of his role as husbander of the country's produce, travelled extensively throughout the land. The most likely representation of his likeness, if any has survived at all, is to be seen on the east wall of the Tomb of Huya in the Northern Hills of El-Amarna. Here the King, Akhenaten, is seen walking with his mother, Tiyi, within the Great Temple walls. They are part of an extensive procession of courtiers, attendants, porters, civil servants and military men which has Huya, the Superintendent of the Treasury and of Queen Nefertiti's household, near the front of the procession – the position of most importance, ahead of the King himself. But the leader of the entire procession is a mysterious, unnamed official.

This figure is clad in Egyptian dress, but has a fillet around his bald head and a curiously plaited bandage on one leg. This puttee-like legging seems to be a decoration rather than an article of apparel, and is not known from any other ancient Egyptian scenes, but it may well just be a bandage. Although he is partly clad in conventional Egyptian dress, these strange accoutrements mark him out as a foreigner, not of Egyptian birth.[5] There is one quite significant description of Joseph, that adds credence to the theory that this bandaged figure is indeed him. In Psalm 105 there is the following passage:

> *He sent a man before them,*
> *Joseph, who was sold as a slave.*
> *His feet were hurt with fetters,*
> *his neck was put in a collar of iron*

If my theories of time and place are correct then this pictorial representation on the wall of Huya's Tomb is the Joseph of the Bible – whose likeness has never before been identified.

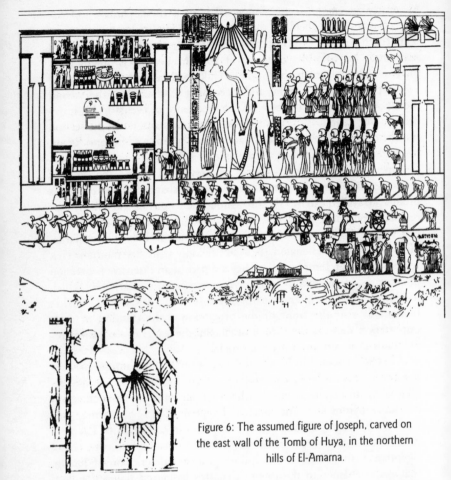

Figure 6: The assumed figure of Joseph, carved on
the east wall of the Tomb of Huya, in the northern
hills of El-Amarna.

There is an alternative historical person in Pharaoh's Court who might
be identifiable as Joseph, who might give an Egyptian name to our
fettered friend – Panehesy.

In religious terms Panehesy was second only to the High Priest of
the Temple – Meryra I. Panehesy's titles were voluminous:

Second High Priest, Chief Servitor of Aten in the Temple, Chief
Servitor, Superintendent of the Granary, Superintendent of the Oxen,
Chancellor of the King of the North, Great favourite of the good
King.[6]

As Meryra I's duties were mainly Temple orientated, Panehesy would have been the most powerful secular administrator in the kingdom, in effect the 'Vizier' of Egypt. Panehesy's name also has a direct link with Joseph, whom the Bible records is re-named by Pharaoh as Zaphenath-paneah (Genesis 41:45). The last syllable of the first part of his name, '...nat', might well refer to his role as 'Vizier', for the Vizier at Akhetaten is none other than a person referred to as 'Nakht'![7]

Panehesy's titles of Superintendent of the Granary and the Oxen is exactly what we would expect as a title for Joseph in his role supervising arrangements for the expected seven-year famine. There are three other clues. Delving again into the Bible,

> And removing his signet ring from his hand, Pharaoh put it on Joseph's hand; and he had him dressed in robes of fine linen, and put a gold chain about his neck. He had him ride on the chariot of his second-in-command, and they cried before him, 'Abrek!' Thus he placed him over all the land of Egypt.
>
> [Genesis 41:42–43]

With the gesture of giving Joseph his signet ring, Pharaoh implied that the Vizier was to be the 'Seal Bearer of the King'. No inscription at Amarna specifically mentions any of Akhenaten's officials as being his 'Seal Bearer', but the title 'Chief Servitor' indicates that Panehesy was in charge of administration and therefore empowered to look after documents, letters and seals. As mentioned previously, it was Akhenaten's custom to lavish gold collars on those he favoured, so we have two good clues for equating Panehesy with Joseph from these Biblical verses.[8]

The third remaining clue concerns the word generally translated from the Hebrew as 'Abrek'. It is thought to be an Egyptian or Assyrian title but its meaning is unknown. I believe its origin and meaning is to be found in 'The Shorter Hymn to Aten', which appears inscribed on walls of the tombs of Apy, Any, Mahu, Tutu and Meryra – all officials at Akhenaten's Court. An oft-repeated phrase, it is translated by de G. Davies as:

> All that thou has made (done) leaps before thee...[9]

This phrase begins and is summarized in the hieroglyph which alliterates in English as 'ary-ek'. What more appropriate phrase to shout as Joseph rides through the city in a procession of honour?

A SURFEIT – THEN FAMINE

Famine and/or flooding were constant cyclical threats to Egypt's prosperity. If the annual inundation from the Blue Nile and River Atbara bringing waters from the Ethiopian plateau, which normally commenced in July and reached its height in September, did not cause the surging rise of waters, drought ensued. We know from evidence from inscriptions that a disastrous succession of low Nile levels hit the country during the 12th century BCE. The national economy went into decline, evidenced by the soaring price of grain.[10]

In Canaan, at the beginning of the famine years, times were also

Figure 7: King Akhenaten with his family handing out gold collars to members of his faithful retinue. From an inscription on a tomb wall found at El-Amarna.

hard and Jacob decided to send his sons to buy corn in Egypt. Joseph learns of their presence and they were brought before him. His brothers who had sold him into slavery do not recognize him. Hardly able to keep back his tears, Joseph enquires of his father. Eventually Joseph reveals himself to his brothers, gives them food and valuables and entreats them to bring Jacob to Egypt as there are still five more years of famine to come. Jacob, overwhelmed when he hears Joseph is still alive, gathers up his family and possessions and travels by way of Beersheba to Egypt.

It is in this part of the Old Testament that Jacob is first referred to by the alternative name of 'Israel'. No particular reason is given for the change, but it is not inconsistent with the theory that it is in Egypt that his destiny is fulfilled.

Jacob and his family are, according to the Bible, settled at Goshen, and prosper under Joseph's filial care. Most authorities state that Goshen was somewhere in the Delta region of northern Egypt. This area was relatively unpopulated but was the traditional land for migrant people who sojourned briefly in Egypt.

But I believe that the initial place the Hebrews settled was further south, although still not far from the Delta region. The place I have in mind was not too distant from Akhetaten, where Amenhotep IV established his capital. One reason I have for this belief is that immediately prior to Akhenaten's reign, the capital was at Thebes; and immediately after his reign, which lasted only about 17 years,[11] the capital reverted back to Thebes. If Joseph was Amenhotep IV's Vizier, and therefore had the power to decide where his family could best be settled, surely he would have chosen a location as near as possible to the new capital, in a place with good soil near to water. The place I believe the Hebrews settled, today in the region known as Faiyum, was about 125 miles (200km) from Akhetaten, whereas the distance from Thebes would have been about 250 miles (500km).

Confirmatory evidence can be found by flying over the area. From the air there appears a westward depression some 25km west of the Nile, extending over 4,500 square km, which formed Lake Moeris in ancient times. To the north-west corner of this area lies the modern-day Lake Qarun. The tributary that feeds this lake leaves the main river at Assiut, just south of Amarna (ancient Akhetaten), and is called…Bahr Yusuf – 'Joseph's River'.

If we put ourselves in Joseph's shoes, bearing in mind that he had been given *carte blanche* by Pharaoh to settle his family anywhere he wished, he would have looked to settle them in a location not too distant from Akhetaten, today's Amarna, if possible accessible by boat, in a place where traditionally foreigners might not cause too much resentment; a region that is agriculturally desirable and able to support cattle, and if he had foresight, which Joseph certainly did, a place able to support a large number of Jacob's descendants.

What would be more convenient than that Joseph should have located his family near a lake which was connected by a river that led from the Nile within a few miles of Akhetaten? An area rich in vineyards and fruit trees – 'one of the most agreeable spots in Egypt'.[12] Quite consistent with the instruction Pharaoh gives to Joseph:

> 'The land of Egypt is open before you: settle your father and your
> brothers in the best part of the land; let them stay in the region of
> Goshen. And if you know any capable men among them, put them in
> charge of my livestock.'
>
> [Genesis 47:6]

According to the Old Testament, the Hebrews numbered 600,000 when they departed from Egypt – an enormous figure in ancient population terms (and in view of the original 70 who comprised Jacob's family). The total population of Egypt is estimated to have been 870,000 in 3000 BCE and only 2.6 million in 1250 BCE. Even allowing for some exaggeration we should expect to find traces of a large settlement in the area of Faiyum.

There is evidence that after the destruction of the First Temple in 586 BCE the Israelites were dispersed and some settled in the Faiyum region, in Egypt. But this settlement is at a far later date than Joseph's time.[13] Archaeological evidence shows that by the time of the New Kingdom (13th century BCE) the population density in the Faiyum region was higher than in the Nile Valley, lending proportionality truth to the Biblical Exodus number. However, the total figure of 600,000 must be viewed with scepticism in view of the known estimates for the total population of Egypt at the time.

Further corroboration that the 'Goshen' of the Bible may not have been the initial place where Jacob and his family were settled, can be found from the residual monuments to Ramses II, traditionally held as the Pharaoh who put the Hebrews through the harshest rigours of bondage and who presided over the Exodus period. At ancient Hermopolis (now called Ashmunein) in the region of Faiyum, two colossal seated figures of Ramses II sit before a ruined temple. The Hebrews already settled in the Faiyum area may have been put to work on this project, before being moved further north to a Delta region Goshen.

JACOB IS WELCOMED BY AKHENATEN

In Genesis 47:7, Joseph brings Jacob to meet Pharaoh and by all accounts they formed a mutual respect, empathy and friendship. This respect Jacob earns is honoured at his death in Egypt, when he is treated like a national celebrity.

In her book *Spoken Choice*, Amy Blank, the American author, quotes a poem which movingly catches the atmosphere of the meeting that might have occurred when Jacob met Akhenaten:

> *I stand before you, Pharaoh, yet I turn*
> *Toward the past, the counting of my days.*
> *Stretched out before my face I see my life,*
> *I see the hungry hills, the well's dusty lips,*
> *The long journeyings; and over-arching all,*
> *Even from first to last of generations spanned,*
> *The God who blessed my way...*
>
> *The moonlight almost spent*
> *Upon the river,*
> *The stars spread far apart –*
> *Jacob, the father, thought into the future:*
> *'My hope is far removed.'*
> *The lissome Pharaoh thought:*
> *'My hope is long fulfilled.'*
> *Deep silence fell*
> *Upon the two old men who understood*
> *Each other's separate earth and separate heaven.*[14]

CROSS-FERTILIZATION OF IDEAS

To summarize, we have Joseph, Pharaoh's most trusted administrator, the second most powerful person in the land. Joseph is married to a woman of Pharaoh's choice – a priest's daughter. He almost certainly socializes with Pharaoh, becomes a close friend, and has the opportunity to assimilate Pharaoh's religious ideas. One can imagine Joseph, Jacob and Akhenaten talking deep into the night on the theory and practice of their 'new' religion. Just like Abraham in his time, Jacob would have emphasized the simpler and more pure nature of his belief in one God, unrequiring of graven imagery etc. The monotheism that the Hebrews eventually take out of Egypt is forged in the furnace of this debate and is closely aligned to the concepts and beliefs of Akhenaten.

The parallels in customs and practices of worship can be seen in many examples of later Hebrew formulations. Guidance on behaviour and ethics were at this stage relatively less well developed, but nevertheless did exist, and would have been mainly influenced by the concepts of 'Maat', as understood by the Egyptians.[15] The essence of early Egyptian 'Maat' – a scheme of how to behave and think in life – was not initially seen as divine law, but as acting in accordance with the anticipated desires of the creator gods. Later however, there are indications that 'Maat' was seen as instruction from God:[16] in the Memphite period, as instruction from Ptah; and later still in Coffin Texts where we find:

> I did not command men that they do evil
> It was their hearts which violated my word.[17]

How much Joseph and Jacob strengthened the determination of Akhenaten to impose monotheism cannot be ascertained, but we do know that in the latter part of the Pharaoh's reign his attitudes hardened. The temples of all the old deities were closed by royal command, their priesthoods disbanded and their property seized and assigned to the local Atenist headquarters. All figures and names of Amun, together with associated deities, were hacked off temple walls and wherever else they were found – to drive the older gods out of existence.[18]

DEATHS AND CATASTROPHE IN THE FAMILY

Before Jacob's death he chose to give preference to Joseph's Egyptian-born sons and blessed Ephraim and Manesseh, empowering them with the torch of Abraham and Isaac. Jacob talks to Joseph in the words of the Koran:

Surah XII, Joseph (Jusuf) Revealed at Mecca
6: *'Thus thy Lord will prefer thee and will teach thee the interpretation of*

events, and will perfect His grace upon thee and upon the family of Jacob,
as he perfected it upon thy fore-fathers, Abraham and Isaac; Lo! thy Lord is
Knower, Wise...'

When he died, Jacob is given full national honours. His body is embalmed in the traditional Egyptian manner over a period of 40 days, and the Egyptians mourn him for 70 days. This could only have happened to someone very close to Pharaoh.

Jacob's last request had been that he should be buried in the cave of Machpelah, near Mamre, Canaan – a request that is readily acceded to by Pharaoh. Such was the importance accorded to Jacob that his funeral cortège was accompanied all the way back to Goren ha-Atad, beyond the River Jordan, by senior Egyptian nobility.

> So Joseph went up to bury his father; and with him went up all the officials of Pharaoh, the senior members of his court, and all of Egypt's dignitaries.
>
> [Genesis 50:7]

Joseph and his brethren returned to Egypt after burying Jacob. Very soon things started to go wrong – Akhenaten died.

The sudden death of Akhenaten in 1332 BCE gave the priests and dispossessed officials of the Amun factions the opportunity to regain power and take their revenge. Egypt began slipping back into polytheism and idolatry.

Immediately after the death of Akhenaten, the mysterious Smenkhkara, believed to have been Akhenaten's younger brother, tries to assume the throne. He is quickly murdered, and the priests of Amun proclaim Tutankhamun as the new Pharaoh. Resistance to the old polytheism from the established officials of Akhenaten will not be immediately crushed, but the omens are bad.

Although most of Egypt returned to the worship of man-made gods – led by Amun, Mut and Khunsu – Tutankhamun appears to have persisted in his belief in one God. It would be surprising had he not been a monotheist. Brought up in Akhetaten – the Holy City – he was immersed in Atenism from birth and took as his child-bride a daughter of Akhenaten, Ankhesenpaten, who must have re-enforced his childhood indoctrination.

Inheriting the throne at the tender age of 11, Tutankhamun was brought back to Thebes by the powerful Ay, who for many years effectively ruled Egypt as Vizier. When Tutankhamun reached his late teens he and his Atenist wife may well have started to agitate for a return to monotheism.

What evidence do I have for this theory?

Apart from his familial grounding in monotheism, Tutankhamun's throne chair testifies to his continued adherence to the 'Aten' disc, which is displayed on its surface *(see Plate 8)*. There is strong evidence that he was murdered by the ambitious Ay at the age of 21. Forcing Ankhesenpaten to marry him to gain the throne, Ay would have found her equally unconvinced that a return to polytheism was desirable. So he probably arranged her death as well.

On the walls of buildings at Thebes and Luxor one would expect to find many inscriptions recording Tutankhamun's reign – especially at the Temple of Luxor, where a processional colonnade begun by Amenhotep III was completed in the reign of Tutankhamun. There are almost none. Even at Abydos, where a comprehensive list of kings is inscribed on the Temple of Seti I, Tutankhamun's name is missing. Just like Akhenaten's name.

Someone went to enormous lengths throughout Egypt to obliterate the memory of Tutankhamun. Ironically, 3,000 years later, his name, of all pharaohs, is probably the most widely known in the world.

Ay, Akhenaten's old Chancellor, was soon to seize the throne for himself and complete the destruction of Akhetaten and the eradication of Akhenaten's name on sites across Egypt. The few examples that can be seen today are on the Great Stele of Geber es Silsila, in upper Egypt, and on the tenth pylon at Karnak, where attempts to remove all vestiges of the 'monotheistic' Pharaoh are still evident.

SO WHAT OF JOSEPH?

According to Philo, the 1st century Alexandrian philosopher, Joseph continued on in a position of authority after Akhenaten's demise. However the Old Testament relates a different outcome:

> A new king arose over Egypt, who did not know Joseph. And he said to his people, 'Look, the Israelite people are much too numerous for us.'…So they set task masters over them to oppress them with forced labour, and they built garrison cities for Pharaoh: Pithom and Ramses.
>
> [Exodus 1:8–9, 11]

Why would Joseph, a successful and proven genius in managing the affairs of Egypt, so quickly fall from favour? The answer lies in his association with the now demoted religion and Pharaoh. Had there been no drastic change in the direction of the beliefs of the royal household, he would have undoubtedly been found a useful position within the state machinery. Or, as the son of a national hero, he would surely have maintained his social position.

This episode is in itself further proof that Joseph encountered Akhenaten. No other pharaoh in this period fell from grace so rapidly after his death, and no other vizier was dragged down so rapidly by what must have been the same stigma.

In the meantime the Hebrew family of Jacob, adherents of the now proscribed religion of 'Aten', are easy scapegoats to capture and set to slavery. For the next 150 years they will toil and suffer under successive pharaohs, whilst secretly sustaining, and being sustained by, their belief in an Omnipotent God who will one day manifest Himself and save them.

For many historians and religious writers, the demise of Akhenaten was the end of a chapter in history and that was that. It was, and is, convenient to compartmentalize and forget about this 'heretic' Pharaoh. I think this is far from the truth. Akhenaten's priests didn't die with him. His writings and works didn't suddenly become obsolete. His ideas lived on.

The death of Akhenaten proved a disaster for his priests and Joseph, but they at least had a forewarning that the Theban priesthood might try to regain power, and the resources to make good their escape…and to bury some of the treasures of the Great Temple and the Treasury that they could not carry with them.

Is there any indication that treasures were buried, as I contend, apart from the logic of the situation? It would indeed be quite remarkable if there were any clues, especially from Jewish literature. Chaim Rabin, Associate Professor of Hebrew Language at the Hebrew University in Jerusalem, is a specialist in the study of the sources from which the Dead Sea Scrolls derived and their ongoing influence on other religions, such as Islam. In a lecture to the Institute of Jewish Studies in Manchester,[19] he drew attention to Yemenite Midrashim (Biblical commentaries), which recall Haman's presence at Pharaoh's Court, in Egypt, and a 16th-century CE Venetian work by Alkaabez,[20] which says Haman found one of the treasures buried by Joseph. Significantly Joseph is threatened that if 'the light of his Lord' is cast away the world will return to chaos.

Taken together, the corroborative testimony of dates, influences, associated place-names, events and circumstantial evidence, the notion that Joseph and Jacob had a direct encounter with Akhenaten becomes overwhelming.

We now have a scenario describing how Joseph acquired vast wealth and almost certainly how he, and/or the priests of Aten also knew where the incredible treasures of the Great Temple and the Treasury at Akhetaten were buried. The places to look for much of the treasures of the Copper Scroll have become clearer – a connection now needs to be found between knowledge of its whereabouts and the Qumran-Essenes.

CHAPTER ELEVEN

THE LONG TREK
SOUTH

After the death of Akhenaten, I believe most of his priests fled, fearing the vengeance of the old Theban guard of priests, who were soon to reassert their power under Akhenaten's successors.

Under cover of darkness a band of these Atenist priests, heavily laden with Temple treasures – gold, jewellery, lapis lazuli, malachite, fine spices, cloth – all that they can carry, steal away into the night. Fortunately the new minimalist religion does not need much paraphernalia. A small symbol of 'Aten', the recordings of the Akhenaten *Amduat* (compendium of texts), simple libation vessels, offering implements, incense, and lamps to illuminate and imitate the glow of the sun. The most precious things that the priests carry away from Akhetaten are in their heads.

Where to go? To the west lies open desert, to the east the Red Sea and hostile tribes, to the far north the difficult Delta lands – no friends and no escape beyond the open Mediterranean Sea. Some of the priests, I believe, went north to On, near modern-day Cairo. The others went south, risking the dangers of travelling the length of Egypt to the possible safety of sympathetic priests known to reside in the region of Ab, in a remote part of Southern Egypt – to an island (the Island of Yeb, or Elephantine Island) that still today has the remains of monuments to Amenhotep III and Akhenaten on it. Some of the Hebrews close to Joseph travel with them, contributing their desert guile to a trek that will last over 40 days and cross 500km of territory.

How long the priests of Aten and their retinue of Hebrew retainers remained in the area of Elephantine Island is uncertain. There is evidence that a remnant of 'Hebrews' lived in the settlement until well into the 4th century BCE.[1]

This strange pseudo-Jewish Community that survived at Elephantine, has always been a puzzle for historians. Most admit they do not know where it came from. Its inhabitants are variously described as militaristic, or priestly, or both, but their presence has never been satisfactorily explained.

We know quite a lot about the Community from numerous papyri found in the vicinity.[2] Its religious and social customs were quite different from those of the Jews in Canaan. The Community did not celebrate the usual Jewish festivals or, apparently, the Exodus of the Hebrews from Egypt.

There is archaeological evidence that the colony existed before 800 BCE. From the papyri documents we learn that the Community was collectively affluent, and its members had built a substantial Temple for worship. It is assumed that when the Temple was destroyed (around 400 BCE), the Community came under mortal threat, because there is no evidence of its existence after 410 BCE. History just does not know what happened to the members of the Community.

ATEN IN HIDING

With the return of polytheism to Egypt after Akhenaten's death, it is inconceivable that the ideas of monotheism just sank out of sight, out of mind. Apart from the circumstantial evidence of the 'Aten' symbol continuing to appear on inscriptions around Egypt (and, for example, on Tutankhamun's throne chair; *see Plate 8 (bottom)*), ideas are universally recognized as the hardest things to kill off.[3]

The priests of Akhetaten who fled north to On, also kept the ideas of Akhenaten alive there.

The City of On was the site of the first known sun temple, dedicated to Ra-Horakhty, *c*.2600 BCE. By the time of Akhenaten (1349–1332 BCE), all of the other major gods of Egypt had been subsumed by the god Ra, indicated by the addition of -Ra to their titles. Akhenaten's concept of monotheism removed all these previous anthropomorphic figures of a universal god and replaced them with an abstract representation, in the form of a sun disc. A temple to Aten had been built at On, and the priests there were known to be sympathetic and receptive to this new concept of one Supreme God.[4]

The pseudo-Jewish Community at Elephantine may be the strongest indication that a form of monotheism survived in Egypt. There is considerable evidence, as we shall see later, that the Community was not the result of re-imported Judaism from the Holy Land. It followed a unique form of Judaism, and originally appeared to have no post-Exodus religious knowledge.

In the rapidity of events that overtook Joseph and the priests of Aten at Akhetaten, there can have been little time to bury all the precious items that had accrued to the Temple and the Treasury: to the Temple through traditional donations of 'tithes' – a tenth of a person's earnings – and to the Treasury through possessions handed down from pharaoh to pharaoh, together with ongoing gifts and levies garnered from throughout Egypt and through foreign tributes. Some of the more portable treasures might have been spirited away; the bulk would have been too heavy to easily remove and would have been buried.

Knowledge of this treasure trove's whereabouts would have gone with the priests of Aten whom, as I have said I believe, fled north to On, or south to the Island of Yeb, in a land also known as 'Cush'.

CHAPTER TWELVE

MOSES
– PRINCE OF EGYPT

The scene now shifts. We have moved on about 150 years from the time of Akhenaten and Joseph to the time of Pharaoh Ramses II. The Hebrews have long been enslaved by the Egyptians, toiling in the fields and building monumental structures for successive Pharaohs. The dust of the quarries and the sand of the desert has ingrained their very being, just as the customs and superstitions of the Egyptians have ingrained their souls. Deliverance is, however, at last approaching with the birth of Moses.

We know Moses was brought up at the Court of the reigning Pharaoh, generally assumed to be Ramses II. His strong personality and outspoken manner won him few friends at Court and his enemies intrigued behind his back to get rid of him. His name itself, is perhaps a clue to his radicalism. There is a linkage to the Tutmoses' family of pharaohs, and we know that this family almost certainly inter-married with, and was familiar with, the Amenhotep family philosophies that culminated in the thinking of Akhenaten.[1]

We also know that after the death of Akhenaten, although there was a return to polytheism there was, nevertheless, a key change in the style of worship and approach to the reinstated old gods. Knowledge of the so-called 'heretic Pharaoh', of whom Moses, as a Royal Prince, might have been a direct descendant, would have been available to him – particularly as there is evidence from Manetho (a high priest of Heliopolis during the 3rd century BCE) that Moses received much of his early education from priests at Heliopolis.[2] If Moses was sympathetic to those ideas he would have been viewed as a radical at Court and made unwelcome.

This historical tradition fits in well with my theory that Moses learned, quite early on in his life, a philosophy of religion which flourished at Heliopolis during the time of a religious revolution in Egypt, and which remained hidden there for centuries after.

Both Josephus and the Old Testament maintain that Moses, later in his life, spent some time in the region of 'Cush' in the extreme southern part of Egypt. According to Josephus, he was sent there at the connivance of Pharaoh's courtiers who wanted to get rid of the 'dissident'. Their solution was to get Moses sent off to fight against the Ethiopians – the people of 'Cush' – in a remote region of Egypt's southern border. Another angle on the story is recorded in the Old Testament and in Midrash, which relate that Moses found a wife in 'Cush'.

It is in this distant land of 'Cush' that, I believe, Moses got more than a wife. He encountered another outpost of monotheism, on the Island of Yeb (Elephantine) where some of the priests of Aten had originally fled to after Ahkenaten's death. The wife he married could indeed have been the daughter of a priest of that colony – especially in view of all the difficulties the Old Testament has in naming his father-in-law, and the incongruity of the Bible's statement that he was a Midianite priest who kept sheep, which I discussed in Chapter 4.

There are, therefore, two defined locations where Moses might have learned about the monotheism of Akhenaten. From the priests of On, and from the priests living on the Island of Yeb. He may also have learned, from one or other of these sources, about the treasures that still remained hidden at Akhetaten.

It is in his period of isolation from Egypt that Moses has his Biblical vision and encounters God in a burning bush. The wording in Exodus 3:6 relating to this event, warrants closer examination.

> Moreover He said, *'I am the God of thy father,* the God of Abraham, the God of Isaac, the God of Jacob…'.

This appears to be an unequivocal statement that God is God of Moses's father, as well as of the Patriarchs. If Moses was a Royal Prince of Egypt, as I maintain, the 'father' being referred to might well be represented by Akhenaten, or a member of his line. We know Akhenaten could not have been his immediate father, but that, as a 'Prince of Egypt', Moses was of a Pharaonic parentage.

The academic Philip Hyatt's analysis of the phrase 'God of thy father' concludes that the use of the Hebrew word 'Jahweh' for God implies that 'Yahweh' may originally have been a patron deity of one of Moses's ancestors – though not necessarily of his father, grandfather or even a more remote patrilineal relation. That the ancestor in question may have been from his mother's side of his family is seen by Hyatt as more probable, because Moses's mother's name was 'Jochebed', a theophoric name* which uses the first element of 'Jahweh'.[3] Could this be the same God of Akhenaten?

On the surface there seems little connection between the name 'Jahweh' and the name Akhenaten uses to address his God – 'Aten', apart from the fact that they both have two syllables. However, a number of scholars have suggested that a name Akhenaten may also have used to address his God transliterates as 'Jati',[4] not a million miles away from the Hebrew name 'Jahweh'.

One only has to look at the works of E.A. Wallis Budge, Keeper of Assyrian and Egyptian Antiquities at the British Museum, who lived from 1857 to 1934, or the American archaeologist James Breasted, to see the large number of Hebrew words that are adopted from the ancient Egyptian language.[5] Irvin Zeitlin, Professor of Sociology at the University of Toronto, agrees with Hyatt: 'Hyatt's thesis commends itself because of the strong support it receives from the texts,' he says.[6]

The implications of this thesis also tie in with the possibility, alluded to in Chapter 8, that Moses might have been a descendant of Sarah, through her encounter with Amenhotep I, and therefore that Moses had a direct lineal link to the Patriarchs.

Bit by bit Moses learns about his ancestor's belief in one God and determines to break out of the yoke of idolatry surrounding him.

THE *ARBEITWERKE***

Now fully immersed in this new philosophy of monotheism, Moses, to his surprise, finds that the Hebrew slaves in his land, who had clung on to their belief in God through the years of slavery, share his beliefs. What more natural, then, than that Moses, a dissident at Court, should adopt the Hebrews as his chosen people? A huge cohesive mass of humanity, a potential army, a potential nation.

Whilst I am on this point, we might just tidy up an anomaly which

---

* A name which combines the name of a god and a human.
** Foreign workers allowed into a country to undertake tasks the indigenous population do not want, or are unable, to perform.

worried Sigmund Freud. He, you will recall (in Chapter 4), postulated that Moses was a contemporary of Akhenaten and had actually encountered him.[7] This theory is inconsistent with an Exodus date of around 1200 BCE, or historically related data. By dating Moses to around 1375 BCE, rather than the now generally accepted dating of around 1200 BCE, Freud set himself a riddle. Why would a high-born Egyptian choose to adopt a throng of 'culturally inferior immigrants'? Especially as there was then a well-known Egyptian contempt for foreigners. Freud cites this riddle as the main reason why historians have tended to reject the idea of Moses as an Egyptian.

The answer to Freud's riddle lies in his wrongly equating Moses with Akhenaten, rather than with Ramses II. If, as I propose, the Hebrews had already come under the influence of a pupative form of Amenhotep I's monotheistic religion, through Abraham, and a refined version through Joseph and Jacob's direct contact with Akhenaten, their attractiveness to Moses becomes much more feasible. Here was a body of people who already had absorbed many of the ideas Moses had imbibed from his Tutmoses/Amenhotep ancestry.

The Name of a 'Hebrew'

I think it useful at this juncture to take a look at the possible derivation of the word 'Hebrew', as it gives us some clues as to how Moses might have viewed what must have been a motley collection of *arbeitwerke* living in Egypt. There is absolutely no record in Egyptian literature or inscriptional works referring to the name 'Hebrew'. If there is mention it is to a class of slaves or foreigners.

There are numerous theories, many of them philologically based, as to how the word 'Hebrew' arose. One of these is that it comes from the name 'Habiru', derived from the Sumerian term for groups of incursive Semites coming into Mesopotamia from the west, around 2150 BCE. From this period onwards a number of different strands of 'Habiru' – some mercenaries, some traders, others semi-nomadic tribes, have been identified.

In the Tel-El-Amarna tablets, discovered in Egypt in 1887, there are requests from Egyptian dependancies in Canaan and Syria, calling for military reinforcements to help repel invaders who are referred to as 'Habiru'. The use of this term, from other references, appears to refer to loose-knit bands of warrior groups that harassed parts of the Near East during the Second Millennium. If it did refer to the Hebrews it would imply that there was more than one group of them (i.e., additional to the Biblical Hebrews), and that they had left Egypt not later than 1350 BCE.

What seems clear is that the Hebrews of Egypt were not the same grouping as the 'Habiru', who continued to maraud in and around Canaan whilst the Hebrews were still kept in slavery.

Another possibility derives from the use of the word 'Aperu', which appears frequently on monuments in Egypt and refers to groups serving as labourers or mercenaries. This may well be the correct explanation.

However, one theory, which does not appear to have been considered previously, is the possible derivation from the Egyptian word 'Khepru'. One has to bear in mind that attempts to spell in English words that have not been heard by a living person for thousands of years are, at best, close approximations and, at worst, suspect. A relevant example is that of the English transliteration of the name of the Amenhotep pharaohs, which is often read as Amenophis.

We know that the 'Highest God', in early Egypt, went through a series of transformations from initial comprehension in the Primeval Waters, and one of these later manifestations was in the form of 'Khnum', the ram god of Elephantine, who shaped mankind on a potter's wheel. Growing alongside all these transformations was the concept of the 'soul', of the divinity in a form no mere human could begin to comprehend. The sun, for example, was the 'soul' of the 'High God'. This 'soul' was called 'Khepru', and in the light of the development of monotheism through the patriarchal descendants in Egypt, it is not inconceivable that Moses looked on his new found people as a collective holy manifestation of God's purpose, and referred to them as 'Khepru' – 'Hebrew' – equating them with the name of God. The idea that 'God gave His name to his people' is a familiar concept in Hebrew literature.

At the emotionally moving 'unconsumed burning bush' encounter, Moses is instructed by God to go to Pharaoh and seek the release of the Hebrews from slavery. He is told that God will support him in his endeavours and lead the people to Canaan, a land of milk and honey.

Moses protests that he is not eloquent enough for the task, so Aaron, his Biblical 'brother', is recruited to be his spokesman.

The excuse that Moses puts forward for needing a spokesman in talking to Pharaoh prepares the ground for the solution to another problem in the Biblical story. How to explain why Moses could not speak easily to the Hebrews? He would have had little difficulty in speaking to Pharaoh, but, brought up as a high-caste Egyptian, his language would be quite different even from the everyday Egyptians, let alone the Hebrews. The Biblical writers could hardly state that he used an interpreter when speaking to the Hebrews, as the story must have come down to them. Their explanation, that he stuttered and needed someone to speak more clearly on his behalf, gets over the reason why Moses could not speak directly to the Hebrews – he did not speak their language.

Fresh from his encounters at the distant southern borders of Egypt, Moses returns to Court bent on obtaining the release from slavery of his new found people.

CHAPTER THIRTEEN

THE EXODUS
– MOSES DOES A SCHINDLER[1]

Moses and Aaron go together to speak to Pharaoh, who does not recognize their God or their plea to free the Hebrews. (Our Biblical writers cannot quite face up to the confusion of whether Moses needs an interpreter or not when he goes to speak to Pharaoh; the Hebrew text refers to them in the singular.) Perversely, the Bible records, Pharaoh takes umbrage at the insolent request and makes the Hebrews work even harder, piling injury on insult by depriving them of straw for their brickmaking. Not surprisingly the Hebrew slaves are none too pleased with Moses, who is himself having doubts about God's support.

However, God reassures him and Moses goes again to see Pharaoh, and this time tries some magic. This doesn't impress Pharaoh too much either, so God sends a succession of ten disasters on Egypt – turning rivers to blood, plagues of frogs, lice, flies, dead cattle, boils and blains on men and cattle, hail and fire, locusts and darkness. With each catastrophe Pharaoh promises to let the Hebrews go, but then reneges on his word. The last plague is the killing of all the Egyptian first-born, whilst the Hebrew first-born are 'Passed Over'. Finally Pharaoh cracks.

Traditionally Ramses II is seen as the pharaoh of oppression, reigning when the Hebrews escaped from Egypt. It is my view that, whilst the environment from which the Hebrews were to emerge was almost certainly established by Ramses II, he was not the pharaoh in power during the Hebrew Exodus. I think the Exodus took place shortly *after* Ramses II's demise in 1215 BCE. His rule was too secure to have allowed a mass escape of slaves.

What kind of a man was Ramses II? He was certainly a prolific builder and left more monuments across Egypt than any other pharaoh of the 19th Dynasty. The evidence of his work can still be seen, a short distance from Medinet-el-Fayuim, where there are over four square kilometres of ancient ruins, known as Crocodilopolis-Arsinoe. Here a Middle Kingdom Temple was restored and expanded by Ramses II. In the adjacent eastern Delta region of Goshen, the Bible records that the Hebrew slaves were put to work on the Pharaoh's construction programme at Ramses and Pithom.

This 'localization' of workers is quite consistent with our understanding of the immobility of labour in ancient Egypt. Very little population movement occurred in Egyptian society, nor would the Hebrews' presence, as 'foreigners', be tolerated in traditional construction areas. The artisan villagers of Deir el-Medineh near Thebes, for example, remained for centuries fulfilling the needs of the Valleys of the Kings and the Queens. Expertise in crafts was handed down from generation to generation of embalmers, coffin varnishers, carpenters, leatherworkers, brickmakers, stone masons, metalworkers and jewellery workers – the latter invariably being dwarfs. All this added up to a veritable team of 'undertakers' for all funereal and tomb requirements.

We know that Ramses was a warrior king from the extensive records carved on the outer walls of the Temple of Luxor, which record his defeat of the Hittites at Kadesh. We also know, from reliefs on the wall of the Great Temple of Amun-Re at Karnak, that he was a pragmatic king who could show mercy on his defeated enemies. This inscription relates details of a complicated peace treaty that was concluded with the Hittites – a wise move, because the Hittites were far from eliminated from the scene by one Egyptian victory. He died *c*.1215 BCE, and his mummified body was discovered in 1881, amongst a cache of New Kingdom pharaohs buried at Deir el-Bahir opposite Luxor.[2]

Eventually, after much entreating and fulfilled threats, the reigning Pharaoh, according to the Bible, accedes to Moses's demand to 'let my people go'. A number of suggestions as to why Pharaoh finally let the Israelites go have been proposed, apart from the Biblical explanation of the ten plagues that were visited on Egypt. These suggestions include the threatening increase in numbers of the Hebrews, and as a pragmatic reward for the work they had done in completing Pharaoh's building programme.

However, if Moses was a Prince of Egypt, he would have been very rich in his own right, and this gives us another intriguing possibility: *Moses did a Schindler and bought the freedom of the slaves.* This type of exchange was a common practice at the time and the only way valuable commodities such as slaves could ever gain their release. The Songs of Deliverance (Exodus 15:16) that Moses and the Children of Israel sang as they left Egypt gives probity to this theory:

> *Terror and dread descend upon them;*
> *Through the might of Your arm they are still as stone;*
> *Till your people cross over, O Lord*
> *Till your people cross whom You have ransomed.*[3]

The word 'ransomed' is, in fact, alternatively translated as 'purchased' in authorized versions of the Bible. The same allusion to the Hebrews being 'purchased' by God at the time of the Exodus occurs in Psalm 74 of the Old Testament, and again in Jeremiah 31:11:

> For the Lord hath redeemed Jacob [the people of Israel], and *ransomed him* from the hand of him that was stronger than he.

In Deuteronomy 28, we have an even clearer hint that Moses paid for the freedom of the Hebrews, as he taunts them in the desert with the penalty awaiting them if they do not keep God's laws:

> God will bring you back to Egypt…and you will offer yourselves for sale as slaves and bondswomen there, but there will be no buyer.
>
> [Deuteronomy 28:68]

So Moses, a wealthy Prince of Egypt and skilled military tactician, leads his newly found people, his Egyptian priests and Egyptian associates, guarded by soldiers of his loyal troop, out of Egypt. Exodus 13:18 puts it as follows, and causes endless confusion for modern translators who strive for all sorts of convoluted explanations to understand why the Hebrews were 'armed':

> Now the Israelites went up armed out of the land of Egypt.[4]

The simple answer is that they *were* 'armed', most probably with lances, and they would have had war chariots in their entourage.

When Pharaoh went in hot pursuit of the departed Hebrews

(Exodus 14) with 600 chariots, it may have been that he had got wind of the enormity of the treasures that Moses had taken with him – or had just changed his mind for the eleventh time. Either way he and his forces met determined resistance and came to a messy end in the marshy Bitter Lakes region north of the Gulf of Suez, somewhere between modern Suez and Ismailia.

Exodus 13 recounts that some 600,000 Children of Israel left from the region of Ramses, in the northern Nile delta, after spending 430 years in Egypt. Both these figures, as I have said earlier, are extremely suspect.

When the Israelites departed from Egypt, we are told (Exodus 3:21–22 and 12:36) that they took with them much plunder and wealth. On the surface this action, like the Bible's recording that they were armed, appears to be a very strange occurrence for slaves leaving in such a hurry that they hardly had time to finish baking their bread.

> And I will give the people favour in the sight of the Egyptians. And it
> shall come to pass that, when ye go, ye shall not go empty [handed];
> but every woman shall ask of her neighbour, and of her that sojourneth
> in her house, jewels of silver, and jewels of gold, and raiment, and ye
> shall put them upon your sons, and upon your daughters; and ye shall
> spoil the Egyptians.
>
> [Exodus 3:21–22]

These passages, repeated again in Exodus 12:36, have presented a real conundrum for religious traditionalists. How could a nation of slaves come away with such wealth? Why should the Egyptians simply let some of their belongings be taken from them? Were the Hebrews stealing from their host nation?

Some of the ideas put forward to explain this rather strange behaviour towards an enslaved community are quite quaint. One idea proposed by Dr Nina Collins at the Department of Theology and Religious Studies, University of Leeds, is that the plunder was only to be borrowed and would be returned after a three-day festival in the desert.[5] The Biblical passage about a festival comes in a section unrelated to the taking of valuables from the Egyptians. Were the Egyptians really that gullible? It also implies that the Israelites perpetrated a deception and knowingly stole the goods.

Even commentators on differing translations of the Old Testament are at odds. In the Soncino version,[6] edited by the Chief Rabbi of the

British Empire, Dr Joseph Herman Hertz (who died in 1946), the translated phrase 'every woman shall borrow of her neighbour', is labelled as thoroughly mischievous and misleading. This is a phrase which, in almost identical form, appears in the later Plaut translation of the Torah.[7]

The favoured explanation by the commentators in the Soncino version, is that the Egyptians demonstrated their humanity and gifted household valuables to their departing slaves in wishing them well on their forthcoming journey. They probably put roses in their hair as well!

This idea that the gold and silver vessels and jewels, were given with formal sanction by the Egyptians just does not ring true. It appears to be the only pleasant explanation that gets around the charge of theft. It is in itself thrown into doubt by the Talmud's recording of a later formal claim for indemnity put forward by the Egyptians before Alexander the Great. Another curious aspect of this story is that we are told that the valuables were to be later employed in the adornment and enrichment of the Sanctuary – the consecrated place for Divine worship. Hardly a role suited to domestic and household jewellery.

However, if my theories are correct there is a very simple explanation. The wealth of the departing group in the Exodus was derived partly from Moses, as a Prince of Egypt, and partly from the accompanying Atenist priests who still retained some of the treasures from the Great Temple at Akhetaten – some of which might even have been described in the Copper Scroll.

This explanation vindicates the Israelites from having 'despoiled, borrowed, or plundered' from the Egyptians. It also explains why vessels of gold and silver, and jewels – effectively a treasure trove – were 'gifted' to the Israelites by a particular group of Egyptians, but not formally sanctioned by the Egyptian authorities.

It also answers the question of how a community of impoverished Hebrew slaves could provide the exotic accoutrements for the Tabernacle, and the large amount of gold required for the Golden Calf some of them temporarily worshipped. Whilst he was away on the Holy Mountain receiving the Ten Commandments, as the Bible describes, Moses would have entrusted the treasures to Aaron, his chief priest – who apparently helped in the making of the Golden Calf.

The treasures that the Hebrews took with them when they left Egypt were not stolen from the Egyptians. They were given to Moses by the Atenite priests and, in addition to his own Princely wealth, were partly used to buy the freedom of the Hebrew slaves and partly to adorn the 'Tabernacle' – a transportable tent that acted as the shrine for the Holy Ark, where the holy written or inscribed laws were kept.

After making good their escape the Children of Israel continued to wander for forty Biblical years in the deserts of Sinai to the east of Egypt. This period of 'purification' seems to imply that an entire generation died out, so that no-one who came out of Egypt, except Joshua and Caleb, survived to reach the Promised Land, not even Moses.

THE TEN COMMANDMENTS

Early in their wanderings the Hebrews made an eternal Covenant with God. The acquiring of the Covenant was the most momentous moment in Jewish history. Traditionally, Mount Sinai, in the Southern part of the Sinai peninsula, is taken as the place for the receiving of the Ten Commandments and the Covenant. (Some historians place it at Jebel Helal in North Sinai, or at a mountain east of the Gulf of Aqaba.)

Figure 8: Egyptian models for the 'Golden Calf'. Divine cow inscribed on the back panel of the outer shrine found in the tomb of Tutankhamun, Luxor.

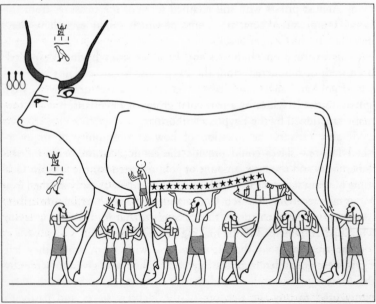

Moses spent forty Biblical days on the Mountain of the Lord receiving from God Ten Commandments written on two tablets of stone, together with details for the construction of an Ark to contain the holy words, a Tabernacle to contain the Ark, and for prayers and sacrifice.

Impatient at the delay some of those waiting prevailed on Aaron to make them a Golden Calf to worship. When Moses came down the mountain he was furious. He broke the two tablets, destroyed the idol and had 3,000 offenders put to the sword.

The design of the 'Golden Calf' that Aaron made for the Children of Israel, and that they danced around whilst waiting for Moses to descend from Mount Sinai (Exodus 32), was almost certainly based on the Theban idol Hathor, goddess of motherhood, gold, revelry, music and dancing.

Moses spent a further forty days on the mountain collecting a duplicate set of tablets inscribed with the Ten Commandments. Then he came down from the mountain:

> And when Aaron and all the children of Israel saw Moses, behold, the skin of his face sent forth beams; and they were afraid to come nigh to him.
>
> [Exodus 34:30]

The Hebrew word translated as 'beams of light' can also mean 'horns of plenty'. The correspondence between this description and the 'beams of light' radiating life and bounty from Akhenaten's vision of God cannot be ignored.

What was the language of the works Moses brought down from Mount Sinai? It is generally assumed to be Hebrew in much the form we have it today. But that just cannot be the case – Hebrew had not yet been invented.[8]

At the time of the receiving of the Commandments at Sinai, therefore, no other form of writing, apart from Mesopotamian cuneiform or Egyptian hieroglyphs, would have been available to the Hebrews. It is therefore inevitable that the tablets which Moses brought down from Mount Sinai were inscribed in Egyptian hieroglyphs, and that in laying the foundations of the 'Torah' Moses would have written on papyrus in Egyptian hieratic.*

It was only after the Israelites settled in Canaan that they developed

---

* Egyptian script form of hieroglyphs, written from right to left.

a paleo-Hebrew alphabet, probably based on Phoenician writing – at the time the Phoenicians lived along the coastline of the Northern part of Canaan. (Like the Phoenician alphabet, derived from 'Ugarit', paleo-Hebrew had 19 letters, but it only crystallized into linear independent Hebrew writing in the middle of the 9th century BCE.)

THE ARK OF THE COVENANT

The Tabernacle and the Ark, which were to house the Ten Commandments, are described in detail in the Old Testament, in Exodus 25:10–40; 26:1–36; 27:1–19; 36:8–38; and in Exodus 37.

> Bezalel made the ark of acacia wood, two and half cubits long, a cubit and a half wide, and a cubit and a half high. He overlaid it with pure gold, inside and out; and he made a gold moulding for it round about. He cast four rings for it, for its four feet: two rings on one of its side walls and two rings on the other. He made poles of acacia wood, overlaid them with gold, and inserted the poles into the rings on the side walls of the ark for carrying the ark.
>
> He made a cover of pure gold, two and a half cubits long and a cubit and a half wide. He made two cherubim of gold; he made them of hammered work, at the two ends of the cover: one cherub at one end and the other cherub at the other end; he made the cherubim of one piece with the cover, at its two ends. The cherubim had their wings spread out above, shielding the cover with their wings. They faced each other; the faces of the cherubim were turned toward the cover.
>
> [Exodus 37:1–9]

The description in Exodus 25 is very similar to that in chapter 37, but is specific in saying that the poles are not removable. Some translations refer to the cover as a 'mercy seat'. The word for 'cherubim' cannot be translated directly, but in Aggadic (oral Jewish tradition) they are conceived as having the body of an animal and the face of a human, rather like the Egyptian sphinx (with the face of a human and body of a lion), whilst in Ezekiel, 1:5–14, they are winged creatures, calf-footed, with the body of a man and the face of a man, or lion, or ox, or eagle.

The question of why the Ark, a supreme vehicle of Hebrew holiness, should be adorned by Egyptian images is perplexing and has never been answered satisfactorily. However, in the light of the comparisons to be discussed here, a plausible explanation for their existence becomes apparent.

The mysterious figure of a creature with the body of a falcon with outstretched wings and the face of a human is seen in the head section of a coffin now in the British Museum. Inscribed on the cartouche, or name plate, of the coffin is the name 'Amenophis ruler of Thebes', who ruled from 1557–1530 BCE.

A similar design can be found on the Canopic Chest of Akhenaten, and many of the treasures of Tutankhamun show the same motif of winged beings spreading their wings in a protective mode – the interior panel of the third shrine, the head of a sarcophagus, the innermost gold coffin. Plate 9 shows a fine example.

When compared to a 'portable chest' found in the tomb of Tutankhamun, the next but one successor to Akhenaten,[9] we find the Old Testament description of the Ark is remarkably similar. Tutankhamun's chest measures 0.830m in length, width 0.605m, height 0.635m, with a ratio of length to height of almost exactly 1.33:1, whilst the Ark, also rectangular in shape, measures 1.275m long by 0.765m wide by 0.765m high, with a ratio of length to height of 1.66:1.[10]

Although there are depictions of such portable chests in tombs of high officials, like Mereruka and Ankhmahor, at Saqqara, dating from c.2300 BCE, the Tutankhamun chest (see Plate 9) is the only one ever to have been discovered.

The Tutankhamun chest is both a magnificent and practical piece of furniture, with ornate carvings and fine embellishments. The lid, or cover, and body of the chest are made from ebony with inner recessed panels of red cedarwood. The joints are close fitting mortise and tenon secured by pegs, or dovetailed. Each panel is bordered by alternate strips of ivory and polished ebony veneer. Solid bronze shoes support the weight of the chest on four curve-edged legs. On top of the cover is a large gilded knob which, together with a similar knob on the upper face of one end, forms a fixing point for a 'tie' to seal the lid. Each knob has the cartouche of Tutankhamun inset on the hieroglyph for gold.

Because of its probable use as a treasure chest, the chest could not easily be carried by simple handles, and is fitted with four poles which can slide under the chest through two bronze rings. Collars on the ends of the poles prevent them from slipping forward. When the chest was placed on the ground, the poles could be pushed back until the opposite

Hieratic Ostracon from Western Thebes, Metropolitan Museum of Art, New York

Egyptian hieroglyphics

8th Century BCE papyrus fragment of Hebrew letter found at Wadi Murrabba'at

Dead Sea Scroll fragment

TEN COMMANDMENTS

c 1200 BCE
Carved on stone in Egyptian Hieroglyphs as part of 613 Commandments

ORAL LAWS →

TORAH →

Dead Sea Scrolls written in Hebrew

1100	Partly written down in Hieratic Egyptian
1000	
900	
800	Translated into pre-Hebrew and Aramaic
700	
600	
500	
444 →	Finalised in Hebrew by Ezra the Scribe
400	
300	Translated into Greek as Septuagint
200	
100 BCE	
0	
CE	
100	
150 →	Earliest New Testament "Ryland" fragment, written in Greek
200	Translated into Coptic, Syriac translation

Part compilation by Rabbi Akiva

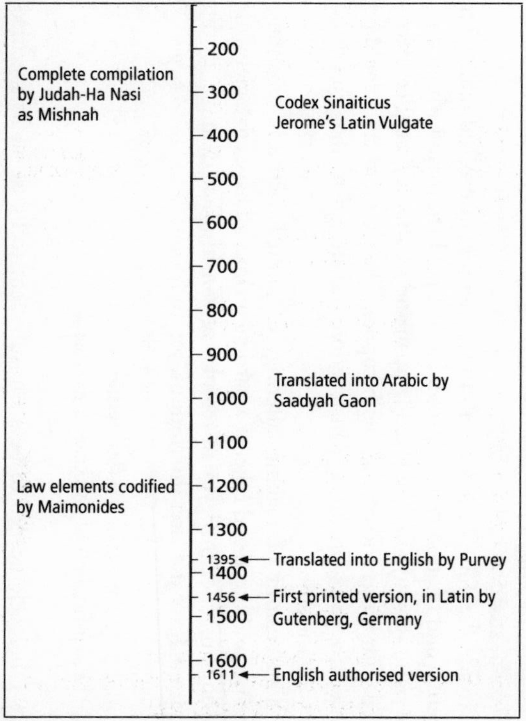

Part of the 4th century CE
Codex Sinaiticus. Copy
Manuscript containing all
of the New Testament and
parts of the Old Testament
(from the Septuagint, an
original translation of the
Torah into Greek by 70
scribes working at
Alexandria, Egypt in the
3rd Century BCE

Ryland fragment,
showing part of the
18th Chapter of the
Gospel According to
St John

15th Century manuscript of
Jonah and the Whale, with
Hebrew letters almost
identical to modern
Hebrew writing

Figure 9: Time line of the Bible.

	Complete compilation by Judah-Ha Nasi as Mishnah
—200	
—300	Codex Sinaiticus
—400	Jerome's Latin Vulgate
—500	
—600	
—700	
—800	
—900	Translated into Arabic by Saadyah Gaon
—1000	
—1100	
—1200	
Law elements codified by Maimonides —1300	
1395 —1400	Translated into English by Purvey
1456 —1500	First printed version, in Latin by Gutenberg, Germany
—1600 1611	English authorised version

Copyright: Robert Feather

poles touched and were out of sight. The poles were therefore not removed, and could not be removed, when the chest was not in use. Compare Exodus 25:14–15:

> ...then insert the poles into the rings on the side walls of the ark, for carrying the ark. The poles shall remain in the rings of the ark: they shall not be removed from it.

When the portable chest of Tutankhamun is verbally described there can be little doubt that it is very similar to the Biblical description of the Ark.

THE TABERNACLE

The 'Tabernacle', or tent in which the Ark was to reside, is described in the Old Testament as being made of blue, purple and scarlet fine linen curtains, worked with cherubims. The curtains were held together by blue woollen loops and gold clasps. The roof of the Tabernacle was made from goats' hair with a covering of tanned ramskins, with a covering of dolphin skins above. The sides of the Tabernacle comprised planks of acacia wood held together with tenons set in silver sockets. On the side walls there were centre bars held in gold rings on planks overlaid with gold. Within the Tabernacle was a curtained off section separating the Holy Place and the Holy of Holies where the Ark of the Covenant stood.

Inside the Tabernacle were also to be set a gold overlaid table with offering and libation vessels, a six-branched gold lampstand with a central stand (giving a total of seven lamps), and an altar for sacrifices decorated with horns and overlaid with copper. The altar and table could be carried by poles similar in construction and design to those used for carrying the Ark.

The custom of making offerings of animal sacrifices, libations, incense, and bread and cake, at a particular time, all have analogies with previous practice in Egyptian temples of worship. For example, in the Pyramid Texts and later inscriptions, we find:

> Your bread of worship is (in) its due time...
> The sacrificial bread and cake in its time...[11]

The Tabernacle needed to be a size sufficient to house all its specified contents and yet be portable in structure. It measured approximately 15.3m x 5.1m x 5.1m high (30 cubits x 10 cubits x 10 cubits – measurements based on plank sizes (being 'upright' planks) and a cubit at 51cm). Biblical descriptions of the Tabernacle show that in the method of linking the wooden planks that formed the walls of the tent using bars, the curtaining, and the cover of cloth and skins, it was very similar to portable tent structures in use in Egypt at the time. They may have been similar to the 'pavilions of life' used for embalming. These were light tents made of rush matting and other materials that could be easily erected and transported or destroyed after use.

The description of the cups on the lampstand (Exodus 37), is particularly reminiscent of the 'Lotiform Chalice' found in the tomb of Tutankhamun, now in the Cairo Museum collection, and seen in a faience plaque owned by Eton College, England. In its white lotus form this type of cup was used for drinking, but in a blue lily form it was used for ritualistic purposes.

This chalice was carved from a single block of alabaster, or calcite, as a single bloom of the white lotus inlaid with blue pigment. It is characterized by 16 to 20 oval-shaped petals and four oval-shaped sepals. Compare the Biblical description:

> There were three cups shaped like almond-blossoms, each with
> calyx [a whorl of leaves or sepal forming the outer case of the bud]
> and petals, on one branch...Their calyxes and their stems were of
> one piece with it, the whole of it a single hammered piece of pure
> gold.
>
> [Exodus 37:19, 22]

The design of the golden seven-branched lampstand ('Menorah') has many pre-Exodus prototypes. One of the clearest of these is to be seen on a bituminous stone bowl from Susa, Elam (Ancient Babylonia), now in the Louvre Museum in Paris. Dated to 2300 BCE, it shows cherubs guarding several identical seven-branched trees which are very close in design to that of the Tabernacle lampstand description.

There are many other correlative comparisons that can be made in other descriptive passages of the Tabernacle adornments and priestly costumes that were to be worn. Almost every single item relating to the Tabernacle, as described in the Bible, can be identified as being uncannily similar to items in the possession of Tutankhamun, Akhenaten's successor.

From the similarity of shape, construction, principles of operation and embellishments it is difficult not to conclude that the 'Tabernacle' and the 'Ark of the Covenant' were, at the very least, based on Egyptian designs and motifs – motifs that are evident in the Temple of Akhenaten. The close similarities of the Ark indicate that it was almost certainly of Egyptian origin and, like the other treasures carried off from Egypt by the departing Hebrews, was probably given to Moses by the surviving priests of Akhetaten.

SACRIFICE

I need to say something here about the Biblical accounts of animal sacrifice, that were apparently part of the Tabernacle and later Temple rituals, as they are inconsistent with my previous contention that Akhenaten abhorred the unnecessary shedding of blood and the practice of 'holocaust' (burnt) offerings (*see Chapter 9*).

The preparations required for sacrifices, as described in the Old Testament, are very similar to pagan sacrifices in ancient Egypt. For example, any animal sacrificed to the Egyptian god Amun had to be scrupulously clean, without any physical blemish and shaved clean of all its hair.

In most respects the Children of Israel remained faithful to the fundamental beliefs advocated by Akhenaten, but there are certain ritualistic and superstitious practices, of which animal sacrifice is the most pertinent, that appear to have resulted from a 'reversion' back into pagan-like behaviour.

I don't claim to have a complete answer as to why this particular type of 'reversion' relating to sacrifice took place, either during the time the Israelites were wandering the deserts of Sinai or, later, when the Temples were built in Jerusalem. Part of the answer, I believe, lies in the fact that amongst those whom Moses led out of Egypt were a number of Ay-type 'paper Akhenatenists', who still hankered after the old rituals of Egypt. Aaron, Moses' Biblical brother, who was appointed High Priest in charge of arrangements in the Tabernacle, was among these 'back-sliders'. Sacrificial rituals are described in the Old Testament as being the responsibility of Aaron and his sons, and it was Aaron who later allowed some of the Israelites to dance around naked in front of an idol – the Golden Calf.

This was not the only incident of major dissent within the camp. Different factions struggled for control of the priesthood and challenged Moses' authority throughout the period in the wilderness, sometimes with fatal consequences.

Wherever the Israelites went the treasures that they had brought out of Egypt were guarded by the most trusted tribe of Levis and the Kohathites[12] – a grouping who in time would be punished for challenging Moses' authority and be removed as exclusive trustees of the Ark of the Covenant.

I am postulating here that the reasons for these squabbles were because the relatively impoverished Hebrew slaves brought out of Egypt by Moses were accompanied by a wealthy class of Egyptians, mainly comprising Egyptian priests – an almost certain scenario for the emergence of group rivalries, jealousies and even violence. All of these emanations were not long in appearing after the Exodus.

The Old Testament adds credence to my contention that there were Egyptian priests amongst the followers of Moses. In Exodus 12 we find that the Hebrews leaving Egypt were accompanied by a 'mixed crowd', and Numbers 16 speaks of two rival factions of priests. One of these factions was led by leaders with Egyptian-style names – Korah, Dathan, Abiram and On, son of Peleth. ('On' being the ancient name for the Egyptian city of Heliopolis.)

THE DNA FACTOR

There is fascinating firm scientific evidence, 3,000 years after the event, that underlines the homogeneity of the Hebrew peoples, but also reveals a genetically separate priestly faction with quite different DNA patterns.

A January 1997 edition of *Nature* carried an article on the 'Y chromosomes of Jewish priests'.[13] The Y-chromosome is inherited paternally and does not recombine. Because of this fact the research teams at the Technion-Israel Institute of Technology, the University of Toronto, University College, London and the University of Arizona who wrote the article, chose to study the genetic coding of Jewish males whose designation to the priesthood, through strict patrilineal descent, has continued for thousands of years right up to this day.[14] The surnames of the priestly strain are generally derivations of the name 'Cohanim'. The researchers concluded that there are clear differences in the frequency of Y-chromosome hapolytes* between an unbroken line of Jewish 'priests'

---

* Hapolytes are molecular groups which characterize chromosome types.

and their lay counterparts. Quite remarkably, the difference is observable in both the Ashkenazi- (Central European) and Sephardi- (North African, Spanish, Middle Eastern) descended populations, despite the huge geographical separations of these original communities.

The study showed that there is a 'relative preponderance of the YAP-DYS19B hapolyte in both Jewish populations, suggesting that this may have been the founding modal hapolyte of the Jewish priesthood'. The presence or absence of the YAP chromosome is thought to represent a unique evolutionary event dated to between 29,000 and 340,000 years ago. The significance of this latter statement is that *the priestly strain must have pre-existed, by many thousands of years, events in biblical times.*

In other words the priestly group that were 'chosen' by Moses to provide the line of High Priests and prime guardians of the holy rituals, were *already* genetically different from the bulk of Hebrews and must have come, or originated, from outside the main Hebrew tribes.

One possible consequence of the genetic-factor evidence is that Aaron and his family, who were designated to fill the role of High Priest, were of a different DNA grouping to the rest of the Hebrews. As the brother of Moses, in Old Testament terms, the proposition that Moses was an Egyptian becomes even more convincing. Another possibility is that Korah, as previously suggested (*see p.139*), was one of the leaders of the Egyptian priests that came out of Egypt with Moses, and that his family gave rise to the line of High Priests. This is quite a seductive theory in view of the similarity of the sound of his name and that of the 'Cohanim' or 'Cohan'.

EVIDENCE FROM THE DEAD SEA SCROLLS

There is more evidence that the secret teachings the Atenist-inspired priests might have brought out of Egypt pre-dated the teachings of Moses. The Dead Sea Scrolls themselves, particularly those from Cave 4 at Qumran, give us very potent evidence. Amongst the fragmentary scrolls are two works known as 'The Testament of Amram' and 'The Testament of Qahat'.[15] The name 'Qahat' is translated by Eisenman and Wise as 'Kohath'.[16] Both these works record that holy texts, written long before the time of Moses, were handed down through the priestly line.

It is worth looking at part of 'The Testament of Amram', which has been translated by Geza Vermes from the Aramaic:

Copy of the book (text) of the words of the vision of Amram, son of Kehat, son of Levi, al[l that] he explained to his sons and enjoined on them on the day of [his] death, in his one-hundred-and-thirty-seventh year, which was the year of his death, [in] the one-hundred-and-fifty-second year of Israel's exile in Egypt…to call Uzziel, his younger brother, and he ma[rried] to him Miriam, [his] daughter, and said (to her), 'You are thirty years old'. And he gave a banquet lasting seven days. And he ate and drank and made merry during the banquet. Then, when the days of the banquet were completed, he sent to call Aaron, his son, and he was…years old.[17]

In the text Amram is said to have died aged 137, indicating that Amram, whom the Bible names as being the father of Moses (and Aaron and Miriam) is, rather, the 'spiritual father' of Moses. Nevertheless we are given a very precise figure, which is not one of our 'magic numbers' conjured up for mathematical convenience (*see Chapter 7*). The place name 'Amram' became closely associated with the area of Akhenaten's holy city of Akhetaten, after its destruction around 1300 BCE. I believe there was a 'mixing' of names, and that the Amram being referred to could well be Akhenaten himself, and the texts his texts.

Akhenaten died *c.*1332 BCE, aged approximately 30, so his allegoric death*some 107 years later, would have meant he lived until 1225 BCE – very close to the dates I propose (and many scholars prefer) for the time of Aaron and Moses. The implication is that the texts being referred to were passed down through a strand of the priestly line, who may have added to them, but that they originated from the time of Akhenaten.

Incidentally, the Amram Testament refers to a seven-day banquet. What on earth were impoverished slaves doing, living it up in such an extravagant manner – unless of course they had loads of money and Royal connections!

MANETHO, MEYER AND MOSES

I have mentioned Manetho, a renowned 3rd century BCE Egyptian scholar and priest, several times before. But this is where Manetho's evidence throws its full weight behind my theories.

---

* i.e., the date visualized by the authors of the 'Testament of Amram' for Amram's death had he lived to be 137.

Manetho was born in the region of the northern Delta, and lived and worked at Alexandria during the time of the Greek rulers. He left us two major treatises which have had a pivotal bearing on our understanding of early Egypt. The first was the earliest, almost complete, chronology of the Pharaohs, which has been crucial in establishing the dates and identities of Egyptian dynastic rulers. His second major contribution was a history of Egypt, of which his details on two versions of the 'Exodus' is of most interest in our search for the links between Akhenaten, Moses and the Qumran-Essenes.

Unfortunately, although considering the 2,300 years that have elapsed since his time it is hardly surprising, none of Manetho's writings have survived in their original form. What we do have are variants of his texts recorded by other Alexandrian historians, such as Chaeremon and Apion, and corroborations from other non-Egyptian writers, like Hecataeus, Diodorus and our old friend Josephus – the 1st century CE Jewish-Roman historian. Josephus recorded details of the 'Exoduses' and his accounts are considered to be derivatives of Manetho's work.

Manetho wrote most of his works at the request of Ptolemy II Philadelphus, one of the new Greek rulers of Egypt, so they have a certain slant. Extracting the truth from Manetho's evidence is therefore not easy; he was writing to cater for Greek sensibilities as well as trying to project historical Egypt as a worthy civilization that the Greeks might be proud to maintain. There is also the consideration that subsequent witnesses also had their own 'hidden agendas' in reworking Manetho's texts. Many scholars have attempted to unravel 'the truth' in Manetho's writings, and modern experts credit Eduard Meyer, a German scholar, as having come closest to the target.[18]

Manetho wrote of two expulsions from Egypt. The first was of the Hyksos 'shepherd-foreigners' in the 16th century BCE, and the later one of foreigners and lepers at the time of Moses. He actually gives us the earliest, and almost certainly clearest, non-Biblical reference confirming an Exodus of the Hebrews under Moses's leadership. Meyer concludes that the two Exodus versions were conflated in Josephus's version, and allusions to 'Solymites' (builders of King Solomon's Temple) and a destination of 'Jerusalem' are more appropriate to the later 'Exodus'.

It is in the personal names that Manetho quotes in association with the later Exodus, that we find clues as to the connection between the

Hebrews and Akhenaten. Clues that show they kept the memory of Aten in their midst.

In the later 'Exodus', Manetho refers to 'Osarsiph' as a leader of a people that can only be the Hebrews. As Lucia Raspe, of Freie University, Berlin, points out,[19] the name has 'long been suspected of being a pseudo-translation of Joseph', and the texts associate Joseph with service to the monotheism of the 'Aten' disc of Akhenaten and to Heliopolis.

Two other names emerge in relation to Joseph and to the Exodus – Amenophis and Ramses. Amenophis has been identified as Amenhotpe, son of Hapu, who served as a royal scribe to Akhenaten's father Amenhotep III (1387–1349 BCE), and was closely associated with Akhenaten. The Ramses of the Exodus period is identified as Ramses III. Immediately prior to the reign of Ramses III there occurred a well-documented period of 13 years' 'chaos and upheaval' during the reign of Ramses III's father, Setnakhte. This anarchical situation is ascribed to a power struggle taking place at Court during what, I believe, was a period when 'Aten' was back in favour, promoted by powerful backers including Moses. There was an atmosphere of resurgent Atenism in the air.

At the end of this period of 'chaos and upheaval' the throne was occupied by Setnakhte, and his name reveals a predilection towards Akhenaten's monotheism. The '*nakhte*' element of his name identifies him with the name 'Nakhte', or Vizier – as Joseph was referred to at the time of Akhenaten. Moreover, his throne name of 'Userkaura Meryamun' identifies him with 'Meryra' – the High Priest at Akhenaten's Court. What better time for Moses to take advantage of 13 years of destabilization and a favourably disposed king to seek release of his adopted people?

Chaeremon's version of Manetho's 'Exodus' quotes Moses as being a leader of the afflicted people whom he leads out of Egypt. The Egyptian name he gives for Moses is 'Tisithen' and this name, as a number of scholars conclude, almost certainly preserves the name of 'Aten' in its etymology, re-affirming the association I have previously made between Moses and Atenism.

To summarize the analysis of Manetho's works, he records:

- Joseph as a contemporary of Akhenaten
- Setnakhte as the probable Pharaoh of the 'Exodus'
- Moses as leading the Hebrews from Egypt somewhere between 1206 and 1189 BCE *Trojan War 1194 – 1184 ?*

- Moses' name testifying to an allegiance to the monotheism of Akhenaten.

I believe that Setnakhte was the Pharaoh of the 'Exodus' and that it was towards the end of this period of 'chaos and upheaval' (around 1200 BCE), under his benign rule, that Moses, a Prince of Egypt, took the opportunity to gain the release of the Hebrews and lead them out of Egypt to the Promised Land.[20]

BACK TO THE COPPER SCROLL TREASURE

From the point of view of our 'treasure hunt', the important feature to be drawn from the Exodus story is that the Israelites took out of Egypt treasures, some of them Temple-related. There were also Egyptians and Egyptian priests amongst their numbers, some of whom came from On, a place known to be a traditional centre for sun-associated religions, the place where the first Temple to Aten was built, and a place likely to be sympathetic to Akhenaten's new religion. These accompanying priests may well have carried with them the *knowledge of where some of the treasure of Akhenaten's Great Temple and Treasury were buried*. They also had access to copper. How do I know that?

The Old Testament gives several clues. In Numbers 21:4–9, for example, there is a curious passage which is quite out of context. The Children of Israel are getting fed up with wandering around in the desert, short of food and water, and they start grumbling at Moses. Worse still, they are suddenly plagued by a horde of poisonous snakes, biting and killing many of them. The Israelites plead with Moses to intercede with God on their behalf to protect them. So what does Moses do? He takes some *copper* and beats it into the shape of a serpent. Anyone who looks at the 'copper snake' is immediately cured of the poisonous-snake bites.[21]

There is a possibility that this copper was obtained from copper mines known to exist at Timna, in the north-eastern part of Sinai, but this would imply that the Children of Israel tarried for a long period in that area to learn the skills required in mining, smelting, purifying and fabricating the product – which seems unlikely. Midianite tribes, who lived east of the Gulf of Aqaba, are said to have had a shrine at Timna where they worshipped a small copper snake measuring 12cm in length.[22] It is possible this is the snake being referred to in the Old Testament, as Moses instructed the Children of Israel to annihilate virtually all the Midianites, and they took bounty from them which may well have included this snake.

However the strange incident of Moses making a copper snake, and other examples of copper being used in the Tabernacle for pans and overlays before any encounter with the Midianites, answers the question. Copper, in raw material form, was available to the people of the Exodus and must have been brought with them when they left Egypt.

CHAPTER FOURTEEN

TOWARDS QUMRAN

A brief journey through history, covering a period of 1,000 years from the time the Israelites entered Sinai from Egypt, bridges the gap between Moses and the tantalizing Qumran-Essenes, inhabiting a remote corner near the Dead Sea in Israel around the time of Christ. Figure 10 gives the historical land-marks on which to pin an evaluation of how the monastic community at Qumran might be related to the priests of Akhenaten. A fuller description is given in note 1.

When Moses left Egypt to lead the Children of Israel towards the Promised Land, I believe he took with him some of the Akhenaten priests amongst a mixed company of Egyptian nobility, soldiers and general helpers. They, in turn, became the natural guardians of the holy treasures, the Ark of the Covenant...and many secrets.

One group of these priests who left Egypt with Moses were known as the Levites. They were consecrated by Moses to serve in the Tabernacle, and eventually formed part of the select priests of the First Temple (built by Solomon in Jerusalem, around 950 BCE).[2]

THE LEVITE PRIESTS

What the precise role of the priestly Levite guards was between the time of Joshua, the 'Conquistador' of Canaan, and the end of Solomon's reign in the time of the First Temple is unclear. The Torah gives differ-ent answers for different periods.

Early on the Levites are assigned the priestly office – the guardians of the Tabernacle (Numbers 1:50) and, in Exodus 32:26–29, as the sons

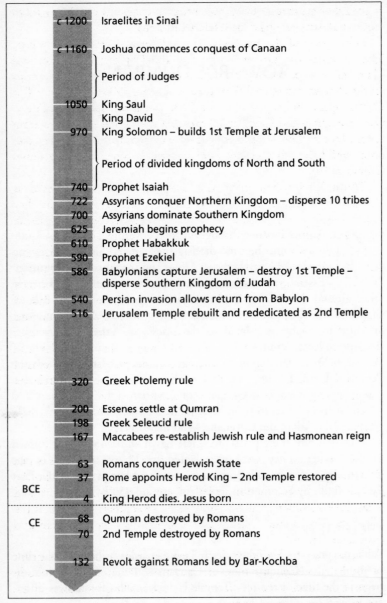

c 1200	Israelites in Sinai
c 1160	Joshua commences conquest of Canaan
	Period of Judges
1050	King Saul
	King David
970	King Solomon – builds 1st Temple at Jerusalem
	Period of divided kingdoms of North and South
740	Prophet Isaiah
722	Assyrians conquer Northern Kingdom – disperse 10 tribes
700	Assyrians dominate Southern Kingdom
625	Jeremiah begins prophecy
610	Prophet Habakkuk
590	Prophet Ezekiel
586	Babylonians capture Jerusalem – destroy 1st Temple – disperse Southern Kingdom of Judah
540	Persian invasion allows return from Babylon
516	Jerusalem Temple rebuilt and rededicated as 2nd Temple
320	Greek Ptolemy rule
200	Essenes settle at Qumran
198	Greek Seleucid rule
167	Maccabees re-establish Jewish rule and Hasmonean reign
63	Romans conquer Jewish State
37	Rome appoints Herod King – 2nd Temple restored
BCE 4	King Herod dies. Jesus born
CE 68	Qumran destroyed by Romans
70	2nd Temple destroyed by Romans
132	Revolt against Romans led by Bar-Kochba

Copyright: Robert Feather

Figure 10: Time line from Sinai to Qumran.

of Templars

of Levi, they are manifestly warrior priests prepared to use the sword to root out idolatry amongst the Children of Israel.

Other parts of the Bible give them different roles. Deuteronomy 33:8–10 allots the Levites a role as keepers of the Thummim and Urim,* teachers of the law, burners of incense and placers of sacrifices on the altar. In earlier traditions they are known as 'Palace guards'. The Levites equated with priests in the Bible are shown special consideration throughout the Torah. It appears that the Levites descended from Aaron, Moses' Biblical brother, and were to perform the priestly functions, whilst the other Levites were to perform other sanctuary duties (Numbers 18).

Whilst King David ruled, the northern Levite priests based at Shiloh (who claimed descent from Moses), were favoured, but they suffered badly under Solomon and even worse under Jeroboam, giving them every reason to become isolated from the community.

In the time of the Judges and the Kings of Israel, the injunction that priests could only be from Levite stock seems to have been varied: Samuel, an Ephraimite, performed the role of priest when the sanctuary was initially established at Shiloh (I Samuel 1 and 2), and in the time of King David the priests were entitled Zadok and Ahimelech (II Samuel 8:15–18).

Ezekiel 40:46 is even more specific in stating that the position of high priest should be reserved for Zadokites, descendants of the sons of Levi, and it appears that the Zadokite priests dominated the role for several hundred years from Solomon onwards.

PORTENTS OF DISASTER

The period before the invasion from the north by the Assyrians is one of prophecy and castigation of the Jewish people for straying from the path of God, by the line of prophets from Amos, Hosea, Micah and Isaiah during the period 800–700 BCE. As we approach the time of the fall of the First Temple, the prophesying becomes more strident and more doom-laden.[3]

We see also, before the period of the next invasion from the north by the Babylonians, that there is a movement from within a priestly group to get 'back to basics', to return to the teachings of Moses in the deserts of Sinai. A 'new' Testament[4] is suddenly discovered in the time

---

* i.e., diviners of God's will by the throwing of dice.

of King Josiah, who ruled from 637 to 608 BCE, and this is the first hard evidence we have that there were secret texts being kept by the priesthood which were not available to the general populace, or even to the monarchy.

After the capture of Jerusalem by the Babylonians (Chaldeans) and the destruction of the Temple in 586 BCE, the majority of Israelites were taken as prisoners to Babylon. Those that were taken comprised mainly the upper classes and intellectual sectors of the community. (This is one of the reasons why the Babylonian version of the Talmud came to dominate Jewish thinking, rather than the Judaean or southern version.[5]) The line of the transitional and post-First Temple prophets, commencing with Ezekiel, Jeremiah, Zephaniah, Nahum and Habakkuk, now sang a different tune. Along with condemnation for pagan practices come the predictions of divine retribution on the enemies of Israel, and the encouragement that the meek and religious will survive.

It is these themes that were taken up, or perhaps originated, by the Essene movement. They are exemplified by the teachings of the Prophet Habakkuk ('The righteous shall live by his faith').[6] These teachings were of profound significance to the Qumran-Essenes, and are given prominence in their recording in one of the Dead Sea Scrolls.

EMERGENCE OF THE QUMRAN-ESSENES

This 'community apart' began transforming itself into a separate religious group which was, I believe, the early Essenes; an ultra-religious faction of this sect eventually evolved to become the Qumran-Essenes of the Dead Sea.

We pick up the thread of the priestly guardians of the Covenant before the destruction of the First Temple in Jerusalem *c*.586 BCE. It is in this period that the line of priestly inheritance came under greatest threat. The sacred Ark of the Covenant and the treasures of the sanctuary were in jeopardy and, whilst some sacred items had already probably been carried off to Babylon, like the bulk of the Jewish tribes (as the Old Testament asserts), the rest of the treasures may have been hurriedly hidden in the vicinity of Jerusalem. Some of the priestly guardians may have been able to remain in Judah, others may well have been carried off to Babylon and the region of Damascus. When the Persian King, Cyrus II, overran the Babylonian Empire in *c*.540 BCE, he gave permission for the Jews to return to their homeland. Not all took up the offer, but of those that did, the priestly guardians would have had every reason to be amongst them. Their first task was to start rebuilding the Temple.

I believe that it was at this stage in history that, under the influence of prophets like Ezekiel and Habakkuk, the Levite priestly guardians became even more estranged from the central control of the Temple's activities and began re-formulating their religious philosophies.

The situation is beautifully summed up by Richard Friedman in his brilliant book *Who Wrote the Bible?*[7] The Aaronic priests had been dominant in the south, in Judah, but are confronted with the arrival of refugees from the fallen northern kingdom. They bring rival priests, who trace their ancestry back to Moses, and Biblical texts that denigrate Aaron. The theme of disputing priests, begun in the deserts of Sinai, continues. The Aaronic priests of the south win the initial struggle and proceed to re-write some of the holy texts to reinstate Aaron and his descendants as the true priestly line that should have the sole right to officiate in the Temple.

Conventional understanding is that the Qumran-Essenes 'emerged' around 300–250 BCE, but a few scholars now accept that their influences and writings are based on much older experience. One of these scholars is the highly respected Ben-Zion Wacholder, a blind Professor from the Hebrew Union College, Cincinnati. At the 'Dead Sea Scrolls – Fifty Years After Their Discovery' Congress, in Jerusalem in July 1997, he created a real stir by standing up and announcing that he believed Ezekiel was 'the first Qumran-Essene'. In his paper Professor Wacholder drew attention to what he called enigmatic lines in the 'Ezekiel' Dead Sea Scrolls, one of which refers to 'the wicked of Memphis whom I will slay'. Enigmatic indeed! Why would God be interested in avenging people in Egypt?

If my contentions are correct, the northern priestly guardians began welding themselves into a very different Jewish sect in Babylon and, on returning from exile around 540 BCE, accelerated that process in reaction to what they termed the mis-rule of the newly entrenched Aaronic Temple priests.

Under the Persians the population was treated with respect. Religious life in Judah continued relatively uninterrupted whilst Aramaic became the predominant language, as opposed to paleo-Hebrew. However, something happened soon after the end of the 4th century that frightened the guardian Levite priests into seeking a safe refuge. That something was the prospect of once again being ruled by 'pagan' Egypt.[8]

The priestly guardians scoured around for a place of refuge. Like their ancient predecessors, they looked for a secretive place which was near to water, to enable them to perform the purification rites that were part of their code. The choice was limited. There was, nevertheless, a honeycomb complex of caves on the shores of the Dead Sea which would serve their purpose well for the next 300 years – Qumran.

Although the Dead Sea was too salty to provide potable water, they chose a place where there was a spring, some 4km south of Khirbet Qumran. Here they worshipped, scribed, studied and died.

A MODERN VIEWPOINT/SECOND OPINION

I have discussed the basic theory connecting Akhenaten's 'new religion' to that of the Qumran-Essenes with Professor George Brooke, Co-Director of the Manchester–Sheffield Centre for Dead Sea Scrolls Research, and a world renowned authority on the subject.* He has recently been appointed editor for a new series of books entitled *The Dead Sea Scrolls* (being published by Routledge), and organized a recent exhibition of the Copper Scroll at Manchester Museum, from October 1997 to January 1998.

Professor Brooke goes along with the general idea that Egyptian influences could well have penetrated into the philosophy of the Qumran-Essenes, and comments 'Egypt would have been a place where a Jewish association would feel comfortable and its religious environment would be consistent with monotheistic traditions.' However, he proposes another route by which the influences might have travelled.

The alternative theory he suggests is that the knowledge the Qumran-Essenes might have acquired about the monotheism of Akhenaten, and Egyptian religion in general, may well have been imbibed at a later date, namely in the 6th century BCE, possibly through the associations Ezekiel and Jeremiah had with Egypt.

As outcasts from Temple life and privilege after the destruction of the First Temple, the priestly group that was eventually to evolve into the Essenes, disillusioned by the failure of God to protect their holiest place, may well have been looking for an alternative form of Judaism to sustain them in their relative isolation, a form which might distinguish them from the mainstream body of Jewish religion.

There was undoubtedly considerable contact between Judaean

---

* George Brooke is Rylands Professor of Biblical Criticism and Exegesis at the University of Manchester.

Judaism and the settlements of Jews who were dispersed to Egypt after the destruction of the First Temple. (Most of the dispersions were to Babylon and to parts of the Babylonian Empire east of Jerusalem. But several thousand captive Jews were taken to the northern Nile delta region of Egypt.)

Professor Brooke maintains that, if my theory that a residual strand of Akhenaten's monotheism survived within a group of priests in Israel is correct, what would be more natural than that they, as a proscribed group of Jewish priestly thinkers, might find sympathetic understanding with another ostracized Egyptian group with similar monotheistic beliefs? Contact between Jews dispersed to Egypt and those remaining in Israel after the destruction of the First Temple is known to have taken place after 550 BCE. There could well have occurred, therefore, an interchange of information, bringing the ideas of Akhenatenism and some of its secrets to this Jewish sect. Professor Brooke notes that:

> At its outset the Essene movement was predominantly priestly and is evidence of a priestly pluralism in the three centuries before the fall of the Temple in 70 CE. The Jewish priesthood in Egypt was clearly revitalised at the time of Onias IV by his move to Heliopolis in the second quarter of the second century BCE,[9] the very time at which the Essene movement was being established in Judaea.[10]

Whilst my view remains that the Essenes (and, subsequently, the Qumran-Essenes) gained their knowledge of Akhenatenism through a direct connection to the Akhenaten period, rather than through Professor Brooke's later and indirect linkage, the net outcome does not alter the essence of the Egyptian influences that I have proposed. However, it would have an impact on how the Qumran-Essenes acquired the knowledge contained in the Copper Scroll.

I also discussed some of my theories with Jozef Milik *(see Plate 10(top))*, the man who led and organized the original Dead Sea Scrolls translation team working on scroll fragments at the Rockefeller Museum in East Jerusalem. Born in the village of Serwczyn, Poland, 76 years ago, he was educated at the University of Lublin and came to Jerusalem from the Biblical Oriental Institute at Rome as a Catholic priest at the end of 1952. He was the doyen of Qumran scroll research, the first person to produce an official translation of the Copper Scroll, and he has dedicated his life to the study of ancient Middle Eastern texts. When I met him in the autumn of 1998 at his Paris home, it was with some degree of awe that I talked with him about my theories and ideas. Although his eyesight is now poor, his mind is still razor sharp and on several occasions he corrected me when I mixed up a name or was unsure about a reference.

When I asked him if he still considered the Copper Scroll to be a fraud, he replied without hesitation, 'No, no, no it is absolutely excluded...it was found under metres and metres of earth...it was found with small fragments of manuscripts of the library.' However, he still considers that the contents of the scroll 'do not correspond to reality' – to be based on legend – and he referred to similar lists of treasure found in Egypt. Why the document was written 'was a problem'.

Jozef Milik agreed that the numbering system in the Copper Scroll could have come from Egypt and could date back to the time of Akhenaten, but found it difficult to make a connection right back from Qumran to Akhetaten, equating the jump as equivalent to the claim of the Freemasons that they can trace their origins back to Solomon's time. When we came to discuss the Copper Scroll translations in detail, he did not find it easy to accept my reasoning for the connections I proposed. However, he was far from dismissive, asking probing questions and acknowledging with surprise that some of the evidence appeared convincing, and yet puzzling. He agreed that there was a lot of concordance between Egypt and the Jewish nation, but suggested the Therapeutae as a possible link between Egypt and the Essenes.[11]

(Currently Dr Milik is working on the decipherment of a bilingual inscription found on a 2nd century BCE temple in southern Syria. The inscription describes four gods who were worshipped there – Ben Shammen, Isis, a local goddess Shiyiah and the Angel of God – Malach el Aha.)

AKHENATEN'S HEIRS

If my assumptions – that the Essenes of Qumran were the heirs of the priestly guardians of the Covenant, and can be traced back to the priests of Akhetaten – are correct, then we would expect to see many 'fingerprints' in their activities and writings to mark them out from the general Jewish population.

These expected fingerprints would include:

- a different version or conception of the generally accepted Torah teachings and a closer relationship with the religion of Akhenaten

- a sense of guardianship and divine mission
- emphasis on the sun – brightness – light
- extreme ritualistic cleanliness
- stronger Egyptian influences.

We might also expect some memory of the original holy city of Akhetaten. The catastrophic destruction of the Temple there would have inevitably left a deep scar on their subconscious. Perhaps, in the extreme, there might also remain some knowledge of the whereabouts of the treasures buried at Akhetaten, or the treasures that Moses and the priests brought out of Egypt.

It would in itself be quite surprising if any of these listed characteristics were found amongst the Essenes – especially that of Egyptian influences – after so long a period of immersion in a foreign culture and a refined Judaism that had 'cleansed itself' of as many foreign influences as possible. One would certainly not expect to see more Egyptian influence within a closed sect than was apparent in the common body of Judaism. *But we do*. In fact, we find the Essenes exhibited many of the characteristics of the priests that came out of Egypt, modified by time in just the form that one might expect.

There are not just 'fingerprints' of the connection between Akhenaten and the Qumran-Essenes, there are 'smoking guns'!

Before going into the 'religious fingerprints', I have uncovered some intriguing visual and pictorial links to Egypt and the City of Akhetaten, which are quite surprising.

ORIENTATIONS AT QUMRAN

The following very strange co-incidences give us visual links between the Qumran-Essenes and Akhenaten. So strange are these links that I do not think they are mere accidents of chance. I believe they constitute a body of evidence which, on its own, clinches the connection between the Qumran-Essenes and Pharaoh Akhenaten. Before reading the next paragraph, turn to the plate section of illustrations and look closely at Plate 10 (bottom) – the hills above the Qumran settlement. What can you see?

When I first noticed the images, I thought I was dreaming. The photograph was printed in a book entitled *The Dead Sea Scrolls Uncovered*, by Robert Eisenman and Michael Wise, first published in 1992. No-one previously seems to have noticed what I hope you have seen for yourself. Amongst the Mount Rushmore-like shapes in the hills directly above Qumran there appear to be faces. For me, these elongated faces look remarkably like ancient Egyptians. If that is what they are, what on earth are they doing staring out over the ruins of a Jewish settlement on the Dead Sea? There are only three reasonable explanations. They were carved, possibly by members of the Essene community; they are the result of weathering and are quite accidental; or they are the work of the hand of God. On closer examination I believe the faces are the result of weathering, but nevertheless their existence is quite unnerving!

The New Jerusalem

The 'orientation' story now shifts back to the Congress held in Jerusalem in July 1997, to celebrate the 50th year of the finding of the first of the Dead Sea Scrolls. Some 300 delegates, including experts from all over the world, gathered in the magnificent setting of the Israel Museum grounds where the Shrine of the Book is located, to indulge in an academic *freudenfest* of learned exchanges.

One of the papers presented at the Congress was given by Joerg Frey, an academic from Tübingen, Germany.[12] His specialism was the so-called 'New Jerusalem' text, which comprises six manuscripts of the Dead Sea Scrolls. Written mainly in Aramaic, they are considered by most scholars to relate to the description of an idealized city which might exist in an eschatalogical period at the end of time, and are identified with the visionary writings of Ezekiel 40–48 (and to Revelations 21).

However, there are serious problems with this identification. The texts (which do not actually mention the word 'Jerusalem'), describe a much larger city than Ezekiel's and cannot be easily related to a plan of Jerusalem at any time in its history. As Herr Frey put it, the plan of the 'New Jerusalem' in the Dead Sea Scrolls is difficult to understand and it is unclear where the people who wrote these particular Qumran-Essene documents got their ideas from. A clue was not long in coming.

My ears pricked up when a delegate in the audience commented during question time that a team of researchers, including Shlomo Margalit, Georg Klostermann and Ulrich Luz had studied the 'New Jerusalem' texts in the 1980s.[13] They had compared the city plan descriptions in the texts with actual cities in the ancient Near East and had come up with a 'best fit' of...Akhetaten! The same Akhetaten that was Pharaoh Akhenaten's holy city on the Nile, situated in lower Egypt, now know as El-Amarna.

If this assertion was correct, what clearer evidence could there be that the Qumran-Essenes knew the plan of a city that existed 1,100 years before their time? A city that had been made desolate very soon after the death of Akhenaten in 1332 BCE, resettled in Romano-Ptolemaic times and then long-since abandoned and forgotten.

I decided to look at translations of the original 'New Jerusalem' texts myself and to make my own comparisons.

Text 5Q15 of the 'New Jerusalem' texts, found in Cave 5 at Qumran, reads as follows:

> [round] = 357 cubits to each side. A passage surrounds the block of houses, a street gallery, three reeds = 21 cubits (wide). [He] then [showed me the di]mensions of [all] the blo[cks of houses. Between each block there is a street], six reeds = 42 cubits wide. And the width of the avenues running from east to west; two of them are ten reeds = 70 cubits wide. And the third, that to the [lef]t (i.e. north) of the temple, measures 18 reeds = 126 cubits in width. And the wid[th of the streets] running from south [to north: t]wo of [them] have nine reeds and four cubits = 67 cubits, each street. [And the] mid[dle street passing through the mid]dle of the city, its [width measures] thirt[een] ree[ds] and one cubit = 92 cubits. And all [the streets of the city] are paved with white stone...marble and jasper.[14]

The Dead Sea Scroll texts conceive the city as covering an area of 25–28km^2, an area very similar to that of the city of Akhetaten, as revealed through excavations.[15] The style and formula of presenting measurements is also quite similar to that used at the time of the city's existence, exemplified in an inscription on a boundary stele, stele 'S', found at El-Amarna, which describes the dimensions of the Akhetaten site.[16]

Excavations at El-Amarna by Sir Flinders Petrie,[17] Professor Geoffrey Martin[18] and, more recently, by Barry Kemp of the Egypt Exploration Society, show that Akhetaten had three main streets running east/west, and three running north/south, almost exactly as described in the Dead Sea Scroll texts. The streets were unusually wide for an ancient city, being between 30m and 47m in width, again closely corresponding to measurements in the 'New Jerusalem' texts, as do the distances between the blocks of houses.

The descriptions of streets 'paved with white stone...marble and jasper' are especially noteworthy. Akhetaten was the 'beautiful gleaming white city' of Egypt. Built on virgin land in a vast sandy plain which formed a natural hill-surrounded amphitheatre on the banks of the Nile, no expense had been spared in its construction. Roads, pavements and buildings were made of the finest available materials. An exquisite example of the craftsmanship that was lavished on the city can be seen in the painted pavings that adorned Akhetaten's main palace, reconstructed in the Cairo Museum. A glowingly beautiful piece showing a blue, green, yellow and red marshland setting for a duck-like bird can be seen in the Metropolitan Museum in New York.

By all accounts the city must have gleamed white in the sunlight, its roads and buildings made from limestone, which had the appearance of alabaster.[19]

The 'Jerusalem text' goes on to describe the dimensions of a huge building, and various houses in the city. A comparison of the archaeological reports of the Great Temple at Akhetaten indicates that this is the building the texts are describing.

A recent comprehensive study of the New Jerusalem Scroll, by Michael Chyutin, also concludes that the city plan of Akhetaten appeared to form a template for the Qumran-Essenes's idealized vision of their Holy City.[20] However, the author can only speculate on the reason for the association: 'Why did the author of the Scroll describe a city planned in an archaic Egyptian style, rather than describing a Greek city or a Roman *castrum*?'

The work by Shlomo Margalit and his colleagues, by Michael Chyutin, and my own cross-checking, can leave little doubt that the Qumran-Essenes had in their possession works handed down from previous guardians of their literature, which must have been composed within living memory of 1300 BCE (the date the city of Akhetaten is thought to have been destroyed by Pharaoh Haremhab).[21] They knew exact details about the geographical layout of Akhetaten, details that appear in no other source.

If the Qumran-Essenes knew the layout of what I believe they considered as their model 'holy city', did they make use of that knowledge in other ways? Was there a connection to the Copper Scroll? Clearly the knowledge of the city layout would have been useful to them in visualizing the whereabouts of some of the treasures described in the Copper Scroll. The city plan was, after all, a reference grid for the description of where some of the treasures were hidden. But there is more.

If, as I surmise, the Qumran-Essenes knew the direction and layout of their 'holy city', wouldn't they have made use of that knowledge

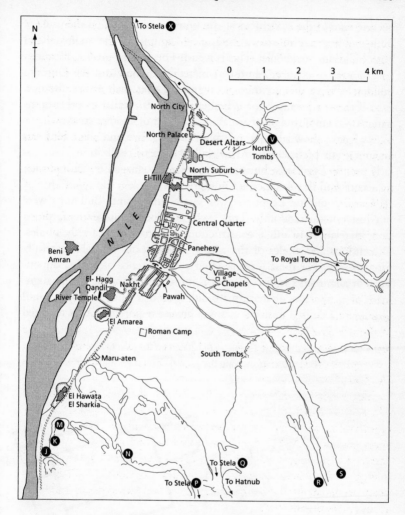

Figure 11: Site of Akhetaten showing outline plan of streets and buildings.

when they came to build their own 'holy settlement'? It would be surprising if it had not had some influence on their constructions. The initial site correspondences were there – a flat area, near to water, backed by hills.

Look at Figure 12 on the next page. The geographical alignment of the Qumran settlement is approximately north-west. If we overlay the reconstructed outline plan of the Great Temple at Akhetaten on the outline plan of the settlement at the Qumran site, we find the walls of both buildings are in *exact* geographical alignment. The main walls of both buildings are parallel. This is weird. The fit is so precise, it cannot be a matter of chance. Almost as incredible is how did the Qumran builders achieve this accuracy in alignment over such a vast distance, even if they had wanted to? Whether some solar, stellar or other comparator was employed must remain the subject of another study.

As I have shown before, relating numbers, size and alignment was an important preoccupation and skill of ancient civilizations, particularly for the Egyptians, but how the Essenes managed to achieve such an accuracy in this instance is a mystery.

Orientation for Egyptians was vitally important. Buildings were not just put up randomly. They were positioned with extreme precision in relation to other constructions and natural heavenly bodies. Dimensions and angles of the actual construction were also carefully programmed. For these reasons when a concurrence of angles, dimensions or alignments is discovered it is immensely significant. The alignment of an aperture or shaft in a building so that sun or starlight could illuminate a desired position at some precise required time, is repeated

Figure 12: Overlay of the Great Temple at Akhetaten on the plan of Essene buildings at Qumran showing the parallel orientation.

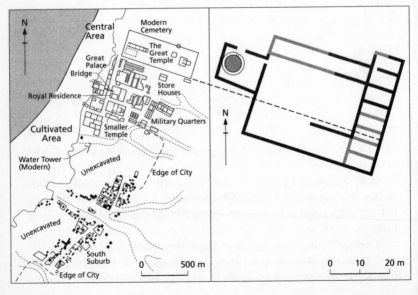

in many settings. A couple of examples will illustrate the point.

Mark Vidler's book, *The Star Mirror*, shows that the builders of the Great Pyramid at Giza were able to measure star angles to an accuracy of 'one arc minute', and used isosceles triangular alignments of pyramids on the Giza plateau to mirror isosceles triangular configurations of stars, in order to highlight special dates in the calendar.[22]

Another example relates to the Great Temple built by Ramses II at Abu Simbel, in southern Egypt. It was deliberately built in such a way that twice a year, on the 22 February (the date of his birthday) and on the 22 October (the date of his coronation), the sun shines directly over the holy shrine, illuminating the Pharaoh's throne.[23]

The 'singing statue' is our last example. Two huge statues of Akhenaten's father Amenhotep III can still be seen in front of the Valley of the Kings, on the west bank at Thebes. When Strabo, the Greek 1st century BCE writer, visited the site, he recorded that every morning when the first rays of the sun struck one of the statues, it let out an audible singing note, which he was at a loss to explain.[24]

The Qumran Cemetery

In May 1998 Dr Timothy Lim, Associate Director of the Centre for the Study of Christian Origins at the University of Edinburgh, organized an international conference on 'The Dead Sea Scrolls in their Historical Context'. The conference was held in the architecturally grandiose Faculty of Divinity building, adjacent to the old Assembly Hall of Edinburgh (where the new Scottish Parliament will hold its initial meetings).[25]

The first presentation was given by Professor E.P. Sanders, of Duke University in America, and during the discussion the question came up of why all the bodies of the Essenes in the graveyard at Qumran were buried with their heads facing south.

The large main cemetery at Qumran faces east and is some 50m from the site of the settlement, in between the settlement and the Dead Sea. Some 1,100 graves have so far been identified. They are arranged in neat, close-ordered rows, contrasting to the usual disorder of cemeteries in ancient Palestine. The graves are simple dug-out trenches marked by a small pile of loose stones. To date about 40 graves have been excavated, and from the random choice of excavation, it is statistically certain that all the bodies in the main cemetery are male. Female and children's bones were found in secondary cemeteries. All the human remains were buried naked, without adornments and with no

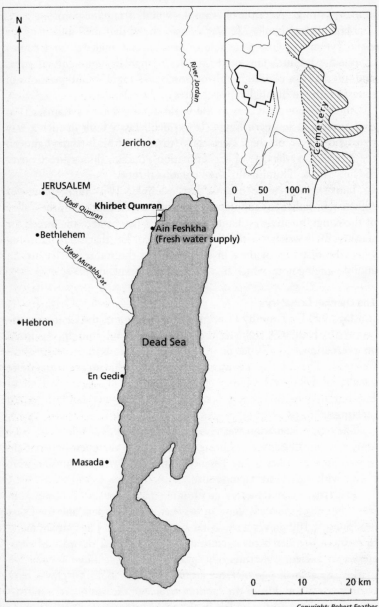

Copyright: Robert Feather

Figure 13: Map showing the location of Qumran, and an enlarged view (inset) of the site remains and cemetery.

worldly goods, apart from a few examples of ink pots and a mattock. The bodies were all buried lying on their backs, with their heads turned carefully in their graves to face south.[26]

Neither Professor Sanders nor anyone in the audience had an explanation for this peculiarity. Jerusalem, the natural direction to face, was, after all, to the west. Absorbed in the repartee of the discussion I literally had to bite my lip to stop myself gushing forth with my own explanation: 'South was the direction of the Qumran-Essenes' "holy city" of Akhetaten!'

LINKS WITH AKHETATEN

As we have seen from the 'New Jerusalem' Scroll, not only did the Qumran-Essenes know where Akhetaten was, a city destroyed 1,000 years before their time and long expunged from Egyptian memory, they had detailed knowledge of its layout.

The form of burial – naked and without any worldly accoutrements – practised by the Qumran-Essenes is quite consistent with the simple style introduced by Akhenaten, who swept away all the accompanying 'furniture for the afterlife' and burial cults associated with tombs prior and subsequent to his reign. Akhenaten, like the Qumran-Essenes, did not believe in a physical resurrection of the body, but in a spiritual re-emergence in the next world: the Qumran-Essenes believed that they would be received into the 'company of angels' after death.[27]

The Essenean asceticism associated with burial was in sharp contrast to the general behaviour and attitude of the Jewish populace in Judaea and elsewhere, which had 'slipped back' into a cult-type reverence for the dead. For them it was a sojourn in the darkness of the underworld, and it became customary to provide:

- food for the journey
- sprinkled water on the grave to provide refreshment
- weapons for men, and ornaments for women to help them in the after-life
- tombstones with names
- protective amulets.

None of these practices or beliefs were held to by the Qumran-Essenes. All of them, however, can be identified with pre- or post-Akhenaten Egyptian practice and belief.

The Qumran-Essenes' belief was in sharp contrast to the Pharisaic belief of bodily resurrection,[28] a belief which prevailed amongst the general population after the destruction of the Second Temple in 70 CE, and predominates in Orthodox Jewry to this day. (Interestingly, the Reform and other Progressive movements of Judaism have, over the last 100 years, moved back towards the original doctrines of the Qumran-Essenes. They have progressively reduced their acceptance of bodily resurrection and now advocate belief in an ongoing spiritual soul after death.)

What then of the Copper Scroll – the penultimate expected 'fingerprint' – and the treasures of the First Temple (or perhaps an even earlier Temple)? If there had been little advanced recognition that the Temple was in danger, the chances of hiding away all the sacred articles would have been reduced. Considering the timescale of advanced warning, from prophets like Jeremiah, there would appear to have been time for the 'priestly guardians' to have hidden some of the treasures of the Temple, and to have written down where they were hidden – perhaps to add these locations to a list of treasures they already knew about from another Temple – before the cataclysmic event that shattered Jewish history and brought the Southern Kingdom to an end.[*]

Many of the scrolls in the possession of the Qumran-Essenes were secretive documents, unknown to the outside world. Like their attitudes towards death and burial, many of the scrolls of the Qumran Community relate to beliefs and activities which were inconsistent with the normative Judaism of the time. These inconsistencies have not been explained satisfactorily, in fact very little attempt has been made to explain them at all. Tracing their underlying meaning back to the time of Akhenaten explains most of the anomalies, and the solution to the enigma of the Copper Scroll.

---

* The destruction by the Babylonians of the First Temple at Jerusalem in 586 BCE.

CHAPTER FIFTEEN

THE
LOST TREASURES
OF AKHENATEN

Prepare for the exciting climax of an extraordinary treasure hunt – a denouement that will irrefutably underscore the contention that the Qumran-Essenes were the direct executors of Akhenaten, with all that that implies about the undoubted influence they had on Christianity and Islam.

In John Allegro's original analysis of the Copper Scroll, he identified four likely locations for the lost treasures listed by the Qumran-Essenes. Namely, in the vicinities of:

- the Dead Sea
- Jericho
- Jerusalem
- Mount Gerizim.*

Quite specific depositories of the treasure are pinpointed by John Allegro within the ruins of the Qumran-Essene monastery at Khirbet Qumran; near Ain Farah; in the Antonia fortress at Haram; at Wilson's Arch in Haram; at tombs in the Kidron Valley; on the Mount of Olives and Mount Gerizim and in Jerusalem.[1]

Many of the locations mentioned appear to refer to Jerusalem, or its close vicinity. Since it would not be wise to go digging at the Temple site – for fear of attracting a hail of machine-gun fire as official permission is difficult to obtain – for reasons of religious sensitivity, I will concentrate on locations that can possibly be explored and excavated. The

---

* See Figure 1, the relational map of the ancient Middle East.

same considerations apply to what are now largely built-up areas of Jerusalem. Although locations in Jerusalem are difficult to excavate, over a period of 45 years none of the suggested locations has yielded any treasures.

From the deductions that I have made and the conclusions reached earlier in this book, there are sufficient clues to identify additional candidate sites where parts of the treasures mentioned in the Copper Scroll may be found. Careful study of these sites will assist anyone determined enough to venture forth with spade, metal detector and the necessary permits.

The sites are within nearby proximity, or easy access, to:

- El-Amarna – ancient Akhetaten – in northern Egypt
- Faiyum, Hawara and the Delta regions of northern Egypt
- Elephantine Island in southern Egypt, and Heliopolis near Cairo
- Lake Tana, in Ethiopia
- The First Temple at Jerusalem
- The Caves of Qumran on the Dead Sea
- Mount Gerizim in northern Israel

You may find it useful to refer back to Figure 1, the relational map of the area, as I discuss the individual sites.

El-Amarna

With the sudden demise of Akhenaten, at a relatively young middle-age, the rule of the Kingdom fell to Tutankhmun, his brother (and husband of his daughter), who was still a child, following a brief interlude by the enigmatic Smenkhkare. Neither of these two pharaohs had the political strength to resist the machinations of the priests of Thebes, who may have started to move against Akhenaten's power bases as soon as they heard of his imminent death.

The time to squirrel away the treasures of the Great Temple, Palace, and Treasury of Akhetaten may therefore not have been too long. The sheer weights and volumes involved could have amounted to several tonnes of precious metals and valuables. The work could not be entrusted to labourers – unless they were to be killed subsequently – so the hard graft had to be done by the caucus of priests. It would also seem inevitable that, with such a volume of treasure, it would not have all been hidden in one location but would have been spread around to increase the chances of some of it remaining undetected.

The greater the weight of treasures to be hidden, the less the likely distance of travel from the source. The most probable areas, therefore, are in the immediate vicinity of the Great Temple.

Stretching half a kilometre to the north and south of the Temple complex before the North and South City suburbs would have been reached, there are two unexcavated areas of land. These are possible sites for treasure burials, but are relatively unlikely in view of the proximity of workmen's villages and the danger of spying eyes.

However, going south of the present day village of El-Till, and following the track beside the edge of the cultivated land, we are walking along what would have been the main street of Akhetaten. Where the city's main administrative centre would have been is now marked by two mud-brick pylons – all that remains of a bridge that connected the 'King's House', to the east, with the Official Palace, to the west. This enormous complex of buildings has never been fully excavated and contains numerous inexplicable features. Here, under cover of darkness, many of the treasures of the Palace and King's residence could have been secreted.

Figure 14: Site of Akhetaten showing view of Great Temple, stelae and tombs.

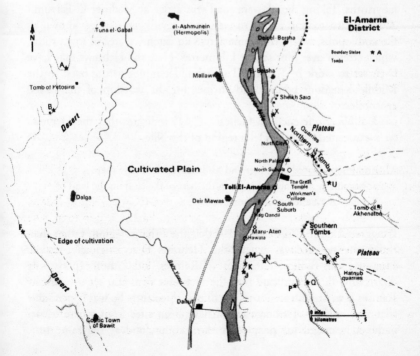

A most promising location for the treasures of the Temple lies in the vicinity of the Tomb of Akhenaten and the southern group of private tombs. Already prepared for him during his lifetime, it would have been a natural place for the priests to consider.[2] It lies a suitably safe and secluded 12km east of Amarna, along the 'Royal Wadi' (today, inaccessible to motor vehicles).

The private tombs, many with sand-blocked entrances, face the village of Hagg Qandil and the public are not allowed access. This, however, is a likely place where some of the treasure of the Temple of Akhenaten may be found.

Faiyum and the Delta Region

Another compelling location for some of Akhenaten's treasure to have been hidden lies some distance from Amarna, at the place where Joseph's family were settled. It is the Faiyum area, adjacent to the outfall of the Bahr (River) Jusuf, at Lake Qarun.

During Joseph's lifetime, Lake Moeris, as it was then known, would have been far more extensive, and I looked for an area which might have contained extensive ruined buildings and temples – hidden labyrinths. Taking the Hawara road you arrive at Medinet El-Faiyum.[3] A secondary road runs north-west to Kiman Fares, once known as Crocodilopolis, where you come across an extensive area of town ruins, which stretch over four square kilometres. Here the Hebrews may have been set to work by Ramses II to rebuild temples dating back to the Middle Kingdom period, and shrines for the worship of the sacred crocodiles.

A Biblical reference, in Genesis 47:11, indicates that the Hebrews were associated with the Delta region of the Nile:

> And Joseph placed his father and his brethren, and gave them a
> possession in the land of Egypt, in the best of the land, in the land of
> Ramses, as Pharaoh had commanded.

I suggested earlier (in Chapter 10) that the Faiyum region, rather than the Delta region, was where the Hebrews were originally settled. However, the Biblical references to Ramses and Pithom (previously Avaris and Tanis), indicate that the Hebrews were also set to work by Ramses II to build storehouses for him at these sites. So it is conceivable that these places of storage could have been sites from where Moses gathered some of his people for the Exodus, and at the same time secreted the details of the treasures that could not be carried with them from Egypt.

Elephantine and Heliopolis

After the priests of Akhenaten fled the destruction of Akhetaten, I suggested that some of them settled at the Island of Elephantine and at Heliopolis, so both these areas warrant re-evaluation and excavation.

Archaeological evidence shows, as we have previously noted, that there was a pseudo-Judaic militaristic community at Elephantine on the extreme southern borders of Egypt, at least as early as the 7th century BCE.[4] The relatively 'certain' early date shows that they were not 'Dispersees' (Diaspora) from the fall of the First Temple in 586 BCE, but had arrived from somewhere other than Israel. Justification for this assertion needs a fuller discussion and I will go into more detail later in Chapter 19.

Lake Tana

When the Community at Elephantine suddenly disappeared in 410 BCE, it is not unfeasible that the survivors journeyed deep into Ethiopian territory, and eventually settled on the shores of Lake Tana in the northern part of the country. Like the Judaic Community of Elephantine, the Community of Lake Tana, now known as Falashas, had, and still have, unusual customs and practices, reflecting a people who had not participated in the mainstream Judaism of Canaan. Like the Essenes they did not keep Purim* or the ceremonies related to the Dedication of the Temple.

It is possible that the ancestors of the Falashas took away to Ethiopia some residual treasures, but their location would and could not have been recorded in the Copper Scroll of the Essenes.

The First Temple at Jerusalem

The impending threat of the destruction of the First Temple by the Babylonians in the years before 586 BCE must have wrought untold anxiety on the population. As guardians of the Holy incunabula and treasures that came out of Egypt, the priests of the Temple would certainly have taken the opportunity to carry many of the sacred and valuable items to hiding places in or near Jerusalem.

When Nebuchadnezzar's iron fist finally reached Jerusalem, those

---

* A festival celebrating the events described in the Old Testament Book of Esther.

treasures that were not saved were carried off by the Babylonians as spoils of war, and are lost to the mists of time.

Whilst it has not been possible to excavate fully at the site where the Temple is thought to have stood, because the Dome of the Rock and Muslim Temple of Al Ahxsa now occupy a large area of the Holy Mound, it is unlikely that any holy relics or treasure described in the Copper Scroll would be found there.

The Caves at Qumran

Many textural treasures have already come out of the finestriated hills of Qumran since the accidental finding of the first of the Dead Sea Scrolls in 1947. There may be more 'textual' treasures to be discovered, but the area has been explored so intensively that the likelihood of large amounts of treasure being found becomes increasingly remote.

CRACKING THE CODE OF THE COPPER SCROLL

At this stage in my researches I went back to the original source – to the Copper Scroll itself – to reconsider the mixture of Egyptian and ancient Hebrew exhibited in it. I came to the intriguing possibility that the Copper Scroll refers to both Israeli and Egyptian locations. Having isolated the most likely general areas for the treasures of Akhenaten to be found, I started to home in on more exact locations, with the help of the Copper Scroll.

Going back to the scroll, I needed to address a number of questions before I could make more progress:

- Does the scroll contain some kind of code that, once solved, will lead to the treasures it describes?
- Were the Qumran-Essenes prone to writing in code?
- If so, are any other Dead Sea Scrolls written in code?

The answer to all these proved to be 'yes'.

When referring to their own Community, the Qumran-Essenes often used cryptic codes, mirror writing and hidden messages within their own texts.

Looking at several examples of other Dead Sea Scrolls, it became immediately obvious that the Qumran-Essenes had a fondness for codes, and this predilection gave me an insight into the quirky minds of these hermit-like people. More importantly, it unambiguously showed the scribes to be familiar with Egyptian symbols in use between 1500 and 1200 BCE, a period comfortably encompassing the reign of Pharaoh Akhenaten.

One example is Scroll 4Q186 (dealing with horoscopes), which includes Greek, square-form Hebrew and Paleo-Hebrew letters encrypted as mirror writing.

Another scroll, known as the 'Admonitions of the Sons of Dawn', was found in Cave 4 at Qumran. This scroll is different from other scrolls. It begins in Hebrew, with a mention of the 'Maskil' ('Teacher'), and then converts to apparently arbitrary cryptic symbols, plus a void character which is quite unknown in the Hebrew alphabet!

Robert Eisenman and Michael Wise[5] deciphered the text of the 'Admonitions' scroll by equating what appeared to them to be '23 more or less arbitrary symbols' with Hebrew letter equivalents. When I looked closely at the apparently random cryptic symbols, it became clear that they are mainly Egyptian in origin. Many of the symbols are based on hieroglyphics or hieratic writing – a cursive form of hieroglyphics used by Egyptian priests. For example, the symbol used for the Hebrew 'aleph' is part of the sound 'meni' made from the hieroglyphic sign '𒍦' turned through 90°. The symbol for the Hebrew letter 'shin' is the Egyptian hieroglyph for a 'wall'. The symbol below – the Hebrew letter 'zahde' – is the Egyptian 'ankh' sign for 'life'.

Why would the Qumran-Essenes still utilize an ancient form of Egyptian writing, closely related to the writing that Moses must have used in recording the early Old Testament texts? The answer can only be that ancient Egyptian writing was still important to them, and part of their inheritance.[6]

An outline of the types of language and writing, in use in the Middle East from earliest times up to the period when the Dead Sea Scrolls were written, will be helpful in assessing the types of writing that were available to the Qumran-Essenes.

These examples of the use of codes by the Qumran-Essenes made me fairly confident that the interspersion of Greek upper case letters in the Copper Scroll, which do not have an immediately obvious meaning, indicated that this Scroll falls into the category of having a hidden meaning. I was already suspicious of the numbering system used in the scroll, as it is not equatable with the Hebrew format in use at the time of its engraving around the time of Jesus, but is identifiable with much earlier dates. The treasure weight dimensions (*see Chapter 2*) are also clearly exaggerations if taken as Hebrew weights. It would therefore be

Table 4: Forms of Writing and Language in the Ancient Middle East

EGYPT

Hieroglyphs	Pictorial symbols from 2nd Dynasty onwards (3000 BCE)
Hieratic	Cursive writing form of hieroglyphs, mainly used by priests from 11th Dynasty onwards (2500 BCE)
Demotic (Enchorial)	Business and social form of Hieratic from 900 BCE–300 CE
Greek	From 330 BCE onwards[7]
Coptic	Egyptian language written in Greek letters 200 BCE onwards

MESOPOTAMIA

Cuneiform	Pictorial symbols pre-1800 BCE
Akkadian	Semitic language, also in international use from 1500 BCE onwards
Aramaic, Ancient	North Semitic pre-1000 BCE

CANAAN

Ugarit	1500 BCE
Proto-Canaanite (Western Semitic)	1400 BCE
Phoenician (form of Proto-Canaanite)	1100 BCE
Paleo-Hebrew	c.800 BCE
Aramaic, Intermediate	c.600 BCE Semitic language Western Aramaic (language of the Palestinian Talmud) Eastern Aramaic (language (with Syriac) of the Babylonian Talmud)
Aramaic, International	Widespread use in and beyond the Middle East from 6th century BCE (language of the Elephantine papyri and parts of the Old Testament)
Hebrew (Square Form)	c.200 BCE
Greek	after 200 BCE
Latin	after 67 BCE

naive to take the locations and related numbers, as described in the Copper Scroll, at face value.

As Greek-language influences in Judaea did not appear until after 250 BCE, it is safe to conclude that the Copper Scroll was not engraved until after this date. Its rough-and-ready writing indicates that it was a copy of an earlier document done with some haste. It is written in a form of Hebrew unlike that used in any of the other Dead Sea Scrolls,

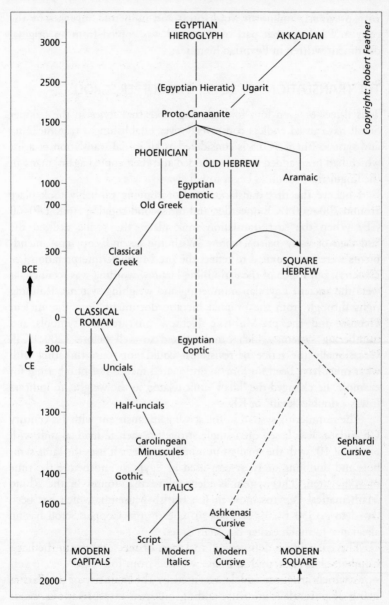

Figure 15: Schematic showing the development of writing forms. (Adapted from an original schematic by Jonathan Lotan in *From A to Aleph: 3 Steps to Writing in Hebrew* (Qualum Publishing, 1996)).

with previously unknown word forms and numerous mistakes by the copyist. I believe that part of the scroll was copied from an original document written in Egyptian hieratic.

THE TRANSLATIONS OF 3Q15 – THE COPPER SCROLL

This three- or even four-fold alloying of textual styles in the Copper Scroll has caused endless controversy over establishing a true meaning and syntax. But if 3Q15 is considered as an initial translation of a list which had been added to and amended and then copied again, many of the linguistic difficulties begin to fall away.

I believe the first translation and/or copying probably took place around 700–600 BCE or earlier, and the second copying around 40–60 CE. When the first translation took place, the scribe utilized the language of early paleo-Hebrew. With the second copying, amendments were incorporated to reflect the pre-Mishnaic interpretation (*see Glossary*), but much of the early Bible Hebrew wording was retained, as were the ancient Egyptian numbering and weighing systems. Running right through from the original hieratic document, into the ancient Hebrew and the pre-Mishnaic Hebrew mixture, are symbols and numbering systems which can be dated to well before 1200 BCE. Occasionally the scribe or revisionist could not resist tinkering with what must have been for him an antiquated method of numbering; for example, he changed the 'khaff' unit related to the weights to indicate it was a double 'khaff' or KK.

The numbering system in the scroll is inconsistent with 1st-century CE Judaea. It is based on a single stroke for each individual unit with breaks of 10, with the smallest number to the left. It uses the same symbols and doubling of 10 system used in Egypt at and before the time of Akhenaten. This system is identical to that found in the Rhind Mathematical Papyrus, now in the British Museum, which has been dated to *c*.1550 BCE[8] (*see Plate 3*). Clearly the Copper Scroll has an allegiance to much earlier Egyptian times.

There is still no definitive translation of the scroll from the large numbers that exist, and so I have worked from four of the main versions which are most widely accepted by the majority of scholars as being of potential authority, adding my own interpretations where I diverge from all of their variants. The four translations I have worked from are by John Allegro, Garcia Martinez, Geza Vermes and Al Wolters.[9] However, I shall endeavour to describe the main reasons for my selections as we go through the relevant parts of the text.

Each of the descriptions of the 64 treasure locations listed in the Copper Scroll are presented in the text in a similar pattern:

a) a specific description of the hiding place
b) a secondary description of the hiding place
c) an instruction to dig or measure
d) the distance from a position by numbers of cubits
e) a description of the treasure
f) Greek letters (after seven of the locations).

A translation of Column 1 of the Copper Scroll text is typical of the style and content.

> *the ruin which is in the valley, pass under*
> *the steps leading to the East*
> *40 cubits (…) a chest of money and its total*
> *the weight of 17 talents.* K є N
> *In the sepulchral monument, in the third course:*
> *one hundred gold ingots. In the great cistern of the courtyard*
> *of the peri-style, in a hollow in the floor covered with sediment,*
> *in front of the upper opening: nine hundred talents.*
> *In the hill of Kochlit, tithe-vessels of the lord of the peoples and sacred*
> *vestments; total of the tithes and of the treasure; a seventh of the*
> *second tithe made unclean. Its opening lies on the edges of the Northern*
> *channel, six cubits in the direction of the cave of the ablutions,* X A Γ
> *In the plastered cistern Manos, going down to the left,*
> *at a height of three cubits from the bottom: silver, forty*
> *…talents…*

The connections I have made back through the Qumran-Essenes to Ezekiel and Habakkuk, the Levites, the priests of On present in the Exodus, and to Akhenaten, means that any interpretation should assume a strong 'Egyptian Effect' on the hidden meanings of the text. The numerical values are also all likely to be Egyptian in origin, rather than Canaanite.

A full translation, in the version given by John Allegro, of all 12 columns of the Copper Scroll, together with the ancient Hebrew text, is given in the Appendix.

THE FINAL HIDING PLACE

To begin at the end, as Lewis Carroll would recommend. The end of the last column of the Copper Scroll, Column 12, refers to a tunnel in Sechab, to the north of Kochlit. It is here, in this last mentioned place, that, we are told, is hidden the key to the Copper Scrolls:*

> In the tunnel which is in Sechab, *to the North of Kochlit*, which opens
> towards the North and has graves in its entrance: a copy of this text
> and its explanation and its measurements and the inventory of
> everything…item by item. (My italics.)

Clearly this confirms that the contents of the Copper Scroll cannot be taken at face value. There is a code, and a key which can unlock the code.

So where is Kochlit? What does the code mean? Where is the key?

In his translation of the Copper Scroll, John Allegro, one of the original editorial team who worked on the Dead Sea Scrolls, is very cautious (and rightly so) in assigning place-names to words which are essentially a grouping of consonants. By the nature of the Hebrew writing at the time, and as still pertains in the scrolls of the Torah, vowels were not included. Usually there is little ambiguity about the pronunciation and meaning of a word, but for unusual words, such as names and place-names, there is ample room for alternatives.

The Geza Vermes translation of 'Kochlit' is also given in the first, second, fourth and twelfth columns of the Scroll,[10] but interestingly John Allegro here translates 'Kochlit' not as a place-name, but as:

…and stored Seventh Year produce…

The 'Seventh Year produce', if it is a correct interpretation, is an unusual term. There is only one reference in the Bible that comes to mind for this kind of far-sighted strategy. Could it be referring to the place where Joseph stored the last year's and previous years' excess gatherings of corn from the seven years of plenty for his Pharaoh, Akhenaten?

Do the Greek letters, which appear in Column 1 and which also contains the word 'Kochlit', have a bearing?

---

* Scrolls, because Column 12 indicates that a second copy of the scroll will be found north of Kochlit.

The Strange Greek Letters

No-one has previously come up with a satisfactory explanation of the meaning of the Greek letters in the Scroll, suggesting that they are indeed some kind of coded message, however many theories have been put forward. They are variously ascribed as referring to:

a) place-names
b) types of treasure
c) quantities of treasure
d) names of people
e) distances from locations
f) scribal marks
g) section divisions.

One of the most recent authoritative translations of the Copper Scroll, *The Copper Scroll, Overview, Text and Translation*, by Al Wolters and published in 1996, refers to the Greek letters as follows:

> Although various theories have been offered to explain the Greek letters, they remain an enigma. It may be significant that they could in each case be the beginning of a Greek proper name.

Studying the Greek letters, and thinking about my theory that Moses, or the priests of Akhenaten who came out of Egypt with him, brought a 'written map' of treasures that remained hidden in Egypt, the solution to the Copper Scroll enigma suddenly dawned on me. A solution that was not inconsistent with Al Wolters' suggestion.

My excitement at the discovery, as the letters fell into place, made the back of my neck tingle. The answer lies partly in the order of the locations described and partly in the cryptic Greek letters appended to some of the columns of text which have long mystified translators. They now began to have some meaning.

Later hiding places for the precious items that were brought out of Egypt and subsequently hidden in Canaan, were added to the original texts being copied.

All the visible Greek coding marks occur in the first four columns of the Copper Scroll.

The letters are interspersed in the columns as:

K ∈ N # X A Γ # H N # θ ∈ # Δ I # T P # Σ K

The first ten letters spell (A)KHENATE!*

I realized that I had cracked one of the most obstinate puzzles of the Copper Scrolls – one which has baffled scholars for decades.

The reaction of Jozef Milik to my explanation was one of wonderment. He was the first person to publish an official translation of the Copper Scroll and is an expert in ancient Middle Eastern linguistics. Whilst agreeing that the letters could relate to Akhenaten, he was puzzled as to 'how the Essenes could know about the Pharaoh or his City'.[11]

In addition to Jozef Milik's affirmation that the first ten Greek letters in the Copper Scroll might refer to Akhenaten or Akhetaten, I now needed to see if there were any references in classical literature that might use Greek letters to spell out these names.

Living in London, I was fortunate enough to be able to consult one of the most knowledgeable authorities on Egyptian and ancient Middle Eastern languages, Professor John Tait of University College London. He was kind enough to direct me towards a number of sources where I might find an answer.[12]

Gauthier's *Dictionnaire des Noms Geographiques* gives the equivalent hieroglyphic sound of Akhenaten as: Ahk (on) t n – Åton, and from Calderini's *Dizionario dei Nomi Geografici e Topografici dell' Egitto Greco-Romano* the nearest equivalent name in Greek is ÅKAN ΘION.

The fact that I could not find an exact Greek rendering of the name Akhenaten or Akhetaten was, as Professor Tait pointed out, not surprising as the Greek world would not have known of a place that had long since disappeared.[13] Also, he added, there would not be Greek letters available to make the sounds equivalent to ancient Egyptian hieroglyphic or hieratic words.

The nearest Greek letters that could have been used to represent pronunciations of Pharaoh Akhenaten's name, or its earlier version of Amenhotep, which the ancient Greeks were familiar with, was Amenophoris or Amenophis. Had they known of the Pharaoh's later name, like the Qumran-Essenes, they might also have come up with the Greek letters:

Å KϵNXAΓHNΘϵ

The meaning of the remaining Greek letters is discussed below, in their context within the book. The reason the Greek letters occur only in the

---

* The Greek letters X, Γ and Θ have English transliterations of kh, g and th, respectively.

earliest part of the Copper Scroll is, I believe, because the earlier columns relate to locations in Egypt and the scroll, being a form of list, has been added to at a later date with locations referring to Canaan.

The Seventh Year Storehouse
The meaning of the term 'Kochlit' as storehouse for the seventh year, as referred to in Column 1, now became clear. It is almost certainly one of the storehouses (probably the main one), next to the Great Temple of Akhenaten, where Joseph would have stored grain during the seven years of plenty in preparation for the seven years of famine. What more convenient place to hide the bulk of the treasures of the Pharaoh than at his capital Akhetaten, modern-day Amarna?

On the Upper Floor of the Museum at Luxor there are several statues of Akhenaten, and a breath-taking reconstruction of a wall from a Temple of Akhenaten at Thebes. Pictured on the *talattat* (blocks) of the wall are scenes of busy life on the Aten estates and, in one, a storehouse crammed full of pots, caskets, metal ingots and precious items. This is the kind of storehouse from which our search can truly begin.

If the reference in the final column, Column 12, does refer to the storehouse at Amarna, as the starting place from where a summary and explanation, item by item, will be found, (and if my theory is correct), I would anticipate finding Greek letters at the end of this passage also, to indicate it was an Egyptian location. There are none. However, this is almost certainly because there is a piece of text missing exactly where one would expect to find the Greek coding letters, with just enough space to accommodate two Greek letters. What those two Greek letters might have been, I will come back to shortly.

My theory is further endorsed by a reference to a place, in Column 4, that John Allegro reads as 'the Vale of Achor', and Garcia Martinez reads as 'the valley of Akon'; I read as 'the valley of Aton'.* From now on the pieces of the jigsaw fall neatly into place, each bit reinforcing the others.

Figure 16: Illustration of text from the last column of the Copper Scroll.

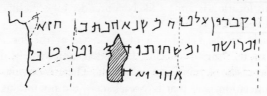

* An alternative spelling of Aten.

The description at the end of the final column, therefore, refers to Egypt, and we start at the storehouses just south of the Great Temple.

> ...In the tunnel which is in Sechab, to the North of the Store House, and opens towards the North and has graves in its entrance: a copy of this text and its explanation and its measurements and the inventory of every thing [blank] item by item [missing piece].
>
> [Column 12]

The Copper Scroll is saying: go due north of the stored seventh year produce and you will find a tomb or tombs.

Bearing almost exactly due north, as instructed, from the storehouses you do indeed arrive at a line of northern tombs, running along the edge of a quarry-ridden plateau just south of modern Sheikh Said. Here the plateau parallels the curve of the River Nile, and comes right down to within about 30m of the river. What more convenient way to transport bulky treasure than by the river which is in close proximity to the Great Temple.

The tomb which has a tunnel opening towards the North, has the key to the Copper Scroll buried in the mouth of the tunnel.

The ridge on which these Northern Tombs are situated faces in various directions following the contour of the hillside. Those of Meryra, Huya and Meryra II (or Kheshi as he has been called), face approximately south, and their tunnel openings run northward. All three persons were key officials in Akhenaten's Court, and their tombs are candidates for determined further excavation.

As far as is known, Meryra was the only High Priest of Aten. His other titles were: 'Bearer of the Fan on the right-hand side of the King', 'Royal Chancellor', 'Sole Companion', 'Sometime Prince', and 'Friend of the King'. He was also an hereditary prince and his tomb reflects his importance, with lavish decorated scenes of local life. About 60m behind his tomb at the top of the hill, is a deep burial shaft, facing north. This location is a most likely contender for secreting the key to the Copper Scroll.

Reference in the translation of *at Sechab* as the location of the tunnel is another important clue. Looked at more closely, the Hebrew word could easily be translated as 'Sechra'. There is one name that fits this pronunciation, and that is 'Seeaakara' – the mysterious King who immediately succeeded Akhenaten and is thought to have reigned as

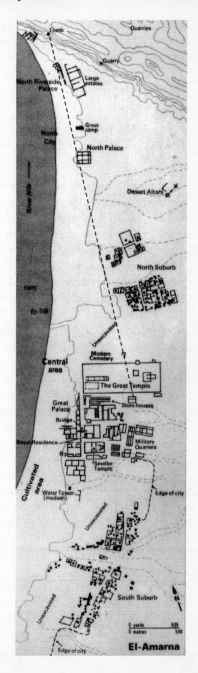

Figure 17: Plan of the archaeological sites at Akhetaten, now known as El-Amarna.

co-regent shortly before Akhenaten's death. Seeaakara, as King, is shown rewarding Meryra II, his scribe and superintendent, on an unfinished picture on the wall of the scribe's tomb.[14]

The tomb of Meryra II, or, if it can be located, that of the mysterious Seeaakara (Smenkhkara), also warrant further intensive investigation.

BACK TO THE BEGINNING OF THE TEXT

Column I

Returning to Column 1, the line *ruin which is in the valley*, puts us, according to John Allegro, in the valley of the seventh year produce, looking for structures built before the time of Akhenaten, or which were then in ruins. There are *steps leading east*. The most likely contenders are the Desert Altars, not far from Akhenaten's North Palace. These were enclosed in heavily buttressed brick walls, alluded to by John Allegro's translation which describes the location as 'fortress-like'. The altars, chapel and pavilion structure were either in ruins or dismantled in Akhenaten's time. The Northern Altar can be approached by a ramp leading to the east. Forty cubits (or 20.4m) along this ramp and beneath it, there should be *a chest of money with contents weighing 17 Talents*.

The next section refers to *the sepulchral monument*, where *there are 100 light bars of gold*. There is only one other reference to gold ingots, and that occurs in the 'Egyptian' Column 2. This talks about the *carpeted house of Yeshu*(?). I take this as meaning in the precincts of Akhetaten city. John Allegro, rather, reads this phrase as *the Old House of Tribute*. In one of the northern group of tombs there is a tomb of 'Huya', Steward to Queen Tiyi, mother of Akhenaten. The decorated chapel to Huya shows a scene of Akhenaten in the 12th year of his reign, being borne on a carrying chair with his wife Queen Nefertiti to the Hall of Foreign Tribute. Below and to the side of the scene are pictures of visiting emissaries paying homage to Pharaoh. The 'House of Tribute' was almost certainly this Hall of Tribute of Akhetaten.

The Hall of Tribute was a large altar area forming part of the enclosure wall of the Great Temple to the north-east end of the building. It is quite likely that the floor would have been carpeted, for the comfort of the dignitaries who must have been constantly prostrating themselves at the feet of Pharaoh. *In the cavity...in the third platform 65 gold ingots.*

Under the raised platform three levels down these gold bar riches must have been secreted.

Too late! Someone has got there first!

'Crock of Gold Square'

In 1926 a team excavating the ancient city of Akhetaten had began a six-year season of work under its leaders, Dr H. Frankfort and J.D.S. Pendlebury.

The dig had reached the Central Western Quarter of Tell el-Amarna and what appeared to be the outhouse of a large estate. In a small court-yard to the east, Mr Pendlebury was supervising a Bedouin workman in what seemed to promise to be a useful day's effort. They had already found a small limestone statue of a monkey playing a harp and a frag-ment of pierced blue faience decorated with spirals and a Nefertiti car-touche.* Digging a foot under the ground the workman unearthed a large buff-clay, matt-brown painted jug. It was about 24cm high and 15cm diameter. As he prised off the lid, out popped a gold bar, followed by 22 more.

By the time they had completed the excavation, the team had also found two silver ingots, silver fragments, rings, ear rings and silver sheet.

Dr Frankfort believed that the silver fragments had been crushed and the rings twisted and broken, to make them ready for melting down, just the way the silver and gold ingots had been produced. Frankfort and Pendlebury considered that the find was part of a thief's loot, and even suggested that the looter, or looters, had raided the Hall of Foreign Tribute, as it was less than a mile away.

The area that they were excavating is now known as 'Crock of Gold Square'. What Dr Frankfort and his team had found was a treasure trove of 23 gold bars of various weights between 34.62g and 286.53g, and weighing 3,375.36g in total.[15]

Before proceeding to assess this find we need to re-examine the question of what the text of the Copper Scroll really means when it refers to a 'Talent'.

The Problem of Weights and the 'Gold Khaff Link'

The difficulties in determining what exactly was meant by the unit of weight which is written in the Copper Scroll texts as 'KK', and

---

* A rectangular inscribed outline with curved corners, inside of which, usually in hieroglyph form, were carved a person's titles.

sometimes just as a single 'K', has continually perplexed translators. The unit is usually translated, and therefore considered to be, a 'Talent'.

The weight term is represented in the text as two Hebrew 'khaffs', for which there is no exact English pronunciation but an approximation would be 'kh kh'. These weight letters have always previously been translated as the Canaanite or Biblical 'Talent' – a unit weighing variously between 30kg and 150kg. For the Copper Scroll, 35kg (equivalent to the weight of 3,000 Shekels), has usually been taken as the guide. Using even the lowest of these units, astronomical financial values and excessive weights are arrived at for the total amounts of precious metals mentioned in the Copper Scroll. Some translators have, therefore, quite arbitrarily downgraded the term to the next Canaanite unit of weight.[16] (For further discussion of this point, see Chapter 2.)

From my standpoint that the texts refer to Egyptian locations, I considered it more logical now to use local contemporary Egyptian units of weight. In addition, drawing on my experience as a metallurgist, I knew (as anyone who has been in an assay office would know), that units of 'kilogrammes' are not the currency for weighing precious metals.

The Egyptian common unit of weight was, until 1795 BCE, the 'Deben' – equivalent to 93.3g. After that period it was supplemented by the 'Kite' of 9–10g – which was exclusively used to weigh gold and silver.[17]

Our worthy gentlemen, Dr Frankfort and Mr Pendlebury, and their team of excavators at Tell el-Amarna, also dug up a number of small decorative figures which they classified as weights. All are in the range of 20g, but only one looks like a standard weight. It is made solely of lead as a plain cuboid and is inscribed with two parallel vertical downward marks 'II'. This was found in one of the most sumptuous houses amongst the large estates. These downward marks are identical to the type of single marks found in the Copper Scroll to indicate one unit of weight.

The weight of this lead cuboid is 20.4g. The two parallel downward strokes on it indicate that it was equivalent to two 'Kite' and must mean that the standard unit of weight – a 'KK' – is represented by the two 'khaffs' in the Copper Scroll.

The Copper Scroll only mentions pure gold ingots twice; on both occasions each reference is in the first two columns, which I have deduced relate to the City of Akhetaten. The total number of gold bars listed, from both locations, is 165. Assuming the gold bars were originally cast in identical, standard moulds, sized to produce gold bars as close as possible to the standard 'KK' unit of weight, the total weight of the 165 gold bars would be:

165 x 20.4g = 3,366g

This is virtually identical to the total weight of gold (3,375g) found at the 'Crock of Gold Square' in Amarna. The correlation is so close in fact (within 0.28 per cent or 99.72 per cent probability of correctness), that, bearing in mind the technical difficulty of consistently pouring the liquid gold into the original standard moulds to the exact level mark, the degree of certainty that they were the same gold bars the Copper Scroll refers to is virtually 100 per cent.

Clearly, as Dr Frankfort surmised, the thief had melted down the 165 light gold bars to produce 23 ingots, of varying sizes and weights, from his crude sand moulds.

If this is what transpired, we would expect some of the new ingots to weigh a multiple of the 'KK' 20.4g unit weight, purely on statistical grounds, particularly the larger ingots. This is just the case, and the largest of the new ingots is almost exactly 14 times the 'KK' unit weight. (The 23 gold ingots from 'Crock of Gold Square' can be seen in the Cairo Museum, and many of the silver items are in the British Museum.)

So, our thief had found the hoards hidden at the *sepulchred monument* and from the *Hall of Foreign Tribute*, and had found a nearby house to sort through his plunder. He was also busy melting down silver, approximating to 40 KK, and other jewellery, perhaps from the hoard at Column 1's *ascent of the staircase of refuge* where there were 40 Talents of silver.

This finding, that the gold bars mentioned in the Copper Scroll weighed almost exactly the same as a hoard of gold bars discovered at El-Amarna in the 1920s, is virtually certain proof that I have made a correct interpretation of the Copper Scroll. More significantly, it puts a lock at the end of a chain stretching through the centuries that links the priests of Akhetaten to the Essenes of Qumran – a 24-Carat gold link!

Are there any other 'finds' in the region of Akhetaten which back up this conclusion? When we come to Column 6 of the Copper Scroll we will discover there is indeed another 'gold link', and although not quite so clear cut as the above example, it is still very convincing.

My conclusion is further reinforced by an astonishing design characteristic of the jar in which the treasures from the 'Crock of Gold Square' were found. All the jars in which the Dead Sea Scrolls of the Qumran-Essenes were found were unusually large. They are unique to the Essene Community who must have made them, and they are not found elsewhere in Judaea or ancient Israel. They have a mottled white coloured exterior with a squat curved lid. They vary in outline shape, maximum diameter and height, but virtually all have a lid diameter of 15cm – exactly the same diameter as the 'Crock of Gold' jar found at Amarna (*see Plate 11*). There is also a marked similarity in base design and size, and in lid design.[18]

Not to worry that some of the treasure has been found. There are still sizeable amounts not yet located!

Returning to the Column 1 text, we are probably still in the city centre and the next description is of a building with a *peristyle* courtyard (i.e., surrounded by columns) with a large cistern and a floor covered with sediment. Assuming the building is the Great Temple, its outer part had a colonnaded court which must have contained the Great Cistern, supplying water to the Temple area and the eight bathing tanks which stood at the back of the Temple. *In front of the upper opening: 900 Talents.*

Still near the Seventh Year Store we are told to look somewhere in the *Place of the Basins*: there, at the bottom of the conduit which supplies the water, six cubits down from the edge of the northern basin we will find vestments and tithes[*] of treasure. The Garcia Martinez translation of the section refers to *the second tithe made unclean*, implying contact with the dead or a sacrifice, and therefore proximity to burial chambers or places where offerings of animals might have been prepared.

These basins, of which there were eight, stood outside the Lesser Sanctuary housing the 'Holy of Holies' or 'Benben' of the Great Temple, and were supplied in series by a main conduit from the Great Cistern. As the Temple was oriented approximately east to west lengthways, the northern-most basin was probably the first one connected to the water conduit. The Garcia Martinez translation can be explained by the proximity of this part of the building to a preparation area.[19] These preparations would also have required large amounts of cleansing water.

---

* Tributes or religious donations amounting to a tenth of a person's income.

It appears, therefore, that 9m from this northern-most basin in, or near, the supplying conduit, the treasures were hidden.

Finally in Column 1 there is a phrase which Garcia Martinez (and Al Wolters) translate as: *in the plastered cistern of Manos*. He has, perhaps, been influenced here by the Greek letters scattered in the text and comes up with a Greek name – which is not very helpful! Manos is a legendary character, portrayed in the film *Manos the Hands of Fate* who encounters Torgo – a type of monster with huge knees who has trouble walking.[20] Somehow I think the translators were on the wrong track here!

John Allegro translated the critical phrase as *Staircase of Refuge*, and Geza Vermes has it as, *In the hole of the waterproofed refuge*; these probably allude to the Temple, and could possibly refer to the screened portico section of the building known as 'The Sunshade'.[21] But as we know, Dr Frankfort's thief has already cleaned out this cache.

Column 2

At the beginning of Column 2 there are said to be 42 Talents (KK), *In the filled tank which is underneath the steps*. John Allegro and Al Wolters disagree with Garcia Martinez and translate *filled tank* as *In the salt pit...* Either way, the steps may well be those depicted on the walls of the Tomb of Panehesy and shown in Plate 18 of N. de G. Davies' *Rock Tombs of El Amarna – Part II*. They are the steps up to the Great Altar of the Temple, which stood in the centre of an open courtyard and was approached by a flight of 17 steps.

The space within the altar and under the steps was used for storing offerings, and if the offerings were meat they would have been preserved by salting. de G. Davies, however, takes this usage as only being 'sculptured on the sides' of the altar. If this assumption is correct then the space under the steps could well have provided accommodation for a water storage tank, to supply the two lavers, or basins, which stood next to the altar. Geza Vermes' translation of *In the cistern of the esplanade* then makes much more sense.

The steps leading up to the altar are illustrated in Figure 6 – the Egyptian tomb inscription showing the assumed figure of Joseph.

Column 2 continues, according to Garcia Martinez: *In the cellar which is in Matia's courtyard*. Two Hebrew letters in the name 'Matia' overlap and appear to have been translated as a *tav* – the Hebrew letter for 't'. Separated, the letters would translate as *raysh* and *vahv*, the Hebrew letters for 'r' and 'v' respectively. This then gives a rather different translation for the name of the courtyard – 'Marvyre'. There is one name that is remarkably close to this sound: 'Meryre' or 'Meryra' – who was the High Priest of Aten. His name has been identified from tomb inscriptions in the group of Northern Tombs at Amarna, described previously. If this translation is correct, there was a *cistern in the cellar* or *lower part of his house* in Akhetaten, and hidden in it were 70 Talents of silver.

Meryra's house in Akhetaten was located near to the Treasury. It stood at the corner of a large walled-in courtyard. Deeper excavation of the house, to locate its cellar, could pay dividends to the tune of 70 Talents (KK) of valuables. Attached to the estate, beside the stables, was an Eastern Garden with a small park of trees, and servicing these trees were two large walled-in water tanks with steps leading down their steeply sloping sides. The tank in the middle of this small grove of trees could also have concealed the 70 Talents (KK) of silver, submerged at the bottom of it.

It would also be worthwhile looking more closely at the tank which stood some 7.65m in front of the Eastern Gate of Meryra's house, for vessels and 10 Talents (KK) of valuables.

John Allegro, however, translates this section in Column 2 rather differently, as:

> In the underground passage which is in the Court a wooden barrel(?) and inside it a bath measure of untithed goods and seventy talents of silver.

I consider that there are two plausible possibilities for this particular hoard of treasure, as, if John Allegro's translations are correct (which I do tend to go along with), then this and the next series of descriptions all relate to treasure still hidden within the Great Temple at Akhetaten. John Allegro's translation of *untithed goods* also implies a location within a Temple environment. The 70 Talents of silver, in John Allegro's version, were therefore hidden in an underground passage of the Temple Court.

The front and back halves of the Great Temple, shown in a modified cross-sectional drawing on the west wall of the Tomb of Panehesy, clearly show activity in subterranean passages, below the line of the Temple. However, these underground passages only appear to emerge in the upper, back-half part of the Temple, in the Court of the Inner Sanctuary, close to where the King sits by the altar.[22] Here, no doubt, was a need for water and other offerings to be 'bucketed up' to the Sanctuary which, in itself, was difficult to reach and heavily secured.

The next three locations from Column 2 are of 10 Talents of metal in a cistern 19 cubits (9.7m) *in front of the Eastern Gate* to the Temple (Garcia Martinez says 15 cubits or 7.65m); 600 pitchers of silver in the cistern under the Eastern wall of the Temple near what was the Great Threshold; and 22 Talents of treasure buried in a hole 2m deep, in the Northern corner of the pool in the Eastern part of the Temple. Archaeological work has shown that the Great Temple may only have had one gate, and that was an Eastern one. I take this as further confirmation that we are at the right Temple. The Copper Scroll descriptions for the above three locations are therefore fairly unambiguous, although there were two Eastern Gates – one outer and one inner. The inner Eastern Gate opened onto the Greater Sanctuary, where there were two lavers immediately in front of the Gate, which would have needed a water supply. It would seem prudent to re-excavate the area between 7.65m and 9.7m going inwards from both gates.

Column 3

Still in the Great Temple at Amarna, Column 3 pinpoints 609 gold and silver vessels, comprising sacrificial bowls, sprinkling basins and libation containers 9 cubits (4.6m) under the Southern corner of the courtyard, and 40 Talents of silver at a depth of 16 cubits (8.16m) under the Eastern corner of the courtyard. Unfortunately the Copper Scroll is too damaged at this point to tell which Court of the Temple is being referred to. It would therefore be sensible to excavate to the recommended depths at the Southern and Eastern corners of all eight courts and forecourts within the Temple!

Continuing in Column 3 there is a very interesting phrase: *In the tunnel which is in Milcham, to the North: tithe vessels and* my garments.

John Allegro translates Milcham as *some funerary structure*. *My garments*, which are elsewhere also called vestments, seems to strongly indicate that the writer of the original Copper Scroll was a priest, and probably the High Priest. This deduction ties in with the description of tithes and the Temple-related locations we have isolated. It could also help unravel the last six Greek letters in the text which I have not yet deciphered:

$$\Delta\ I\ \#\ T\ P\ \#\ \Sigma\ K$$

The Puzzle of the Remaining Greek Letters
Σ K are the last of the Greek letters to appear in the first four columns

which relate to Egypt. Perhaps these two letters are also the missing ones from the very end of the document, which I would expect to have been signed off on behalf of the High Priest. Σ K would then have been the most appropriate Greek abbreviation for the Qumran copyist to have used for the traditional name of the High Priest of the Jewish Temple…Zadok. *Zedek*, from which the word Zadok was derived, also meant priest in ancient Egyptian.*

What we also have is a title closely associated with the Qumran-Essenes. The connection of 'Zadok' to the Qumran community was made well before the discovery of the Dead Sea Scrolls, in Genizah fragments** found in Cairo in 1896, confirming the affinity between the two sources.[23] These Genizah fragments have variously been referred to as 'The Zadokite Fragments'[24] or 'Cairo-Damascus' texts, and it has been generally accepted that the Qumran-Essenes were a 'Zadokite Priestly Sect'[25]. In their own writings the Community refer to themselves as the 'Sons of Zadok'[26] and some interpreters have equated their leader – 'The Teacher of Righteousness' – to 'The Zadokite High Priest'[27] with a sequential role for the 'Sons of Zadok' as guardians of the Ark and the Commandments, going back at least to the time of Aaron. Column 7 begins *Priest dig for nine cubits…*

The four Greek letters which still remain, and which may not be complete, are somewhat puzzling.

Δ I # T P

To try and solve the problem I again approached it from the end – using the clues I already had to work backwards toward the answer. On the basis that the original document from which the Copper Scroll was copied was written by the High Priest of Akhenaten, and from those texts I had deduced that some of the locations described were in the Great Temple of Akhetaten, I felt that the four remaining undeciphered letters could well be a more general reference to the location of the Great Temple.

Going back to the original text, only the Δ T P are clear and unambiguous. The second letter, which has been taken to be the Greek capital letter 'Iota', is nothing more than a tiny 'floating' vertical line. It could quite easily have been part of a capital Greek 'Lambda'. The four

---

* The Greek letter sigma Σ has an 'sz' sound.
** A cache of documents, see Chapter 16 for further details.

letters would then come out as pronouncing the word: DELTRE.

If, however, the Qumran-Essene scribes wished to use a Greek word for 'Temple' there are few more appropriate than the most famous Greek temple that would have been within their purview – DELPHI. For the ancient Greeks, this was the centre of the world, and was once the site of an oracle of the goddess Gaea, subsequently replaced by that of Apollo and Dionysus.

If the fourth letter had been a Greek 'Phi' this explanation would have been a lot more convincing. So possibly the four letters do simply refer to the DELTA area in which Akhetaten was located.

Going back to Column 3, the location for *tithe vessels and my vestments* is at the entrance to a funerary structure, beneath its western corner. The scroll goes on to describe a tomb to the north-east of the structure where there are 13 Talents of valuables buried 1.5m below the corpse.

We appear to be back at the Northern Tombs. The 13 Talents are described by John Allegro as being *In the tomb which is in the funerary structure, in the shaft, in the north.* If the original scribe is the High Priest Meryra, talking about his vestments, we must be at his tomb and looking for a shaft. John Allegro's translation seems to be correct, as directly beyond Meryra's tomb, some 61m to the north, there is indeed a deep burial shaft on the summit of the ridge. Although this shaft has been plundered, it could pay dividends to dig further down this shaft, well below where a corpse would have lain.

The *vessels and vestments* are therefore located at the western corner of the entrance to Meryra's tomb.

Column 4

Unfortunately a number of words are missing in the first part of Column 4, and we can only interpolate the textual description of where *14 Talents* are hidden. We are directed to:

> The large (great) cistern in the…in the pillar
> of the North…

We seem to be back in town now, or near it, as the next passage refers to 55 Talents of silver in a man-made channel. We can only speculate that the Great Temple and the Great Palace needed a Great Cistern to supply them both with water. If this is the case, then there are 14 Talents in the hole of a pillar near the Great Cistern of the Palace or

Temple at Amarna. The 55 Talents of silver are 20.9m up the channel from the Great Cistern.

Further out from town there are *two jugs filled with silver, between two buildings* [possibly oil presses] *in the valley of Aton*. They are buried mid-way between the two oil presses at a depth of 1.53m.

Still near presses, but this time ones used for wine, and in the *Clay tunnel* [or pit] *underneath it there are 200 Talents of silver*. The location of these 'presses' is discussed more fully in Column 10.

Penultimately, in the *eastern tunnel to the North of the Store House of the Seventh Year produce: 70 Talents of silver*. Perhaps this is the tunnel that ran east to west under the front section of the Great Temple, or might even have connected the storehouses with the Temple.

For the final paragraph of Column 4 we appear to be in a different valley:

> In the dam sluice [burial mound?] of the Valley of Secacah, 1 cubit down there are 12 Talents of silver

Column 5

Column 5 also talks about Secacah, and it is tempting to associate this translation with the Old Testament reference where the land of Canaan is being allotted to the tribes of Israel. Judah are to take control of land:

> In the wilderness, Beth-arabah, Middin, and *Secacah*, and Nibshan,
> and the city of Salt, and En-gedi; six cities with their villages.
> [Joshua 15:61–62, my italics]

There is archaeological evidence that Khirbet Qumran was occupied in the Israelite period as early as the 9th century BCE,[28] and that Secacah might have been the ancient name for Qumran. (The site was apparently deserted between 600 BCE and the time of the arrival of the Qumran-Essenes, *c.*200 BCE.) Unfortunately the exact whereabouts of ancient Secacah is unknown and in his search for the city John Allegro, like many others, was unable to locate it.

However, even though there is also an adjacent translated reference to *Solomon's trench*, I am not convinced we have yet left Egypt. John Allegro, in fact, annotates his translation of *Solomon's reservoir (or trench)*, which occurs in conjunction with the word 'Secacah', as a technical description of the shape and function of this type of reservoir. If we are still in Egypt, 'Secacah' could easily be to the north of Akhetaten, at 'Sekkara', or Saqqara.

Saqqara was the main cemetery for Memphis, dating back to 3000 BCE, and contains burial sites from the 1st to the 6th Dynasties, and enormous shaft-tombs from the 26th Dynasty. It is dominated by the huge step pyramid of King Djoser of the 3rd Dynasty, dating to 2700 BCE. Much of the area is still unexcavated. Work that has been done, digging down through the layers of Roman and quarry debris, shows the remains of 18th Dynasty chapels and burial chambers, indicating that burials were taking place here at the time of Akhenaten.

Reference in the Copper Scroll to *burial mound* (as opposed to tomb), is perhaps significant. The earliest part of the cemetery is to the north, and is densely packed with mudbrick Mastaba or burial mounds. Plate 13 shows the burial district at Saqqara.

Column 6

Column 6 brings us back to the Temple, *In the inner chamber of the platform of the Double Gate, facing East...* This is fairly unambiguous. There was only one Double Gate facing east in the Great Temple of Akhetaten, and the inner massive doors consisted of two solid, corniced towers with jambs projecting from the inner face. To quote N. de G. Davies:

> The Passage (to the Outer Court) was barred by two double-leaved gates. The inner one being high and unwieldy, a similar but smaller gate was set within its jambs, contracting the passage.[29]

The location for our treasures is therefore: 'In the Northern entrance (tower), buried three cubits (1.5m), is a pitcher containing one scroll, and beneath that 42 Talents (KK).'

Paraphrasing the next piece of text, we have *Buried nine cubits (4.6m) under the inner chamber of the watch tower that faces East, there were 21 Talents (KK).* Security of the Great Temple was obviously of prime importance, and as well as double protective walls and gates, armed guards would have been on constant duty. The 'watchtower' is depicted in various inscriptions of the Great Temple as a Pylon-like structure, 'formed by a portico of columns, eight in line and two deep, broken by the entrance (to the East), and with towers and masts reaching high above it in the centre'.[30]

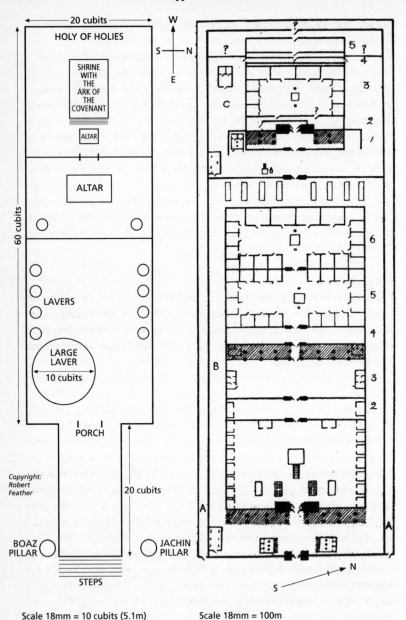

Scale 18mm = 10 cubits (5.1m)   Scale 18mm = 100m

Figure 18: Schematic of Solomon's Temple and the Great Temple at Akhetaten.

You will recall that after the 'Crock of Gold' find pinpointed in Column 1 *(see p.183)*, I mentioned there was another convincing 'gold link' between the Qumran-Essenes and Akhetaten. The next part of Column 6 takes us to this link: *In the Tomb (?) of the Queen, in the western side*, in John Allegro's version. This phraseology must be assumed to refer to the burial place of either Queen Tiyi, or Queen Nefertiti, respectively Akhenaten's mother or his wife.[31]

Garcia Martinez takes the key word to be her *'residence'* rather than *'tomb'*, and John Allegro is not too happy with his own translation of *'tomb'* as he equates the word here with 'dwelling'. However there is no evidence that Nefertiti (or Tiyi) had her own Palace, other than the one she shared with Akhenaten in Central Akhetaten – unless the Northern Palace was her preferred place of residence, some 3.2km to the north.

A deeper excavation, down to 6.1m (12 cubits) in the western section of Nefertiti's Tomb, located in the Royal Wadi, might reveal the 27 Talents (KK) buried there.

Royal tombs would, of course, be the most vulnerable to tomb robbers and I fear that is exactly what has happened to the 27 KK. I consider that this reference in Column 6 is once again to items that have already been found; the items now reside in Edinburgh, Scotland and in Liverpool, England!

In 1882 local grave-robbers found a number of articles of gold jewellery near or at the tomb of Nefertiti. Villagers of Hagg Qandil, near El-Amarna, later sold them to the Reverend W.J. Loftie, a collector of Egyptian relics. He, in turn, sold the trove to W. Talbot Ready in London. Loftie kept back two rings for himself, which later came into the possession of the author Sir H. Rider Haggard, and eventually the City of Liverpool Museum where they now reside. The London dealer sold the balance of jewellery to the Royal Museum of Scotland, Edinburgh, where they might have lain unrecognized to this day were it not for the astuteness of Professor A.M. Blackman. Re-examining the find in 1917, he concluded that some of it was from the 18th Dynasty, particularly a heavy gold signet ring incised with the cartouche of Nefertiti, a ring with a frog-shaped bezel inscribed 'Mut Mistress of Heaven', and two ear studs embossed in the shape of a flower bloom. The jewellery from Hagg Qandil is shown in Plates 14 and 15.

Considering this information, my guess was that if the 18th-Dynasty items were separated from the non-18th-Dynasty items in the

Edinburgh collection, and the two rings that our reverend gentleman kept back were added back in, the total weight would come to either 183.6g or 550.8g – these weights being specified in the Copper Scroll according to the three main translators, when using my Egyptian value of 20.4g for the term KK. John Allegro reads the reference to the weight of the treasure in Column 6 of the scroll as 9 KK, whilst Garcia Martinez and Geza Vermes (whom I go along with on this occasion for technical reasons), translate it as 27 KK.

When we add up the weights of all the 18th-Dynasty gold items and the gold/precious bead necklaces that came from the original Hagg Qandil find, the total weights come remarkably close to 560g – almost exactly the weight specified in the Copper Scroll.[32]

Column 7

Finally in Column 6 and at the beginning of Column 7 we are led by John Allegro to: *the dam-sluice(?) which is in the Bridge of the High Priest...*

Meryra's house has already been mentioned. It was probably next to the Treasury, and as High Priest he commanded a view overlooking the Nile and would have had a private walkway access to the Great Temple. His extensive eastern gardens were watered by a large storage tank, served by water from the River. An indecipherable number of Talents (KK) are buried perhaps 4.6m down, by the sluice gate feeding the two large walled-in tanks.

The next injunction, at the beginning of Column 7, is: *Priest, dig for nine Cubits: 22 Talents in the channel of Qi...* Much of the Scroll is missing here and any interpretation is guesswork. If the injunction applies to the previous location, then there may be valuables anywhere along the length of the channels feeding Meryra's garden tanks.

The Northern reservoir or cistern for this garden to the East of Meryra's residence has 400 Talents (KK) somewhere within 10.2m of its perimeter.

Apparently still in the garden of Meryra, there was an *inner chamber which is adjacent to the cool room of the Summer House, buried at six cubits: six pitchers of silver.* One of the buildings in this garden area is described in the *Rock Tombs of El Amarna – Part I* as being 'of striking security'. It was built to be impregnable – a very unusual structure to find in a garden. From its description getting inside this building must have been like navigating the Maze at Hampton Court Palace.

The only access is by the triple entrance in front, and he who passed it was immediately confronted by another and similar one. This also passed, the visitor was in an open square with thirteen almost identical doors to choose from, and only the three (two?) least promising of these enabled him to gain the innermost rooms, twenty-one in number. Moreover, each one of these only led into one of three blind corridors, flanked on one side with rooms...[33]

The innermost chamber of this building must have had a large amount of silver buried 3m under its floor.

The next instruction is to look *In the empty space under the Eastern corner of the spreading platform, buried at seven Cubits: 22 Talents.*

There were two large walled-in watering tanks feeding the garden, and each had a small enclosure opposite its steps which suggest some additional purpose. These enclosures appear to have provided a table or platform, used preparatory to sliding something into the water. There is only one eastern table, which must be the one being referred to in the scroll. Buried 3.6m under it there could be 22 KK.

Assuming the water tanks were fed in series there was an outlet pipe, or conduit, from an overflow tank, and 1.5m back from this outlet were buried 80 KK of gold or, according to Garcia Martinez, 60 KK of silver and two KK of gold.

Column 8

Not far from the Great Temple and the Royal Palace, perhaps even interconnecting with the Palace, was to be found the Treasury. On a private connecting road to the Palace running east from the Treasury there must have been a channel or drain pipe going into the building just by its entrance. Here, buried by this 'drain pipe', were tithe jars and scrolls and possibly silver.

Further afield, we are in an *Outer valley* looking for a *Circle on the Stone*, or circular shaped stone. Deliberately shaped ancient circular stones are not that common a sight in Egypt. The one described must have been immediately recognizable as being unique.

The most notable of these that comes to mind is a huge, monolithic, alabaster circular slab whose remains can be found at Abu Gurab on the West Bank of the Nile, between Giza and Saqqara (*see Plate 13 [bottom]*). In the centre of the ruins sits a massive circular disc surrounded by four *hetep* (offering) tables. The slab served as an altar at the Sun Temple of the 5th-Dynasty King Nyusserra, who lived from 2445 to 2412 BCE:[34] 17 cubits (8.7m) under the slab there could be 17 KK of silver and gold.

ON INTO ISRAEL?

John Allegro now conveys us to Israel and the Kidron gorge, but Garcia Martinez reckons we are still: *In the burial mound which is at the entrance to the narrow pass of the potter.* John Allegro's clues prove not very useful. Taking the second translation, *burial mound* generally implies older or more modest tombs. If we assume we are still looking at the burial areas of Akhetaten, the smaller Northern Tombs become possible candidates for investigation. Beside the series of tombs that run along the hillside to the north of the City, there are a few of unspecified date within the hills.

By a gap in the hillside and a central ravine, there is a track which leads up into the hills towards a tomb N. de G. Davies classifies as No.6.[35] To the right of this path is a burial place and there are four more ancient burial sites scattered along this part of the hillside. In front of these tombs there are traces of a small community settlement. There is evidence that within this community, living by a narrow pathway that led up into the hillside, there was an active pottery utilizing local clay materials. This site has also been identified as being in use as a pottery in late Roman times by Professor W. Petrie.[36] The burial mound nearest to the street of the *potters' pass* is the the most likely place to *dig for three cubits; four talents.*

The subsequent descriptions of Column 8 are particularly intractable and vague. We are in the *Shave* – a plain or cultivated area which perhaps lies to the *South-West* of the Northern hills. In an underground *cellar or passage* which faces north there are *67 Talents.* Nearby in the irrigated part of this cultivated area there is a *landmark*, and there are *70 Talents buried at 11 cubits.*

The first direction could be referring to a set of isolated altars that lie south-west of the Northern hills of Akhetaten in the open plain. A dry watercourse runs out from the hills in this direction, indicating that irrigation water was available. Excavation of the altar and chapel buildings shows that they were used in the time of Akhenaten and fragments of gold leaf have been found near the Northern Altar.[37] Some 600m from the Northern hills, near to the path of the watercourse, there is a brick platform which might well be the *landmark* of the second direction. Buried 5.6m under, or by an irrigation channel near this platform, are 70 KK of precious metal.

Column 9

Column 9 is again particularly obtuse. John Allegro guides us back to the First Temple at Jerusalem. Here he locates various likely places for treasures. Whilst I have already indicated that I believe some of the treasures of the Copper Scroll originated from the First Temple, the possibility that some may also have come from the Second Temple cannot be completely ruled out. Unfortunately both sites, which must have been fairly adjacent, are either inaccessible for excavation for religious reasons, or have so far proved fruitless.

However, assuming we are back at the Great Temple of Akhetaten, Garcia Martinez gives some additional clues by imputing a *dovecote* as being mentioned at the beginning of the paragraph. The first Hebrew word reads *bsovak*, and almost certainly means dovecote. We know that doves formed part of the Temple ceremonies so it is reasonable to assume that they were kept in the vicinity. However, the usual place for a dovecote would be in the upper part of a building near to the altar

Figure 19: Plan of the Second Temple at Jerusalem, dating from 515 BCE. It was fully restored by Herod the Great in 20 BCE.

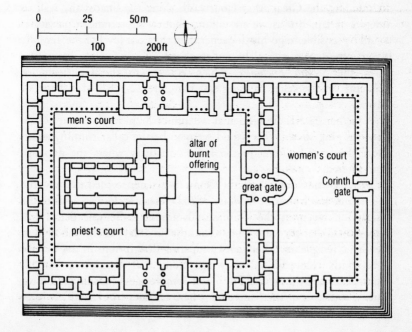

courtyard. The instruction to dig for 1m *under seven slabs* would seem, therefore, rather incongruous.

I believe the solution lies in the representational form of many ancient Egyptian drawings, where the artist combines external images into his perspective.

The drawings on the east wall of Huya's tomb at El-Amarna show what appear to be pastoral activities at the base of the Temple, but the only scene that contains a defined enclosure has doves flying inside and around it. In the lower sections of the drawing all the figures are stooping, indicating that they are working in underground cellar levels of the Temple. The positioning of the framed dovecote drawing implies a device of the artist who wanted to represent it as being both under and outside the Temple. A possible conclusion is that the main storage place for the doves was in an underground passage of the Temple, but some were kept at the top of the Court of the Great Altar. In fact a straight line connects the drawing of the doves at the bottom of the Temple to the symbol of a dove at the top of the building.[38]

The most likely place, therefore, to dig for *four bars* of precious metal would be approximately 6.6m in from each corner of the wall surrounding the Great Altar Courtyard, along the line of the wall to a depth of 1m. But as we are talking about a subterranean passage it would be sensible to go much deeper than the floor level of the Temple. If you come across seven slabs you are there!

In the *Second Enclosure*, which equates to the Courtyard of Rejoicing, in the cellar running east there are 22.5 KK at a depth of 4.1m.

A further 22 KK are hidden at a depth of 8.2m in *the passage of the Holes* running south. This would seem to be the cellar running south under the laver building in the Inner Sanctuary where the drainage shaft entered.

I have already noted how the Qumran-Essenes seemed to know the orientation and layout of the City of Akhetaten. A close analysis of the description given in the Qumran Community's Temple Scroll will demonstrate that they also knew about the inner layout and function of the Great Temple at Akhetaten. Comparing descriptions in the Temple Scroll with reconstructed drawings from wall inscriptions at El-Amarna, it can be seen that The Great Temple had a 'washing building' to the south-east of the Sanctuary, where residues from sacrifices were dealt with by channelling them down a shaft into deep holes in the ground away from the Temple.[39] Compare this to sections from Columns 31 and 32 of The Temple Scroll:

> You shall make a square building for the laver, to the south-east, all its sides will be twenty-one cubits, at 50 cubits distance from the altar…

> You shall make a channel all round the laver within the building. The channel runs from [the building of the laver] to a shaft, goes down and disappears in the middle of the earth…

In the shaft or *funnel* itself were secreted silver offerings. 'Funnel' might also be translated as *bekova* or helmet, implying a location at the top of the drainage shaft. The outlet to this conduit must have led to a drainage basin and to the east of this, at a depth of some 3.6m, was buried 9 KK of metals.

More *consecrated offerings* were to be found *in the sepulchre that is in the North, at the mouth of the gorge of the Place of the Palms*. We now appear to be back at the foothills to the north of Akhetaten, looking for another burial monument. The narrow pass appears to be the same 'potter's pass' we encountered in Column 8. Reference to *a Place of the Palms, at the outlet of the valley*, indicates we are on lower ground, near water. This therefore may be in the area of the community that lived by this pass entrance, perhaps in the vicinity of the same burial mound indicated in Column 8.

Four options face us for the last clue in Column 9. The key words from Garcia Martinez are *dovecote* and *Nabata*, whilst John Allegro comes up with *gutter* and *Sennaah*. Both agree that the location is a fortress or stronghold.

Could it possibly be the Castle or Fort of Aten? This was located about 500m south of the Great Temple of Akhetaten. The second floor gutter or dovecote of this building is, of course, long gone and the chances of finding the 9 KK stored there negligible…but somewhere in close proximity?

Column 10

Column 10 presents its own problems. From the last six lines, through to the last few lines of Column 12, the instructions have almost certainly switched to locations in Canaan/Israel. There are pointed references to Absalom's tomb, the Siloam conduit of Jerusalem, Zadok's tomb, Jericho and Mount Gerizim.

Assuming, however, that the first lines of Column 10 still refer to Egypt, we are initially looking for a cistern or irrigation structure by a *great stream* and a *Ravine of the Deeps*.

The translation of the Hebrew '*nahal hagadol*' as *great stream* or *great river* has been studied in great detail by many researchers, including B. Pixner, J. Lefkovits, Jozef Milik, F. Cross, and Stephen Goranson.[40] To quote Lefkovits, 'it is a mystery to which river or wadi the "Great River" refers'. With our Egyptian perspective the 'Great River' can surely be none other than the River Nile – a term which was often used by the ancient Egyptians to describe it.

One can only imagine that the *Ravine of the Deeps* must have been what is now a very large (and for most of the year), dry watercourse that runs south from the Northern hills through a deep ravine mid-way between the line of Northern Tombs at Akhetaten, alongside the Nile. In ancient times this ravine was swept by occasional torrential rains collected on the limestone hillside. Somewhere along the line of this *dry watercourse* is hidden the remains of an ancient irrigation waterwheel; buried *at its foot* lies 12 KK of treasure.

Both Garcia Martinez and John Allegro agree that the key phrase in the next section of Column 10 is '*Beth Keren(m)*' – the *House of the Vineyard*. By its water reservoir are hidden 62 KK of silver. The lower slopes of the Northern Hills of Amarna have, through the ages, sustained continuous weathering and denudation of topsoil. It is only in the well-watered, cultivated areas nearer to the Nile and to the large watercourse, which must at one time have provided good water supplies so that substantial cultivation could be sustained.

Here the 'North City' suburb of Akhetaten nestled between the curve of the River and the beginnings of the meandering slopes of the Northern Hills. On the gentler slopes at the foot of the Northern Hills, olive trees could have been sustained and vines cultivated on the facing plain. Perhaps the brick platform, located along the line of the watercourse in this vineyard region, was the structure which supported the heavy stone slab measuring *two cubits* across needed to press the precious oils from the olives. In one of the large storage vats of this agricultural area 300 KK of gold and some 20 libation vessels were secreted.

ON INTO CANAAN?

The Copper Scroll text now appears to move irrevocably into Canaan, with a reference to 'Absalom's memorial'. One would therefore expect some (if only a cryptic) marker to that effect. Untidy as our scribe (or scribes) was, he never placed a letter completely out of alignment – except at this item where a Hebrew 'kaff' appears at the side of the Column – the same sound that starts the Hebrew word for Canaan. This is presumably the scribe's 'marker' which indicates that we have moved to Canaan. The treasures we are looking for are therefore, either treasures that have been dug up and brought from Egypt or, more likely, treasures hidden at the time of the destruction of the First Temple in 586 BCE.

There are three possible candidates for Absalom's Monument. One is a structure built in the 1st century BCE, in the Valley of Kidron, for King Alexander Jannaeus – a descendant of the House of Absalom. The second is the tomb of Absalom, the third son of King David, and the last is the resting place of a patriot rebel leader named Absalom, who fought the Romans at the beginning of the Jewish uprising. Both of our last two candidates died in battle and there are no known monuments to them or their deaths.

The first location is the most northerly of the Hellenistic tombs to the east of the Kidron Valley, which is associated with a marble column that Josephus mentions as being 'two stades' distant from Jerusalem. We are told by the Copper Scroll to dig *on the west side for 12 Cubits (6.2m)*. There is indeed an opening on the western side of the Monument. The opening leads to an underground cistern which is almost exactly 6.2m deep, giving credence to this as the location mentioned in the Scroll for 80 KK of treasure. No trace of the treasure has so far been found at this site.

Without the excess 'Kaff', the next line then begins '*bivot*' or *In the ducts* of the water system at Siloam. The word Siloam comes from the Hebrew 'Shiloah' or 'Pool'. Around 700 BCE the forward-thinking King Hezekiah, of Judah, had a tunnel cut through under Jerusalem to tap the waters of the Gihon Spring, in the event of a siege. At the centre of the duct there is an inscription in Hebrew commemorating the completion of the construction. It is one of the oldest known recordings of Hebrew writing (*see Chapter 14*) and can today be seen in the Istanbul Museum. Under the *water outlet* from the storage tank there were hidden 17 KK, and in the four corner inner buttresses of the pool, *tithe vessels and figured coins,* according to John Allegro.[41]

Column 11

The next item, in Column 11, identifies a location of tithes: *under the corner of the southern portico at the tomb of Zadok, under the pillar of the covered hall: vessels of offering of resin and offering of senna,* according to Geza Vermes. Zadok was the High Priest at the time of King Solomon and King David, *c.*1000 BCE. The whereabouts of his tomb is unknown. However, if the use of the name 'Zadok' is merely generic then there are two other likely possibilities.

As has been discussed previously, 'Zadok' is also the name used for the title of High Priest in Egypt. If, therefore, we are back in Egypt, at Akhetaten, the High Priest's tomb would be that of Meryra, located in the Northern Hills of El-Amarna. Meryra's tomb is altogether one of the most substantial and artistic tombs of all, except for those of the royals. Sure enough, the tomb has a southern entrance, and we are told by John Allegro to look *below the Portico's Southern corner, in the Tomb of Zadok, under the platform of the exedra [vestibule].* The portico or porch entrance to the tomb leads into a spacious vestibule, which had two large ornately inscribed columns (there were probably originally four). *Underneath the column of the exedra* we are told will be found *tithe vessels.* Not only does the exedra have columns, as described, but one of them is towards the southern corner of the room. The description fits so precisely that Meryra's Tomb becomes a prime candidate for re-excavation.

Our second locational possibility – that Zadok's Tomb is that of the High Priest at the time of Solomon and David – led John Allegro to home in on the double-columned arcade running along the eastern side of the Temple. However, the religious restrictions preventing tombs inside the city walls, pushed his search outside to the eastern side of the Kidron Valley, where precise orienteering becomes tenuous and he gave up the search.

The next proposition: *opposite Zadok's garden, under the large slab which covers the water outlet* also presents insurmountable difficulties in identifying the garden of the High Priest near Jerusalem. Nor does the added descriptive restraint, that the garden is cut into *the cliff facing west,* help much in the search.

However, lo and behold, when we return to Egypt we find that Meryra's tomb does have a walled garden outside its entrance, which is cut deep into the cliffs. A tomb with a frontal garden is in itself quite unique. Because of the orientation at this curve of the hillside the garden faces roughly west. As N. de G. Davies relates:

> The cutting back of the rock slope, in order to gain the elevation for
> the facade, has formed a level court more than twenty feet wide in

front of the tomb, and this was further marked off by leaving a low enclosing wall of rock on the outer side, with a broad gap in the centre for entrance. The court has thus the appearance of the walled-in garden before a modern double-fronted house.[42]

The precise location of the consecrated offerings, in relation to Zadok's garden, is not easily ascertained from the translation. Above the tomb a cutting of rock frontage was begun and abandoned, perhaps as it involved too ambitious a task...*in the concession at the tip of the rock* might be a reference to the upper limit of jutting-out rock in this area allocated for Meryra's tomb. Then again: *under the large slab which covers the water outlet* or *under the great sealing stone that is in its bottom*, appear to refer directly to the garden and the water drainage channel that must have nurtured it. Closer investigation of Meryra's tomb garden, which measures 30m x 10m (the same proportions as the Great Temple), would seem highly appropriate.

John Allegro's version of the next item, points to 40 KK *In the grave which is under the paving stones*. Whether this means under the paving stones of the garden, or under Meryra's actual grave, or in another grave which is under the garden, is unclear. All three possibilities warrant investigation.

The next passage appears to read: *In the grave of the sons of Ha'amata of Jericho(?)...there are vessels of myrtle(?) there, and of the tithe of pine(?) [resin]*.[43] The translation of 'Jericho' by Garcia Martinez is none too certain; the Hebrew looks more like 'orho' or a word related to 'luna'. John Allegro has it as:...*of the common people...*; Geza Vermes doesn't really know but plumps for *the Sons of... (?) the Yerahite*. My own interpretation is as follows.

The area of Akhetaten takes its modern name of El-Amarna from a nomadic Arab clan 'Beni Amran', who settled in an area straddling both sides of the Nile River. (Is it merely a strange coincidence that the Biblical name of Moses' father was Amram?!)

A traditional name for one of the Amran tribe's villages was Hawata.[44] Whether this traditional name is an echo from the dim and distant past of a village of 'Ha'awata', and one of the officials was named 'orho', is conjectorial. The location of Hawata is today marked by a boundary inscription, known as Stele J, in the hills to the south of El-Amarna, high on the north side of a ravine. Excavation of tombs in the area of modern day Hawata, especially near Stele J, might yield the *tithe vessels* we are seeking.

The Boundaries of Akhetaten

The name 'Akhetaten' meant 'Horizon of Aten', and the complete boundaries of the City were delineated by huge monolithic tablets, or stelae carved from cliff faces. This procedure was unique to Akhetaten and not found elsewhere in Egypt. The 14 boundary stelae encompassed what was, for Akhenaten, the holy place wherein his God's purposes could be enacted. Inside the boundary was holy ground, outside was not.

Akhenaten's affiliation to the area bounded by the stelae was reiterated on the stelae themselves and other monuments, where he makes it clear no other place on earth was as spiritually important. If he, or any of his family, were to die outside the holy enclosure, it was to Akhetaten that their bodies must be returned.

The 14 stelae, some as high as 26 feet, were cut into the cliff faces. The cliffs formed a natural boundary to the east and west of the district of Akhetaten and the stelae marked the 'Horizon of Aten' within its northern and southern limits. In all the area encompassed was about 14.4km x 25.5km. Inscriptions on the stelae generally relate to the worship of Aten:

> ...his is my testimony, forever, and this is my witness forever, this
> landmark...I have made Akhetaten for my father as a dwelling for...
> I have demarked.

Within this 'special' area religious activities could be performed which were not acceptable outside the area.

Whilst we are talking about stelae we might take a look at a Jewish 'chok' – a ritual which has no defined instruction in the Bible. (Another is the prohibition of wearing wool and linen together.) This particular tradition relates to the possibility of creating a local 'holy enclosure' within which acts normally forbidden on the Sabbath can safely be performed – like carrying a key or umbrella, or pushing a wheelchair. The boundaries of this 'eruv' or area, can be defined by natural geographical features, sometimes supplemented by man-made demarcations.

There is no coherent explanation as to why an 'eruv' can be created, or its precedent. In the light of my theories and knowledge of the layout of the City of Akhetaten, we have a possible explanation related to the stelae.

I believe this idea of boundaries marking a holy area, centred on the Great Temple, is the template for the modern Jewish idea of an 'eruv' centred on a synagogue. They exist in Toronto, Phoenix, Memphis, Los Angeles, Boston, Chicago, Providence, Miami, Washington DC, Johannesburg, Melbourne, Gibraltar, Antwerp, Strasbourg, and other cities around the world, and one has been sanctioned for north-west London.

MOUNT GERIZIM AND THE FINAL DESTINATIONS

We now enter the last lap of our journey, in the second half of Column 11. Here, as John Allegro points out, there is a strange upper case Greek letter 'gamma', a 'Γ', after the first word of the next item, which he concludes is an erroneous mark. However it might well be that it is not erroneous, and instead marks the beginning of the last tranche of descriptions of locations in the region of Mount Gerizim, which is clearly identified in the final passages of the Copper Scroll. We are in Israel, near modern day Nablus, which sits in a valley between Mount Gerizim and Mount Ebal some 56km north of Jerusalem.

It was here, when they first entered Canaan in *c*.1200 BCE, that the Children of Israel assembled for a blessing of all those who observed the laws that Moses had brought to them from God. What more appropriate place for the designated custodians of those laws to hide some of the treasures they brought out of Egypt? This was a place of enormous spiritual significance for the Hebrew people.

From the 4th to the 2nd centuries BCE, Mount Gerizim was the traditional place of worship of the Samaritans, who established a rival Temple to that in Jerusalem. An altar was originally erected on Mount Gerizim, near Shechem (today's Nablus), at the beginning of the Second Temple period (538–515 BCE), and the rival Temple was built by Sanballat, the Samaritan leader, in the 4th century BCE. The Samaritan sanctuary was destroyed by the Priest-King John Hyrcanus in the early part of the 2nd century, and tradition relates that treasure was hidden nearby. It is still a place of gathering for the few remaining Samaritans in the world today, who celebrate Passover on the Mountain with a midnight vigil and the sacrifice of a lamb.

Such are the similarities between the Samaritans and the Qumran-Essenes that one might postulate a sympathetic connection between the two sects. The Samaritans (or 'Shamerim' as they were originally known), also styled themselves 'keepers of the Law', rejected the conventional Temple customs and had many parallel beliefs to those of the

Qumran-Essenes. In the Dead Sea Scrolls that refer to the Book of Joshua,[45] the Qumran-Essenes relate the implementation of the law in Deuteronomy 27:5–8 which commanded the building of an altar of unhewn stones on Mount Ebal, and the inscription of a copy of the Torah of Moses upon it. A ceremony (Deuteronomy 27:11–13), is described where the people are arrayed on both sides of the valley of Shechem, one half facing Mount Gerizim and the other half facing Mount Ebal. The ceremony involves the reading of blessings and curses to the assembled tribes. The validation of a holy site, other than at Shilo or Jerusalem, appears to pre-date this Deuteronomic law that there should only be two holy places.

Mount Gerizim is cited in Column 12 as a place where a chest with 60 Talents of silver will be found. The clues are sparse: *underneath the staircase of the upper [pit] tunnel.*

The area on Mount Gerizim held sacred by the Samaritans was enclosed by a wall, and covered the entire summit of the mountain. Worshippers ascended to it from the City's western quarter by a broad staircase some 10m wide. The line of the Temple wall is well-defined and some 120m still remains. Excavations to date have revealed the nucleus of an ancient settlement dating back to the 4th century BCE, but little detail of the Temple. Somewhere on the huge area at the top of the mountain there are treasures – perhaps, near the top of the broad staircase, there is the beginning of a tunnel that ran under the Temple.

The four previous items of location, prefixed by the Greek Gamma, could also relate to the area around Mount Gerizim.

In the first instance we are looking for either the house of *Esdatain* or a house of *two pools.* Two of the buildings in the settlement at Mount Gerizim conform to the requirement of having *a cistern at the entrance to the smallest water basin,* and the *tithes of aloes and white pine* may, at one time, have been amongst the remnants of coins, pottery, basalt and metal vessels found here.[46]

Very close by at the West entrance of the sepulchre room, there is a platform for the stove above…900 talents of silver. Could this have been the Samaritan sacrificial oven found in a complex building in the northern quarter of the city? If it was, 900 KK of silver and a considerable amount of gold are nearby.

Column 12

A further 60 KK are to be found at the western entrance to a burial monument under a *black stone* or *blocking stone*. Close by *under the sill* of the tomb chamber or *at its side underneath the threshold of the burial chamber*, there are 42 KK.

Also in the final Column: *In the mouth of the Spring at Beth-Sham: silver vessels and gold vessels for the tithes; in total 600 talents.* John Allegro translates 'Beth-Sham' as 'the Temple' and we can take this phrase as meaning 'House of the Shom-erim' the original name for the Samaritans.

For a mountain reaching to a height of 895m there would inevitably be a water source near the top for the beginnings of a stream which descends into the valley. At the original source of this stream the treasures are to be found.

The penultimate location of the Copper Scroll is given by Garcia Martinez as: *In the large conduit of the burial-chamber up to Beth-Hakuk.* This latter word could easily be read from the text as 'Habukah' and, as such, makes much more sense. Habakkuk was a Prophet of the Old Testament, believed to have lived at the time of the Chaldean siege of Nineveh, around 612 BCE. He was of particular interest to the Qumran-Essenes.

The Dead Sea Scroll 'Habakkuk' document is a 'Pesher', or commentary-cum-interpretation of prophecies, sometimes explaining hidden meanings of the Prophet Habakkuk. The 'Pesher' has two themes: the threat of the 'Kittim' – foreigners who will come and threaten Judea; and the 'Wicked Priest' (of Jerusalem) who threatens the 'Righteous Priest'. There have been many attempts to identify these characters. One possibility is that they were, respectively, the Samaritan High Priest at the time of the destruction of the Temple at Gerizim by the 'Wicked Priest' King Hyrcarnus. Another possibility is that the 'Righteous Priest' was Sanballat, the Samaritan leader who built the Temple at Gerizim.

Unfortunately the whereabouts of the tombs of both these 'Righteous' contenders are unknown, as is the burial place of the Prophet Habakkuk. All that can be concluded is that somewhere in the region of Mount Gerizim, or the tomb of Habakkuk, there is a burial chamber that contains 72 KK and 20 Minas of treasure.

Just as Alice predicted, having commenced at the end of the Copper Scroll, we have finally finished just before the end.

What then are the chances of finding some of the Copper Scroll's hidden treasures which have not yet been found? After nearly 3,500 years, for much of the remaining treasure, not too good. The most fruitful places to search may well be those in Egypt, as the locations in Israel are less well-defined and, as has already been said, it is not permissible to excavate burial sites or many of the holy places that might yield further clues.

The excavations that need to be carried out to find the remaining treasures will have to be done by professional archaeologists. Recovery will not be a simple matter, given the current political situation in the Middle East, and I don't recommend rushing off with bucket and spade as part of a transitory tourist excursion! All that is still to be found will automatically become the property of the country from where it is excavated anyway. Some may already have been lost to grave robbers and thieves. Some will not be easy to dig up, as it is located within sites sacred to both Jews and Muslims, such as at the Temple Mount in Jerusalem. Finally, some may still be languishing unrecognized in private collections.

Nevertheless, I calculate that an enormous amount of treasure is still just waiting to be excavated. Apart from the monetary value, items such as ritual vestments, unguents and scrolls could add considerably to our knowledge of the society that produced them.

An indication of the content and weight of treasure still to be recovered is as follows:

Table 5: Indication of treasure that remains to be discovered

Type of treasure remaining to be discovered	Weight according to new interpretation
Gold	38.74kg
Gold vessels	1 lot
Silver vessels	3 lots
Precious metals	42.68kg
Tithe vessels	6 lots
Ritual vestments	2 lots
Jars/pots of silver	16.92kg
Consecrated offerings	3 lots
Unguents/oils	1 lot
Scrolls	3

It is difficult to estimate the material value of the precious metal and jewellery that remains to be discovered, but at today's prices, bearing in mind that much of the material is unspecified, a conservative estimate would put it at between £5,000,000 and £10,000,000. Actual values could multiply this figure ten-fold.

The region of Elephantine and around Lake Tana, in Ethiopia, are other likely venues for further researches!

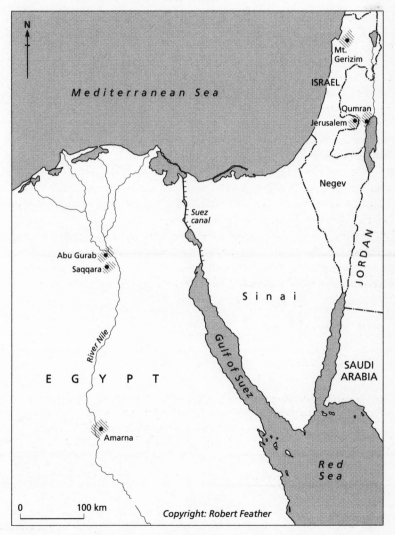

Figure 20: Sites where treasures of the Copper Scroll that have not already been found were hidden.

Some of the treasures of the Copper Scroll have now, I believe, been positively identified. The probable locations of many of the remaining treasures have also been detailed.

Exciting as these discoveries are, it is far from the end of the story. There are vastly more significant and profound implications to be discerned as a consequence of these discoveries. The Copper Scroll now underlines a connection from the religion of the Qumran-Essenes to the religion of Akhenaten and Egypt. This connection has been suggested by Sigmund Freud, in his book *Moses and Monotheism*, and hinted at by Jeffrey Katzenburg in his film *The Prince of Egypt*. The further, 'hard' evidence I have gathered together in the final chapters of this book confirms, I believe, that connnection.

CHAPTER SIXTEEN

THE
LEGACY OF
AKHENATEN

Inque brevi spatio mutantur saecla animantum
Et quasi cursores vitai lampada tradunt.

And in a short space the tribes of living things are changed, and
like runners hand on the torch of life.

[Lucretius, *De Rerum Natura*, II, line 77][1]

I believe that I have now established beyond the balance of reasonable
doubt that the early Patriarchs (Abraham, Isaac and Jacob), Joseph and
Moses were all heavily influenced by the religion and culture of early
Egypt – particularly that of the Amenhotep family and Pharaoh
Akhenaten.

The endorsement of the Copper Scroll's connection between a sect
at Qumran that guarded the scroll's secrets inherited over 1300 years
earlier, and Akhenaten, can leave little doubt that there was a common-
ality between the two communities. That connection extended to
religious beliefs which, in turn, affected the formative principles of the
three great monotheistic religions of the world.

The connections between Akhenaten and the Qumran-Essenes are
too numerous to be mere coincidence, and there are more to come!

When Akhenaten died, attempts were made by other Egyptians
to remove all traces of his inscriptions and of his teachings. The
monotheistic 'torch of light' that the followers of Akhenaten picked up
was eventually to become bifurcated – carried by the priestly heirs of
Akhenaten in Egypt, and by Moses and the Hebrews into the deserts
of Sinai.

Akhenaten's religious revolution left an indelible mark on the development of early Judaism, and the record of those early, formative years has been preserved for us in the Dead Sea Scrolls.

As descendent authors and guardians of the holy texts, it therefore would not be surprising to find characteristics of Akhenaten's beliefs and other Egyptian influences evident amongst the Essenes, even after so long a period of immersion in a foreign culture and a refined Judaism that had cleansed itself of as many foreign influences as possible. If my assumptions are correct, it should be possible to detect a greater Egyptian influence within the closed sect than was apparent in the common body of Judaism. And we do.

In fact the Qumran-Essenes exhibited many of the characteristic beliefs of the Atenist priests that came out of Egypt – modified by time, but still in a very recognizable form. Their strong sense of an inherited mission, mysterious customs and exclusivity can all be fully explained in terms of their sacred connection to the priests of Akhenaten.

As well as the influences carried over from the Akhenaten period, there are also 'overlaying commonalities' of more general Egyptian effects, garnered from across the spectrum of Egyptian paganism and social practice.

Three main subjects remain on the agenda. I have presented the weighty evidence linking Akhenaten and the Qumran-Essenes, mainly through the unravelling of the Copper Scroll, and I will now delve further into the body of the Dead Sea Scrolls to see what additional evidence can be found from them. I will then take a more general look at how many of these 'overlaying commonalities' from Egypt have entered the conscious and sub-conscious mind of the western world and its religions. Finally, there are two loose ends relating to the mysterious pseudo-Jewish communities of priestly-soldiers at Elephantine, in Southern Egypt, and to the Falasha Jews of Lake Tana in Ethiopia, that need tying up.

These two latter locations are, as I have already suggested, possible places where residual treasures of the Copper Scroll might still be found.

ADDITIONAL EVIDENCE FROM THE DEAD SEA SCROLLS

The contents and format of the Dead Sea Scrolls, commentaries by contemporary writers and the findings of archaeologists at the Qumran ruins, provide a vast number of threads from which to weave a tapestry depicting the lives and thinking of these hermit-like people. At the time of Jesus they numbered about 4,000 across Judaea, with some 200 resident and working in the area of Qumran at any one time.

They talked in terms of apocalyptic events and of a 'last days' eschatological philosophy. Their 'War Scroll' speaks of the final battle in which two Messiahs – one kingly, one priestly – will triumph. Their way of life was geared to preparing themselves for this great event. They were the 'righteous ones' whose mission was to preserve and protect the true faith.

Excavations at Qumran have shown that there was a settlement there between the 8th and 6th centuries BCE, shortly before the Babylonian exile. This was destroyed during the fall of the Southern Kingdom. Several centuries later, around 200 BCE, it was resettled by the Essene Community and remained occupied until a severe earthquake in 31 BCE badly damaged the buildings, causing the inhabitants to leave Qumran for a short period.[2]

No-one seems to know quite where they went in the interim period between 31 and 4 BCE when they returned. One suggestion is that the Qumran-Essenes journeyed to Damascus, because the city finds mention in their texts. But this seems very unlikely. Earlier on I proposed an association with Damascus during the previous Babylonian exile, which seems a much more plausible explanation for its mention.

The archaeological evidence finds them returned to Qumran at a peculiarly coincidental date. The Community that was to so markedly affect the teachings of Jesus returned to its home in the year 4 BCE, the year now accepted by most scholars as that of Jesus's birth. Those writers that attempt to make close links between the Qumran-Essenes and Jesus might even postulate that they went to visit Jesus at Bethlehem in the meantime, but there is no evidence to that effect. The Community site was eventually destroyed in 68 CE by the Romans.

COMMUNITY RULES AND LIFESTYLE

A passage from Josephus gives an insight into the daily lives of the Qumran-Essenes:

> Before the sun is up they utter no word on mundane matters, but offer
> to him certain prayers, which have been handed down from their
> forefathers, as though entreating him to rise. They are then dismissed
> by their superiors to the various crafts in which they are severally
> proficient and are strenuously employed until the fifth hour, when they

again assemble in one place and, after girding their loins with linen
cloths, bathe their bodies in cold water. After this purification, they
assemble in a private apartment which none of the uninitiated is
permitted to enter; pure now themselves, they repair to the refectory, as
to some sacred shrine. When they have taken their seats in silence, the
baker serves out the loaves to them in order, and the cook sets before
each one plate with a single course. Before meat, the priest says a grace;
thus at the beginning and the close they do homage to God as the
bountiful giver of life. Then laying aside their raiment, as holy
vestments, they again betake themselves to their labours until evening.
On their return they sup in like manner.

[*The Jewish War* II]

Some of the Essenes' main characterizing features were that they did
not recognize the Temple practice in Jerusalem, they held all goods in
common (a theme picked up in the New Testament, Acts 2:44) and disapproved of sacrifices. They stressed prayer, study, ennoblement of
the spirit, and ritual purity and cleanliness through the purification of
bathing. They maintained an hierarchical structure of discipline, had a
different calendar from the general Jewish population and therefore celebrated their festivals at different times from the rest of the population.[3]

Our knowledge of the behavioural requirements of the members of
the Community throws intriguing light on what lay behind their thinking and beliefs. Much of this knowledge comes from a Dead Sea Scroll
which deals with Community Rules. It has been identified as the final
part of the Damascus Document, and is corroborated by another version from the Egyptian Genizah Collection.[4] The piece deals with a dis-
ciplinary convocation of the Council of the Essenes which is addressed
by 'the Priest commanding the many'. His role can be discerned (from
analysis of both documents), as that of Head of the Community, the
final arbiter of the law, the knower of all the 'secrets', and the senior
priest. He is referred to variously as the 'Mebaqqer' or 'Hamerverkah' –
'The Merverkyah'. How long this title had existed is not certain, but in
sound it has a remarkable resemblance in the role to the name of the
High Priest of the Great Temple to Aten, at Akhetaten. His name
can be found inscribed on his tomb at Amarna and transliterates as
'Mervyre'. The Council are the 'sons of Levi', the priestly strain of Israel
from which the High Priest would be drawn.

Curious as to why documents found in Egypt should corroborate
scrolls found by the Dead Sea, the next step in my journey took me to

Cambridge, courtesy of two rather eccentric Scottish Presbyterian ladies – Mrs Agnes Lewis and Mrs Margaret Gibson.

The Genizah Fragments

It was customary in Victorian times (and earlier in the 18th century) for British gentry to make the 'Grand Tour' of famous foreign landmarks and historical sites. Our two inveterate ladies, however, were more than just casual tourists, and made themselves learned in the history of the Middle East. Their journeys took them off the beaten track, ferreting out the mysteries of the Biblical lands. One such mission led them to an obscure part of Fostat, Old Cairo, into the dingy dim interior of a thousand-year-old synagogue named 'Ben Ezra'. High in the wall of a back area of the building they discovered a 'Genizah' – a place of safe-keeping for documents. There they found a cache of papyrus, vellum and paper, unparalleled in importance and comparable in significance to that of the Dead Sea Scrolls. They carried some of the fragments back to England and, in May 1896, Agnes Lewis brought them to the attention of Dr Solomon Schechter, Reader in Talmudic Literature at Cambridge University (who later became President of the Jewish Theological Seminary of America).

Dr Schechter's excitement can be imagined. Realizing the possible ramifications of the find, he enlisted the moral and financial support of Dr Charles Taylor, Master of St John's College, Cambridge. Together they journeyed to the synagogue in Cairo and were given permission to bring all the remaining fragments back to England.[5]

Why was this discovery so significant, particularly in relation to the Damascus Scroll? The Collection has within it an enormous archive of religious and secular documents, much written between the 10th and 12th centuries CE; some dating back to 600 CE and others up to the 19th century. They illumine Jewish religious experience of these periods and refer back to Biblical times. There are hand-written letters and manuscripts by some of the most influential Hebrew scholars of the Middle Ages, including Moses Maimonides and Jehudah Halevi; Zadokite documents; ancient liturgy; poetry; music; and letters from Palestine, Babylonia and Spain.[6]

Some of the oldest papyrus documents are pages from the Old Testament Book of Kings and Psalms. They are written in Greek, and are copies of the 2nd-century Aquila version of the Bible.

Among many Hebrew texts is a 10th century CE copy of the 'Wisdom of Ben Sira', which dates back to the 2nd century BCE. It contains poetic syllogy or reasoning, and proverbs that advocate a life of moderation. The texts were translated into Greek by Ben Sira's grandson in 132 BCE and incorporated into the Apocrypha as Ecclesiasticus. The Hebrew text of this work was previously thought lost, and therefore it was not included in the Hebrew Bible. Authenticity of the Genizah copy was later confirmed by its similarity to finds amongst scrolls excavated from Masada, in Israel. Although basically the same, there are differences in the Genizah text when compared to the Greek from which our modern Apocryphal Ecclesiasticus is translated.

The fragments of Jewish prayers and commentaries prove, as the Director of the Genizah Research Unit at Cambridge, Dr Stefan Reif (now Professor of Medieval Hebrew Studies at Cambridge University), put it: 'that there had been at the least an intermittent active Jewish presence in Israel, since biblical times right through the early centuries up to the time of the Crusaders in the 13th century CE.'

What was most significant, for my line of enquiry, was a reference amongst the Genizah fragments to the mysterious Zadokite brotherhood of scribes that we now know as the Qumran-Essenes, some forty years before the discovery of the Dead Sea Scrolls.

The Genizah contained two copies of the so-called Damascus Document, similar to ones found amongst the Dead Sea Scrolls. How this document, which was obviously a sectarian text peculiar to the Qumran-Essenes, could turn up in a Cairo synagogue 2,000 years after it was thought to have been composed has proved, as one can imagine, somewhat of a conundrum. The conventional explanation is that a version was discovered in the caves of Qumran around 800 CE and somehow found its way to Egypt.

This idea is based on the contents of a Syriac letter sent by Timotheus I, Patriarch of Seleucia (726–819 CE), to Sergius Metropolitan of Elam (who died *c*.805 CE).[7] The letter refers to the finding, by an Arab, of Hebrew and other scrolls in a rock-dwelling near Jericho.[8] According to the letter's contents, Jews from Jerusalem came out to study the documents and found them to be ancient books of the Old Testament, together with over 200 Psalms. There is no known reference in Jewish literature to the find which, considering the apparent excitement amongst those who rushed out of Jerusalem when they heard about it, and its obvious importance, is rather surprising.

The supposition that somehow the Damascus Document of the Cairo Genizah was a later copy of the Dead Sea Scroll version of the Damascus Scroll, which also happened to be hidden in caves near the Dead Sea, and this latter document (or a copy of it), eventually found its way from this find in the 8th century to Cairo, seems rather fanciful. Especially as the Timotheus episode makes no mention of the Damascus Document, which would have been one of the more significant finds, and that the dates of the Genizah Damascus Documents (there are two differing versions of the original composition) are 10th and 12th centuries CE respectively.

From the content of the Dead Sea Scrolls versions and the Cairo Genizah versions (which collectively are generally referred to as the CD (Cairo–Damascus) scrolls), it is apparent that the original Damascus Document may have been written soon after the destruction of the First Temple, from its references to Damascus and King Nebuchadnezzar. But there are also 'exhortations' on how to obey God's laws which seem to date from much earlier times.

How the Damascus Documents found in the 8th century actually made their way to Cairo is a matter of conjecture; I am not convinced by the conventional explanation.

One possible scenario that gets over these difficulties goes like this: the Damascus and Psalms scrolls found in the hills near Jericho in the 8th century CE, were originally written by the Qumran-Essenes and were subsequently lost. We know that the Qumran-Essenes wrote copies of the Damascus document and knew more psalms than the canonical 150. The Damascus scrolls found in Cairo were copied from much earlier examples of the text written shortly after the destruction of the First Temple in Jerusalem, which found their way to Heliopolis (Cairo) through the interaction of residual Atenist priests at Heliopolis with the old strand of priestly guardians in Judah from whom the Qumran-Essenes were descended.

We know that Heliopolis was the first place where an Atenist temple was built and that it was likely to have remained a centre for secretive monotheistic worship.

THE MESSIANIC 'SOLDIERS OF LIGHT'

Buffeted from desert to Temple and Temple to desert by the sandstorms of time, the 'Priestly Essenes' had seen their sacred place of worship desecrated by Nebuchadnezzar in 586 BCE. After returning from exile in Babylon, they had preserved their beliefs and way of life and eventually found sanctuary in the forbidding reaches of the Dead Sea.

Now, near the turn of the Millennium, their successors had

witnessed the restoration of their sacred Temple by Herod – only to see others not of the Zaddokic line of high priests usurping the role, and a golden Roman eagle perched on the roof.

Therefore to the Essenes the Second Temple was a place of intense contradiction. The holy place, central to their inheritance, was occupied by alien forces and governed by the whims of Herod, a lackey of Rome. Its size and shape were not to their liking and, worse still, from around 31 BCE onwards two lambs were sacrificed every day by the Temple priests for the 'well-being' of the Roman Emperor and the Roman Empire – anathema to many Jewish groups and especially to the Qumran-Essenes. No wonder they took the earthquake of 31 BCE, that caused widespread destruction in the area of the Judaean Desert (and their own settlement), as a portent that they were right, and that their belief in an imminent apocalypse was justified.

It soon becomes apparent from reading the Dead Sea Scrolls that the Essenes of Qumran considered themselves an elite messianic group, who had retreated from the fray of the Temple and the priesthood, and who sought refuge in the wilderness in order to protect their piety. Isaiah aptly describes their role:

> The voice of him that crieth in the wilderness, Prepare ye the way of
> the Lord, make straight in the desert a highway for our God.
>
> [Isaiah 40:3]

The need 'to retreat' for some of the Essenes was part of their searching for a re-affirmation of the divine Covenant given to Moses on Mount Sinai – a searching for the purity and essence of Torah and Hebrew teachings. They looked on themselves as the ancestral custodians of the 'light of truth'.

The Qumran Dead Sea Scroll known as the 'Manual of Discipline' (The Community Rule), sets out the requirement for a 10-year period of study, after which, at the age of 20, students have to undergo a test of public examination to verify their understanding of the law and their own integrity.[9] A year of 'probation' followed, after which the student was again examined. If he passed this test he served a further year of probation before a proposal for full membership of the Brotherhood was put to the vote. If accepted, the student was made to swear an oath of loyalty. The minimum age to hold office in the Brotherhood was 25, and the 'fourth degree of holiness' (referred to by Josephus) could not be reached before the age of 30. (It is interesting to note the similarity in the use of the terms 'Brotherhood', 'degree', and 'master' to those used in the Masonic movement, where members refer to each other as brothers and utilize biblical titles.[10]) The Essenes' spiritual leader was known as the 'right teacher' – a title identified with Moses in his final blessing to the children of Israel (Deuteronomy 33). Successive 'right teachers' had the role of holding the community to the true interpretation of the Torah whilst they awaited the coming of a prophet like Moses and 'two Messiahs'.

This waiting was accompanied by an immersion in the holy scriptures and by the following of an ascetic way of life. Each year a cumulative total of 120 nights were to be spent in prayer and study. Personal possessions and income were to be given to the Community; in turn the Community looked after the individual's needs. Living and eating was communal, and garments were plain and purely functional. (There are many similarities in this 'unselfish' way of life to the modern 'Ashrams' of America, the 'Kibbutz' of modern Israel, and in Christian monasteries over the ages.)

There was a strong hierarchical structure within the community. At the top was the 'right teacher'. Priests, aided by Levites, dictated the doctrine of the group. All members could vote in an assembly on other, non-doctrinal matters, whilst general day-to-day administration was in the hands of a triumvirate of priests and 12 helpers. Everyone had a 'pecking order' in relation to their level of learning and holiness, as determined by their peers.

Throughout the scrolls describing the feelings and activities of the Essenes, there is a connective embodiment of repeated themes and motifs, which endow these works with a sense of collective purpose: 'Sons of Light' fighting 'Sons of Darkness', messianic portents, battles with evil, the fruits of righteousness.

The scrolls' fundamental themes are of persons who are:

- Righteous – Zaddikim
- Pious – Hassidim
- Holy – Kedushim
- Meek – Anavim
- Endowed with God's Spirit – Roucha Hakedushim
- Faithful – Emunim

The first three of these themes are recognizably strongly Jewish, the latter three carry Christian overtones.

It is the transitional/post-First Temple prophets that the Essenes looked to for their inspiration. They closely associated themselves with the 'Sons of Zadok' – the select priests of the Temple – using the term 'Zaddikim' as having an alternative meaning of 'the righteous ones' to describe themselves. They are the holy caucus who carry the true torch of light handed on to them through Moses.

There is continual references through the Scrolls to the part played by the Temple priests, and it is clear that the Essenes considered themselves the keepers of the Covenant – part of the direct line of priests that attended the Holy Shrines. This can be seen in the Scrolls dealing with the Testament of the priestly Levi, of Aaron and of Kohath. These are the 'Righteous seed' – Zaddikim – which the Essenes continually claim as their birthright.

> ...and God of gods for all eternity. And he will shine as a Light upon
> you and He will make known to you His great name and you will
> know Him, that He is the Eternal God and Lord of all creation, and
> sovereign over all things, governing them according to his will...Thus
> you will grant to me a good name among you, together with joy for
> Levi and happiness for Jacob, rejoicing for Isaac and blessing for
> Abraham, inasmuch as you guarded and walked in the inheritance. My
> sons, your fathers bequeathed to you Truth, Righteousness,
> Uprightness, Integrity, Purity, Holiness and the Priesthood.
>
> ['Testament of Kohath', Fragment 1, Column 1][11]

Even after some 1,500 years there is still recognizably an Egyptian style of phrasing, and the continual allusion to light reiterates the significance of the sun and light in Akhenaten's theology.

MYSTICISM AND KABBALAH

In some of the Dead Sea Scrolls there is a visionary mysticism that borders on 'Kabbalah' (*see Glossary*), whilst mysticism and allusions to magic are not excluded.

Practices of divination, magic, astrology, spells and the wearing of magic amulets were still not uncommon amongst the Jewish people at the time of Christ, but they were frowned upon by the Rabbinic teachers.*

---

* To this day some Jewish Orthodox women will wear an amulet during childbirth to ward off evil spirits (see Chapter 9).

On the surface, this makes it all the more surprising to find from scrolls 4Q318, 4Q560 and 4Q561 that the Essenes – a fervently devout, God-fearing group – may have followed, or at least documented these kinds of cultist beliefs.[12]

The fragmentary documents are difficult to understand in detail, but the document catalogued as 4Q560, is an amulet warning against evil spirits. It seems to be an incantation for a spirit to protect a body from male and female demons who might poison or invade it. The echoes of Egypt are not difficult to discern. The use of amulets in ancient Egypt was, as discussed earlier, very common for the living and for the dead. For example, in Chapter 156 of the 'Book of the Dead', or in Chapter 151 of the Papyrus of Ani, we find amulet incantations by 'two Heart-souls' called to bring spirits to protect the body and drive away devils that may wish to destroy it.

Belief in evil spirits and mysticism was a necessary part of the Qumran-Essenes' dualistic concept of the universe. There were for them two spirits created by God: good and evil. These forces vied to influence man in his behaviour. All that was good came from the dominion of light. All that was evil came from the dominion of darkness. (This idea has been echoed in the Persian 'Zoroastrian' idea of the supreme deity – Ahura Mazda – but in this philosophy it is he, rather than man, who must choose between good and evil.)

The Book of Hagu

Rabbinic teaching and the Torah both denounce study of mystic 'hidden secrets' as dangerous. The Qumran-Essenes' philosophy reject-ed magic, but positively required study of these mystic 'hidden secrets'. Many of these Kabbalistic-like mysticisms can be traced back to early Egyptian traditions and the idea that Pharaoh and the select priests were entrusted with such hidden secrets.

This hidden knowledge must have been handed down by word of mouth or by secret texts, but were there any secret texts kept even from the ordinary Qumran-Essene members?

The question brings us to the mystery of the Book of Hagu (or Hagi). The book is mentioned in the Damascus Scroll and in the Manual of Discipline (1QS) as being fundamental; it was mandatory to understand it for anyone who wished to act as a judge of the congrega-tion. So far, no-one has identified what the Book is or where it came from. Some scholars, such as Yigael Yadin,[13] consider it might be the Temple Scroll or another, as yet undiscovered, scroll. Either way it appears to be a Book of Divine Law dating back to the time of Moses and Joshua – known to the Qumran-Essenes, but not known to the general Jewish community of Canaan or Israel.

Most of the Dead Sea Scrolls were, as previously mentioned, written in Aramaic square script, paleo-Hebrew (much older lettering), or Greek. There are however some examples in Nabatean Note A,* and ten manuscripts written in 'Cryptic A', 'Cryptic B' and 'Cryptic C'. These have been partially deciphered, but reference is made in the Damascus document and other Dead Sea Scrolls to a mysterious 'Midrash Sefer Moshe' (MSM) text. This text is known to have been written in 'Cryptic A' and was personal to the 'Maskil', or leader, of the community – 'for his eyes only'. This document (catalogued as 4Q249) which, unfortunately, has not yet been found, could well be the key to the secret 'knowledge' of the community, and appears to be the basic source of rules and authority for the community.[14]

I do not have a firm view as to what form the Book of Hagu really took. It was undoubtedly of tremendous importance in the eyes of the Qumran-Essenes. The references to it demonstrate that this lineage of devout, priest-like people possessed exclusive religious works, which must have come from outside traditional Jewish knowledge and been in their keeping for many centuries. The vows that new entrants to the Order were required to take (attested to by Josephus), were lengthy and mainly about piety towards God, observing the community's rules and maintaining righteous thoughts and behaviour. However, the Qumran-Essenes undoubtedly had secrets to hide, because one of these vows was: 'to safeguard the secret books'.

THE QUMRAN-ESSENE CALENDAR

As I looked for other Egyptian antecedents amongst the Dead Sea Scrolls, one of the most startling I found relates to the calendar used by the Qumran-Essenes. As mentioned in Chapter 1, it is solar based, relying on the sun's movement, and gave them a year that contained 364 days. The 12 months each had 30 days and one of four extra days were added at the end of each three-month period. The basis for the Qumran-Essene solar calendar is spelled out in detail in their Book of Jubilees, the Book of Enoch and in the calendrical texts (4Q320–30).

---

* The Nabatean were Arab tribes who occupied Edom (part of today's Jordan) in the 6th century BCE, establishing their capital at Rekem (Petra).

The solar calendar was physically confirmed by Father Roland de Vaux in 1954, by the finding of a stone 'sundial' in the Qumran ruins.

The 'sundial' was almost certainly used by the Essenes to enable 'physical' measurement of days and intervals in a solar calendar.[15] Not only were explicit details of the solar calendar given in the Dead Sea Scrolls, it was a mandatory requirement that it be followed. Those who did not follow the original (solar) calendar are harshly castigated in the Damascus documents.

The intriguing thing is, the Essene calendar was quite different from the Rabbinic Jewish calendar, which was, and still is, based on lunar movements, giving a year of 354 days.*

For the ancient Egyptians their year was, like the Qumran-Essenes, solar based – made up of 12 months of 30 days with five intercalary days added. These additional days were related to festivals for the birthdays of Osiris, Horus, Seth, Isis and Nephthys.[16]

The question I asked myself was, why did the Qumran-Essenes only add four extra days rather than the conventional Egyptian calendar's five? I believe a likely answer is that when Akhenaten became Pharaoh, these five traditional gods were *persona non grata* and he needed other festivals to equate with the intercalary days. There were many other traditional Egyptian festivals to choose from, the most important being the New Year Festival, the Festival of Sokar, the Festival of the Raising of the Sky and the Festival of the Potter's Wheel. The choice, however, was severely limited as most of the major and minor festivals were built around pagan gods. The most likely outcome therefore, was that Akhenaten opted for the three traditional 'crop'-related festivals of the Nile's inundation, spring and harvest, supplemented by the Festival of the New Year.

This would explain why the Qumran-Essenes only added four intercalary days to their solar calendar – a procedure which was in tune with their stated affiliations to order and conformity with 'the natural laws', and in non-conformity 'with the festivals of nations'. The four festivals the Qumran-Essenes celebrated were Passover (Pesach), the Feast of Weeks (Shavuot, Pentecost), the Day of Atonement (Yom Kippur) and the Feast of Tabernacles (Sukkot) – all equivalent to those celebrated by the normative Jewish community, but all celebrated on different dates.[17]

The fifth Jewish festival, 'Purim', traditionally dating back to the

---

* This was modified around 400 CE by the addition of an extra seven lunar months in every 19 years to harmonize the cycle with the seasons – see the Glossary for more details on Calendars.

5th century BCE Persian period of Jewish history, was celebrated in the general community, but would have been superfluous to the calendrical needs of the Qumran-Essenes. This could explain why the Dead Sea Scrolls – which contain two almost complete versions of Isaiah and passages from every single book of the Old Testament, as well as apocryphal, pseudepigraphic and sectarian works – have nothing from the Book of Esther for which Purim is the related Festival.[18]

The life-cycle of any community is critically controlled by the calendar it follows. The ability of the Qumran community to maintain their own version of the Israelite calendar is indicative of their extreme independence from mainstream Judaism – theirs was the same solar-based calendar that Akhenaten and the early Egyptians used.

FESTIVALS AND JUBILEES

Another calendrical difference from mainstream Judaism, maintained by the Qumranites related to Festivals or 'Jubilees'. These significant years for priestly celebration are documented in a Dead Sea Scroll known as 'Heavenly Concordances' (4Q319A).

Taking their guidance from the creation story of Genesis 1:4, the Community looked for signs in the sky:

> And God said, 'Let there be lights in the firmament of the heaven to
> divide the day from the night: and let them be for signs, and for
> seasons, and for days, and years.'

Because their calendar was solar, rather than lunar based, years in which the sun and moon were aligned at the beginning of a year were signs of momentous portent worthy of celebration. For the Qumran-Essenes that happened in years one and four of six-year rotations. There is no mention in the scrolls of a first Jubilee, but a second Jubilee is listed as commemorable after a period of 48 years. The first Jubilee period must therefore have been a lesser number of years, but nevertheless a significantly long period to justify celebration, and to be divisible by six. It could have been after 30, 36 or, perhaps, 42 years. Lesser Jubilees would then fall in the fourth year of a six-year period, and at the end of the cycle or at the beginning of the seventh year.

This system of Jubilees was quite unique to the Qumran-Essenes and not part of normal Jewish practice. The 'Book of Jubilees', which describes these requirements, is considered pseudepigraphic, i.e., non-canonical anonymous writings, thought to be from the period 200 BCE to 200 CE. But the system was not unknown in Egypt a thousand years earlier.

By now this phrase is becoming quite repetitive, but the evidence is, again, very convincing.

The 'Sed' or 'Jubilee' festivals celebrated in ancient Egypt were an ongoing tradition that can be traced back well before the period of Akhenaten, and were considered of fundamental importance for the 18th-Dynasty pharaohs.

The main Jubilee was celebrated in year 30 of a pharaoh's reign; a lesser, secondary Jubilee was celebrated in the 34th year, and a tertiary Jubilee in the 37th year. These ceremonials are well documented, for example those in the reign of Amenhotep III, Akhenaten's father.[19] They involved long-range planning and preparations, erection of statues, large building projects, and the design of new clothing and apparel. The event itself took the form of regal processions, a re-enactment of the pharaoh's enthronement, feasting and national events.

For Akhenaten, 'celebrator of Jubilees'[20] who only reigned long enough to celebrate lesser Jubilees, they were opportune occasions for his multi-talented abilities in literature, design and architecture to be exploited. Under his instructions, Akhenaten's chief sculptor created new forms of 'expressionism' previously unseen in Egyptian artform. Portraits and statues appeared with elongated, Modigliani-like features. Figures were no longer represented in a rounded form, striving for realism, but as aquilinized creations with sharp features and enlarged heads. One can imagine that the inspiration for Akhenaten's new perspectives may have been related to his worship of Aten, and came to him when he gazed at the long shadows cast by solid objects illuminated by an oblique sun.

However one looks at the celebration of Jubilees as they are described by the Qumran-Essenes at the time of Christ, they have a striking resemblance to practices only too familiar to the Egypt of 1,500 years earlier.

There are other similarities between the Essenes' culture and philosophy and that of ancient Egypt, for example seen in the way the Qumran-Essenes viewed the forces of 'light' and 'darkness'.

THE SCROLL OF MOSES' BIBLICAL FATHER

The Dead Sea Scroll of the 'Last Words of Amram' – the Biblical father of Moses – describes two forces struggling over possession of the spirit of his dead body. Both beings exhibit the reptilian features of an asp and a viper, whilst the one of 'darkness' is known as 'Belial' and the one of 'light' is known by three names. They 'watch' over the dead body, but inner knowledge will save Amram from the 'King of Wickedness'.

Many interpretations have been made of the origins of this passage, but one possibility which does not seem to have been examined is its parallels to the Egyptian myth of Osiris. All the elements are there. Horus, the redeemer, 'watches' over Osiris in his state of suspended death to protect him from the god of darkness, Seth, whilst the serpent doors are guarded by the gods. The serpent was from ancient times an emblem of moral evil and therefore dread for the Egyptians, and they had long believed in a 'limbo filled with snakes'.[21] The combining of gods into three was, as has been seen previously (in Chapter 5), a common feature of Egyptian lore, and a body in limbo was to be revived by 'three entities' – the soul (ba), intelligence (xu), and genius (ka).[22]

If this scroll is referring to the Biblical father of Moses, as the name implies, it is certainly saying that he was not a Hebrew.

BEYOND REASONABLE DOUBT

So many are the conventionally inexplicable passages of the Dead Sea Scrolls and the life-patterns of their authors, the Qumran-Essenes, which can be clarified by comparison with ancient Egyptian custom – particularly that of the Akhenaten period – that it becomes irresistible to link the two.

I think it is quite reasonable to say that the proposition that Judaism emerged out of Akhenatenism, has many justifications, just from the evidence already cited. The deep philosophical bases of monotheistic religion, evident even at the time of Moses, is unlikely to have emerged from a group of nomadic Patriarchs. We have already seen how Egyptian religion had moved inexorably towards a consensus that there was only one supreme God. The development of that conviction accelerated with the Amenhotep pharaohs, culminating in Akhenaten's complete break with multi-deity worship and idolatry.

The Essenes were the children of the Akhenaten priests in the same manner as Christianity and Islam are the children of Judaism – the torch bearers of the eternal light of God.

If Moses did acquire his depth of monotheistic understanding from

Egypt, then the obvious question arises – is there any other evidence or acknowledgement, from within the Bible or other related sources, that the Biblical Commandments and Laws, other than the very early 'Noahite Laws', pre-dated Moses?

If I am correct, there should be. If there is such evidence, it would be powerful additional proof of my suppositions.

The immediate answer is a qualified 'No' – at least as far as conventional Torah and the Bible admit. However, as already mentioned, religions tend to be selective in their memories and distance themselves from their early antecedents! This apparent lack of confirmation of an earlier structure of Laws is therefore only to be expected. Later Rabbinic teaching does, however, tend to talk in terms of Noahite Laws and Mosaic Laws, as if to half-heartedly admit: 'Well, if there are any pre-Moses laws they were basic and quite under-developed.'

The pre-Moses 'Noahite Laws', which have been deduced from Genesis 9:4–7, etc., are considered to number seven in total, and forbid:

- idolatry
- blasphemy
- murder
- adultery
- robbery
- eating flesh from a living animal.

The seventh requires the establishment of courts and justice. There is no specific mention of keeping the Sabbath holy, or other precepts.

When, however, one looks at the oldest known Hebrew and Aramaic sources of the Bible – the Dead Sea Scrolls – and especially those of them which do not relate to specific descriptions of the Qumran Community, but to pre-Exodus references, there is a clear, unambiguous acknowledgement that the Commandments of Moses were extant and operative *before* the time of Moses. This conclusion is not just my own interpretation; it is the view of eminent scholars like Professor Ben-Zion Wacholder of the Hebrew Union College in Cincinnati, Dwight D. Swanson, and Philip R. Davies,[23] the latter being published within a programme of Judaic Studies sponsored by Brown University in America.

These pre-Exodus references are to be found in the Qumran-Essene 'Jubilees Scroll', in the 'Damascus Document' and in the 'Temple

Scroll'. 'Two of these scrolls represent the law as having been fully known before Sinai.'[24]

Many derivations of 'the laws' can be seen in pre-Sinai writings of Egypt. As Raymonde de Gans expresses it in his work *Toutankhamon*,[25] referring to post-1422 BCE and moral concepts which are:

> curieusement formulée en termes négatifs à la manière des Dix Commandements de Moise. Souvent très long et très détaillé, ce plaidoyer nous fournit des indications précises sur le Code Moral de l'Egypte antique.

> curiously formulated in negative terms in the style of the Ten Commandments of Moses. Often very long and very detailed, this pleading gives us a precise indication of the Moral Code of ancient Egypt.

'Jubilees'

The Jubilees Scrolls of the Qumran-Essenes record that the Sinai law was known, and observed, by the Patriarchs.

> And He said to us: I am going to take for Myself a people among my peoples. And they will keep the Sabbath and I will consecrate them as My people and I will bless them. They will be My people and I will be their God. And I chose the descendants of Jacob among all those I saw. And I confirmed him for Me as the first-born son and consecrated him to Me for ever and ever. The seventh day I will teach them so that they keep the Sabbath on it above all . . . And this is the testimony of the First Law.
>
> [Jubilees, Fragment 1]

In Fragment 7, Terah is talking to his son Abraham:

> You my son, keep His precepts His decrees and His judgements; do not go after idols or after carved or cast effigies. And do not eat any blood of an animal, cattle or any bird which flies in the air.

Other commandments in Jubilees include prohibition from: accepting a bribe; evil deeds; abominations; and defiling the Holy of Holies.

The Damascus Document

The Damascus Document is independently corroborated by the Genizah version found at the Cairo Synagogue,[26] and many of its passages can be found in the Torah. There can be little doubt as to its validity in our investigations, or to the authenticity of the other texts. All three scrolls confirm the Mosaic Laws as having been fully known before Sinai.[27] It is also apparent that these documents did not originate with the Qumran-Essenes, but are copies of much earlier texts.

Columns 2 and 3 of the Damascus Document read as follows:

> because they did as they wanted and did not keep the commandments of their maker, until His anger was aroused against them. Because of it the children of Noah went astray, as did their families; through it they were cut off.

> Abraham did not follow it, and he was accounted as a friend because he kept the commandments of God and did not choose what he himself wanted.

> And he passed on [the Commandments] to Isaac and Jacob, and they kept [them] and were written down as Friends of God and covenant partners for ever.

> The children of Jacob went astray because of them and were punished according to their error. And their children in Egypt walked in the stubbornness of their heart in taking counsel against the Commandments of God and doing each one as he thought right.

Columns 5 and 6 read:

> For in ancient times there arose Moses and Aaron, *by the hand of the Prince of Lights,* and Belial,* with his cunning, raised up Jannes** and his brother during the first deliverance of Israel...

> And in the age of devastation of the land there arose those who shifted boundary and made Israel stray.

> And the land became desolate, for they spoke of rebellion against God's precepts through the hand of Moses and also of the holy anointed ones.

> (My italics)

---

* A wicked person. Satan in the New Testament.
** An Egyptian magician who, in the Bible, confronted Moses.

The phrase: 'by the hand of the Prince of Lights' as the force behind Moses and Aaron, is, I believe, a deeper reference to the Pharaoh Akhenaten, for whom rays of light in the form of a hand with out-stretched fingers were symbolic of his belief in God. (Although it is even more likely that it is a reference to 'Meryra', the High Priest of Akhetaten, who was also an hereditary Prince.) Figure 5 shows Akhenaten worshipping Aten at the Great Temple of Akhetaten.

The Temple Scroll

Still on the theme that the Mosaic Commandments pre-dated Sinai, the balance of authoritative opinion is that the 'Temple Scroll' was not an internal Qumran Community document, but derived from much earlier times. The assertions within the Temple Scroll itself, that the commandments and Covenant that the Israelites were ordered to follow pre-date Sinai, are most intriguing, especially when compared to the Old Testament Book of Jeremiah. Jeremiah 31:31–33 talks of a new Covenant between the Lord and Israel.

> Behold, the days come, saith the Lord, that I will make a new covenant with the house of Israel, and with the house of Judah: not according to the covenant that I made with their fathers in the day that I took them by the hand to bring them out of the land of Egypt; which my covenant they brake, although I was an husband unto them, saith the Lord: but this shall be the covenant that I will make with the house of Israel. After these days, saith the Lord, I will put my law in their inward parts, and write it in their hearts; and will be their God, and they will be my people.

The theme is taken up in the New Testament, in Hebrews 8, and is generally seen in Christian theology as the pivotal point of a 'new beginning'.

However, in the Temple Scroll, the covenant for the new Temple is not the covenant made with those who led the Hebrews out of Egypt, but with the original patriarchs of Leviticus:[28]

> Like the covenant which I made with Jacob at Bethel…

The Temple Scroll contradicts Jeremiah, and maintains that there is no new Covenant. It does, however, clarify Jeremiah's meaning of a 'new Covenant' as referring to a new inward understanding of the old Covenant.[29]

THE TEMPLE

Intriguingly, the above quotation from the Essene Temple Scroll, '...the covenant for the new Temple...', suggests the possibility that there was an older Temple – one prior to Solomon's First Temple.

This apparent knowledge of an older Temple makes the attitude of the Qumran community to the Temple at Jerusalem all that more easy to understand. It has already been noted that the Qumran-Essenes were not at all happy with the manning, procedures and geometry of the Second Temple. Their dissatisfaction must also have been directed at the First Temple which, although not as elaborate, was dimensionally essentially the same.

The Essenes considered the priests corrupt, the festival rituals inappropriate and the size of the building too small, with the wrong number of courtyards. They wanted it to have three courtyards, rather than two. Detailed measurements of the First Temple are given in I Kings 6 and 7, II Chronicles 3 and 4, and are referred to in I Chronicles 28 as being given to Solomon by his father David. The description in Ezekiel, 40–47, appears to differ from the earlier Biblical descriptions, and seems to be rather more a 'vision' of a hypothetical temple rather than a real one. Most scholars, in fact, view Ezekiel's description as a half-remembered idyllic vision of how the Holy Temple should be constructed. Without going into the complexities of this description, there is one feature which has convinced most scholars that Ezekiel was fantasizing.

And when the man that had the line in his hand went forth eastwards, he measured a thousand cubits, and he brought me through the waters; the waters were to the ankles. Again he measured a thousand, and brought me through the waters; the waters were to the knees. Again he measured a thousand, and brought me through; the waters were to the loins. Afterwards he measured a thousand; and it was a river that I could not pass over; for the waters were risen, waters to swim in, a river that could not be passed over.

[Ezekiel 47:3–5]

Ezekiel's guide is telling him that the Temple is 510m (taking a cubit as 0.51m) from a very wide river. The description bears no relation at all to the geography of the Temple mound at Jerusalem. However, look again at the maps showing the position of the Great Temple of

Akhenaten in Figures 12 and 17. Of course, rivers change course over thousands of years, but as far as we can tell if you walked 500m from the Great Temple you would be up to your ankles in the water of the River Nile!

There are many other features of Ezekiel's vision that are reminiscent of the Great Temple at Akhetaten and its surroundings. There are also some that are quite confusing and which do not appear to relate to the Great Temple. To analyse them in detail would take another book, but his description of the proximity of a large river to the Temple, and its precise distance, could well indicate that it was Akhenaten's Temple that he was talking about.

According to I Kings and II Chronicles, the First Temple at Jerusalem was effectively an enlarged edition of the desert Tabernacle, and measured 60 cubits (30.6m) in length, 20 cubits (10.2m) in breadth and 30 cubits (15.3m) in height. (This is based on the Egyptian cubit measurement of 51cm; however it is likely that by the date of the building of the First Temple, *c.*940 BCE, the 'Royal Cubit' of 53.3cm may have been used.) The inner sanctuary was 20 x 20 x 20 cubits.

Surrounding and abutting the Temple were storehouses, priests' quarters, service buildings and Solomon's Palace, in a similar structural complex to that seen at Akhetaten.

Notable differences from the Tabernacle descriptions were the addition, by Solomon, of a large brazen altar, ten lavers (rather than one) in the outer court – plus a very large one for the priests, ten seven-branched candlesticks rather than one, and two huge cherubim with 20-cubit long wings forming a protective shade over the Ark in the inner sanctum, which was in total darkness.

cf Ark of
(Hancock)

Similar outline designs of temples built in the same period have been found in Canaan and Syria, but it is interesting to draw a comparison between the much earlier Great Temple at Amarna. Whilst Solomon's Temple appears to have been considerably smaller, there are some remarkable similarities. The Great Temple was oriented north-west–south-east, whilst Solomon's Temple was probably oriented east to west, and their overall plan sizes are in almost exact proportion – 1:3. The parallel requirement for utter darkness in the inner sanctuary of Egyptian temples has already been remarked on in Chapter 5.

p 61-2

One puzzle, however, is that the 'Temple Scroll' found at Qumran goes into great detail on the forms of animal sacrifice that are to be carried out in the Temple, and animal sacrifice continued in the Temple at

Jerusalem throughout the period of the Qumran-Essenes. The legislative requirements for sacrifice are repeated in parts of the Books of Exodus, Leviticus and Deuteronomy, and all these books were of importance to the Qumran-Essenes. However, I have previously suggested that, not only did the Qumran-Essenes, like Akhenaten, not practice holocaust sacrifice, they were against it.

For the Qumran-Essenes, their rules required the Community to be 'without the flesh of holocausts [burnt offerings] and the fat of sacrifices'. A 'sweet fragrance' was to be sent up to God, and prayer was to be 'an acceptable fragrance of righteousness'.[30] No evidence of sacrificial shrines, rituals or sacrificial remains have ever been discovered at Qumran.

The view has been advanced that the Temple Scroll is not a Qumran composition; I tend to go along with this view in relation to the descriptive passages dealing with sacrifices, which are clearly rooted in a post-exilic Canaanite setting. A possible explanation is that whilst one group of the conflicting strands of temple priests, who influenced the writing of the Old Testament, condoned animal sacrifice (and the worship of the god Astorath in conjunction with God), the other group of temple priests abhorred it. Going back to the 'Golden Calf' incident in Sinai, the condoners were most likely derived from the Aaronic priestly line, as opposed to those who traced their ancestry back to Moses. The passages in the holy texts that advocate holocaust sacrifice could therefore have been promoted by the writers that supported this view.

SQUARING THE CIRCLE

One can postulate from our new understanding of their heritage that, with their disenchantment with the Second Temple from both a religious and structural viewpoint, and their separation from normative Judaism, the Qumran-Essenes felt increasingly marginalized. Their only hope for a return to authentic monotheism – Atenism – was in the return of their 'Messiah of Holiness'. When the Damascus Document of the Dead Sea Scrolls and the Genizah collection cite both Moses and the 'hands of the anointed Messiah of holiness' as the givers of the Commandments, they are almost certainly referring to Moses and another lawgiver – Akhenaten? – who had the status of a Kingly Messiah. The Priestly Messiah in this context can only be Meryra, the High Priest of Akhetaten, who was also an hereditary Prince.

As a corollary to the above conclusion, it becomes evident that many other of the controversially perplexing statements and attitudes expressed in the Dead Sea Scrolls, which have not been easy to explain previously, now have very plausible explanations.

For example, there must have been a reason for the 'catastrophic messianic' perspective of the Community. It could have been related to the destruction of the First Temple in Jerusalem in 586 BCE. However, although the Qumran-Essenes venerated the concept of the Temple, they did not approve of the First (or Second) Temple and anticipated an imminent messianic age when all would be put right. Why should they be upset over the destruction of a Temple that they detested? Another, more likely, explanation can be proposed: the death of their King and loss of the Temple at Akhetaten, as the centre of their religious world, left an abiding memory of how their world should have been and that only dreams of the future could offer them the catharsis of re-instatement.

As guardians of the original covenant, the Qumran-Essenes were convinced that they were the only true Israelites and that all other Jews were in the wrong. Their messianic fervour foresaw two Messiahs coming to save them: one Kingly and the other Priestly, with Aaronic connections – i.e., a saviour dating back to the times in Egypt.

The Dead Sea Scroll texts written in the 3rd century BCE referring to a King as 'Son of God' are, as Lawrence Schiffman, Professor of Hebrew and Judaic Studies at New York University asserts: 'the statement of a notion already in existence, and not a reference to Jesus'.[31] This notion is entirely consistent with the concept of the King, or Pharaoh, being the appointed human representative of God on earth, and of his High Priest being the second of the Messiahs they awaited.

The imagery of a Messiah who '…will extend his hands to the bread', described in the Messianic Rule of the Dead Sea Scrolls, is unmistakably reminiscent of the extended hands of Aten towards the bread of offering. The Community's conviction of a future that was ordained confirms their overt belief in predestination, in direct contradiction of Jewish teaching at the time and of today. Needless to say, belief in predestination was the current canon in the religion of Akhenaten.

Suddenly a lot of other things fall into place. Many references in the New Testament not only allude to the coming of the Messiah, but state that the Messiah took an active part in the Old Testament. Professor A. Hanson, of Hull University, writing in the 1960s about 'Jesus in the

Old Testament', put it more strongly: 'Paul (and John) frequently perplexes us by apparently throwing Christ's activity back into the Old Testament'.[32] Perhaps they are merely reflecting an older tradition that one Messiah had already been on earth.

Polygamy, The Gander and The Goose

The rules applying to the Qumran-Essenes on marriage are spelled out in the Damascus Document. They prohibit a man to take two wives and positively reject polygamy. The practice is condemned by the Document as unacceptable fornication. (King David, c.1000 BCE, is exonerated apparently because he was not privy to the laws, which were kept hidden in the Ark of the Covenant.)

Marriage between uncle and niece is not forbidden by the Mosaic Law and seems to have been quite acceptable in normative society, but marriage between aunt and nephew is forbidden. What was sauce for the gander was not sauce for the goose. The Damascus Document, however, maintains that the Law applies equally to males and females, and that both connubia are forbidden.[33]

The Temple Scroll of the Essenes also confirms this sanction, and makes it clear that whilst marriage after the divorce or death of a first wife is acceptable, polygamy is not.

The attitude of the Egyptians, particularly the Pharaohs pre- and post-Akhenaten, appears to be rather similar to that of the Kings of Canaan. They were polygamous and could take numerous wives, for sexual pleasure and to procreate the dynastic line.

Akhenaten appears to have taken a different stance – a stance echoed by the Qumran-Essenes. As far as is known he only had one wife at a time to bear his children throughout his life, and there is no mention of another sexual relationship in Egyptian chronicles (although there is mention in the Tell-Amarna Letters of a 'diplomatic' wife). The circumstantial evidence that he practised and preached monogamy can be discerned from the fact that whilst his wife, Nefertiti, produced six daughters for him (there was possibly a seventh), he did not 'do' a Henry VIII and get rid of her in order to obtain a son. Nor did he take additional wives – despite the inevitable pressure to ensure the continuity of his dynastic line through a son.

A Second Torah?

It is amongst the Essene writings on marriage that further strong evidence can be found of the extreme antiquity of the texts of these

'Guardians of the Ark of the Covenant'. We come back to the enigmatic statement in the Damascus Document that King David was apparently unaware of the 'hidden laws' that related to marriage and other divine injunctions. How could it be that the general populace, many of the priests and the King of his people were not acquainted with a huge chunk of divine writ?

Carbon dating and palaeographic comparisons place the writing of the earliest Dead Sea Scrolls at 250, possibly 300 BCE. The Damascus texts, which apparently existed at the time but were not available to King David, make the link from these dates back to the time of David, and to the time of Joshua before the entry of the Hebrews into Canaan, *c.*1200 BCE, as the following passage reveals:

> And about the Prince it is written: he should not multiply wives to
> himself. However, David had not read the sealed book of the law
> which was in the ark, for it had not been opened in Israel since the day
> of the death of Eleazar and of Jehoshua, and Joshua and the elders who
> worshipped Ashtaroth had hidden the copy until Zadok's entry into
> office.
>
> [Damascus Document, Column 5]

The Torah confirms the Damascus texts in relation to David's 'taking of more concubines and wives' (II Samuel 5), and also tends to confirm the implication that the contents of the Ark were, at that time, privy to a select priestly line only and not available to David. II Samuel 6 describes how the Ark of the Lord was brought from Baalim, but that David was initially afraid to go near it, or to bring it to the tent he had prepared for it in the City of David. The Ark was left in the keeping of Obed-edom until David changed his mind.

The references to Baalim, which indicates an association to idolatrous worship of Baal, and to Ashtaroth, a favoured god of the Amenhotep faction, also supports the contention that David had not yet seen, or taken to heart, the contents of the Ark and had allowed a degree of backsliding amongst his people.

Even with the Ark of the Covenant in his possession it is not clear that David had an understanding of all the laws. Later Biblical writings also confirm the assertion of the Qumran-Essenes that the priests kept at least some of the Torah hidden from the people. This can be clearly deduced from the Second Book of Kings, and to an event which, in itself, led to profound changes in the way Judaism was practised.

And it came to pass in the eighteenth year of King Josiah, that the
King sent Shaphan the son of Azaliah, the son of Meshullam, the
scribe, to the house of the Lord, saying, 'Go up to Hilkiah the high
priest, that he may sum the silver which is brought into the house of
the Lord, which the keepers of the door have gathered of the people…'
…And Hilkiah the high priest said unto Shaphan the scribe, 'I have
found the book of the law in the house of the Lord.' And Hilkiah gave
the book to Shaphan, and he read it.

[II Kings 22:3–4, 8]

What on earth was going on here? Does this mean that one of the Five
Books of Moses, apparently given to him on Mount Sinai, had been
lost for at least 400 years? You may well ask, but that is exactly what the
Bible is saying. It means someone or some persons were privy to a different and sometimes contradictory, version of the laws and commandments, versions which may have been as old as 1200 BCE but also
incorporated new ideas developed around 600 BCE.

Alternatively, this Book was fully originated around 600 BCE, and
did not exist before. Because this 'newly found book' is written in a
style consistent with the 7th century, it is believed by most scholars to
have been a product of that era, developed by its authors to put across
their own contemporary programme of views and given authority by
pretending it was a work of Moses.

The Scroll that Shaphan read and brought to the King was almost
certainly, in essence, what we now know as the Book of Deuteronomy.
When King Josiah, who was in the 18th year of his reign in 621 BCE,
read the Scroll he immediately realized its significance, and decreed that
sacrifices should henceforth only be performed at Jerusalem, and immediately stopped sacrifices everywhere else in Israel. According to II
Kings, he destroyed all the other shrines and altars sited on high places,
at Beth-El, Ahaz, Carmel and on the hills around Jerusalem, and had all
the associated priests put to death. (It appears he left Mount Gerizim
untouched.)

This measure had the effect of controlling sacrifices which, up until
that time, had been subject to local cultic abuse and pagan practices –
worship of Baal, Astarte, and even possible child sacrifice to Moloch, by
earlier Kings in times of dire trouble. (All sacrifices within Judaism were
finally ended with the destruction of the Second Temple in 70 CE.)[34]

We can date the finding of the Scroll of Deuteronomy by King
Josiah reasonably precisely to 621 BCE from excavations at Megiddo,

where the King was slain by the Egyptian Pharaoh Nechoh in 608 BCE.

The conclusion must be that a priestly group, which I believe can only have been the predecessors of the Qumran-Essenes, were aware that David was in the wrong in 1000 BCE, and that their 'Second Torah' held additional and sometimes contradictory details of the Pentateuch which derived from well before 1000 BCE.

There is not enough space in this book to consider all the detailed similarities that exist between the writings and prayers of Akhenaten and those of the Qumran-Essenes (and on into Hebrew, Christian and Muslim texts). It will suffice to cite the generality of themes running throughout both varieties of texts. Themes of reverence to light, truth, peace, predestination, ritual washing, and admonitions against the forces of darkness, lying, insincerity, serpents and vipers.

One specific example illustrates the flavour of these similarities. The Dead Sea Scrolls record 'daily prayers' that the Qumran-Essenes followed every morning and every evening, as did the priests of Akhenaten.

Longer Prayer found at the tomb of Panehesy at El-Amarna, Egypt[35]	*Daily Prayers of the Essenes, found in Cave 4 at Qumran*[36]
Homage to Thee! Thou dawnest in the sky and shinest in the morning on the horizon of heaven, coming in peace the Lord of Peace.	And at the rising of the sun . . . to the vault of the heavens, they shall bless.
All mankind lives at sight of Thee, the whole land assembles at Thy rising; their hands salute Thy dawning.	They shall say: Blessed be the God of (Israel). Today He renews in the fourth [gate of light . . .] for us the rule [. . .][. . .] teen [. . .] the heat of the [sun] when it crosses [. . . with the streng]th of His powerful hand [peace be with you].[37]

We see in 4QFlorilegium, one of the Dead Sea Scrolls from Cave 4 discussed by Professor George Brooke in his extensive work on the subject 'Exegesis at Qumran',[38] another reference to light, in Fragments 6–7:

They shall cause your laws to shine before Jacob and your laws before Israel.

THE LINKS FROM AKHENATEN TO THE QUMRAN-ESSENES

It is now possible to summarize the essential and exclusive elements that connect the Qumran-Essenes to the priests of Akhenaten. We find that the Qumran-Essenes:

- believed God's commandments pre-dated Sinai
- did not recognize the Jewish Oral Laws, and had their own version of the Laws
- rejected the conventional Temple cult priests
- rejected any form of necromancy
- rejected polygamy
- rejected, at least temporarily, ritual animal sacrifice
- venerated light, calling themselves the 'Sons of Light'
- followed a solar calendar and recognized 'Jubilees' related to the sun's movements
- only recognized four festival days
- believed in pre-destined fate
- wanted the Temple to be the same design as the Temple at Akhetaten
- included reference to Akhenaten and Aten in their texts
- called their leader by a similar name to that of the High Priest of Aten, i.e., 'Merkabah' for 'Meryra'
- used numerous Egyptian phrases and literal forms, particularly those extant at the time of Akhenaten
- possessed a detailed description of the location of the treasures of Akhetaten, engraved on a Copper Scroll.

All of these elements, apart from the penultimate one, were quite contrary to the practices and beliefs of mainstream Judaism that the Essenes were surrounded by.

Taken *en masse*, it is evident that the Qumran-Essenes were aware of and pursued a number of characteristic religious practices and rituals, many in fundamental contravention to mainstream Judaism, that can only be explained as being derived from practices and beliefs of the Egyptian Akhenaten period.

CHAPTER SEVENTEEN

PHYSICAL, MATERIAL AND TECHNOLOGICAL LINKS BETWEEN QUMRAN AND AKHETATEN

Historians and archaeologists have noted many differences in various technical aspects of the scrolls' manufacture between techniques used by the Qumran-Essenes and those of mainstream Jewish society, and in the design of structures and other objects used at Qumran. These differences have just not had any satisfactory explanation. Virtually all of these 'mechanical' anomalies can, however, be explained by the connections that I have made between the Qumran-Essenes and the Egypt of Akhenaten.

WRITING MEDIA

The majority of the Dead Sea Scrolls were written on leather or skins, except for a few fragments written on papyrus or pieces of ceramic and, of course, one engraved on copper. Papyrus was not used in the Holy Land until around 190 BCE. Prior to that time writing was on potsherds (pieces of broken pottery); one assumes there was some use of leather, but no examples are known from Israel prior to the finding of the Dead Sea Scrolls. Examples from outside Israel of the use of leather date back to 2000 BCE Egypt.[1]

Ruled Lines

An intriguing characteristic seen in some of the Dead Sea Scrolls (notably the Commentary on the Book of Habakkuk), is the use of vertically ruled lines to separate columns, and horizontal ruling. It is extremely rare for papyrus (or leather) to be ruled horizontally in this manner, as the lines of fibre are sufficient guide to writing in straight lines. Ruled Aramaic or Hebrew papyri are virtually unknown prior to 68 BCE.[2] There are however examples of Egyptian papyri ruled both vertically and horizontally, in the British Museum's collection from the 'Book of the Dead'.

The Red Ink Mystery

Another link can be made from the strange existence of apparently random passages and words written with red ink in three of the Dead Sea Scrolls. Most notable are the examples in the scroll 4QNumbers, shown in Eugene Ulrich and Frank Moore Cross's book *Discoveries in the Judaean Desert VII, Qumran Cave 4*.[3] However, the significance of this phenomenon has not yet been determined.[4] The practice was unknown in Israel or in any other country, except ancient Egypt.[5] Coincidentally the main source of red pigment in Egypt was from the Elephantine region, and one can conjecture a connection between the Jewish Community at Ab, utilizing the local red ink, and a harking back to this old usage by the Essene Community at Qumran.

Analyses using energy-dispersive X-ray fluorescence (XRF) have shown that the inks used in writing the Qumran Dead Sea Scrolls were all based on carbonaceous pigment – either lampblack or soot, with traces of copper, lead and bromine[6] – not unusual for the period or location of the scribal activity. What *is* surprising, however, is their use of red ink to highlight sections of some of the scrolls – a practice unknown in Judaea at the time, or previously. XRF analysis has shown the red ink to contain mercury in the form of its sulphide compound (HgS), which derives from a naturally occurring mineral known as cinnabar. This finding was totally perplexing, as cinnabar is not present in Israel.

Why would the Qumran-Essenes go to the trouble and expense of importing red pigment, or even want to use it in the first place?

The answer is by now all too familiar. Red ink was selectively used in ancient Egypt for scribal texts, and was in use at the time of Akhenaten. There are good examples of scribal palettes from this period in the Museum of Liverpool, and in the Tutankhamun collection in the Cairo Museum. These examples show the use of two separate palette containers for black and red ink, and many Egyptian religious documents, dating back to at least the 15th century BCE, show red ink being used to highlight sections of text.

TEXTILES

In the spring of 1949, Lankester Harding and Father Roland de Vaux collected samples of textiles from the floor of Cave 1 at Qumran, which were carbon-14 dated in 1950, by Dr W.F. Libby at the University of Chicago, to between 167 BCE and 237 CE. Samples were subsequently sent to England for analysis.[7]

When the first box of samples was opened, at HM Norfolk Flax Establishment, it gave off a smell 'like that of an ancient Egyptian tomb'. Much of the material was identified as being fine-quality flax of natural colour or with blue-dyed lines, which had been used as scroll wrappers or jar covers for some of the Dead Sea Scrolls. There are *no known examples* of similar wrappers from Judaea of the period, or prior to it, and exact dating of the material is therefore quite a problem. However, because the material is entirely of flax and contains no wool, there is one indicator of its date. To quote Dominique Barthélemy and Jozef Milik:

> The indigo lines suggest at once the blue of the fine linen of Ancient
> Egypt, where until the Coptic period [395–641 CE], there was a
> strong religious prejudice against the use of wool. Perhaps it was the
> conservatism of Jewish piety that assured the continuance of the
> Ancient Egyptian practice into the last centuries BC and even later.[8]

As in ancient Egypt, the Qumran yarn was all spun with the natural twist of the fibre (S-spun), and some of the cloths had fringes. Barry Kemp, an eminent Cambridge University archaeologist, has been excavating at the site of Akhetaten for many years, and in his study of the local textile industry he noted that it was normal to weave fringes onto the bottom hem of flaxen cloths.[9]

Yet another, crucial, factor entered my analysis of the linen cloth wrappers found with some of the jars of the Dead Sea Scrolls: they bore an embroidered pattern of concentric squares, which appeared to the original investigators to allude to 'the ground plan of some religious building'. The embroidered weave consists of six concentric rectangles, and 'presents a most intriguing problem, for the blue weft threads actually turn round corners and become warps'. Clearly great effort and technical skill was employed to achieve the desired design.

Comparisons with a description of the 'idealized temple' in the Temple Scroll show that the 'ground plan' bears a remarkable resemblance to the ground plan of this 'hypothetical' temple described in the scroll. I have already suggested there is evidence that the Temple Scroll contains a description of the City of Akhetaten, and further comparison of this 'hypothetical' temple shows it, in turn, to have remarkable correspondences to the Great Temple of Akhenaten.

So where does that leave this particular investigation? It seems to me that the skills and technology needed to produce the woven materials associated with the Dead Sea Scrolls, found in Cave 1 at Qumran, cannot have been acquired from other local craftsmen. All the indications are that the weavers of Qumran used similar techniques to those used in ancient Egypt – techniques existing at the time of Akhenaten some 1,000 years earlier – and that there are many similarities in the Essenes' type of woven cloth to that produced at Akhetaten.

The material the Qumran-Essenes used to wrap their holy texts makes a strong link back to Akhetaten; the pattern they wove on to the material also makes a strong link back to the idealized temple of the Temple Scroll and the actual temple at Akhetaten.

The intense prejudice amongst the Egyptian priesthood against mixing wool and flax, by the way, helps to explain another modern 'chok' (forbidden thing) that has no accepted reasoning. Orthodox Jewish law forbids the mixing or wearing of wool and linen together. There is also a Biblical injunction regarding the wearing of prayer shawls, for example in Numbers 15:37–41:

> And the Lord spoke to Moses saying: 'Speak to the children of Israel
> and bid them that they make fringes on the corners of their garments
> throughout their generations, and that they put upon the fringes of the
> corners a thread of blue...'

One can thus also conjecture that the type of textiles used at Akhetaten was a fore-runner for the present-day prayer shawls that are used in synagogues by congregants, and that the 'Biblical blue' is the same as that preserved in the linen fragments found at Qumran.

HYDROMECHANICS AND CLEANLINESS

When the Essene sect's obsession with ritual washing is considered, the close proximity to water of Qumran, Elephantine Island, and Lake Tana in Ethiopia, should not be overlooked. The thread of ritual cleansing by water, as part of religious practice, and the need for a readily available water supply, may well be traceable back from these locations to the sacred pools of the Egyptian temples, and again more specifically to the Great Temple at Akhetaten.

As a result of Roland de Vaux's first excavations at Qumran in the early 1950s, he came to the conclusion that the large number of 'cisterns' within the buildings' grounds had been installed as a means of storing water, and that only two were possibly for ritual washing. This was despite the fact that Josephus, the Damascus Document, and the 'Rule of the Community' (now generally known as the 'Manual of Discipline'), spoke of the need for frequent purification by water.

Modern scholars now consider almost all the 'cisterns' to be 'Mikvah' – baths specially designed for ritual washing. Ronny Reich, of Haifa University and the Israel Antiquities Authority, counts ten stepped 'Mikvaot' at Qumran.[10] They are not dissimilar to others excavated at Jerusalem and elsewhere in Israel, except for one – which has its stepped area divided into partitions making it a four-section bath. Quite why the Qumran-Essenes should have required so many 'ritual bath' constructions is uncertain.

Knowing what I have discovered about the orientations of the buildings at Qumran, and how they are closely aligned to those of the Great Temple at Akhetaten, it is, perhaps, no surprise to find that there were also ten 'lavers' or ritual baths within the Great Temple area. Eight of these 'lavers' were in the Second Sanctuary and the other two in the court of the Great Altar.

> At the back of the temple are seen eight oblong lavers or bathing tanks, and all the material for a ceremonial offering, a rite prescribed perhaps before entering the second sanctuary…Near the altar are four erections, two of which appear to be lavers, divided into four basins each, corresponding to those at the smaller temple.[11]

The similarity in numbers of the ritual baths at Qumran to those at Akhetaten, and the 'unique' construction of four-section baths at both sites, cannot be a coincidence.

The ritual use of water and cleanliness is taken up, in turn, by the Essenes, John the Baptist and Jesus in spiritual baptism, by the Jews in spiritual and ritual cleansing in the 'Mikvah' or place of washing, and by the Muslims in their triple washing ritual prior to prayer.

Still on the subject of cleanliness, Josephus, talking about the ablutionary habits of the Qumranites, quotes:

'...[they] wrap their mantle about them so that they may not offend the rays of the deity...'

(Again, we cannot escape the allusion to God as being represented by the hands of the sun.)

The Qumran-Essenes were in the habit of carrying a mattock or hoe-like tool, which they used for tidying up after relieving themselves. Once again I did not have to look too far to find an explanation for this unusual practice – quite unique to the Qumran-Essenes in Judaea. It was during the 18th Dynasty in Egypt that 'shabti' (small statues) are first seen carrying mattocks![12]

Table 6: Summary of the mechanical and technological concordances between Qumran and Akhetaten.

	Use at Qumran 200 BCE–68 CE	Use at Akhetaten in Egypt c.1350 BCE	Use elsewhere in Judaea or Israel prior to 68 CE
Measuring Systems and Units			
Calendar	Solar	Solar	Lunar
Numbering	Decimal/repetitive	Decimal/repetitive	Alphabet based
Weighing	Khaff	Kite	Talent
Materials and Writing Techniques			
Leather skins	Used	Used	No examples
Papyrus	Used	Used	Rare
Red ink	Selective use	Selective use	Unknown
Ruled manuscripts	Common	Common	Rare
Copper engraving	Selective use	Selective use	Unknown
Copper rivetting	Selective use	Selective use	Unknown
Writing tables	Used	Used	Unknown
Design Techniques			
Qumran-style jars	Used	Similar designs	Unknown
Jar textile wrappings	Linen S-weave	Linen S-weave	Unknown
Four-section baths	Used	Used	Unknown

Why would the Qumran-Essenes, a relatively poor and isolated community, go to the trouble and expense of importing these materials and applying these techniques when other, local alternatives were available? Where did they get the knowledge required to utilize these relatively unknown materials and techniques? Unknown not just in their native land but also in the rest of the Middle East, apart from Egypt.

The only logical conclusion that can be reached from the evidence is that the Qumran-Essenes deliberately chose to use Egyptian materials and techniques because they had a determined affinity to Egypt, and to a period dating back a thousand years before their time.

They either went to the extreme expense and inconvenience of importing the materials and learning the technologies from contemporary Egyptian sources, or (and I believe this is the much more likely explanation), they had the materials and technical knowledge already in their possession – handed down to them by their Egyptian predecessors who left Egypt with Moses.

CHAPTER EIGHTEEN

EGYPT, ISRAEL AND BEYOND – THE OVERLAYING COMMONALITIES

I believe I have shown that many features of Akhenaten's monotheism later became exclusive to the Qumran-Essenes, when compared to the practices of the surrounding Israelite community. However, many more 'overlaying commonalities' of general Egyptian beliefs and traditions were, and still are, practised by mainstream Judaism. Tracing back these 'commonalities' shows that the Essenes undoubtedly formed a music workshop for the orchestra of Christianity and, by extension, of Islam.

BEYOND THE 'REED CURTAIN'

Although mainstream Judaism has always acknowledged an ancestral relationship with pharaonic-Egypt, it has never acknowledged any fundamental religious derivations, nor any cultural, social or doctrinal factors. Any discussion of the possible derivation of these from Egypt is cut off by a 'Reed Curtain', which rarely takes account of pre-Exodus Egypt. Nevertheless, the heritage and religious importance of Egypt is unambiguously spelled out in Isaiah 19. We are told (in verses 18–25) how the spirit of God, having descended onto the Egyptians, is soon abused and they return to their idols. Later, when five cities* speak the language of Canaan and there is an outpost on the border (probably referring to the Island of Elephantine, see

---

* Interestingly, the Revised Standard Version of the Bible has one of these cities called 'the City of the Sun' (Isaiah 19:18).

Chapter 19), Isaiah predicts that the Egyptians will begin the process of returning to God. Eventually, when Israel, Assyria and Egypt are at peace:

> In that day shall Israel be the third with Egypt and with Assyria, even a blessing in the midst of the land: whom the Lord of hosts shall bless, saying, 'Blessed be Egypt My people, and Assyria the work of My hands, and Israel Mine inheritance.'[1]
>
> [Isaiah 19:24–25]

The Bible, in the words of Isaiah, is saying that Christians, Jews and Muslims are equally acceptable in the eyes of God and, by inference, peoples of all religions and nations throughout the world. (*See Glossary on 'Contemporary Movements'.*)

There is not space here to analyse all the analogies of the characteristics of Egypt that have been absorbed into Judaism, and then often forward into Christianity and Islam. Some of them have already been discussed briefly, and other writers cover them in much more detail – writers such as Sir Ernest Wallis Budge,[2] Dr H. Brugsch,[3] Robert Eisenman and Michael Wise,[4] Theodor Gaster,[5] Irving Zeitlin[6] and Siegfried Morenz.[7]

These, and others, have long recognized that there are extensive commonalities between the pharaonic-Egyptian religions and the roots of western religions. These commonalities have been acknowledged by historians and academics, but only in a limited way by modern religious writers.

Sir Ernest Wallis Budge (Keeper of Egyptian and Assyrian Antiquities at the British Museum in the late 19th and early 20th centuries), one of the most venerated historians of his day, had no doubts about the concepts ancient Egyptians had about God.

> A study of ancient Egyptian religious texts will convince the reader that the Egyptians believed in One God, who was self-evident, immortal, invisible, eternal, omniscient, almighty, and inscrutable.[8]

One of his contemporaries, Dr H. Brugsch, collected epithets from the histo-Egyptian texts, which led him to conclude that:

> ...the ideas and beliefs of the Egyptians concerning God were identical with those of the Hebrews and Muhammadans at later periods.[9]

The idea that the writings of the ancient Egyptians were no more than isolated collections of stories, and that their scribes did not have the inclination to collate them into an overall pattern of scriptures is incorrect.

Apart from the Pyramid and Coffin Texts, which have been gathered together and, in themselves, form an interlocking picture of ritual life, there is the New Kingdom period 'Amduat' or 'Book of That Which Is In the Otherworld'. This attempts to encompass not only ideas of the royal resurrection but also the basic structures behind the resurrection and the calendar that controls the cyclical pattern of life. Versions appear in many royal tombs of the New Kingdom, including that of Tutmoses III, and they were a stage in the progressive development towards the simplicity of Akhenaten's religion. Unlike the post-Akhenaten tomb of Tutankhamun, which held all manner of adornments and numerous shrines and representations of the gods attending the sarcophagus* of the dead king, Tutmoses III's tomb is empty of garnishings and stripped of ritual furnishings. As John Romer put it in his BBC television series:

> The religious 'books' of the New Kingdom theology, of which the
> Amduat is but one example, were a codification and unification of
> these age-old beliefs, made by the priests pressurized by the acute
> enquiries of a new era.[10]

There was, therefore, ample precedent for the production of a codified work, encompassing the religious beliefs of the age.

A specific example which links Biblical texts to a body of Egyptian texts (significantly, precisely dated to the time of Akhenaten), can be seen in the similarities between Psalm 104 of the Old Testament and the Great Hymn to Aten found at the tomb of Ay at El-Amarna.

Psalm 104[11]	*Hymn to Aten*[12]
Bless the Lord, O my soul	An adoration of Aten...
O Lord my God, thou art very great;...	Lord of all...Lord of heaven, Lord of earth...
Thou art clothed with honour and majesty.	Thou are splendid, great, radiant, uplifted above every land.

* Stone coffin.

Who coverest Thyself with light as with a garment:	Thy rays embrace the lands to the extent of all that Thou hast made.
...Who laid the foundations of the earth... ...He causeth the grass to grow for the cattle, and herb for the service of man:	...Thou layest the foundations of the earth...Animals of all kinds rest on their pastures: trees and herbage grow green:
...O Lord, how manifold are Thy works! In wisdom hast Thou made them all	...How manifold are the things which thou hast made!
...There go the ships:	...The ships, too, go down and up the stream;
...That Thou givest them they gather:	...The land depends on Thee, even as Thou hast made them;
Thou openest Thine hand, they are filled with good.	When Thou dawnest they live,
Thou hidest thy face, they are troubled: Thou takest away their breath, they die, And, return to their dust. Thou sendest forth Thy spirit, they are created...	When Thou settest they die.

Thou in Thyself are length of days; life is from Thee... |

The Psalms, as a body of works, encompass a wide period of Biblical history, and many have distinctive overtones of ancient Egyptian style, content and feeling. They have had a profound effect on western religious belief and therefore have considerable significance to my narrative.

THE MUSICAL PSALMS

The 150 Psalms in the Old Testament form a unique corpus of literature, comparable with the Sonnets of Shakespeare in their profoundly beautiful imagery, literary quality and intellectual depth. In his classic work on Jewish music, Professor A.Z. Idelsohn, of the Hebrew Union College in America, calls them: '...the fountain from which millions of souls draw their inspiration and through which they have voiced their devotion for more than two thousand years'.[13] The reason for their power is expressed by many Church Fathers, such as Athanasius, Bishop of Alexandria, who lived from 295–373 CE. He said of the Psalms: 'They embrace the entire human life, express every emotion of the soul, every impulse of the heart.'[14]

The Psalms were written down somewhere between 800 and 200 BCE, but some are associated with even earlier periods.[15] Their content and phraseology find their way into many other sections of the Bible. They were employed in Israel as songs or chants to be performed in the Temple at Jerusalem as processions wound their way within the Temple during sacrificial, coronation, or offering ceremonies.

Whilst the lyrics of these 'processionals' were well documented, from other descriptions and depictions, and because many are introduced as 'songs' or as dedicated 'to the Chief Musician', it is certain that music accompanied the words. What this music was like is not known, although the nearest tunes in existence today are thought to be those preserved in the traditional chants of Yemeni Jewish ceremonies. However, circumstantial evidence and rhythm analysis indicates that the 'singing' was derived from ancient Egyptian temple music, dating back beyond the 18th Dynasty.

Professor Idelsohn refers to Egyptian temple music as having 'a certain dignity and holiness', with the priests resisting any attempts to change the sacred melodies. He concluded, as did Alfred Sendrey in his *Music in Ancient Israel*,[16] that ancient Egyptian music and instrumentation were the primary influences on the music of Israel, with some borrowings from Assyria, and virtually none from Phoenicia – Israel's nearest neighbour. With regard to the music of the Psalms Idelsohn states: '…from the composition of the orchestra of the First Temple, we learn that Israel accepted some of the arrangements of the religious orchestra used in Egypt at the time of its cultural height'.[17]

Many of the 'orchestral' instruments used in the Jewish Temple, such as the silver trumpet (*chatzotzera*),* the ten- and twelve-stringed lyres (*kinnor* and *nevel*), the flute (*uggav*) and the cymbal (*metziltayim*) were replicas of Egyptian instruments. In addition, little bells (*paamonim*) were attached to the skirts of the High Priest, as described in Exodus 28:35:

> …and his sound shall be heard when he goeth in unto the holy place
> before the Lord, and when he cometh out, that he not die.

---

* The Triumphal Arch of Titus in Rome shows treasures being borne away, which include silver trumpets from the Second Temple.

This custom is very reminiscent of the Egyptian usage of 'Sistrum' (tinkling bells) which, according to the Greek historian Plutarch (46–120 CE), were used to call the attention of worshippers to the sacred function in their sanctuary, and to drive away the evil spirit. Other instruments particularly associated with Egyptian temple worship included clappers, cymbals and bells.

The similarities between instruments used in the Temple at Jerusalem and Egyptian instruments, are evidenced by numerous archaeological and inscriptional discoveries. The earliest form of *kinnor*, for example, is illustrated on a vase dated to *c.*1025 BCE, found at Megiddo in Israel, which bears a striking resemblance to a lyre illustrated on a tomb wall at Thebes, dating to *c.*1420 BCE.[18]

Themes in the Psalms

The proximity of ideas between the Wisdom books of Egypt* and the Bible – which are particularly notable in the Book of Proverbs – are also touched on in areas of the Psalms. The bulk of the Psalms, however, have a much more similar ring to the prayers to Aten of the 18th Dynasty, and other prayers to be found in older tomb texts. The themes of light and shadow, praise to God, love of righteousness, hate of wickedness and judgement run through the Psalms, and can be readily identified with the themes contained in processional prayers performed in earlier Egyptian temple ceremonies.

Almost half of the Psalms are attributed to King David; significantly, the only one attributed to Moses – Psalm 90 – is, as would be expected, redolent with references to light and the effects of the sun.

> *For a thousand years in Thy sight*
> *Are but as yesterday when it is past,*
> *And as a watch in the night.*
> *Thou carriest them away as with a flood; they are as sleep:*
> *In the morning they are like grass which groweth up.*
> *In the morning it flourisheth, and groweth up; in the evening it is cut-*
> *　　down, and withereth.*
> *For we are consumed by Thine anger,*
> *And by Thy wrath are we troubled.*

---

* Collections of instructions and discourses dating from c.2250 BCE to the 11th century BCE. The 'Instructions of Any' and of Amenemipet son of Kanakht, composed during the New Kingdom period (1150–1069 BCE), bear most similarity to Biblical wisdom texts such as Proverbs.

Thou hast set our iniquities before Thee,
Our secret sins in the light of Thy countenance.

[Psalm 90:4–8]

King David himself, according to tradition, went into battle with a shield inscribed with the words from Psalm 67: 'May God be gracious to us, and bless us and make His face to shine upon us.'

This theme of light and the sun's influence runs throughout the Bible: it brightly colours the writings of the Qumran-Essenes, occurs in numerous prayers in all three monotheistic religions, and persists today in the Jewish celebration of 'Blessing the Sun'. This takes place every 28 years – the last one was in 1981 and the next is due in 2009.

The origins of monotheism in Egypt can be traced back to the sun worshipping priests of 'On' at Heliopolis, culminating in the full emancipation of the belief with Akhenaten. His praise in the Hymns to Aten, the sun as Creator, can readily be compared to the Psalms of praise to God of the Old Testament, in terms of the intensity of feeling and devotion. But it was not the old sun god of Heliopolis that Akhenaten was worshipping. He had made the religious, and scientific, breakthrough of realizing that the sun merely represented the power of an abstract, supreme God.

Cave 11 at Qumran yielded the so-called 'Psalm Scroll', which was translated by James A. Sanders, Professor of Old Testament at the Union Theological Seminary, New York, between 1965 and 1967.[19]

The 'Psalm Scroll' mixes details of Psalms, supposedly composed by King David, into a setting of the Qumran-Essenes' unconventional 364-day solar calendar, making it difficult to reconcile the supposed dates of their original composition. Unless the solar calendar was in force at the time of King David, in 1000 BCE, for which there is no Biblical evidence, one is forced to look further back in time to when a solar calendar might have applied, and is led inexorably to a period when the Hebrews were still in Egypt.

SOCIAL MORALITY

Examples of Egyptian social conventions that have penetrated through into the religious morality of Judaism, Christianity and Islam today, are not easily detected. There are some, however, which can be readily identified.

Homosexuality

In orthodox Judaism homosexuality is looked on as a sin. This follows on the injunction in the Bible which labels the practice as 'an abomination' in the sight of God. Modern 'Progressive' movements of Judaism, such as Reform and Liberal in Britain, and Conservative in America, are more tolerant, but generally still will not sanction any formal acknowledgement of homosexuality within a synagogal environment.

In the surrounding, and often dominating cauldron of ancient cultures that helped shape Jewish social attitudes, there was little objection to homosexuality. It was fully accepted in the ancient Greek world of Pericles and Plato, and even encouraged between teenage boys and older men. The one adjacent culture that did condemn homosexuality, and had done so for a time well before the Exodus, was that of Egypt.[20] It is not unreasonable to assume that this is a possible source from where the Judaic antipathy emerged.

THE EGYPTIAN 'WISDOM' WRITINGS AND ARCHETYPE STORIES

Many of the Hellenistic influences that colour the New Testament are well documented. Some of the Egyptian influences are also a consequence of the original translation of the Torah – as it was translated into Greek by a team of seventy scribes working at Alexandria, in Egypt in the 3rd century BCE. This 'Septuagint' is the Old Testament 'gospel' that all three of the great monotheistic religions refer to.

Whilst stories from Egyptian literature are relatively easy to identify earlier on in the Old Testament, they become less obvious as one goes further into the Book. This has led some historians to doubt the significance of Egypt and to look for other sources. I believe the more obscure correspondences have always been there but were not recognized by earlier researchers, and that their lack of findings discouraged others from looking more intensely for a number of decades. One of these researchers was Siegfried Morenz, a Director of the Institute of Egyptology in Leipzig, who concluded:

> Unfortunately the degree to which this influence [Egypt's on the Old Testament] is perceptible stands in indirect proportion to the significance of the facts.[21]

He even postulates that this 'influence' might have been in reverse – the Old Testament on Egyptian religious literature! Even after quoting endless citations of Egyptian socio-religious correspondences, he still did not appear to believe his own evidence.

Others, like myself, do not agree with this viewpoint.

The influence of 'Wisdom writings' from Egypt can still be seen quite far on into the Old Testament; for example, in the so-called 'Succession Narratives' in the Books of Samuel and I and II Kings, where the author (probably a contemporary of King David), draws heavily on Egyptian style and insights. As R.N. Whybray puts it in his book on the Succession Narratives: 'Whether the author of the Succession Narratives knew the Egyptian literature of the 12th Dynasty [or not]…that such a literature was among his models must be regarded as extremely probable.'[22]

It is not only the philosophical and religious patterns which have been imported into the Old Testament, but also local stories, expressions and phrases. A number of examples of this type of 'story copying' have already been cited – the Two Brothers' story (*see Chapter 10*), and the tradition of seven lean years followed by seven years of plenty – seen in a modified form in the Biblical texts – are but two of them.

EGYPTIAN INFLUENCES ON THE NEW TESTAMENT

There are also instances where Egyptian influences have 'jumped' the Old Testament to arrive in the New. We find this in the Gospel of St Luke, 16:19–31. This is the Parable of the Rich Man and Lazarus, where Lazarus, a wretched sick beggar, is left to rot outside the gate of a very wealthy man. Both die, but the beggar is carried up to Abraham's bosom whilst the rich man goes to hell. The rich man sees Abraham in the distance and cries out for mercy and for Lazarus to bring him water. Abraham tells him that the gulf between them is too great. Again the rich man calls to Abraham, asking if he will at least send Lazarus to his house to warn his five brothers of the torment that lies ahead if they behave the way he himself had done.

Abraham's reply speaks volumes:

> And he said unto him, 'If they hear not Moses and his prophets,
> neither will they be persuaded though one rose from the dead.'
>
> [Luke 16:31]

When this parable is compared to the ancient 'Setna Story', which was written in demotic Egyptian, there are notable similarities. Here, the hero learns that in the realm of the dead a sinful rich man has lost all the ostentation and finery on his tomb to a poor but righteous man. The poor man is comforted beside Osiris, whilst the rich man is relegated to the terrors of hell.[23]

The idea behind Jesus' parable of the rich man and Lazarus has been shown to have been transmitted through Jewish literature from Egyptian origins,[24] as was the acclamation by early Christian communities of 'God is One'.[25]

The non-canonical saying attributed to Jesus: 'Nothing is buried which will not be raised up',[26] is found inscribed on a mummy bandage from an 'Oxyrynchus' fish, sacred to the goddesses Hathor, Isis and Mut, of which there is an example in the British Museum.

The sentiment of heaping 'coals of fire' on one's enemy's head, which occurs in the Epistle of Paul the Apostle to the Romans (Romans 12:20), is very reminiscent of the Egyptian reverential rites. When St Paul talks of the absolute power of the Creator to confer honour and dishonour, he is paraphrasing thoughts in the 'Instruction of Amenemope' dating from 8th-century Egypt:[27]

For man is clay, and the God is his builder.
He is tearing down and building up every day.
He makes a thousand poor men as he wishes,
He makes a thousand men as overseers.

Hath not the potter power over the clay, of the same lump to make one vessel unto honour, and another unto dishonour?

[Romans 9:20]

Picked up in Judaic philosophy, this idea sharply delineates the line between Creator and created.

The 'second death' judgement of the already dead, in the Revelation of St John the Divine (20:14), can be linked directly to the Egyptian concept of 'second mortality' in the Coffin Text – a 'Spell of not dying a second time in the realm of the [already] dead', and in the Papyrus of Ani, Chapter 44.[28] As can the 'crown of righteousness' of II Timothy 4:8 and the First Epistle of Peter 5:4 be linked to the 'crown of life' of Egyptian theology.[29]

The concept of the trinity, already discussed in Chapter 5, which entered into Greek tradition a century or so before Christ, was well known in Egypt many years earlier. In Egyptian theology three gods were often combined as one and addressed in the singular. As Siegfried Morenz puts it:

> In this way the spiritual force of Egyptian religion shows a direct link with Christian theology…The multifarious links between Egypt and Judaeo-Christian scriptures and trinitarian theology can already be traced with some degree of plausibility.[30]

STYLISTIC ASPECTS

In addition to these examples of Egyptian influence on Judaism, it is possible to note many conceptual and stylistic effects on the Old and New Testaments.

Gathering these examples together, they can be listed as follows:

- The Egyptian Court 'chronicles' style of literature influenced the chronicled accounts of David and Solomon in the Bible.
- Isaiah's list of appellations for the Prince of Peace were derived from the five titulary ways of addressing the Egyptian King.[31]
- Wisdom literature, which Siegfried Morenz calls 'a gift of Egypt',[32] can be seen in many parts of the Bible, particularly in the Book of Proverbs.
- The 'Instructions of Amenemope' and the Biblical Book of Proverbs bear remarkable similarities.
- The Book of Psalms echoes many Egyptian temple prayers. A specific example being Psalm 104.
- Musical instruments used in both the First and Second Temples to accompany the Psalms were similar, if not the same, as those used in Egyptian temple ceremonies.
- Egyptian lists of knowledge formed the basis of the proverbs of King Solomon.[33]
- The Koheleth teachings of Solomon in Ecclesiastes, exemplified by the 'Horace–Williams'-type injunction, '*carpe diem*' – 'seize the day',* which appeared in the 'Songs of the Harpers', had long influenced Egyptian thought.[34]

    Another example is the idea current in the 'Songs of the Harpers' from the Middle Kingdom period of Egypt (and as

---

* A saying of the Roman poet Horace (65–8 BCE), popularized by Robin Williams in the film *Dead Poets Society*.

testified to by the Greek historian Herodotus), that it was the fashion to pass around a casket at a banquet, containing the remains of a dead person, with the reminder: 'gaze here, and drink and be merry; for when you die, such will you be'.[35]

- The concept of 'do not change any of the words, and add nothing thereto, and put not one thing in the place of another', which comes at the end of the 'Instructions of Ptah-hotep', has been taken up in Deuteronomy, and in the Revelation of St John the Divine at the very end of the New Testament.[36]

- The appellations for God. For example, in the earliest known translation of the Old Testament, the Septuagint, we find in Deuteronomy 9:26: 'Lord, Lord, king of the gods…'. This is an unknown phrasing for Israelite literature, but was a normal invocation for the High God in ancient Egypt.

- As said above, the trinity of Egyptian gods and their precedence for Christian theology has already been commented on.

- Well over 40 Egyptian words can be identified as being adopted into the original translation texts of the Bible.[37]

One could go on and on, and I am sure readers will discover many for themselves, by accident or design.

THE BODY OF EVIDENCE

Look at the evidence presented here. Weigh it all up and see what conclusion you come to. I believe the evidence I have presented is overwhelming.

The close resemblance of Psalm 104 and a hymn dating back to the time of Akhenaten (and very possibly composed by him), has been remarked on before, but the connection has never been explained. How could it be that a psalm, supposedly written down after 800 BCE, is so similar to a work written in hieroglyphs at least 500 years earlier, which was found in a place unfrequented by Egyptians and inaccessible to Hebrew scribes hundreds of kilometres distant – unless awareness of Akhenaten's Hymn came out of Egypt with the Exodus? The breadth of influence of 'wisdom literature', too, and the proverbs that can be traced back to ancient Egyptian lore, is so extensive that one has to pose the question: 'Was not the famous wisdom of Solomon really the concentrated wisdom of Egypt?'

There will inevitably be those who cannot, or dare not, take on board the conclusions that emerge, because they present too many challenges to traditional beliefs. But look for one moment at a couple of 'what ifs'. 'What if I am correct?' 'What if the origins of monotheism do go back to the time of Akhenaten?' Does this knowledge change fundamental religious beliefs? Not really. It does, however, change the perspective of how some customs and practices have become erroneously entrenched in modern attitudes. The misconceived role of women and the need for animal sacrifices are obvious examples. It does also give us the opportunity to look at texts and prayers in an Egyptian context and, in many instances, to discover emotive and moving passages which are still relevant today.

Let me make an analogy. The contemporary phrase 'Can the Ethiopian change his skin, or the leopard his spots?' is quoted in the *Oxford Dictionary of Quotations* as coming from Jeremiah 13:23. A similar phrase, deriving from an apparently much earlier date than Jeremiah (who fled to Egypt *c.*650 BCE), appears in an Egyptian papyrus in the British Museum known as 'The Instructions of Ankhsheshonq'. Here we read: 'There is no tooth that rots and stays in place. There is no Nubian [the ancient term for Ethiopian] who leaves his skin.'[38] All right, so the origins of the phrase may be much earlier than most people have acknowledged, and it may come from Egypt not Israel, but the essence of the saying and its validity remain unaltered.

FINAL CLUES FROM THE COPPER SCROLL – ELEPHANTINE ISLAND AND THE FALASHAS OF ETHIOPIA

The locations indicated by my new interpretation of the Copper Scroll, for the hidden treasures described in it, have led to descriptions of a number of novel places *(see Chapter 15)*. Sometimes these descriptions are in the same areas indicated by previous translations, but often they are of places that have not so far even been considered, let alone excavated. Some four-fifths of the locations I identify are different from those given in conventional interpretations.

I do not believe the Copper Scroll refers to locations other than in Israel or northern Egypt, but by tracking the 'footprints' left by the Atenist priests who did not travel out of Egypt with Moses, it is quite possible that other treasures from the Great Temple of Akhetaten may still remain to be discovered.

One of these likely locations is at the ancient temple at On, modern-day Heliopolis. Two others are Elephantine Island in southern Egypt, and near Lake Tana, in northern Ethiopia.

The link that has been made between Akhenaten and Judaism, reinforced by the decoding of the Copper Scroll, is instrumental in explaining two long-standing mysteries – that of why Jewish-style settlements existed at Elephantine Island and at Lake Tana. Both communities at these sites practised forms of Judaism quite different from that of the mainstream. The Jewish community at Elephantine, for example, did not know about the Exodus – not surprising, if my theories are correct, since they had not been part of it. Nor did they follow Jewish law, but based their ideas on Egyptian experience. Similarly the Ethiopian Jews had no knowledge of the Oral Laws of Judaism and followed different religious practices.

The presence of these two 'residual' pseudo-Jewish enclaves are loose-ends of history. There has never been a satisfactory, agreed explanation of how either of the settlements came into existence. The sequence of events and the circumstantial evidence (previously related) that connects the priests of Akhenaten to Elephantine Island gives, I believe, a convincing explanation, which is verified by the unusual nature of the Judaism practised by the inhabitants of the settlement.

ELEPHANTINE ISLAND IN THE ANCIENT LAND OF AB

The ancient Island of 'Yeb', known to the Greeks as the 'Island of Elephantine', encompasses a narrow strip of land measuring 2km by 500m at its widest *(see Plate 16)*. The location is usually on the tourist itinerary to see the best example of an ancient Nilometer. Looking rather like a flight of steps, the structure was rebuilt during the Roman period and still shows the level markings which were used to monitor the height of the Nile's inundations. There are, however, other curiosities, hidden away, which most tourists do not see or learn about.

Excavations on the Island have revealed an Egyptian presence dating as far back as the 1st Dynasty, c.3000 BCE, to the time of Pharaoh Naqada II. In the centre of the Island there once stood a Temple of Tutmoses III, and to the north, a Temple of Amenhotep III, Akhenaten's father. Both these temples were totally destroyed in the civil conflicts which occurred not long after their construction. There is also evidence that a very ancient pseudo-Jewish Community lived on the Island.

This pseudo-Jewish Community at Elephantine Island, near modern Aswan, suddenly disappeared around 400 BCE. Where did it come from? Where did it disappear to? How long had it been there?

Historians and commentators writing about the members of the Community, and trying to answer these questions, fall into three distinct groups:

- those who say they are the result of 'dispersions' of Jews from Israel
- those who ascribe them to be mercenaries, or troops from Israel who came to help defend Egypt's southern borders sometime after 730 BCE
- those who say no-one knows where they came from.

These views are patently mutually exclusive and therefore they cannot all be correct.

What then is the explanation for the existence of this strange, anachronistic settlement? I looked first at the idea that it resulted from 'dispersed' Jews from Israel.

Dispersion Explanations

The cartophilic official biographer of Winston Churchill, Sir Martin Gilbert, ascribes the colony to the Dispersions of 722 and 586 BCE – the periods of Assyrian and Babylonian conquests of the Northern and Southern Kingdoms of Israel. However, to make the point he has to place Elephantine 550km further north than it really is!

Sir Martin illustrates the explanation in his *Atlas of Jewish History*, first published in 1969,[1] where a map of the 'First Dispersions' of 722 and 586 BCE, shows the position of the 'Jewish' colony at Elephantine as being some 300km south of Alexandria. Syene, the ancient name for the area of Elephantine Island, is also shown on the same map, but this time some 500km south of Alexandria. The actual positions of Elephantine Island and Syene are some 850km south of Alexandria![2]

This explanation of how this strange pseudo-Jewish settlement came into existence, gratefully accepted by most religious observers and, through inertia, by many historians, just cannot be correct.

Consider the background history of Israel that led up to this weird situation, where a 'Jewish' settlement is said to have suddenly appeared in one of the remotest parts of ancient Egypt.

When King Solomon died in 928 BCE, his son Rehoboam, and one of his officials, Jeroboam – 'the champagne boys' – didn't get on too well and squabbled over control of the Kingdom. In the end they decided to divide the Kingdom, so that Jeroboam and ten of the tribes of Israel took control of what became the Northern Kingdom, with their capital at Shechem, whilst Rehoboam, leading the tribes of Judah and Benjamin, set up the Southern Kingdom with its capital at Jerusalem.

Trouble was not too long in coming. In 722 BCE the Northern Kingdom was conquered by the Assyrians, who dragged most of the Jewish population northward to other parts of their empire – the beginning of the mythology surrounding the ten lost tribes of Israel had been enacted. At the same time the Southern Kingdom came under the domination of Assyria but, although Jerusalem was besieged in 701 BCE, it managed to hold out against complete subjugation.

No sooner had Assyrian power started to wane, than the dark shadow of the Babylonians loomed on the horizon. Their forces, under Nebuchadnezzar II, captured Jerusalem and destroyed the First Temple in 586 BCE. Once again most of the Jewish population was carried off, this time north to locations immortalized in the song *By the Rivers of Babylon*.

The problem with the Sir Martin-type scenarios is that in both of these 'dispersals' virtually all the Jews were taken northward. Even if some were taken south, the Assyrian conquest of Egypt, at its height, never extended beyond Thebes, some 200km north of Elephantine, and the Babylonians did not even invade Egypt.[3]

Those Jews that might have fled to Egypt would surely have stayed in the traditional Northern Delta region, just beyond the Egyptian border. In the Old Testament, Jeremiah 43:7 and 44:1 confirms this with his references to reluctant settlers at Tahpanhes, Migdol and Noph (Memphis) – all in northern Egypt; but he does also refer to Pathros in Upper Egypt south of Thebes.

Military Explanations

The military garrison theory is discussed very fully by Bezalel Porten in his *Archives from Elephantine*.[4] From all the historical evidence, if there was a Jewish military establishment made up of troops from Israel, they would need to have arrived at least prior to 700 BCE. The only reasonable scenario for this possibility would be that it occurred during the mid-7th century BCE, when Israel attempted to throw off the Assyrian yoke by aligning itself with Egypt. Why they would want to send soldiers to the remotest part of Egypt, ostensibly to defend that country's borders, is difficult to justify logically. Jewish soldiers, or even mercenaries, would not have been good at defending someone else's country anyway – they would have been reluctant to fight on the Sabbath unless attacked first. Nor was Elephantine the effective military southern limit of Egypt.

The idea that there was a military garrison in the area is attested to by Herodotus, the 4th century Greek historian, but the garrison he was talking about appears to have been at nearby Syene, modern Aswan, and was manned by Aramaen soldiers.

There is no archaeological evidence of any military connection to the pseudo-Jewish Community, and little mention of such activity in their writings.

The Don't Knows

Other historians, such as Reuven Yaron, Lecturer in Roman Law at the Hebrew University in Jerusalem, and G.W. Anderson, Professor of

Hebrew and Old Testament Studies at the University of Edinburgh, are much more cautious in their opinions, and admit that the Jews of Elephantine are an historical loose-end. Professor Anderson states: 'This settlement [Elephantine] dated from before 525 B.C. but unfortunately we do not know exactly when or how it was founded.'[5]

This view is endorsed by Reuven Yaron: 'We do not know whence the original Aramaic-speaking settlers came to Egypt and Elephantine.'[6]

THE ELEPHANTINE COMMUNITY

A close analysis of the nature of the 'Judaism' practised on Elephantine Island shows that it originally bore almost no similarities to the Judaism practised in the Holy Land at any period before 525 BCE: the 'Jews' of Elephantine Island cannot conceivably have come from the Holy Land.

After the Babylonians, the Persians became the power in the Middle East, and by 525 BCE their troops had conquered the whole of Egypt and reached Elephantine Island. When they arrived they found a priestly colony that followed a very unusual form of Judaism. Their religious practices appear to have comprised a mixture of Judaism with the worship of Yaweh and of the Egyptian goddess Astarte.[7] They did not follow and were not aware of the Oral Laws, nor did they appear to celebrate Passover – the great festival of the Exodus of the Hebrews from Egypt.

How do we know all this? Much of our knowledge of the Elephantine settlement comes from Aramaic papyri discovered at the turn of the 19th century. Dated to the 5th century BCE these documents are now to be found in the museums of Brooklyn, Turin, Paris and Berlin. Major parts of these amazing texts are in the Staatliche Museum in Berlin and in the New York Brooklyn Museum, and they comprise some 30 almost complete documents and additional fragments written by the Jewish priestly settlement at Elephantine. They are mainly letters and legal documents concerned with court actions, marriage contracts and property law – there were obviously solicitors around even in those days as we have one of the earliest known examples of a conveyancing document, dated to about 470 BCE, and a lease dated 515 BCE![8]

The Elephantine papyri paint a colourful picture of the Community's activities, but they throw up numerous unanswered problems.

- Why would a group of devout Hebrews settle, or re-settle, in such an obscure place?
- Why did their form of Judaism differ from the mainstream, to the extent that they did not appear to accept, or have knowledge of, the Oral Laws, did not keep the Passover, did not follow the requirements of Deuteronomy and did not know the Pentateuch!
- Why would the Elephantine Islanders still encompass Astarte, and other deities, within their monotheistic beliefs?
- Why did they practise slavery?
- Why did they follow Egyptian legal, fiscal and social precedents – some dating back to 1700 BCE?
- Why did the members of the Community not understand Hebrew?
- From where did the Community obtain its wealth?

The Community spoke and wrote mainly in Aramaic, with the occasional use of Egyptian demotic writing. Early Aramaic was the *lingua franca* of the Middle East in the 1st millennium BCE down to Christian times and was in use in Israel from the 8th century BCE alongside Hebrew. (After the return of 'the intellectual Jews' from exile in Babylon, Aramaic dominated in everyday discourse, until the time of the Hasmonean uprising when Hebrew came back into fashion.) Eric Peet notes, in his *Egypt and the Old Testament*,[9] the paradox that any settlers coming from Israel prior to 525 BCE would have written in early Hebrew, whereas the Elephantine Community wrote and communicated in Aramaic.

They used virtually no Aramaic names and used pre-586 BCE pagan-like non-Hebrew names. They organized themselves in *degels*, or social groupings, along similar lines, significantly, to those employed at Qumran.

Like their ancestors, who first came into Egypt as shepherds, they also were sheep keepers. Many were financially well-endowed property-owning members of the upper classes, able to afford lavish gold, silver and the finest Lebanese cedarwood to adorn their Temple. Services in their Temple included meal and incense offerings, but there did not appear to be holocaust offerings.[10]

Their Temple itself is a mystery, as its very existence is quite anomalous. It just should not be there. The Community had built, at great cost, their own magnificent Temple for worship[11] – something very unlikely for anyone to do outside Jerusalem at any time, and certainly after King Josiah (*c.*640–609 BCE) forbade the building of a Temple anywhere but in Jerusalem. The Temple is dated to at least the 7th century BCE,[12] precluding any possibility that the priestly-militaristic Community at Elephantine derived from the Babylonian dispersal.

Unfortunately, despite intense archaeological work by German and French teams, the exact location of the Temple, somewhere in the Jewish quarter of the Island, has not been discovered. It is known, from descriptions in the Elephantine papyri, that the Temple was a substantial building with stone pillars, and that it had five gateways with bronze-hinged doors. Its size and orientation can roughly be deduced from descriptions of adjacent buildings, and it measured 60 cubits by 20 cubits (approximately 30m by 10m). Bezalel Porten equates the Temple's proportionality to that of the First Temple in Jerusalem (built *c.*950 BCE).[13] He takes its apparent orientation to be towards Jerusalem. Much of this deduction is conjectural, but in my own analysis of the Temple's orientation I found the most probable orientation was in fact north-west–south-east, similar to that of the Great Temple at Akhetaten.[14]

The assumption that the Elephantine Temple was modelled on Solomon's Temple might, after all, be the other way round! The Elephantine Temple may well have been based on Egyptian designs, as its dimensions are exactly in proportion to the Temple at Akhetaten – 3:1, length to width. However, for any Judaic community which originated in Canaan, after the Exodus, to have built a Temple outside the 'Holy Land' after the First Temple was constructed (to the specific and unique instructions of God), would have been unthinkable.

It was only when rivalries, much later in Israel's history came to the surface, that anyone could contemplate building a Temple anywhere but in Jerusalem. The inevitable implication is that the Temple at Elephantine must have pre-dated Solomon's Temple of *c.*950 BCE, and that the original Elephantine religious–militaristic Community must have been established prior to 950 BCE at least.

Michael Chyutin, in his study on the New Jerusalem Scroll from Qumran, published in 1997, confirms my suspicion when he concludes that the town built by the pseudo-Hebrew community at Elephantine Island is a copy of the city plan at Akhetaten. The streets bear similar names, and the structures of the buildings have special characteristics similar to those at Akhetaten. Although there are similarities in the layout at Elephantine to some other orthoganol-design cities in ancient Egypt, the essential features are uniquely comparable to Akhetaten.[15]

The inhabitants of the Community followed Egyptian legal, fiscal and social customs – fundamentally different from those in Israel – and their religion was quite different from mainstream Judaism. They had a concept of a personified 'Maat', and the principles of religious behaviour reminiscent of the Egyptian ideals discussed in Chapter 5. In legal matters, for example, the marriage contract gave equal status, and in some instances superior rights, to the wife; used Egyptian phrases; and was typical of that existing in Egypt in the 12th century BCE. Women also had equal dissolution rights. These freedoms were quite contrary to Jewish custom. No written marriage contract is ever mentioned in the Old Testament, and Jewish law gives power of dissolution to the husband only.

There are also examples, in the Elephantine papyri, of the undisguised taking of interest on outstanding debts. This type of practice is strictly against Jewish law.[16]

The literary style of the legal and other Aramaic papyri is quite different from that of texts from the Holy Land, and far older in derivation than their time of writing. Reuven Yaron cannot find any reasonable explanation for this feature, and prefers to leave the matter open:

> It is typical of Egyptian formulaty style, for many centuries prior to the
> Aramaic papyri, that deeds of sale are drawn up *ex latere venditoris*
> (from the point of view of the seller).[17]

In 407 BCE the Elephantine Community wrote to the Persian Governor of Jerusalem, Bagoas, relating that their Temple had been destroyed three years earlier by agents of the nearby Egyptian priests of Khnum, whilst the local Persian governor was absent. Their letter maintained that the Temple had been '...built in the days of the Kings of Egypt, and when Cymbyses [the Persian King Cyrus II, *c.*525 BCE] marched into Egypt he found the Temple already built'.[18]

At the same time they also wrote asking for help to rebuild their Temple, to the sons of Sanballat, Governor of Samaria. This is another puzzle – because Sanballat had been adamantly opposed to the building of a Temple in Jerusalem, let alone in Egypt, and his sons would not have been in any position to influence the High Priest at Jerusalem. The answer is simply that the Elephantine Community were not 'diaspora' Jews, and they did not know about what had been going on in Israel.

Another text recounts the Persian King Darius II, in 419 BCE, granting the Community permission to hold a feast of 'Unleavened Bread' and instructions on what to do. The Festival of Unleavened Bread is the Festival of 'Passover' – when the Jewish people remember their miraculous escape from bondage in Egypt. The clear implication of these letters is that the Community at Elephantine had not before celebrated, and did not know *how* to celebrate, the Exodus from Egypt, because they had never left that country.

A.E. Cowley, who did much of the original translation work on the Aramaic papyri, went as far as to say that, 'The Pentateuch, both in its historical and legal aspects, was unknown in the 5th century to the Jews of Elephantine.'[19]

Biblical testimony also corroborates the very early existence of the Community. The prophet Amos, who lived from 783–743 BCE, well before the Assyrian dispersals, recalls:

> Are you not as children of the Cushites unto me, O children of Israel? saith the Lord…'[20]

> [Amos 9:7]

There are two other firm clues which tend to indicate a tribal 'Hebrew' presence at Elephantine well before 750 BCE worth mentioning. The so-called 'Elephantine Stele', dated to *c*.1186 BCE, in the time of Pharaoh Setnakhte, recalls an Egyptian rebel faction who bribed certain 'Asiatics' with silver, gold and copper to help them in their plot against the reigning Pharaoh. Were these 'Asiatics' some of the inhabitants of the colony at Elephantine? One also has to wonder if, in adopting the name 'nakht' into his title, this particular Pharaoh was not harking back to an allegiance with Joseph and his form of monotheism; the Joseph who, as I have suggested earlier, was vizier to Akhenaten and who bore the title 'nakht'?

The second 'documentary clue' sits calmly in the Brooklyn Museum, New York. It is one of the Elephantine papyri that a certain Anani b. Azariah wrote as an endorsement on a 'Document of a House'. It has two seals, one of them is the scarab (ring-bezel) of Tutmoses III, an 18th-Dynasty Pharaoh, dating to some 1,000 years before the time of the writing of the Azariah papyrus.[21] Why would a member of the Elephantine Community be making use of a seal from the 18th Dynasty, unless he felt some association with the Amenhotep family continuum? A seal that Akhenaten, as a close family descendant of Tutmoses III, might well have had in his possession.

Although the Elephantine Community later had apparently good relations with their distant cousins in Israel and were on corresponding terms, the worship of Yahwe (the Hebrew God) together with Astarte and Ashambethel, indicates that theirs was not a re-imported version of Mosaic Judaism, but a transmuted version of the original Egyptian-Judaism which had become corrupted by its close proximity to Egyptian paganism.

There is, however, some evidence mitigating against part of this theory, which can be found in the Israel Museum, an enormous complex of buildings standing in 22 acres in the heart of Jerusalem. Set on a hillside the Museum stands imperiously gazing out over the panoramic vista of the Israeli Knesset building (Parliament) in front, to the left the Hebrew University, and to the right the Monastery of the Cross or Crusader Monastery, standing in the Valley of the Cross. The museum buildings comprise the Bezalel Museum of Fine Arts, the Shrine of he Book (which houses many of the Dead Sea Scrolls), the Rose Art Garden, and the Biblical and Archaeological Museum. In this latter building there are numerous examples of Egyptian objects – small votive offerings from a temple of the Hyksos period, found on the shore north of Haifa at Nahariya, and examples of Egyptian pottery attributed to the early third millennium BCE, found at Tell Eirani and Tell Arad.

However, there is very significant evidence of Egyptian influence, long after the Exodus, in the form of a collection of cult objects that include 'Astarte' figurines from the period of the destruction of the First Temple. The goddess Astarte was therefore a stubborn addendum to the worship of one God by the Hebrews long after they entered the Promised Land.

Some additional light can be thrown on the adherence to Astarte by skipping back to Akhenaten's father, Amenhotep III. The conquests of Syria by Egypt had resulted in the incorporation of certain Syrian gods into the Egyptian pantheon. One of these was 'Ishtar' a goddess of life and good health. Ishtar has been equated with the goddess Astarte, and the fondness of Amenhotep III for this goddess could explain the continued affinity of the Elephantine sect to this deity. In his last years of illness, when he was in the 36th year of his reign, Amenhotep III made an urgent request to his father-in-law, Prince Tusratta of Mitanni, to send him a statue of 'Ishtar of Nineveh'.[22]

It may seem dichotomous to contemplate a belief in one God with the continued adherence to previous gods. This would not be inconsistent with the thinking of the Egyptian mind at the time. To them, everything was seen as a continuing process of inter-related entities and when change was envisaged it could be seen as not necessarily invalidating, or even conflicting, with previous beliefs. Rather like the twitching of a chicken's legs after its head is cut off, it would be too much to expect that a mental clean sweep could be made – suddenly forgetting all previous knowledge, superstitions and beliefs.

It was not inconsistent therefore, that gods such as Astarte, a particular favourite of the Amenhotep faction, could survive alongside monotheism. A degree of backsliding was inevitable, and there are numerous examples subsequent to the Exodus. The making of an idolatrous Golden Calf, whilst the Hebrews waited in the desert for Moses to bring down the Ten Commandments from Mount Sinai, was a reflex action understandable for a people who, for thousands of years, had been in contact with such practices.

A close study of the form of worship that was observed at Elephantine was made by E. Maclaurin at the University of Sydney, Australia. He concluded:

> …that it was of a form which could not have existed in a Hebrew
> group which had been exposed to the influences of Sinai and Canaan
> after the settlement[23]

In other words Maclaurin rules out any possibility of the Community at Elephantine having derived from outside Egypt after the Exodus, let alone at the time of Solomon or the kings of Israel.

ELEPHANTINE ISLAND AND AKHETATEN

The main similarities between the religious life at Elephantine and at Akhetaten can be summarized, bearing in mind that for a 'rogue' community of priests and their followers to have survived for so long, at times isolated but at later periods surrounded by Egyptians worshipping conflicting deities, cannot have been easy. Their original well-being and security would have been strengthened by armed Hebrew soldiers, but strategic acquiescence to local customs may have become a necessity as the Island itself became more populated and developed into the centre of worship of a local plume-bedecked, ram-headed god, Chnemu, who moulded man out of clay on a potter's wheel.

- The Community's Temple was in exact proportion to the Great Temple at Akhetaten, and its orientation appeared to be the same.
- There is no indication of holocaust sacrifices taking place. Offerings were similar to those made at Akhetaten.
- Men and women had equal status in marriage.
- Monogamy seemed to be the rule.
- Their phraseology in writing was similar to contemporary writing at Akhetaten.
- They communicated in Aramaic, the successive *lingua franca* in Egypt to the Akkadian language used at Akhetaten.

The stark conclusion must be that the pseudo-Jewish priestly Community that existed at Elephantine at the southern extremity of Egypt, exhibited many ancient Hebraic-like religious attitudes but also had so many differences from the mainstream Israelite religion as to have derived its original beliefs from a common source. This source, however, was not from post-Exodus Israel, but was from the monotheistic Egypt of Akhenaten.

When the banished priests of Akhetaten fled to safety, they made what, in retrospect, can be seen as a sensible choice – a remote part of Egypt, relatively unknown and inaccessible to pursuers. It was also a logical choice – a place 'opened-up' by Akhenaten's grandfather, Amenhotep II, in which perhaps lay a secluded location better known to him than to any other then living Egyptian.[24] What better place for the priests of Akhetaten to flee to, accompanied by a band of Hebrew bodyguards whom Joseph might have helped them to enlist, to guard them in their perilous journey? To a land bordering Cush, at the outermost extremities of the Egyptian Empire, with the Nile cataracts as added protection.

If my suppositions are correct, the Akhetaten priestly sect and their Hebrew bodyguards arrived in Elephantine Island around 1330 BCE, still carrying some of the treasures of the Great Temple at Akhetaten. This was a place where the Amenhotep family ideas might still have had some sway. For a time this is where the fleeing priestly group hid until the crisis was ameliorated.

It was from this land of Cush that Moses, 150 years later, was to take a wife and study under the priesthood of his father-in-law – in an enclave of monotheism. At the time Moses was 'in the land of the Kush', around 1240 BCE, his interaction with the Elephantine

Moses in Cush - of Jesus & the Essenes - but Moses setting up community rather than student of it?

Community would have re-inforced his already established radical ideas of monotheism. When he left Egypt for the last time, leading the Children of Israel toward the Promised Land, Moses perhaps took with him some of the Akhetaten priests and their Hebrew bodyguards. They, in turn, became the natural guardians of the holy treasures, the Ark of the Covenant...and many secrets.

Moses took away with him the fundamental beliefs of Egyptian-Judaism into the desert, and refined and expanded them during the forty years of wandering into the Ten Commandments, and the additional 603 Commandments delineating how a Jew should live and behave. These refinements were unavailable to the Community at Elephantine until they re-established contact with their ancestral compatriots in the Holy Land during the time of the Persian conquests.

Of course, there has to be an element of conjecture in the sequence of events I suggest, but they do fit the known facts more closely than any other theory. They also give an explanation of how the prophets Isaiah and Amos knew – through Moses – about a religious outpost in southern Egypt, especially as there was no contact between that outpost and Israel until the 5th century BCE.

It also neatly explains the strange mystery of why there was a Jewish-style settlement at Elephantine: why, when the Persians conquered Egypt and arrived at Elephantine around 525 BCE, they discovered this peculiar religious Community that worshipped the same invisible God of the Hebrews. They had their own Temple, but followed a quite different form of Judaism to that of Israel. Why they were so wealthy and had been able to furnish their Temple with gold, silver and precious materials. Why they did not appear to have kept the Passover festival or know the Oral Laws or Torah, why their legal, fiscal and social customs were predominantly Egyptian – dating back to at least the time of Akhenaten – and why they communicated in Aramaic and not Hebrew.

The fascinating thing about this lost people is that, when knowledge of their 5th century BCE version of monotheistic Judaism became known to us through the Aramaic papyri, it differed from the mainstream in just the kind of aspects that one would expect had they not to have experienced the post-Egyptian Exodus developments in their beliefs.

Although the Community eventually disappeared from Elephantine Island, a thread of Jewish presence in Egypt continued through to the 13th century CE, as demonstrated in the 'Cairo Genizah' collection, and right up until today.

There remains the knotty question of 'What happened to the Jews of Elephantine after the 5th century BCE?' It is not thought that they were slaughtered by their enemies, but after 410 BCE they were gone. Did they just vanish?

With the return of Egyptian power to the area after Persia's influence waned, perhaps the Community came under threat from the indigenous population. The Egyptians may well have determined to take their revenge on an alien enclave they saw as allied to their previous conquerors – a Community which, moreover, corresponded with foreign cousins in another land. Once before they had sought sanctuary by travelling south. Could it be that the pseudo-Jews of Elephantine now moved even further south for greater safety? I believe the answer is yes, they did.

To the south of the Aswan region, beyond the borders of Egypt, lies more of the Biblical land of 'Cush' or 'Kush', also variously referred to as 'Nubia'. Even further south lies 'Meroe', today's northern Sudan, and 'Abyssinia', today's Ethiopia.

Whether the Community at Elephantine's departure was *force majeure*, or a more controlled retreat, would indicate whether they were obliged to hurriedly hide any remaining treasures of Akhetaten in their possession which were too cumbersome to take with them, or to take everything. If it was the former, further and deeper excavations at the site of the Jewish quarter on Elephantine Island or places previously known to their ancestors – the priests of Akhenaten – are well warranted. The fact that the area has been extensively excavated, particularly by German archaeologists, and has so far revealed nothing of the treasures described in the Copper Scroll does, however, have a positive side to it. It may mean that the remainder of the treasure of the priests of Akhetaten, if their successors still possessed any, travelled with the remnants of the Community when it departed for Ethiopia.

Ark
– Hancock 'Sign + seal'

CUSH AND BEYOND TO LAKE TANA

The small band of travellers who made the long trek, probably took the well-known route following the river valley southward, parallel to the cataract, and rejoined the river at Konosso, from whence navigation further upstream was relatively unimpeded until the second cataract at Wadi Halfa and beyond. Or perhaps they took the long route through the western desert. Eventually, perhaps still carrying their treasure, they would have journeyed through Nubia to Lake Tana, in today's Ethiopia, where their descendants – the Falashas – remained until the 20th century, still practising a form of the Hebrew religion. The island that they colonized, once known as Debra Sehel, is now known as Tana Kirkos.[25]

This is the site where the descendants of the priests of Akhetaten settled and hid their remaining treasures, where their descendants took wives from among the people of Cush and spread their religious customs and wisdom amongst the indigenous population, yet kept themselves apart as a separate foreign 'Falasha' Community.

If this residual Community was a tributary of Akhenatenism that had retreated further up the Nile to Ethiopia, one might expect to find some manifestation of the monotheistic principles that existed at Elephantine carrying on for a period, or even surviving to this day, in the region of Lake Tana. These expectations are not disappointed on either count.

The Community of Lake Tana had similar customs and practices to the pseudo-Jewish Community of Elephantine, reflecting a people who had not participated in the mainstream Judaism of Canaan. They too were devoid of post-Mosaic knowledge, the Oral Laws or knowledge of the significant festivals. Like the Essenes, they did not keep Purim or the ceremonies related to the Dedication of the Temple.

There is to this day a small group of 'Falasha' Ethiopian Jews living in Ethiopia – a residue of the many who have now migrated to modern Israel. They originally lived north of Lake Tana, in the northern part of Ethiopia, near to the Choke Mountains. It is at the very time that the Elephantine Community can no longer be traced that the existence of the Falashas in Ethiopia becomes apparent. Can it really be that the descendants of the priests of the City of Akhetaten, later to be known as 'Amarna', finally settled here? Is it just another coincidence that the area near Lake Tana is today still known by the name 'Amhara'? I don't think so.

We are now, however, taking up the religious and cultural threads of a people that have, I postulate, been twice removed geographically from their original source of inspiration at Akhetaten, in northern Egypt, and 'corrupted' by centuries of overlays of other religions and cultures. If there are any commonalities that are unique to the Falashas, the Elephantine Community and Akhenatenism, and different from the normative Israelite form of Judaism, they will be highly significant and difficult to explain, except as proof of a common religious ancestry.

How this proto-Jewish Community arrived in Ethiopia is, for most historians, still shrouded in mystery. There are three main theories that try to explain their origins and arrival. A measure of how correct these theories are can be gained by assessing how the Judaism of the Falashas differs from normative Judaism, and if those differences exhibited commonalities with Elephantine pseudo-Judaism, with Akhenatenism, and perhaps to the Qumran-Essenes' unique form of Judaism and *its* parallels to Akhenatenism.

The main theories suggest that the Falashas are:

- related to Jews who travelled across from the Yemen or southern Arabia
- related to Jews who travelled up the Nile from Egypt
- descendants from the time of King David, or King Solomon, or King Manasseh.

Yemen and Southern Arabia

Historical evidence makes it reasonably certain that a form of Judaism was fairly widespread in Ethiopia before the coming of Christianity to the country in the 4th century CE. Some authoritative sources[26] put this presence down to the arrival of Jews from southern Arabia sometime after 70 CE, and perceive that the Falashas were there some 2,000 years ago. There is, however, diversity of opinion as to whether the Falashas were Ethiopians 'converted' by diaspora Jews, or the result of assimilation.

Professor Clapham from the University of Lancaster, England, thinks it is extremely doubtful that the Falashas 'can be regarded either as descendants of any part of the Jewish diaspora, or even as authentically Jewish converts'.[27]

The David, Solomon and Manasseh Theories

Some legends speak of Solomon and the Queen of Sheba's son, Prince Menelik, migrating to Ethiopia with a number of Israelites, including priests and Levites, around 900 BCE. At the same time he is said to have surreptitiously removed the Ark of the Covenant and the Tablets of the Law from Jerusalem and brought them to the then capital of Nubia (equatable with Ethiopia), Aksum.

To have removed the sacred objects without anyone noticing, or recording, the event seems rather fanciful. Nevertheless legends of this type invariably contain an element, if only a grain, of truth and this one gives added support to the idea that priests, Levites and Hebrews were amongst the Falashas' ancestors.

There are many other legends, including one that members of the tribes of Dan, Naphtali, Gad and Asher left Israel during the rift between Solomon's son Rehoboam and Jeroboam, and travelled up through Egypt and then into Cush.[28]

Graham Hancock, in his book *The Sign and the Seal*, proposes that the ancestors of the Falashas fled Israel at the time of the 'evil' King Manasseh, *c.*650 BCE, taking the Ark of the Covenant with them, and built a Temple at Elephantine to house the Ark. This, he suggests, they then took with them when they fled again to Ethiopia around 400 BCE. However, the hypothesis is predicated on the idea that Levite priests removed the Ark from the First Temple at Jerusalem in order to avoid it being 'in the same place as the idol Asherah'.[29] The hypothesis becomes very shaky when it is considered that the idol Astarte appeared to be worshipped alongside Yahwe at the Elephantine Temple.

In modern times, the erstwhile leader of Ethiopia, Emperor Haile Selassie, calling himself the 'Lion of Judah', claimed direct descent back to King David. This claim would seem to imply that the Jews had been in Ethiopia for at least 3,000 years!

'Along the Nile' Theories

More concrete reports come from the Greek historians Herodotus, Eratosthenes and Strabo,* who all attest that during the Persian occupation of Egypt a sizeable number of people, probably Aramaen mercenaries, from the area of the Jewish-style settlement at Elephantine, migrated to Ethiopia between 594 and 589 BCE.[30] When the Community at Elephantine finally 'disappeared' around 420 BCE, what would be more natural than that the survivors would follow the path of predecessors (who they may even have kept contact with), to Ethiopia?

These legends, together with references in Isaiah 18:7 and Zephaniah 3:10, tend to confirm that the Falasha Community originated before the Babylonian exile period. Any possibility of the Falashas being part of the 'dispersions' are refuted by the same arguments that I have previously applied to the Assyrian and Babylonian 'dispersion' theories in relation to Elephantine, but even more so because of the added distance.

So here we find a community in Ethiopia, which I surmise was drawn from the most advanced society in the world suddenly transplanted into

* Lived c.485–424 BCE, c.276–194 BCE and 60 BCE–21 CE respectively.

a relatively uncivilized environment. It would not be surprising to find that, with their superior base of knowledge, they would have had a profound effect on the development of Ethiopian society. In fact, one would expect that to be the case, and so it was.

Whilst a caucus of Falasha-Hebrews have remained devoutly faithful to their beliefs through the centuries, their influence on the surrounding 'Amhara' people and their culture led them to dominate the entire country. Their Semitic-based language, which is still spoken by 50 per cent of Ethiopians, became the dominant language of the country.[31] When Christianity finally arrived, in the 4th century, it found Hebrew-type teachings so strongly entrenched in Abyssinian society that it was obliged to adopt many pseudo-Jewish practices. Even today, the Ethiopian Church follows many Judaic customs, including circumcision, a form of Sabbath and dietary laws similar to those in the Torah.

There are, however, many differences in the form of the Judaism practised by the Ethiopian Jews from that practised by mainstream Jews at the time of Kind David (or since), and there are in fact strong links to the type of Judaism prevalent in the Elephantine region. Except for a handful of words the Falashas do not speak Hebrew, but the dialects of their neighbours instead. Their religion is based on an essentially literal observance of the Old Testament injunctions. They do not know anything about post-biblical Hebrew writings.

Their priests read from scriptures written in Old Ethiopic, and offered sacrifices on the Biblical feasts. Like the Qumran-Essenes they did not observe the festivals of Chanukah or Purim. They had no knowledge of Hebrew as a language. Groups of priests lived in monastic communities, observing particularly rigorous purification ceremonies. Ritual washing and immersion was an essential part of the Falasha regime, as was animal sacrifice. Family life was strictly monogamous, and circumcision was performed on male children on the eighth day after birth. Most significantly, wives had equal rights to their husbands in marriage, just as in the Elephantine Community.

The Bible the Falashas now follow was translated not from Hebrew but from a version of the original Greek Septuagint, made about the 5th century CE. It is written in classical old Ethiopian Ge'ez, as are a number of specifically Falasha manuscripts, such as their 'Precepts of the Sabbath' and 'Book of Angels'. They are strongly influenced by the Books of Jubilees and Enoch – books which trace their antecedents back well before the times of King David – and which were also of particular significance for the Qumran-Essenes.

They celebrate a November festival called the 'Seged'. It involves a 'pilgrimage' or processional in which members of the Community carry stones up a hill, as an act of contrition, place them in a circle around the priests and recite prayers. Three times during the day handfuls of seed are placed on the stones to commemorate the dead and for birds to eat. On returning to their 'synagogue' prayers are said over bread and beer.[32]

The festival appears to be quite unique, although one scholar, Shoshana Ben-Dor, relates the 'Seged' to the Atonement Festival performed by the Qumran-Essenes.[33] There is another connection to the Qumran-Essenes which, I believe, may be of significance. In the cemetery at Qumran, at its western extremity, there is a group of three tombs which are different from the other types so far excavated. One of the bodies in these tombs was found to have been buried (unlike all the others at Qumran) in a wooden coffin. The tombs are marked by a 'circle of stones'.[34]

TOMB KV55

This brings me to another mystery worth mentioning at this juncture, related to the body mentioned above buried under the 'circle of stones'.

The body of Akhenaten has never been positively identified, although his fragmented red granite sarcophagus was found at Amarna. A Royal Tomb, cut into the eastern cliffs, had been prepared for him and his wife Nefertiti at Akhetaten, but if it was occupied, their bodies were not found there. Don't worry. I am not going to propose that the body found in the cemetery at Qumran was that of Akhenaten! There was a body in the Royal Tomb at Amarna, but it has been identified as that of one of the King's six daughters, Meketaten, who died at some 12 years of age.

In 1907 a tomb was discovered in the Valley of the Kings, near Thebes, which has caused endless controversy. The tomb, now known as KV55, had been prepared for Tiyi, Akhenaten's mother, but the coffin bore the insignia of Akhenaten. The body in the tomb has proved to be that of a male, aged about 25 – too young to be that of Akhenaten. The general consensus is that this body was that of the transient pharaoh Smenkhkare, Tutankhamun's brother. Without going into the complexities of the arguments, it looks as though someone, probably Tutankhamun, arranged for the bodies of his Royal relatives to be taken from Akhetaten (El-Amarna) and re-interred in a tomb closer to his capital.

When the body in KV55 was discovered, the left arm was bent with the hand on the breast and the right arm was straight with the hand on the thigh.[35] These hand positions were usual for female corpses but not for males. Royal male corpses which are found *in situ* invariably have their hands crossed at the wrists and lying centrally on their chests. I make the observation, and do not profess to have an explanation, but the skeleton found at Qumran under the 'circle of stones' 'was lying on its back, its head to the south, the left hand on the pelvis and the right on the chest'.[36]

What are we to make of the behaviours and beliefs of the Falashas, in the light of my suppositions about their beginnings? Their religious characteristics are a peculiar mixture of selective Judaism, with local Christian descriptive words and pseudo-Egyptian customs. Many of their religious practices are, however, entirely consistent with Akhenatenism:

- monogamy
- equal rights for women
- excessive washing and cleanliness
- circumcision
- ritual immersion
- extreme sabbatical reverence.

And with the practices of the Qumran-Essenes:

- non-observance of Purim and Chanukah[37]
- a unique 'Seged' Festival equatable to the Atonement Festival of the Qumran-Essenes
- their texts refer to the struggle between angels of light and angels of darkness.

Animal sacrifice is the one obvious exception to the teachings of Akhenaten, and one must assume that the misinterpretation arose from the instructions on sacrifice received at Elephantine from Jerusalem in relation to the 'Passover' sacrifice, or from their later readings of the translated Old Testament in the 5th century CE.

Until the arrival of Christianity in Abyssinia in the 4th century, whatever religious books the Falashas possessed would not have referred to anything beyond the time of Moses. This helps to explain why they did not celebrate the Jewish Festivals of Chanukah (the re-dedication of the Second Temple *c.*164 BCE) or Purim (Esther saving the Jews from persecution during the Persian period, pre-330 BCE). They would instantly have recognized the earlier parts of the Bible (the Pentateuch) as being part of their own people's story and would, quite naturally, have adopted a version (translated into Ge-ez), as their own religious template. This they have preserved faithfully up to the present day.

Their own manuscripts, versions of which have survived up to today, are another matter. They might well have originated from an earlier era, prior to any contact with the outside worlds of Christianity or Canaanite Judaism. Their 'Book of Angels' is of particular relevance in this context. It describes the fate of the soul after death when the Angel of Light and the Angel of Death struggle for its possession – themes very reminiscent to the teachings, unique in Jewish experience, to the Essenes but entirely Egyptian in their origin. During prayers, the Falasha priests wave a fly whisk or flail (*nekhakha*), similar to that held by pharaohs as a sign of high office.

The DNA Factor

This, I believe, is one of the most telling pieces of evidence that demonstrates the 'separateness' of the Falashas' form of Judaism, and that they originated from an hereditary lineage quite different from the rest of the Jewish population.

The Ethiopian Jews physically resemble their non-Jewish countrymen, and they practise an unconventional form of Judaism; but through Israel's laws of return they are recognized as Jews, and are entitled to Israeli citizenship. War, famine and oppression in Ethiopia prompted Israel to stage two massive airlifts, in 1984 and 1991, to rescue 50,000 Falasha Jews from Ethiopia and settle them in Israel, leaving only some 100 who did not wish to return. The fairytale soon became tarnished, however, as the new immigrants encountered serious problems in their welfare, treatment and acceptance into Jewish society.

In January 1996 the Hebrew daily newspaper, *Ma'ariv'* reported that blood donated by Falashas had been routinely and secretly destroyed. This disclosure exacerbated an ongoing outcry that the Ethiopian Falashas were not being allowed to integrate into Israeli society. No official explanation was given for the action, until a later investigative report noted that Falashas accounted for more than a third of the 1,386 HIV+ cases identified in Israel up to 1997.[38] In his explanation to the Ethiopians for the non-use of their blood donations, the President of

Israel, Mr Weitzman, made the enigmatic comment, 'They had reasons, harsh, basic reasons.'

It could be that there are other reasons behind the action being taken, and that it is a measure to keep what is conceived of as Jewish and non-Jewish blood from mixing. It has also been the practice for blood from non-Israeli donors to be taken and then to be disposed of, and the State refuses to import blood from other suppliers, such as America. One explanation for the action taken against the Falashas' blood donations could be that it is the genetic difference of the Falashas, revealed by DNA testing, that has caused the authorities to try and keep their blood out of general circulation. The government's Navon Commission, set up to study the problem, recommended a policy which identified blood donors not on the basis of ethnic origin, but on the basis of a series of questions regarding residence in countries where HIV was prevalent.

Genetic evidence does show, however, that the Falashas are different from the Jews of Israel and from those elsewhere in the world. Work on DNA, in Israel, indicates that all groups of Jews throughout the world are genetically connected, except for those from the Yemen – who show similar genetic coding to Arab peoples – the Samaritans, and the Falasha from Ethiopia.[39]

All this lends credence to the previous conclusion, that Ethiopian Jews could not have originated from Jews dispersed subsequent to the exodus from Egypt. In fact, they could well be the direct descendants of the priests of Akhenaten and the ancient Hebrews who did not leave Egypt with Moses, and in some ways have more claim to be the original Jews than any other modern group.

If the Falashas were Holy Land migrant Jews who came from the time of King David, or King Solomon, via Southern Arabia, or down the Nile Valley to Ethiopia, they would not have had different DNA typing, nor would they have followed all the non-mainstream forms of Judaism they practised. They would have had Hebrew as their traditional language, maintained the traditional festivals, known about the Oral Laws, and would not have had affiliations to Akhenatenist ideals.

If the Falashas were ethnic Ethiopians who were converted by Holy Land migrants, the same observations would apply, except that their DNA typing would be different from mainstream Jews.

The histories of the monotheistic communities at Elephantine Island and Lake Tana are further evidence that fundamental Judaistic beliefs came out of Egypt and were later refined into the pure stream of

Judaism. These communities were not re-introduced Jews, who came back into Egypt or Ethiopia at a later date, but were descendants of a residual people left behind at the Exodus. They did not follow the beliefs that Moses can only have taught the Hebrews after the Exodus.

The Prophet Hosea talks about God's dissatisfaction with the Children of Israel, when they do not follow his Commandments:

> *'How can I give you up, O Ephraim?*
> *How surrender you, O Israel?*
> *How can I make you like Admah?*
> *Render you like Zeboim?*
> *I have had a change of heart.*
> *All my tenderness is stirred.'*
>
> [Hosea 11:8]

Ephraim is the younger son of Joseph.

> *'I the Lord have been your God*
> *Ever since the land of Egypt.*
> *I will let you dwell in your tents again*
> *As in the days of old.'*
>
> [Hosea 12:10]

Hosea therefore confirms that the progeny of Joseph are his 'special' people, and the time that the beginning of God's special relationship commences is not, as referred to in previous books of the Old Testament, in the time of Abraham, but 'ever since the land of Egypt'.

There is indeed a reference to the Ethiopian Jewish settlement by the Prophet Amos in the Old Testament, which dates the settlement to pre-Diaspora times. Amos lived from approximately 783 to 743 BCE and wrote:

> 'Are ye not as children of the Cushites [Ethiopians] unto me, O
> children of Israel?' saith the Lord. 'Have not I brought up Israel out of
> the land of Egypt? and the Philistines from Caphtor, and the Syrians
> from Kir?'
>
> [Amos 9:7]

Cush (Ethiopia) also finds mention in a number of Psalms, including Psalm 68 and 87, both of the early Biblical period: 'Princes shall come

out of Egypt; Ethiopia shall soon stretch out her hands unto God.'
(Psalm 68:31, from the Authorized Version of the Bible.)

Both these Psalms are attributed to be of the earliest date and pre-
Exilic times, and Psalm 68 is considered one of the oldest known
psalms.

The lifeline of the Akhetaten priests which runs through the history of
Judaism, on into Christianity and Islam, explains so many puzzles in
the Biblical texts and in religious behaviours that its essential truth is
hard to discount. Many of these puzzles have been discussed in this
book, others remain for the reader and others to consider and resolve.

The place the predecessors of the Falasha people originally sought
out, from the myriad of havens they might have chosen, was not, I
believe, a random choice. They settled on the shores of Lake Tana,
in complete isolation, close to an abundance of water. Water in large
quantities was a vital requirement for their frequent ritual immersions –
as it had been on the Island of Elephantine – as it had been at
Akhetaten on the shores of the Nile – as it was on the shores of the
Dead Sea at Qumran – the place where a quirk of fate had left hidden
for 2,000 years one of the oldest and strangest relics of our time – the
Copper Scroll – the key to unlocking so many mysteries.

A SEURAT[40] OF POINTS TO COMPLETE THE PICTURE

In retrospect it might be said that the examples of correlation between
Egyptian experience and Biblical scriptures have been carefully selected
to fit the 'Proposition' that Egypt and Egyptian religious/cultural ideals
have had a more profound effect on the Old (and to a lesser extent) the
New Testaments, than any other country or culture. More effect than
contemporary commentators care to admit. The 'Proposition' is that
those ideals were the result of development and refinement over thousands of years in the white hot furnace of Egyptian civilization, and
which reached their peak in the time of the 18th Dynasty. During that
period, Akhenaten took the essential wisdoms of his country's religious
philosophies and distilled them into a defined belief in one God, to the
exclusion of all others. A century and a half later, Moses, imbued with
the same belief, brought out from Egypt not just the Children of Israel,
but the fundamental ideals of monotheism as well.

It is certainly the case, as we have seen, that the Bible has borrowed
from the mythologies of Sumerian, Mesopotamian and other Eastern

cultures, but the correlations tend to be weaker in content, and limited to the very early parts of the Old Testament. This is exactly as one would expect. The pre-1500 BCE myths and experiences, garnered from the regions of the rivers Tigris and Euphrates, feature less and less as the recollections of Abraham's clan become increasingly more vague in the process of being handed down from generation to generation.

The points of correlation with Egypt do not need probing selection. They are on record in prolific profusion. Most of the points of non-correlation with the Bible have been omitted because they are inconsistent with the overall progression of monotheism, are cluttered by complex idolatry, do not contribute to a progressive representation of man's struggle towards God, or are plainly pornographic in modern terms.

However, the points of correlation have, I believe, undoubtedly coloured the Biblical stories from those of creation onwards, and are far too numerous to be put down to mere coincidence. The consequential deductions answer many previous conundrums in the Bible. For these combined reasons the points of correlation, which together form a Seurat-like pointillistic picture, create an overall coherent feeling of veracity, which in itself is far more convincing than the sum of the individual points.

I believe these deductions justify a re-appraisal of how the roots of monotheism were originally nurtured, and how they relate to views currently held by Judaism, Christianity and Islam. The links that have been drawn and which are self-evident between the three great monotheistic religions, are profound, forming chains that unite their adherents together as true brothers and sisters – bonds far stronger than any of their differences.

Apart from the potential 'literary' gains that come from the golden era of the 18th Dynasty of Egyptian pharaohs, there are potential religious and social gains.

- The enactment, or contemplation, of any form of animal sacrifice is to be rejected.
- All forms of superstition and magic, verbalizations or emblems attached to religious beliefs are to be rejected.
- Monogamy and familial affection are ideals to be striven for.
- Complete female emancipation and equality in religious, domestic and social matters is an ideal to be striven for.

Another conclusion, perhaps the most important of all, to be drawn from the accounts I have portrayed in this book, is that they tie in early Biblical personalities to real, historical people and events.

There is almost no textual, archaeological or comparative evidence that has been found to date that verifies the existence of the main Biblical characters and their stories, prior to the 10th century BCE. Dame Kathleen Kenyon, a pre-eminent archaeologist who made a special study of the subject, concluded:

> there are virtually no extra-Biblical texts of sufficient direct relevance to
> test the Old Testament's value as a reliable historical source in the
> period before about 900 BCE, the opening of the Divided Monarchy.[41]

A view, not untypical of many historians, was recently expressed by Thomas Thompson, Professor of Old Testament Studies at Copenhagen University, who cannot find any Biblical fact before 300 BCE.[42]

My 'linkages' give historical credence to Biblical characters as far back as Joseph and Jacob, and give the story of Moses a real historical setting.

Whenever and wherever Jews, Christians or Muslims gather to pray, in groups or alone, from time immemorial, a word is intoned whose Hebrew root also gives rise to the words 'faith' and 'faithfulness'. Could it be that the word also recalls the name of the prime mover of these three great world religions: Akhenaten – known as Amenhotep IV – and only to his intimate close circle as Amen-hetep-neter-heqa-Uast?[43]

Amen.

APPENDIX

The following translation of the Copper Scroll is from *The Treasure of the Copper Scroll* by John Marco Allegro (Routledge & Kegan Paul, 1960), reproduced with the kind permission of Mrs Joan R. Allegro.

COLUMN I

COLUMN I

line transcription

1. bḥrwbh šb'mq 'kwr tḥt
2. hm'lwt hbw't lmzrḥ 'mwt
3. 'rwḥ 'rb'yn šdt ksp wklyh
4. mšql kkryn šb' (')śrh   KεN

5. bnpš bndbk hšlyšy 'štwt
6a. zhb zll . . .

6b.   bbwr hgdwl šbḥṣr
7. hyrsṭlwn bzrb qrq'w stwm bḥl'
8. ngd hptḥ h'lywn kkryn tš' m't

9. bḥl šl bḥlh kly dm' blgyn w'pwryn
10. hkl šl hdm' wh'ṣr hšbw' wm'sr
11. šny mpyt lptḥ wbšwly h'm' mn hṣpwṅ
12. 'mwt šš 'd nyqrt hṭbwl   XAΓ

13. bśy' hmsb' šl mns byrk' lsml
14. gbh mn hqrq' 'mwt šlwš[k]sp 'rb'yṅ
15. [ ]kkr

translation

ITEM 1. In the fortress which is in the Vale of Achor, forty cubits under the steps entering to the east: a money chest and its contents, of a weight of seventeen talents. KεN

ITEM 2. In the sepulchral monument, in the third course of stones: - light bars of gold.

ITEM 3. In the Great Cistern which is in the Court of the Peristyle, in the plaster of its floor, concealed in a hole in front of the upper opening: nine hundred talents.

ITEM 4. In the trough (?) of the Place of the Basin (?): tithe vessels, consisting of *lôg* vessels and amphorae, all of tithe and stored Seventh-Year produce and Second Tithe, from (the) mouths to the opening, and in the bottom of the water conduit, six cubits from the north towards the hewn immersion pool. XAΓ

ITEM 5. In the ascent of the Staircase of Refuge, in the left-hand side, three cubits up from the floor: forty talents of [sil]ver.

נכורחבלי חאתח ת חבעלות

בלרן 33 וי   מא

בבצלתבית דכלי חחוצ ולרונר

חשלעצרית וחב אצין חכלא ۳۵

בצליחאנ חצל בת וחעצין וכתבו

גב בצבין וכסף נכלין שבעין

נבוי שער חשע צ חבורחו

רחוף אמית חשע גרא בולין

יבמוקא אבננברן עסר יא

נבר ש מתתחו ב אבן חבזוח

בצן חסלעבריצאלנסף פ ۴

מאות זוחחחסןחחדריל

כ כרב שנכזר חנחלת בלבקצע

חצפונחבור אצח שפ ארבע

בנויאגן

Right margin column:

רתחח
חאבית
ולליח
אא
שתיות
נקיער
תנ מבוא
וח שצלבאמד
בל בון שמאא
ולעובצעבר
יכואב ודצב ן
ול
XA
ובציא לסבל
שקן אלבצי

Left margin column:

בו
בותאב
דבעבז
קסאור
תחת
יתחפז
נבגג
בשות
ללור
תח
בקו
פצע
תשז

COLUMN II

COLUMN II

line transcription

1. bbwr hmlḥ štḥt hmꜥlwt
2. kkryn 42   HN

3. bmꜥrt byt hmdh hyšn brwbd
4. hšlšyl ꜥštwt zhb ššyn wḥmš   Θε

5. bṣryḥ šbḥṣr mtwḥ ꜥsyn ubtkw
6. bꜥ m꜠blyn wksp kkryn šbꜥyn

7. bbwr šngd hšꜥr hmzrḥy
8. rḥwq ꜐mwt tšꜥ (꜐)sr꜐ bw klyn
9. wb(꜐)mwq꜐ šbw kkryn ꜥsr   ΔI

10. bbwr š꜐ꜝt hḥwm꜐ mn hmzrḥ
11. bšn hslꜥ kdyn šl ksp šš
12. m꜐wt wtḥt hsp hgdwl

13. bbrk꜐ šbmzrḥ bḥlh bmqṣ꜐
14. hṣpwny hpwr ꜐mh syṭ ꜐rbꜥ
15. kkryn 22.

translation

ITEM 6. In the salt pit which is under the steps: 42 talents. HN

ITEM 7. In the cavity of the Old House of Tribute, in the Platform of the Chain: sixty-five bars of gold. Θε

ITEM 8. In the underground passage which is in The Court: a wooden barrel (?) and inside it a *bath* measure of untithed goods and seventy talents of silver.

ITEM 9. In the cistern which is nineteen cubits in front of the eastern gateway, in it are vessels, and in the hollow that is in it: ten talents. ΔI

ITEM 10. In the cistern that is under the wall on the east, in a spur of rock: six hundred pitchers of silver (and under the Great Threshold).

ITEM 11. In the pool which is in the east, in a hole in the northern corner, buried at one cubit: four *sȋṭ's*: 22 talents.

COLUMN III

COLUMN III

line transcription

1. bḥ[. . .]ẽ tḥt hpn' hdrw
2. myt 'mwt ẽš' kly ksp wzhb šl
3. dm' mzrqwt kwswt mnqy'wt
4. qs'wt kl šš m'wt wtš'h

5. tḥt hpn' h'ḥrt hmzrḥ
6. yt ḥpr 'mwt šš 'srh ksp
7. kk 40   TP

8. bšyt šbmlḥm bṣpwnw
9. kly dm wlbwhšyñ by't'
10. tḥt hpn' hm'rbyt

11. bqbr šbmlḥm byrydw
12. bṣpwn 'mwt tḥt hm
13. t šlwš kk 13+

translation

ITEM 12. In the C[ourt of (?) . . .], nine cubits under the southern corner: gold and silver vessels for tithe, sprinkling basins, cups, sacrificial bowls, libation vessels, in all six hundred and nine.

ITEM 13. Under the other, eastern corner, buried at sixteen cubits: 40 talents of silver.   TP

ITEM 14. In the pit (?) which is in (the) MLHM, in its north: tithe vessels and garments. Its entrance is under the western corner.

ITEM 15. In the tomb which is in the MLHM, in its shaft in the north, three cubits under the corpse: 13+ talents.

COLUMN IV

COLUMN IV

line transcription	translation

line transcription

1. bbwr hg̊d̊[wl (?) . . . b]l̊ḥ̊lh b'mwd
2. bṣpwnw kk[. . .]　ΣK

3. b'm' hb' [h (?) . . .] bby'tk
4. 'mwt 'rb['. . .] ksp
5. kk 40 (?) [. . . b]s̊̊d'

6. byn šny hbdyn šb'mq 'kwn
7. b'ms'n ḥpwn 'mwt šlwš
8. šm šny dwdyn ml'yn ksp

9. bšyḥ h'dm' šbšwly h'ṣ
10. l' ksp kk m'tyn

11. bšyḥ hmzrḥyt šbṣpwn bḥ
12. lh ksp kk šb'yn

13. bygr šl gy hskk' ḥpwr
14. 'mh ksp kk[. . .] 3+

translation

ITEM 16. In the Gr[eat] Cistern, [. . . in] a hole (?) in a pillar in its north: [. . .] talents. ΣK

ITEM 17. In the water conduit which en[ters (?) . . .] as you go in four [. . .] cubits [. . .] 40 (?) talents of silver [in a] chest(?).

ITEM 18. Between the two oil-presses (?) that are in the Vale of Achor, midway between them, buried at three cubits, (hidden) there are two pots filled with silver.

ITEM 19. In the clay pit which is in the bottom of the wine-press: two hundred talents of silver.

ITEM 20. In the eastern pit which is in the north, in a hole: seventy talents of silver.

ITEM 21. In the dam-sluice (?) of the Valley of Secacah, buried at one cubit: [. . .] 3+ talents of silver.

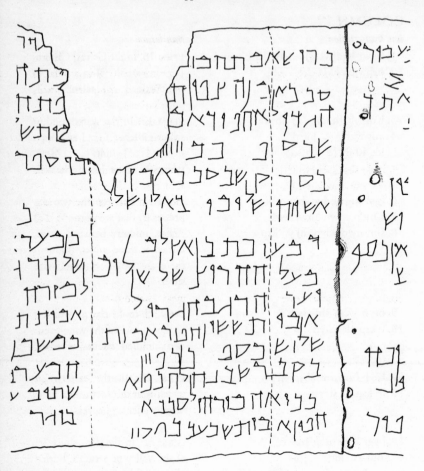

COLUMN V

COLUMN V

line transcription

1. brwš 'mt hmyr̊n [hb'h (?)]
2. skk' mn hṣpwn t[ḥt hym' (?)]
3. hgdwl' ḥpwr 'm[wt šlw (?)]
4. š ksp kk 7

5. bsdq šbskk' bzr̊[b (?)]
6. 'šwḥ šlwmw k'lyn šl
7. dm' wbtkn 'ṣlm

8. m'l hḥrwṣ šl šlwm
9. w'd hrgb hgdwl
10. 'mwt ššyn ḥpwr 'mwt
11. šlwš ksp kk 13

12. bqbr šbnḥl hkp'
13. bby' hmzrḥy lskk'
14. ḥpwn 'mwt šb' kk 32.

translation

ITEM 22. At the head of the water conduit [which penetrates (?)] Secacah from the north, buried u[nder (?)] the great [settling basin (?)] at t[hree (?) cu]bits: 7 talents of silver.

ITEM 23. In the fissure that is in Secacah, in the pla[ster (?)] of the "Solomon reservoir": tithe vessels and in them figured coins.

ITEM 24. Sixty cubits from the "Solomon trench" towards the great watchtower, buried at three cubits: 13 talents of silver.

ITEM 25. In the tomb which is in the Wady *Kippā'*, in the eastern road to Secacah, buried at seven cubits: 32 talents.

COLUMN VI

COLUMN VI

line transcription

1. [bm]ʿı̊t hʿmwd šl šny
2. [h]ptḥyṅ ṣwpʾ mzrḥ
3. [b] ptḥ hṣpwny ḥpwr
4. [ʾ]mwt šlwš šm qll
5. bw spr ʾḥd tḥtw
6. kk 42

7. bmʿrʾ šl hpnʾ
8. šl hrgb hṣwpʾ
9. lmzrḥ ḥpr bptḥ
10. ʾmwt tšʿ kk 21

11. bmškn hmlkʾ bṣd
12. hmʿrby ḥpr ʾmwt
13. štym ʿsrh kk 9

14. bygr šbmgzt hkwhn

translation

ITEM 26. [In the inner cha]mber of the platform of the Double Gate, facing east, [in] the northern entrance, buried at three [cu]bits, (hidden) there is a pitcher; in it, one scroll, under it 42 talents.

ITEM 27. In the inner chamber of the corner of the watchtower that faces east, buried in the entrance at nine cubits: 21 talents.

ITEM 28. In the Tomb (?) of the Queen, in the western side, buried at twelve cubits: 9 talents.

ITEM 29. In the dam-sluice (?) which is in the Bridge of

COLUMN VII

PLATE 1

Above View of Qumran, looking out towards the Dead Sea. ©*Robert Feather*

Below Aerial view of the ruins at Qumran. ©*Chris Bradley/Axiom*

Left Henri de Contenson, leader of the archaeological team that found the Copper Scroll in a cave overlooking Qumran, in 1952. © *Robert Feather*

Right The Copper Scroll, restored by Electricité de France, Paris, as it would have appeared in its original engraved form. © *Robert Feather*

Below The Copper Scroll being examined by John Marco Allegro at Manchester College of Technology, shortly after the scroll's opening in 1955, showing sections 1–15. *Reproduced courtesy of the Manchester Museum, The University of Manchester.* © *Estate of John M. Allegro*

PLATE 3

Part of the Rhind Mathematical Papyrus, discovered at Thebes and dated to c.1550 BCE, showing a numbering system similar to that used in the Copper Scroll. **Right** An example of the ancient Egyptian numbering system, showing that the symbols for 1 and 10 are identical to those used in Column 6 **(below right)** and elsewhere in the Copper Scroll. ©The British Museum

1	l
10	∩
100	
1000	
10,000	
100,000	
1,000,000 (often meaning 'more than I can count')	

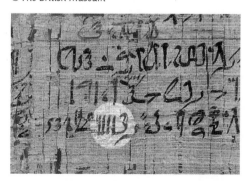

PLATE 4

Pictures of circumcised penises found on inscriptions from Ancient Egypt

Above Detail from an inscription on the east wall of the Tomb of Nefer-Seshem-Ptah at Saqqara. *From 'Une Rue de Tombeaux a Saqqarah, Volume II' by Jean Capart, Vromont & Co. Brussels, 1907. Reproduced courtesy of The Egypt Exploration Society*

Left Priest circumcising a boy, shown in a relief from the mastaba tomb of Ankhmahor, at Saqqara, dated to the 6th Dynasty *c.*2300 BCE. *© Werner Forman Archive*

Below Meatus dating to *c.*1300 BCE found at El-Amarna. *From 'The Royal Tomb at El-Amarna, Part 7' by Geoffrey Thorndike Martin 1974. Reproduced courtesy of The Egypt Exploration Society*

PLATE 5

The Osiris mythology, showing Osiris attended by his wife Isis and son Horus. From a piece of jewellery made for Pharaoh Osorkon II, c.860 BCE. Now in the Louvre Museum. © Ronald Sheriden/Ancient Art & Architecture Collection

PLATE 6

Examples of statues showing the facial features of Amenhotep IV and Queen Nefertiti.

Above left Colossal statue of Akhenaten. Now in the Cairo Museum. ©*Werner Forman Archive*

Above Colossal statue of Akhenaten from the Temple at Karnak, now in the Cairo Museum. ©*Robert Partridge/The Ancient Egypt Picture Library*

Left Akhenaten kisses his daughter. Now in the Cairo Museum. ©*Werner Forman Archive*

PLATE 7

Above Nefertiti, Akhenaten's wife, wearing a curled wig and diadem with uraeus, kissing her eldest daughter Meritaten. From a limestone block found at Hermopolis and now in the Brooklyn Museum. © *Werner Forman Archive*

Right Painted limestone bust of Nefertiti. Thought to have been created by Thothmes at Akhetaten. Now in the Berlin Museum. © *John Stevens/Ancient Art & Architecture Collection*

PLATE 8

Left Amenhotep II. ©*Robert Partridge/The Ancient Egypt Picture Library*

Right The only known example of an ancient Egyptian portable chest. Measuring 83cm long, 60.5cm wide and 63.5cm high. It was found on the floor of the antechamber of the tomb of Tutankhamun, discovered in 1922 in the Valley of the Kings, Luxor, Egypt. Now in the possession of the Department of Antiquities, Cairo.

Below The throne chair of Tutankhamun showing him and his wife Ankhesenpaten with the Aten disc. Now in the Egyptian Museum, Cairo. ©*John G. Ross/Egypt Mediterranean Picture Archive*

PLATE 9

Top right Lotiform 'Wishing' chalice, measuring 18cm in height, carved from a single block of alabaster. The lotus bloom has 16 ovoid petals and four ovoid sepals, with supports of single blue lilies.

Above right Triple lotus oil lamp, 27cm in height, carved from a single block of calcite (alabaster).

All reproduced courtesy of The Griffith Institute, Ashmolean Museum, Oxford

Below Example of 'protective wings' used in Egyptian design found, for example, on the canopic chest of Akhenaten and in the tomb of Tutankhamun. ©*James Morris/Axiom*

PLATE 10

Left Jozef Milik, leader of the translation team at the École Biblique, Jerusalem. He was the first person to publish a translation, in French, in 1959 of the Copper Scroll. ©*Robert Feather*

Below View of hills immediately behind Qumran. From Robert Eisenman and Michael Wise's 1992 book, *The Dead Sea Scrolls Uncovered.* ©*Robert Eisenman. Reproduced courtesy of Element Books*

PLATE 11

Right The Shawabty figure of Meryra, High Priest of Aten. Now in The Metropolitan Museum of Art, New York. *© The Metropolitan Museum of Art, Rogers Fund, 1944 (44.4.71)*

Below Treasure jar found in the remains of a building on the 'Crock of Gold Square' at El-Amarna immediately after being opened. *From 'The City of Akhenaten, Part 2' by H. Frankfort and J. Pendlebury. Reproduced courtesy of The Egypt Exploration Society*

PLATE 12

PLATE 13

Above Archaeological sites in the Saqqara burial district, with the step pyramid of Djoser (*c.*2650 BCE) in the foreground. © *Gwil Owen*

Opposite Site of the Great Temple at El–Amarna, ancient Akhetaten. Showing outline perimeter of the temple and courtyard areas. © *Gwil Owen*

Below The Sun Temple at Abu Gurab, Egypt, built by King Nyuserra (2445–2421 BCE). In the centre of the altar is a massive alabaster circular slab surrounded by four offering tables. © *Dr Paul T. Nicolson F.R.G.S*

PLATE 14

Left Two gold signet rings from Hagg Quandil, El-Amarna, now in the City of Liverpool Museum, England. One depicts 'Bes', the family protector, between two 'life' 'ankh' signs; the other a dancing lion with a tambourine. *Reproduced courtesy of National Museums & Galleries on Merseyside, Liverpool Museum*

Below and Opposite Jewellery from Hagg Quandil, El-Amarna, now in the Royal Museum of Scotland. © *The Trustees of the National Museums of Scotland 1999*

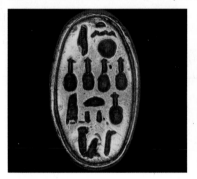

a) Gold signet ring incised with the name Nefertiti.

b) Gold ear stud decorated with herringbone and scroll pattern.

c) Finger ring in gold with bezel shaped as a 'wadjet' protective 'eye'.

d) Finger ring in gold with swivelling bezel in the shape of a frog.

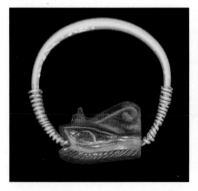

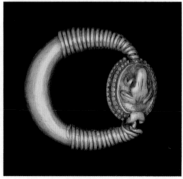

PLATE 15

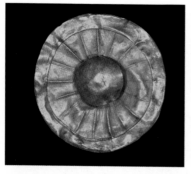

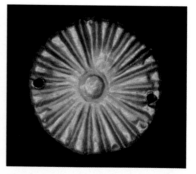

e) Gold ear stud in the form of a roundel with marguerite-shaped boss.

f) Gold sequin in the shape of a marguerite.

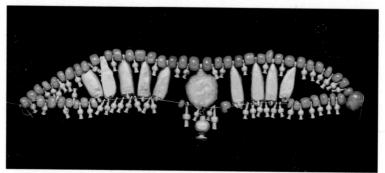

g) Necklace or collar comprising gold convex disc and chevron decoration below, with nine husk-shaped pendants looped above and below, 53 gold pomegranate beads and large gold drop bead attached by copper wire.

h) Gold spacer bead or fastener.

i) Gold ear stud.

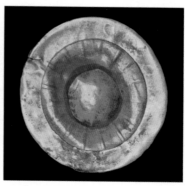

PLATE 16

View of Elephantine Island, in Southern Egypt. ©*Ronald Sheriden/The Ancient Art*
& Architecture Collection

COLUMN VII

line transcription

1. hgdwl h[. . .]
2. tš' k[k . . .]

3. b'm' šl [. . .]
4. h'šwḥ ḥṣpw[ny (?) . . .]
5. b'rb' dwdẏ[n (?) . . . lsm (?)]ẇlẇ
6. mšḥ 'mwt 'sṙyn[syṭ 'r(?)]b'
7. kkryn 'rb' m'wt

8. bm'r' š'ṣl hmqṙ[t (?)] šl
9. byt hqṣ ḥpwr 'mwt šš
10. kdyn šl ksp šš

11. bryq ṭḥt pnt hmšṭḥ
12. hmzrḥyt ḥpwr 'mwt šb'
13. kk 22

14. 'l py yṣy't hmym šl hby
15. b' ḥpwr 'mwt šlwš 'd ḥṭyp
16. kk 80 zhb bkdyn štym

translation

the High Priest that [. . .] nine [. . .] tal[ents . . .]

ITEM 30. In the water conduit of [. . .] the north[ern] reservoir [. . .] in four po[ts (?) . . . to its l]eft (?), a distance of twenty cubits fo[ur *sit's* (?)] four hundred talents [. . .]

ITEM 31. In the inner chamber which is adjacent to the cool room of the Summer House, buried at six cubits: six pitchers of silver.

ITEM 32. In an empty space under the eastern corner of the spreading platform, buried at seven cubits: 22 talents.

ITEM 33. By the mouth of the water outlet of the drain pipe, buried three cubits towards the overflow tank: 80 talents of gold in two pitchers.

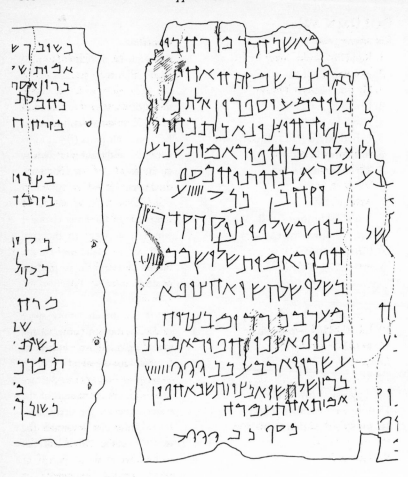

COLUMN VIII

COLUMN VIII

line transcription

1. [bby(?)]b' šbdrk mżrḥ by [t]
2. 'wṣr šmyd h'twn
3. kly dm' wspryn 'l hklyṅ

4. bgy hḥyṣwn' btk hdṙ
5. 'l h'bn ḥpwr 'mwt šb'
6. 'sr' tḥtyh ksp
7. wzhb kk 17

8. bygr šl pyswq hqdrwn
9. ḥywr 'mwt šlwš kk 7

10. bšly šl hšw' hṣwp'
11. m'rb bdrwm bṣryḥ
12. hṣwp ṣpwn ḥpwr 'mwt
13. 'sryn 'rb' kk 67

14. bryw(?) šl hšw' bṣẙh šb' ḥpwn
15. 'mwt 'ḥt 'srh
16. ksp kk 70

translation

ITEM 34. In the [drain]pipe (?) which is in the eastern path to the [T]reasury, which is beside the Entrance: tithe jars and scrolls in amongst the jars.

ITEM 35. In the Outer Valley, in the middle of the Circle-on-the-Stone, buried at seventeen cubits beneath it: 17 talents of silver and gold.

ITEM 36. In the dam-sluice (?) of the mouth of the Kidron gorge, buried at three cubits: 7 talents.

ITEM 37. In the stubble field of the Shaveh, facing south-west, in an underground passage looking north, buried at twenty-four cubits: 67 talents.

ITEM 38. In the irrigation cistern (?) of the Shaveh, in the outlet that is in it, buried at eleven cubits: 70 talents of silver.

COLUMN IX

COLUMN IX

line transcription	*translation*
1. bšwbk šbšwly hnṭp mšḥ mšwlw	ITEM 39. In the gutter (?) which
2. 'mwt šlwš w'štyn ḥywrwrwt bšy̆'h šb'	is in the bottom of the (rain-
3. bryn 'ystryn 'rb'	water) tank, buried at a distance
	of three cubits and two (*sit's* (?))
	from its bottom, in the plaster
	lining the sides: four staters.
4. bḥblh hšnyt bṣryḥ ḥṣwp'	ITEM 40. In the Second Enclo-
5. mzrḥ ḥpwn 'mwt šmwn'	sure, in the underground passage
6. wmḥṣ' kk 24	that looks east, buried at eight
	and a half cubits: 24 talents.
7. bṣryḥy hḥwryn b(ṣ?)ryḥ ḥṣwp' dr̆wm	ITEM 41. In the underground
8. bzrb ḥpwr 'mwt šš 'srh	passages of The Holes, in the
9. kk 22	passage looking south, buried in
	the plaster at sixteen cubits: 22
	talents.
10. bqym'h ksp mn hḥrm	ITEM 42. In the "funnel": silver
	from the consecrated offerings.
11. bqyl hmym hqrybyn lkp hbyb	ITEM 43. In the pipe of waters
12. mrḥb lpyhm ḥpwr 'mwt	that run to the basin of the
13. šb' kk 9	drain, buried seven cubits from
	the wide part towards their
	mouth: 9 talents
14. bšyt šybṣpwn py ḥṣwq šl byt	ITEM 44. In the sepulchre (?)
15. tmr bṣy't gy pl'	that is in the north, at the
16. blškh ḥrm	mouth of the gorge of the Place
	of the Palms, at the outlet of the
	Valley of PL', all in it are conse-
	crated offerings.
17. bšwbk šbmṣdn' ptḥ	ITEM 45. In the gutter (?) that
	is in the Stronghold of Senaah
	(?), opening to the south, in

COLUMN X

COLUMN X

line transcription

1. drwm bʿlyʾh hšnyt yrydtw
2. mlmʿlʾ kk 9

3. bbwr gy (ʿ)mwqwt šrwy mhnḥl
4. hgdwl bqrqʿw kk 12

5. bʾšwḥ šybyt hkrm kbwʾk
6. lsmwlw ʾmwt ʿsr ksp
7. kkryn ššyn wšnyn

8. bym šl gy żyṫ bṣdw hmʿṫby
9. ʾbn šḥwryt ʾmwt štyn
10. hy hptḥ kkrýn šlš mʾwt
11. zhb wklyn kwpryn ʿsrh

12. tḥt yd ʾbšlwm mn hṣd
13. hmʿrby ḥpwr ʾmwt štyn ʿsrh
14. kk 80

15. bym byt hmym šl żḥyl tḥt
16. hšqṫ kk 17

17. [. . .]ḥ bʾrbʿt

translation

the second storey as it runs down from above: 9 talents.

ITEM 46. In the cistern of the Ravine of the Deeps which is fed from the Great Wady, in its floor: 12 talents.

ITEM 47. In the reservoir which is in Beth Kerem, ten cubits on its left as you enter: sixty-two talents of silver.

ITEM 48. In the vat of the olive press (?), in its western side, a plug-stone of two cubits (it is the opening): three hundred talents of gold and ten serving vessels.

ITEM 49. Under the Monument of Absalom, on the western side, buried at twelve cubits: 80 talents.

ITEM 50. In the settling tank of the Bathhouse of running water (?), under the gutter: 17 talents.

ITEM 51. [In the . . .], in its four inner corner buttresses:

COLUMN XI

COLUMN XI

line transcription	*translation*

1. mqṣwʿwtyh bkly dmʿ btkn ʾṣlm

tithe vessels, (and) inside them figured coins.

2. mtḥt pnt hʾsṭʾn hdrwmyt
3. bqbr ṣdwq tḥt ʿmwd hʾksdrn
4. kly dmʿ syḥ dmʿ snh (w?)btkn ʾṣlm

ITEM 52. Below the Portico's southern corner, in the Tomb of Zadok, under the platform of the exedra: vessels for tithe sweepings, spoilt tithes, (and) inside them, figured coins.

5. bʾksdrʾ š(l) hslʿ hṣwpʾ mʿrb
6. ngd gnt ṣdwq tḥt hmsmʾh
7. gdwlʾ šbšwlyhy ḥrm b-

ITEM 53. In the exedra of the cliff facing west, in front of the Garden of Zadok, under the great sealing-stone that is in its bottom; consecrated offerings. In-

8. bqbr štḥt hspyn kk 40

ITEM 54. In the grave which is under the paving stones: 40 talents.

9. bqbr bny hʿm ṭhwr ḥw
10. bw kly dmʿ ʾw dmʿ syḥ
11. btkn ʾṣln

ITEM 55. In the grave of the common people who (died) absolved from their purity regulations: vessels for tithe or tithe refuse, (and) inside them, figured coins.

12. bbyt ʾšwḥyn bʾšwḥ
13. bbyʾtk lw mymwt
14. šlw kly dm (ʿ) lʾḥ dmʿ swrʾ
15. btkn ʾṣln

ITEM 56. In the House of the (Two ?) Pools, in the pool as you enter it from its settling-basins: vessels for liquid tithe, degenerated tithe, (and) inside them, figured coins.

16. bmkʾrw[t] ḇyt hmškb hmʿrby
17. ṭwp ʿl[. . . kkryn (?)] ṱšʾ mʾwt

ITEM 57. In the hewn chambers of the western tomb, scattered over [. . . n]ine hundred [talents of] gold; in jug-

COLUMN XII

COLUMN XII

line transcription

1. zhb b̊k̊ẘz̊ẙn̊ kkryn ššyn by'tw mn hm(')rb
2. ṭḥt h'bn hšḥwrẙ' kwzyn ṭḥt sp
3. hkwk kkryn 42

4. bhr gryzyn ṭḥt hm'lt' šl hšyḥ h'lywn'
5. šd' 'ḥt wkl klyh wksp kk 60

6. bpy hmbw' šl byt šm kl(y) ksp wkly zhb
7. šl dm' wksp hkl kkryn šš m'wt

8. bbyb' hgdwl' šl hbzk kl(y) byt hbzk
9. hkl mšql kkryn 71 mnyn 'sryn

10. bšyt škynh bspwn bḥlh ptḥh spwn
11. wqbryn 'l pyh mšnh hktb hzh
12. wprwš wmšḥwtyhm wpryṭ kl
13. 'ḥd w'ḥ[r]

translation

lets, sixty talents. Its entrance is from the west. Under the blocking-stone are juglets. Under the sill of the tomb chamber are 42 talents.

ITEM 58. In Mount Gerizim, under the entrance of the upper pit: one chest and its contents, and 60 talents of silver.

ITEM 59. In the mouth of the spring of the Temple: vessels of silver and vessels of gold for tithe and money, the whole being six hundred talents.

ITEM 60. In the Great Drain of the Basin: instruments of the House of the Basin, the whole being of a weight of 71 talents, twenty minas.

ITEM 61. In the Pit (*Shīth*) adjoining on the north, in a hole opening northwards, and buried at its mouth: a copy of this document, with an explanation and their measurements, and an inventory of each thing, and oth[er things].

230 CASH-1   2065 0102 002

COPPER SCROLL DECO   1   8.99
                    TOTAL   8.99

    Cash   20.00
              CHANGE   11.01

                        5/07/01 17.21

CHAPTER NOTES

CHAPTER 1   The Copper Scroll – Two Thousand Years in Hiding

1. Some definitions of the term 'Dead Sea Scrolls' use it in a general sense, meaning any scrolls found along the shores of the Dead Sea or even relating to them. In this book the term 'Dead Sea Scrolls' applies specifically to those discovered between 1947 and 1956 in the 11 caves near to Qumran on the Dead Sea.

2. Scorification is a refining process which removes impurities from metals. It is usually applied to the purification of copper, gold and silver ore and involves mixing the impure ore with granulated lead and borax as a flux. The mixture is heated in a muffle furnace to volatilize low melting point impurities and to combine the rest with lead oxide and borax to form an easily removable slag.

3. My last publishing venture involved the purchase of an old Robert Maxwell company, which published magazines on chess and bridge!

4. Mohammed edh-Dhib and his brother, Bedouin from the Taamirek tribe, were searching for two lost black-haired goats in the hills that run along the shores of the Dead Sea. Climbing up the lower slopes of a hillside they entered a dark musty cave and stumbled against a pile of sherds, around which lay clay pots, pieces of leather and some jars...

   Without realizing it, they had discovered the first tranche of the most important biblical texts ever found. Between 1947 and 1956 a further 10 caves, all within a few kilometres of each other, were to yield up an historian's dream, ranging from complete scrolls to tiny fragments, in all some 80,000 items. The caves are located close to the site of an ancient settlement of ultra-religious Jewish Essenes, at Qumran, on the north-western shore of the Dead Sea. The place is known to the Bedouin as Khirbet-Qumran – the Stone Ruins of Qumran.

   The brothers, not knowing what to do with the seven scrolls they had found, in what is now known as Cave 1, showed them to a Syrian shoemaker in Bethlehem, nicknamed 'Kando', whom they knew dealt in antiquities. Kando took four of the scrolls to the Archbishop-Metropolitan of St Mark's Monastery in Jerusalem, who promptly acquired them for the equivalent of £24. This priceless acquisition must rank as one of the bargains of all time.

The Metropolitan had in his possession the oldest complete Hebrew version of the Old Testament Book of Isaiah. (Two versions of Isaiah were found in Cave 1, given the superfixes ª and ᵇ, which were written in ancient forms of Hebrew. 1QIsaª, dated to 202–107 BCE, contains all 66 chapters of Isaiah, apart from a few missing words. It has 13 significant variations from the Hebrew Masoretic text in use today, but otherwise is remarkably similar. 1QIsaᵇ was written around the time of Jesus and is less complete, but it is closer to the traditional Hebrew text. Prior to the discovery of these Isaiahs, the oldest known Hebrew version was in the Cairo Codex, dated to 895 CE.) The Metropolitan had also acquired a Manual of Discipline for the Qumran-Essenes, a commentary on Habakkuk – a minor 7th-century BCE prophet, and a Genesis Apocryphon, which retells and enhances the Old Testament Book of Genesis.

The three other scrolls from Cave 1 comprised an incomplete version of Isaiah (1QIsaᵇ); a War Scroll, which describes how the Qumran-Essenes (as 'the sons of light'), were to wage a final battle against the 'sons of darkness' – those who did not follow their beliefs; and a scroll of Thanksgiving Psalms. These three scrolls were acquired by Professor E.L. Sukenik, of the Hebrew University of West Jerusalem, on 29 November 1947.

Shortly after this purchase, on 14 May 1948, Israel declared its indepedence and war broke out between Arabs and Jews. The Archbishop-Metropolitan, Mar Athanasius Yeshue Samuel (whose name testified to his allegiance to Arab, Christian and Jewish traditions), lived up to his pragmatic nature and promptly fled, via Syria, to Lebanon. One can visualize him scurrying across the runway to catch his plane, with four priceless scrolls tucked under his billowing cassock. It was not until June 1954 that our mercurial Metropolitan popped up again, this time in America. He had placed the following advertisement in the *Wall Street Journal:*

> **"The Four**
> **Dead Sea Scrolls"**
> Biblical Manuscripts dating
> back to at least 200 BC, are
> for sale. This would be an
> ideal gift to an educational
> or religious institution by
> an individual or group.
> **Box F206, The Wall Street**
> **Journal.**

Here fate intervened. As my story unfolds you will find that I am quite a fan of fate and coincidence. By chance Professor Sukenik's son, Yigael Yadin (an Army officer who would later rise to become Deputy Prime Minister of Israel), was in New York and managed, after a hectic scramble around for money, to acquire the scrolls for $250,000.

After the Six-Day War of 1967, when Israel occupied the West Bank of the Jordan, the caves and ruins at Qumran came under their control and subsequently have been the subject of continuous archaeological activity. It was also in 1967 when the last remaining major scroll, the Temple Scroll, was acquired from our ubiquitous friend Kando, who was still living in Bethlehem and had secreted the 9m long scroll under his bed for 11 years!

All seven major scrolls from Cave 1, and the Temple Scroll, now reside in the Shrine of the Book, at the Israel Museum in Jerusalem. Other fragments from Cave 1 have found their way to the Museum of the Department of Antiquities, Amman, Jordan; the Palestine Archaeological Museum, in East Jerusalem (now renamed the Rockefeller Museum); and to the Bibliotheque Nationale, in Paris.

5. G. Bonani *et al.*, Radiocarbon Dating of the Dead Sea Scrolls. *Atiqot* 20, 1991; A.J.T. Jull *et al.*, Radiocarbon Dating of Scrolls and Linen Fragments from the Judean Desert. *Radiocarbon* 37, 1995.

6. Israel Carmi, 'Dating Dead Sea Scrolls by Radiocarbon', The Dead Sea Scrolls – Fifty Years After Their Discovery, International Congress at Jerusalem, July, 1997.

7. Jull *et al.*, *op.cit.*

8. Prior to their discovery the oldest Hebrew versions of the Old Testament were the Aleppo Codex, dating to the 10th century CE, preserved in the Shrine of the Book in Jerusalem, and the Ben Asher text, dating from 1008, now in the Russian State Library at St Petersburg. The Aleppo Codex was written in Palestine, taken to Egypt in the 11th century and found at Aleppo, Syria, in the 14th century. It has suffered fire damage and is not complete.

Virtually all previously discovered Biblical documents, apart from the Dead Sea Scrolls, are known to us from copies or references to earlier documents by later writers. They have therefore been subjected to inaccuracies in copying and adjustments by the writers to meet doctrinal objectives. George Brooke, 'The Treasure under your Noses: 50 Years of Manchester and the Dead Sea Scrolls'. Lecture at The Manchester Museum, 6 December 1997.

9. Flavius Josephus (37–100 CE), a Jewish historian who became a Roman citizen and wrote, amongst other things, about the Essene community and their settlement on the Dead Sea.

Pliny the Elder (23–79 CE). Gaius Plinius Secundus was born in Como, Italy, of an aristocratic Roman family. After a spell in the Roman army he later devoted himself to writing historical treatises on subjects like oration, and the history of Rome. A friend of Emperor Vespasian, he died during the volcanic eruption of Mount Vesuvius in 79 CE.

Judaeus Philo (*c.*20 BCE to *c.*40 CE), a Jewish-Egyptian philosopher and Greek scholar, who was born in Alexandria. He worked at Alexandria on Bible commentary and law, and mentions the Qumran-Essenes in his writings.

10. Josephus, *Wars of the Jews*, II.

11. Pliny the Elder, *Nat. Hist.*

12. Philo, *Quod Omnis Probus Liber Sit.*

13. *Ibid.*

14. There has been considerable argument about whether there was a scriptorium at Qumran. In particular, Norman Golb (*Who Wrote the Dead Sea Scrolls?* Touchstone/Simon & Schuster, 1996), does not believe that there were writing tables. As de Vaux (R. de Vaux, *Archaeology and the Dead Sea Scrolls.* Oxford University Press, 1959) pointed out, received opinion is that scribal tables did

not come into use until the 8th–9th centuries CE, but he cites examples as early as the 3rd century CE. Nevertheless, de Vaux is convinced that the Qumran tables were for writing, not eating, and most scholars today accept his interpretation. There are, in fact, examples of tables being used as early as the 14th century BCE, as illustrated in the tomb of Huya at Amarna, Egypt, which shows scenes from the workshop of Iuty, chief sculptor of Queen Tiyi. See Joyce Tyldesley, *Nefertiti, Egypt's Sun Queen*. Viking, 1998.

15. References in the literature differ about the date the Copper Scroll was discovered. John Allegro, in his book *The Treasure of the Copper Scroll* published in 1960, gave the date as 14 March 1952, other historians quote 20 March. I obtained a definitive date from the person who found the Copper Scroll, Henri de Contenson, Directeur de Recherche Honoraire au CNRS. According to him three excavation teams, led by J.T. Milik, D. Barthélemy and Monsieur Contenson himself, began work in March 1952 on various sections of the hills overlooking Qumran. M. Contenson, with a team of ten Bedouin, arrived on site on 10 March and, after preparatory clearing work on Cave 3, found the Copper Scroll on 20 March. Robert Feather, Recorded Interview with Henri de Contenson. Paris, 16 January 1999. See also E.-M. Laperrousaz (ed.), *Qoumran et les Manuscrits de la Mer Morte*. Les Editions Du Cerf, 1997.

CHAPTER 2 Bullion by the Billion

1. The original international team working on the Dead Sea Scrolls at the École Archéologique Française de Jerusalem (sometimes referred to as École Biblique) and the Palestine Archaeological Museum – later renamed the Rockefeller Museum – comprised Father Jozef Milik and Father Dominique Barthélemy of the École Biblique; John Strugnell and John Allegro from Oxford University; Patrick Skehan and Frank Moore Cross from the Johns Hopkins University, Baltimore; Claus-Hunno Hunzinger from Germany; and Jean Starcky from France.

2. Mishnaic Hebrew is not known as a fully recognizable form of language until the Rabbinic period of 200 CE onwards, but its early development can be seen in a number of Dead Sea Scroll texts and in the Copper Scroll, which was thought to be copied at least some 140 years earlier. Textual comparisons with the Bible have shown usages drawn, for example, from Ezekiel and Isaiah, therefore indicating an allegiance dating back to at least 700 or 800 BCE.

3. The language and writing system of 'Ugarit', in northern Syria, developed around 1500–1400 BCE under the influence of cuneiform (a wedge-like lettering); Akkadian from the Mesopotamian and Sumerian regions. Ugarit reduced the number of letters required from the many hundreds in use in other languages, to a mere 27. Under the influence of Ugarit and Egyptian hieroglyphs, 'Proto-Canaanite' writing was developed in Canaan around 1400–1300 BCE, initially using 27 letters, but by the 13th century BCE 22 letters. By the 11th century BCE, Phoenician influence established a normal form of Proto-Canaanite (subsequently referred to as 'Phoenician'), of 22 letters written horizontally from right to left. 'Paleo-Hebrew' evolved largely from this form of 'Phoenician', around the 9th century BCE.

4. 68 CE is the last possible date for the Copper Scroll to have been engraved by the Qumran-Essenes, as their settlement was destroyed by the Romans at that

time. Apart from evidence of a few Qumran-Essenes turning up to help the Zealots resist the Romans at the mountain fortress of Masada near the Dead Sea, where, in 73 CE, 960 Jews committed suicide to avoid capture, history knows nothing more about the Qumran-Essenes.

5. There are at least a dozen authoritative translations available of the Copper Scroll and between each of them there are many variations on phrases, individual words and letters which give completely different readings to the meaning of the text. As an example of the differences of opinion amongst scholars, Jonas Greenfield (*Journal of the American Oriental Society* 89, 1969), in criticizing the official translation of the Copper Scroll, disagreed with 13 per cent of the vocabulary.

6. J.T. Milik, Le Rouleau du Cuivre de Qumran (3Q15). *Revue Biblique* 66, 1959.

7. John Marco Allegro, *The Treasure of the Copper Scroll.* Routledge & Kegan Paul, 1960.

8. M. Baillet and J.T. Milik, Les 'Petites Grottes' de Qumran. *Discoveries in the Judaean Desert.* Oxford University Press, 1962.

9. Whilst most scholars now agree the Copper Scroll was engraved by the Qumran-Essenes and relates to real treasure, some of the early workers at the École Biblique in Jerusalem, such as Father de Vaux and Father Jozef Milik, did not take its contents seriously and thought them to be based on fable. A small minority, including Norman Golb of the University of Chicago, and Manfred Lehmann (*Revue de Qumran*, October, 1964), maintain that the Copper Scroll was not a work of the Qumran-Essenes.

10. Allegro, *op.cit.*; Florentino Garcia Martinez, *The Dead Sea Scrolls Translated.* E.J. Brill, 1994; Al Wolters, *The Copper Scroll.* Sheffield Academic Press, 1996; Geza Vermes, *The Complete Dead Sea Scrolls in English.* Penguin Books, 1997.

11. John Allegro, the first translator of the Copper Scroll, could not understand the values the Biblical Talent was giving (even though he was using a Talent of 45lb, rather than the more usual value of 76lb), so he quite arbitrarily downgraded the estimates of weights by 1/60 by applying the next Biblical unit down.

12. Geoffrey Wigoder, *The New Standard Jewish Encyclopedia.* Facts on File, 1992.

13. According to Joseph Fitzmyer – *Responses to 101 Questions on the Dead Sea Scrolls* (Paulist Press, 1992) – the Copper Plaque (as he calls it) contains no sectarian terminology and does not mention anything connected with the Community. Professor Lawrence Schiffman, of New York University, identifies numerous words in the Copper Scroll which do not appear elsewhere in the Dead Sea Scrolls ('The Vocabulary of the Copper Scroll and the Temple Scroll', International Symposium on the Copper Scroll at The University of Manchester Institute of Science and Technology, 8–11 September, 1996).

14. Theodor H. Gaster, *The Dead Sea Scriptures.* Doubleday, 1975.

15. Norman Golb, *Who Wrote the Dead Sea Scrolls?* Touchstone/Simon & Schuster, 1996. John Allegro thought that the treasures were hidden by Zealots – a fanatical band of Jewish rebels who fought against the Romans from 66–73 CE, when they were finally crushed at Masada.

16. M.R. Lehmann, Identification of the Copper Scroll Based on its Technical Terms, *Revue de Qumran* 17, October, 1964.

17. Thomas Bradshaw, *Works of Flavius Josephus*. Alex Hogg, 1810.
18. John Marco Allegro, *The Dead Sea Scrolls*. Penguin Books, 1956; P. Kyle McCarter, The Mystery of the Copper Scroll, *The Dead Sea Scrolls After Forty Years*. Biblical Archaeology Society, Washington DC, 1991; J.K. Lefkovits, 'The Copper Scroll Treasure: Fact or Fiction?', International Symposium on the Copper Scroll, The University of Manchester Institute of Science and Technology, 8–11 September, 1996; Michael O. Wise, *David J. Wilmot and the Copper Scroll*. Bloomington, Minnesota, 1996; Al Wolters, History and the Copper Scroll, *Annals of the New York Academy of Sciences 722*, 1994.
19. Joseph Conklin and Michelle Andrea, 'Jeremiah's Wheelbarrow: The First Temple Treasure of the Copper Scroll of Qumran and the Land of Redemption.'
    (http://shell.idt.net/conklin/jeremiah.html).
20. Conklin and Andrea have Ezra returning from Babylon some 70 years after the destruction of the First Temple, i.e., in 516 BCE, whereas most authorities date their return to around 458 BCE.
21. André Dupont-Sommer, Les Rouleaux de Cuivre Trouvé a Qoumran, *Revue de L'histoire des religions 151*, 1957; Bargil Pixner, Unravelling the Copper Scroll Code: A Study of the Topography of 3Q15, *Revue de Qumran 11*, 1983; Stephen Goranson, Sectarianism, Geography, and the Copper Scroll, *Journal of Jewish Studies 43*, 1992.
22. J.F. Elwolde, '3Q15: Its Linguistic Affiliation, with Lexicographical Comments', International Symposium on the Copper Scroll, Manchester–Sheffield Centre for Dead Sea Scroll Research, 1996; J. Lefkovits, 'The Copper Scroll Treasure: Fact or Fiction – The Abbreviations KK vs KKRYN', International Symposium on the Copper Scroll, Manchester–Sheffield Centre for Dead Sea Scroll Research, 1996.
23. In Chapter 3 I include comments from Dr Rosalie David, Reader and Keeper of Egyptology at The Manchester Museum, on the peculiarity of the numbering system used in the Copper Scroll.

CHAPTER 3 Metallurgy and Metrology

1. There were two systems of measuring length in use in ancient Israel. The ordinary cubit (*ammah*) – the length of a man's elbow to his second knuckle – was equal to 45.8cm and the large cubit measured 52.5cm. Geoffrey Wigoder (ed.), *The New Standard Jewish Encyclopedia*. Facts on File, 1992.
2. The main sources of gold in the ancient Middle East were in the regions below Thebes, in Egypt, stretching south to lower Nubia and east to the Sudan desert. The earliest forms of gold were found pre–3000 BCE in alluvial beds, and were later mined from veins in quartz rock. Gold from these sources, in its uncombined form, was simply beaten into the desired shape. Combined ores were crushed into fine particles, separated by washing and, as heating technology improved, melted and refined in clay cupolas with the assistance of air blown onto the molten metal. After about 1300 BCE 'Ketem' gold began to be imported from Asia.

   Silver, which does not normally occur in an uncombined state in the Middle East, was much rarer than gold up until about 1300 BCE, having a value approximately twice that of gold. Examples of silver objects that have been found were usually associated with gold sources, or obtained by separation from Galena (lead sulphide) ores containing silver mined in the eastern desert in southern Egypt.

Although gold and silver are still relatively valuable materials today, with gold fluctuating in price between $280 and $500 an ounce between 1985 and 1998, and silver currently around $6 an ounce, with the protracted difficulties of refining in ancient times they were rare commodities of extremely high value.

3. Giulio Morteani and Jeremy P. Northover (eds), 'Pre-historic Gold in Europe. Mines Metalurgy and Manufacture', *Proceedings of the NATO Advanced Research Workshop on Prehistoric Gold in Europe.* Seeon, Germany, 1993, published by Dordrecht Kluwer Academic, 1995; C.H.V. Sutherland, *Gold: Its Beauty, Power and Allure.* Thames & Hudson, 1959; Timothy Green, *The World of Gold.* Rosendale Press, 1993.

4. Silver was more valuable than gold in the Egyptian New Kingdom period (from 1550 BCE), in line with their relative availabilities of 2:1 in favour of gold. This ratio was slowly reversed, reaching approximate parity around 900 BCE, from which time silver became more abundant than gold.

5. Michael O. Wise, 'David J. Wilmot and the Copper Scroll', at the International Symposium on the Copper Scroll, Manchester–Sheffield Centre for Dead Sea Scrolls Research, 1996.

6. *Ibid.*

7. One of the best translations of the Harris Papyrus was done by the great pioneering archaeologist, James Henry Breasted. Born in Rockford, Illinois, in 1865, he became the first Professor in America of a 'Chair of Egyptian' at Chicago University, and was called 'one of the prophets' by J.D. Rockefeller, who was later to endow the Rockefeller Museum in Jerusalem.

8. James Henry Breasted, *Ancient Records of Egypt, Vol. IV.* Russell & Russell, 1912. (My italics.)

9. All references to 'brass' in the Old Testament, and there are many, are erroneous. They should be read as 'bronze'. Brass was not in use until Roman times.

10. There are numerous examples of pharaohs taking over their predecessors' goods, by right and by plunder, and taking over tomb furnishings and materials, as well as building structures. A good example is Haremhab who usurped many of Tutankhamun's possessions and monuments. See, for example, Peter A. Clayton, *Chronicle of the Pharaohs.* Thames & Hudson, 1998.

11. *A General Guide to the Egyptian Collections in the British Museum.* British Museum Publications, 1975.

12. H. Garland and C.O. Bannister, *Ancient Egyptian Metallurgy.* Charles Griffen & Co, 1926.

13. Mummification, involving removal of internal organs and embalming to preserve the dead body, was common amongst Egyptian royalty and upper classes from the Old Kingdom (*c.*2550 BCE) down to the Greco-Roman period (332 BCE–300 CE).

14. Garland and Bannister, *op. cit.*

15. In addition to the restoration work and analyses of the scroll carried out by Electricité de France, Paris, in the early 1990s, splinters of copper from the scroll were, according to P. Kyle McCarter of Johns Hopkins University,

Baltimore, sent for analysis to Harvard University prior to 1955. The results showed some residual tin and 99.9 per cent copper. The remaining splinters are apparently still in the Freer Gallery, Washington DC. P. Kyle McCarter, 'The Anomalous Spelling of the Copper Scroll', The Dead Sea Scrolls – Fifty Years After Their Discovery, Congress, 1997. See also Al Wolters, *The Copper Scroll Overview, Text and Translation*. Sheffield Academic Press, 1996; D. Brizemeure and N. Lacoudre, 'EDF et le Rouleau de Cuivre (3Q15)', International Symposium on the Copper Scroll, Manchester–Sheffield Centre for Dead Sea Scrolls Research, 1996.

(http://www.edf.fr/html/en/mag/mmorte/intro.htm)

16. Wolters, *op. cit.*
17. Ian Shaw and Paul Nicholson, *The British Museum Dictionary of Ancient Egypt*. BCA/British Museum Press, 1995.
18. Breasted, *op. cit.*
19. Correspondence between Dr Rosalie David and the author, 21 December 1998–18 January 1999.
20. There is evidence at Qumran that the inhabitants had developed skills in leather-working and pottery making, so they could well have adapted these skills to metal-working.

CHAPTER 4 The Hebrew Tribes and Egypt

1. The Judaean Essene movement during the 2nd century BCE to the 1st century CE, is described by Josephus, Pliny the Elder and Philo as being made up of static and mobile groupings, perhaps numbering 4,000 in all at any one time. Their testimony never indicates that the Essenes were recruited from anything other than Jews of Hebrew stock.

2.

Genesis 12:10	'There was a famine in the land, and Abram *went down to Egypt* to sojourn there, for the famine was severe in the land.'
Genesis 37:23–24, 28	'When Joseph came up to his brothers, they stripped Joseph of his tunic, the ornamented tunic that he was wearing and took him and cast him into the pit. The pit was empty; there was no water in it....When Midianite traders passed by, they pulled Joseph up out of the pit. They sold Joseph for twenty pieces of silver to the Ishmaelites, who brought Joseph *to Egypt.*'
Genesis 42:3	'So ten of Joseph's brothers went down to get grain rations *in Egypt...*'
Genesis 46:6	'...and they took along their livestock and the wealth that they had amassed in the land of Canaan. *Thus Jacob and all his off-spring with him came to Egypt.*'
Jeremiah 43:5–7	'But Johanan the son of Kareah, and all the captains of the forces, took all the remnant of Judah, that were returned from all nations whither they had been driven, to dwell in the land of Judah; even men, and women, and children, and the king's daughters, and every person that Nebuzar-adan the captain of the guard had left with Gedaliah the son of Ahikam, the son of Shaphan, and Jeremiah the prophet, and Baruch the son of Neriah. So *they came into the land of Egypt*: for they obeyed not the voice of the Lord. Thus came they even to Tahpanhes.'
Matthew 2:13	'And when they were departed, behold, the angel of the Lord appeareth to Joseph in a dream, saying, "Arise, and take the young child [Jesus] and his mother, *and flee into Egypt*, and be thou there until I bring thee word; for Herod shall seek the young child to destroy him."'

3. The concept of Abraham as the founder of monotheism is based on the Biblical story that God first appeared to him in a vision and promised that his descendants would inherit the lands from the river of Egypt to the Euphrates. The dating of Abraham by various authorities varies from *c.*1900 to 1400 BCE, and the evidence for my preference of *c.*1500 BCE is discussed in Chapter 7. He offered his son, Isaac, as a sacrifice to God, reputedly on a site now known as the Dome of the Rock in Jerusalem. Abraham's other son, Ishmael, is believed to be the father of the Muslims.

4. As his father's favourite son, Joseph aroused his brothers' jealousy and was sold by them to Ismaelite traders, who in turn sold him into slavery in Egypt, around 1350 BCE. A slave in the house of Potiphar, Pharaoh's captain of the guard, he prospered until Potiphar's wife took a fancy to him. When Joseph rejected her sexual overtures, she denounced him to her husband who had him thrown into prison. It was while in prison that Joseph's reputation as an interpreter of dreams came to the attention of Pharaoh.

5. The most notable of the early commentators on the Old Testament, who all held the belief that Moses was educated as an Egyptian and held high rank in that country, were:
    a) Manetho – a 3rd century BCE Egyptian author and high priest of Heliopolis
    b) Philo Judaeus – a 1st century BCE Jewish writer and philosopher
    c) Flavius Josephus – a 1st century CE authoritative Jewish writer
    d) Justin Martyr – a 2nd century Father of the early Christian Church.

6. Josef Popper-Linkeus, Der Sohn des Konigs von Egypten. *Phantasieen eines Realisten.* Carl Reisner, 1899.

7. Sigmund Freud, *Moses and Monotheism.* The Hogarth Press, 1951.
    Sigmund Freud, as well as being the father of psychoanalysis, had an abiding interest in ancient religions and archaeology, particularly Egyptian. In 1931 he wrote a study on the origins of Moses, entitled 'Moses and Monotheism', which attracted considerable criticism and reprobation, largely because he portrayed a first Moses as having been murdered by the Hebrews and the arrival of a second Moses. The work was heavily influenced by his own *angst* over his Jewish parentage and feelings of guilt about his own non-conformity. Interest in the original concept of Egypt and monotheism died away, submerged in the controversy engendered by Freud's extreme interpretation. See also Yosef Hayim Yerushalmi, *Freud's Moses.* Yale University Press, 1991.
    A major collection of Freud's papers and manuscripts are housed in the Library of Congress, Washington DC. His passion for collecting ancient relics can be seen in his family house in Hampstead, London, which is open to the public, and still contains many of the personal possessions he lived and worked amongst.

8. Although this book was written before the release of the Jeffrey Katzenberg, Dream Works SKG, animated film version of the life of Moses, *Prince of Egypt*, it is apparent that the film also challenges the conventional view of the origins of Moses.

9. Martin Noth, *Exodus: A Commentary.* SCM Press, 1962.

10. E. Otto, *Die Biographischen Inschriften der Ägyptischen Spatzeit.* Leyden, 1954.

11. Siegfried Morenz, *Egyptian Religion.* Cornell University Press, 1994.

12. R.T. Rundle Clark, *Myth and Symbol in Ancient Egypt.* Thames & Hudson, 1978.

13. Alfred Sendrey, *Music in Ancient Israel.* Philosophical Library, New York, 1969.

14. *Ibid.*

15. Paul Goodman, *History of the Jews.* Office of the Chief Rabbi, Soncino Press, 1941.

16. Julius Wellhausen, *Prolegomena zur Geschichte Israels.* Edinburgh, 1885. Julius Wellhausen was a 19th-century scholar who identified at least four different authors of the Pentateuch, to whom he assigned the letters: J – Jaweh, *c.*950 BCE, by Judaean sources; E – Elohim, *c.*850 BCE, Ephraim sources; D – Deuteronomy, *c.*640 BCE; P – Priestly, *c.*550 BCE, priestly sources.

17. When Moses was banished from Court he heads for the land of Midian, somewhere in North-west Arabia, and there marries the daughter, Zipporah, of a Midianite priest (Exodus 2). He has a son by her who is named Gershom – alluding to the fact that Moses is 'a stranger in a strange land', and referring to the land of Goshen in Egypt, where foreigners traditionally settled.

   In the Bible there is serious confusion as to who Moses married in Midian. Moses's father-in-law is variously given as 'Reuel', a Midianite, in Exodus 2:18; as 'Jethro' in Exodus 3:1; as 'Raguel' in Numbers 10:29; and 'Hobab' in Judges 4:11.

18. The Bible (Exodus 2:16) confirms that it was a Bedouin custom for daughters of the tribe to look after the flocks.

19. Thomas Bradshaw, *Works of Flavius Josephus.* Alex Hogg, 1810.

20. *Ibid.*

21. E.A. Wallis Budge, *The Mummy.* Outlet Book Co Inc, 1989.

22. Exodus 4:24–26.   'At a night encampment on the way, The Lord encountered him and sought to kill him [Moses]. So Zipporah took a flint and cut off her son's foreskin, and touched his legs with it, saying, "You are truly a bridegroom of blood to me!" And when He let him alone, she added, "A bridegroom of blood because of the circumcision."'

23. Charles Weiss, *The Journal of Sex Research*, July, 1966; Julian Morgenstern, *Hebrew Union College Annual*, 1963.

24. E.A. Wallis Budge, *The Papyrus of Ani.* Gramercy Books, 1995.

25. Geoffrey Thorndike Martin, *The Royal Tombs of El-Amarna – I: The Objects.* Egypt Exploration Society, London, 1974.

26. In order to trace back to the roots of why circumcision was practised at all in Egypt, we need to look at the ancient creation stories of Egypt, to the Papyrus of Ani, written during the 18th Dynasty, in the 14th century BCE. In it we find that Re, the creator God, initiated the process of bringing other beings into existence:

   It is the blood that descended from the phallus of Re
   After he proceeded to circumcise himself,
   And these gods are those who came into being after him.

   This was the myth of how Re, or Ra, brought other gods into existence, from the droplets of blood which came forth.

27. Nicholas de Lange, *Atlas of the Jewish World.* Phaidon, 1985.

28. Bruce M. Metzger and Michael D. Coogan, *The Oxford Companion to the Bible.* Oxford University Press, 1993.

29. Pat Alexander, *The Lion Encyclopedia of the Bible.* Lion Publishing, 1994.

30. Irving M. Zeitlin, *Ancient Judaism.* Polity Press, 1991.

31. John Rogerson, *Atlas of the Bible.* Facts on File, 1991.
32. Morenz, *op. cit.*
33. Other quotes from Zeitlin underline the lack of influence of Canaan on the Hebrews:
    'Thus, there appears to be no resemblance whatsoever between this form of social organization (primitive democracy) and that of the Canaanites which was feudal and hierarchical.' '…no evidence exists of a Canaanite-Israelite syncretism in technology and social organization', '…where the primeval legends of Genesis are concerned, there is no apparent Canaanite influence'. Zeitlin, *op. cit.*
34. '…Israelite military technology was quite different from that of the Canaanites' (Yehezkel Kaufman, *Toledot Ha-emunah Hayisraelit.* The Bialik Institute and Devir, Jerusalem, 1971); '…prophecy of the word, which is so distinctive a feature of Israel, was non-existent in Canaan' (John Gray, *The Legacy of Canaan: The Ras Shamra Texts and Their Relevance to the Old Testament.* Leiden, J. Brill, 1965).
35. Richard Elliott Friedman, *Who Wrote the Bible?* HarperSanFrancisco, 1996; Wellhausen, *op. cit.*
36. Pope Pius XII referred to the writers of the Bible as 'the living and reasonable instrument of the Holy Spirit'. His encyclical, *Divinio Afflante Spiritu*, ended:
    > Let the interpreter then, with all care and without neglecting any light derived from recent research, endeavour to determine the peculiar character and circumstances of the sacred writer, the age in which he lived, the sources written or oral to which he had recourse and the forms of expression he employed.
37. John Marco Allegro, *The Treasure of the Copper Scroll.* Routledge & Kegan Paul, 1960.
38. John Marco Allegro, *The Sacred Mushroom and the Cross.* Hodder & Stoughton, 1969.

CHAPTER 5   The Cocooned Cauldron of Egypt – Hotbed of Civilization

1. Siegfried Morenz, *Egyptian Religion.* Cornell University Press, 1994; H. Junker, Die Gotterlehre von Memphis, *APAW* 23, 1939; H. Kees, Der Gotterglaube im Alten Agypten, *Mitteilungen der Vorderasiatisch-Agyptischen Gesellschaft* 45, Leipzig, 1941.
2. The Hyksos were semitic invaders from the east who dominated most of Egypt from about 1640 to 1538 BCE. They made their capital at Avaris in the delta region of the Nile, and worshipped Seth, Anath and Astarte.
3. James Henry Breasted, *Development of Religion and Thought in Ancient Egypt.* Hodder & Stoughton, 1912.
4. E.A. Wallis Budge, *Egyptian Religion.* Gramercy Books, 1995.
5. Dates of pharaohs are averages from those given by a number of studies quoted in *The Sceptre of Egypt – a Background for the Study of the Ancient Egyptian Antiquities in the Metropolitan Museum of Art*, by William C.Hayes. Metropolitan Museum of Art, 1990.
6. R.T. Rundle Clark, *Myth and Symbol in Ancient Egypt.* Thames & Hudson, 1978.
7. *Ibid.*
8. E.A. Wallis Budge, *The Book of the Dead.* Gramercy Books, 1995.

9. Rundle Clark, *op. cit.*
10. The 'snake', the 'word', and the 'eye' appear in many guises in Egyptian mythology.

Assuming you have a strong stomach, lift the musty lid of a typical coffin of the 9th Dynasty, or just examine the texts running around the outside if you feel too queasy, and you will find references to the 'Primeval Serpent', who can speak and who delineates the limits of existence. Here the 'serpent' appears to be an agent of God and on the side of good. In contrast, in Hebrew theology the 'snake' is viewed in a rather odd way. In the Garden of Eden it is seen as an evil tempter, but in the Midrash (*see Glossary*) interpretation and in commentaries on the Hebrew Scriptures, the snake is referred to as an agent or messenger of God, rather than his opponent.

One possible explanation of this contradiction is that the 'evil snake' derives from the ancient Babylonian Gilgamesh-type myths, whilst the 'favourable serpent' (who is also a protector), derives from an early Egyptian tradition which percolates in at a later date.

The 'snake' is indeed an ongoing creature of fascination in Egyptian mythology. It appears on inscriptions with beards, as the male 'serpent', and in the form of a cobra as the female version, later coming to represent female gods. In its many forms it also plays a dangerous role, as shown in this Pyramid Text, Spell 664:

> If you become dangerous to me I will step on you,
>
> but if you recognize me I will not tread on you,
>
> for you are that mysterious and shapeless thing,
>
> of whom the gods foretold that you have neither arms nor legs
>
> on which to go following your brother gods...

Here is a clear reference to how the snake obtained its form, re-echoed in the Bible in Genesis 4:14:

> Then the Lord God said to the serpent,
>
> 'Because you did this, More cursed shall you be,
>
> Than all cattle. And all the wild beasts: On your belly shall you crawl, And dirt shall you eat,
>
> All the days of your life.'

In another facet of the Memphitic doctrine, the definitive 'motor' of creation was seen as the 'word' that God gave to name everything in the world – without which there would be nothing.

> And then Ptah rested after he had created everything and every Divine Word.

These concepts are again closely echoed in the Old Testament story of the Creation and Adam.

Genesis 2:19   And out of the ground the Lord God formed every beast of the field, and every fowl of the air: and brought them unto the man [Adam] to see what he would call them; and whatsoever the man would call every living creature, that was to be the name thereof.

Genesis 2:3   And God blessed the seventh day, and hallowed it; because that in it he rested from all His work which God in creating had made.

'The Divine Word' features strongly throughout early Egyptian thought, almost as a spiritual force with a power of its own, and associated with the good and favourable act of creation. Intimately associated with the Egyptian idea of the 'Word' being the vehicle of God's creation is the moral concept of good deeds furthering the 'Word', and bad deeds harming the 'ka' and hindering divine redemption – concepts readily picked up by Judaism and Buddhism. From Pyramid Text 1098 we find:

> When the doing of what was to be done was in confusion,
>
> when the doing and the commanding of that which was to be done was asleep.
>
> I create and command for him who commands the good;
>
> My lips are the Twin Companies,
>
> I am the great Word.

Compare this with the beginning of the Gospel of St John in the New Testament:

John 1:1–3
> In the beginning was the Word, and the Word was with God, and the Word was God.
>
> The same was in the beginning with God.
>
> All things were made by him; and without him was not any thing made that was made.

Whilst 'the Word' is the speaking or naming element the Supreme God uses in creation, 'the Eye' is the seeing element. It is dispatched by Atum to seek out 'Shu' and 'Tefnut', subsidiary creative-vehicle gods, of air that separates earth and sky, and of cosmic order, respectively.

Coffin Texts, Spell 80 (from Rundle Clark, *op. cit.*):

> …after the appearance of my Eye, which I dispatched while I was still alone in the waters in a state of inertness, before I had found anywhere to stand or sit…

In the Egyptian 'order' of creation, which the Bible closely follows, the seeing Eye (which is the third procedure of creation), is followed next by the creation of light. As we have seen, and will see further on, the Bible faithfully follows the subject and approximates the order of creation in Egyptian cosmology. Immediately prior to the creation of light, there is a reference for the first and only time in the Biblical story, to God's seeing and that what He sees is favourable.

Genesis 1:12–14
> The earth brought forth vegetation: seed-bearing plants of every kind, and trees of every kind bearing fruit with the seed in it. And God saw that this was good.
>
> And there was evening and there was morning, a third day.
>
> God said, 'Let there be lights in the expanse of the sky to separate day from night; they shall serve as signs for the set times – the days and the years.'

Later on, in the time of the Egyptian New Kingdom, the 'Eye' takes on a deeper meaning, and becomes a symbol of realization and complete awareness of a higher form of existence beyond mere earthly trappings. Its rebus (representation) appears in numerous Egyptian inscriptions.

Another, more enigmatic, Biblical reference to the power of 'the Eye' occurs in Zechariah 3:9.

> For behold the stone that I have laid before Joshua; upon one stone shall be seven eyes: I will engrave the graving thereof, saith the Lord of hosts – and I will remove the iniquity of that land in one day.

This is an apparent reference to the requirement that the coping stone of the Second Temple should have seven eyes to watch over its well-being – seven being a highly significant number in Egyptian and Hebrew belief, *viz* the seven forms of Osiris, the seven days of creation, etc (Rundle Clark, *op. cit.*).

It is impossible to avoid the realization that there are direct Egyptian parallels for all the essential elements of the Biblical story of creation:

a) creating the sky
b) making man in the image of God
c) breathing life into the nostrils of man
d) creating the birds, fish and animals for the benefit and pleasure of man.

The Egyptian texts continue in the vein of the Prophet Ipu:

> Consider mankind as the flocks of God. He made the sky for the enjoyment of their hearts, he repelled the greed of the waters, he created the breath of life for their noses;
>
> His images are they, the products of His flesh. He rises in the sky for their hearts' desire, for them He has made the plants, animals, birds and fish – all for their delight.

11. Morenz, *op. cit.*; Rundle Clark, *op. cit.*

12. Formation of the planets in our solar system is now believed to have come about by the condensation of massive dust and gas clouds that enveloped the sun. The theory has been re-enforced by the prediction and confirmation that all the planets should have the same chemical composition as the sun. For example, the amounts of oxygen and hydrogen, as free molecules, hydroxyl radical (OH) or water (H_2O) in the planets and in the sun are similar.

    It may seem strange to think of water existing on the sun, but it can retain its molecular bonding as superheated steam up to about 3900°K, and the temperature of sunspots are at about 3300°K compared to a surface temperature of 5785°K. NASA, in Houston, Texas, has recently reported that the Galileo space probe to Jupiter shows only 10 per cent of the expected water content in its atmosphere. Steve Connor, Jupiter Probe Upsets Theories. *The Sunday Times*, 21 January 1996.

13. R.O. Faulkner, *The Ancient Egyptian Pyramid Texts*. Oxford, 1969.

14. The elements of the new doctrine are preserved for us in texts written in the time of Pharaoh Shabako, around 700 BCE.

15. Trinities of gods were formed by a grouping of three Egyptian gods, often as father, mother and child figures comprising a divine family, who were worshipped on a localized basis. The practice arose during the New Kingdom period of the Amenhotep pharaohs. Examples were the combination of Amun, Mut and Khons at Thebes; Ptah, Sekhmet and Nefertum at Memphis; Horus, Hathor and the young Horus at Edfu; Khnum, Satet and Anuket at Yeb (Elephantine). A triad worshipped on a national basis was that of Osiris (worshipped locally at Abydos), Isis (worshipped locally at Philae), and Horus (worshipped locally at Edfu).

16. J.B. Pritchard (ed.), *Ancient Near Eastern Texts Related to the Old Testament*. Princeton University Press, 1955.

17. A. de Buck and A.H. Gardiner (eds), *The Egyptian Coffin Texts*. Oriental Institute Publications 34, 1935.

18. Faulkner, *op. cit.*

19. By the end of the 18th Dynasty, *c.*1296 BCE, Osiris is superseding Re as the judge of the dead. The continued adherence to Osiris is attested to by an Osireion (subterranean cenotaph) built in 1290 BCE by Seti I, at Abydos.

20. Morenz, *op. cit.*

21. Papyrus 3284, in the Louvre Museum, Paris.
22. Morenz, *op. cit.*
23. A.Moret, *Le Rituel du Culte Divin Journalier en Egypte*. Paris, 1902.
24. Morenz, *op. cit.*
25. Geraldine Pinch, *Magic in Ancient Egypt*. British Museum Press, 1994.

CHAPTER 6   The Amenhotep Family Continuum

1. Peter A.Clayton, *Chronicles of the Pharaohs*. Thames & Hudson, 1998. Siegfried Morenz, *Egyptian Religion*. Cornell University Press, 1973. R.T. Rundle Clark, *Myth and Symbol in Ancient Egypt*. Thames & Hudson, 1978.
2. John Romer, *Romer's Egypt*. Michael Joseph/Rainbird, 1982.
3. N. de G. Davies, *The Tomb of Rekh-mi-Re at Thebes*. The Metropolitan Museum of Art, Egyptian Expedition Publications, New York, 1943.
4. James B. Pritchard, *Ancient Near Eastern Texts*. Princeton University Press, 1955.
5. The Egyptian goddess Hathor took various bovine forms, including one of motherliness as a suckling cow. In her vengeful aspect of 'Seven Hathors', she enacted what was ordained by fate.
6. Morenz, *op. cit.*
7. *Ibid.*
8. Pritchard, *op. cit.*
9. Morenz, *op. cit.*

CHAPTER 7   Abraham – Father of Three Religions, Founder of None

1. Israel Eldad and Moshe Aumann, *Jerusalem Chronicles – News of the Past, Vol. 1*. Reubeni Foundation, Jerusalem, 1954.
2. Paul Goodman, *History of the Jews*. Office of the Chief Rabbi, Soncino Press, 1941.
3. The most likely date for the completion of the Torah – the first five books of the Bible (Genesis, Exodus, Leviticus, Numbers and Deuteronomy), in substantially the form in which we know it today, comes from a Biblical reference in Nehemiah 8:1–10. This relates to a public reading of the Torah in Jerusalem, conducted by Ezra the Scribe, which is believed to have taken place in 444 BCE. A preponderance of modern scholars, emboldened by the dates of the Dead Sea Scrolls, take this date as marking the completion of the written down Torah. Inevitably, the 'old' story became embroidered with the rosy tint of hindsight and the message that the then writers wished to convey.
   One historian, John van Seters, takes an extreme view that the texts were not completed until the 5th century CE, but in the light of modern thinking this view is hardly tenable. John van Seters, *Abraham in History and Tradition*. Yale University Press, 1975.
4. J.B. Pritchard (ed.), *Ancient Near Eastern Texts Relating to the Old Testament*, 2nd edn. Princeton University Press, 1955.
5. *Ibid.*
6. G.W. Anderson, *The History and Religion of Israel*. Oxford University Press, 1996.
7. J.Bronowski, *The Ascent of Man*. Book Club Associates, 1974. Dr Jacob Bronowski was an Honorary Fellow of Jesus College, Cambridge, and Director

of the Council for Biology in Human Affairs at the Salk Institute for Biological Studies, San Diego, California. His television series was first screened in the early 1970s.

8. *Ibid.*

9. *Ibid.*

10. Hans Eysenck, *Test Your IQ*. Thorsons, 1994.

11. David Rohl, in his book *A Test of Time* (Century, 1995), postulates, with some efficacy, wild divergences in the conventionally accepted dates of Egyptian dynasties from the 2nd millennium BCE onwards. He suggests that some of these dates are as much as 200–300 years out of phase, but his theory finds little support from other historians, and his date of c.1450 BCE for the Exodus is unconvincing.

12. Irving M. Zeitlin, *Ancient Judaism*. Polity Press, 1991.

13. Goodman, *op. cit.*

14. David Alexander and Pat Alexander (eds), *Encyclopedia of the Bible*. Lion Publishing, 1978.

15. Anderson, *op. cit.*

16. Obviously these longevities are suspect and, in contemporary terms, impossible. *The New Guinness Book of Records* (Guinness Publishing Ltd, 1995) gives the oldest authenticated age of a human as 120 years and 237 days, for Shigechiyo Izumi, who lived on Tokunoshima Island, Japan. Born on 29 June 1865, he died in 1986 and attributed his longevity to God, Buddha and the Sun. Jeanne Louise Calment, of Arles, in France, who was reputed to have been born on 21 February 1875, died on 4 August 1997 at the age of 122 years and 164 days. The Bible itself, in Psalm 90:10 states that:

> The days of our years are threescore years and ten;
> And if by reason of strength they be four score years…

17. By the year 2100 BCE the Sumerians were using a 360-day year, based on a 12-month solar calendar. The ancient Egyptians also used a solar calendar, and later added a 'little month' of five days – each of which celebrated the births of Osiris, Horus, Seth, Isis and Nephthys. Around 2773 BCE, and possibly as early as 4228 BCE, they cottoned on to the helical rising of Sirius as occurring at the same time as the annual flooding of the Nile and the conjunction of the sun, thus giving them a regular interval of 365 sunsets and sunrises, which they took as the length of their year. See Alexander Hellemans and Bryan Bunch, *The Timetables of Science*. Simon & Schuster, 1988.

Hellenic astronomers added the missing quarter day to the Egyptian calendar by adding a leap day every four years. This addition was only fully accepted by the civilized world when Julius Caesar made it a mandatory part of the Roman Calendar in 46 BCE, and to correct for the seasons had to make that year last 445 days – the longest year on record! The final 'tweaking' was made by Pope Gregory XIII in 1582, who decreed the dropping of the leap year in years that end in two zeros. (See the *Glossary* for further details on calendars.)

Another explanation for the anomalous Biblical years is that the chroniclers of the Old Testament needed to fit the ages of Biblical characters to a time-scale that allowed them to count back, generation by generation, to a pre-conceived idea of the date of creation at 3760 BCE.

This pre-conceived date is in itself, a source of difficulty for Biblical fundamentalists. 'Big Bang' , the currently accepted scientific theory of the beginnings of the universe, occurred about 15 billion years ago. The earliest earth life forms are dated to 3.5 billion years ago – 1 billion years after the earth was formed. Animal life-forms started emerging onto the land from the seas about 450 million years ago, and the human species began to evolve away from their ancestral chimpanzees about 8 million years ago, began walking upright about 4 million years ago, and started making stone tools about 2.4 million years ago.

18. Starting with the first man in the Bible, Adam, we find:

Adam: $930 = 5^2 + 6^2 + 16^2 + 17^2 + 18^2$

Seth (Adam's son): $912 = 5^2 + 6^2 + 9^2 + 15^2 + 16^2 + 17^2$

Enosh (Seth's son): $905 = 6^2 + 16^2 + 17^2 + 18^2$

Kenan (Enosh's son): $910 = 2^2 + 6^2 + 10^2 + 15^2 + 16^2 + 17^2$

Mahalalel (Kenan's son): $895 = 2^2 + 11^2 + 15^2 + 16^2 + 17^2$

Jared (Mahalalel's son): $962 = 2^2 + 14^2 + 15^2 + 16^2 + 17^2$

Enoch (Jared's son): $365 = 10^2 + 11^2 + 12^2$

Methuselah (Enoch's son): $969 = 10^2 + 16^2 + 17^2 + 18^2$

Lamech (Methuselah's son): $777 = 8^2 + 10^2 + 17^2 + 18^2$

Noah (Lamech's son): $950 = 9^2 + 16^2 + 17^2 + 18^2$

Terah (Abraham's father): $205 = 3^2 + 14^2$

19. H. Kees, *Gottinger Totenbuchstudien*. Berlin, 1954.

20. The authors of the early biblical texts were fascinated with square numbers. By looking at their utilization of mathematics and geometry we can get an interesting insight into their minds. We can also discern, from the knowledge they exhibited and by reference to other sources, the minimum lapsed time between the events recorded and their transcription.

The ratio of the circumference of a circle to its diameter was first given the term '*pi*' by William Jones, an English writer, in 1706.

Pi = Circumference/Diameter

This equation was shown by Lindemann, in 1882, to be incapable of solution as a polynomial equation with integer coefficients. In other words, the division gives you an endless number of figures after the decimal point. The world record for memorizing '*pi*' is attributed to Hideaki Tomoyori, of Japan, who in 17 hours of recitation in March 1987, got to 40,000 decimal places!

The Old Testament, in describing the building of the First Temple at Jerusalem, refers to a bowl having a circumference three times its diameter:

I Kings 7:13–14,23   And king Solomon sent and fetched Hiram out of Tyre.

He was a widow's son of the tribe of Naphtali, and his father was a man of Tyre, a worker in brass: and he was filled with wisdom, and understanding, and cunning to work all works in brass: and he came to king Solomon, and wrought all his work. ...

And he made a molten sea, ten cubits from one brim to the other: it was round all about, and its height was five cubits: and a line of thirty cubits did compass it round about.

This is a clear statement that the authors knew '*pi*' as equal to 3.

The Babylonians were somewhat adrift in calculating '*pi*' as 2.518. The

Egyptians, however were much more accurate with their value of 256/81 = 3.1605.

The Greek, Archimedes, arrived at 22/7, which comes to 3.1428. The Chinese got nearest to the value in 500 CE, with their ratio 355/113, which comes to 3.14159. The ancient Indians used the square root of 10, and came near at 3.16.

21. Anderson, *op. cit.*

CHAPTER 8　Abraham at Pharaoh's Palace

1.　Genesis 20:1–2,　　'And Abraham journeyed from thence toward the land of the South, and dwelt
　　14, 16:　　　　　between Kadesh and Shur; and he sojourned in Gerar.

　　　　　　　　　　And Abraham said of Sarah, his wife: "She is my sister." And Abimelech king of
　　　　　　　　　　Gerar sent, and took Sarah...

　　　　　　　　　　And Abimelech took sheep and oxen, and men-servants and women-servants,
　　　　　　　　　　and gave them unto Abraham, and restored him Sarah his wife...

　　　　　　　　　　And unto Sarah he said: "Behold, I have given thy brother a thousand pieces of
　　　　　　　　　　silver; behold, it is a covering of the eyes to all that are with thee; and before all
　　　　　　　　　　men thou art righted".'

Other faults in Abraham's character are pointed to by several commentators, who suggest that when his faith in God was tested, by seeing if he would give his son Isaac (his most precious possession) to God, he 'failed the test'. Failed, because he acted in blind faith, without reasoning. See S.H. Bergman, *Faith and Reason*. Hebrew University, Israel, 1975; Jacqueline Tabick, Sermon on 'The Binding of Isaac', West London Synagogue, 1995.

Nevertheless Abraham, on another occasion, demonstrates fearless physical loyalty to his family in coming to the aid of his nephew Lot when he is in trouble (Genesis 14). Powerfully built, he is somewhat of a 'merchant adventurer', living on his wits, ready to adapt to new situations and come out winning. He is brave and effective in the face of danger, not hesitating to come to the aid of his brethren. He leads a sizeable force of retainers and provides amply for his family and loyal servants.

2.　Irving M. Zeitlin, *Ancient Judaism*. Polity Press, 1991. Abba Eban, *Heritage, Civilization and the Jews*. Weidenfeld and Nicolson, 1984.

3.　Ernst Sellin, *Mose und Seine Bedeutung für die Israelitisch-Jüdische Religionsgeschichte*. Leipzig and Erlangen, A. Deichertsche Verlagsbuchhandlung, 1922.

4.　Sigmund Freud, *Moses and Monotheism*. The Hogarth Press, 1951.

5.　J. Bronowski, *The Ascent of Man*. Book Club Associates, 1974.

6.　Zeitlin, *op. cit.*

7.　After leaving Egypt the Bible relates that for much of his life Abraham was without a male heir. His wife Sarah undermined her own position by allowing her handmaiden Hagar to sire Abraham's first son Ishmael. Sarah's trust in the Almighty is rewarded by the miraculous birth of a son Isaac, when she is 90 years of age. Abraham's own faith in one omnipotent God is put to the ultimate test when God demands of him the sacrifice of his beloved son Isaac. The story has all the elements of true drama – love, anguish, deception, a miraculous birth, suspense, a supreme act of faith in an Almighty God through a human sacrifice with the heightened tension of a last minute reprieve.

Despite a tremendous internal struggle, Abraham's faith is strong enough for him to apparently be prepared to fulfil God's demand and kill his own son. At the very last minute, even as Abraham's hand is raised to stab his son to death, God intervenes and commands Abraham to stop, content that Abraham's faith is secure, and a ram is substituted as the sacrifice.

This story, and its demonstration of 'a supreme act of faith', is the basis of the magic that sparked the evolution of not only the Jewish religion, but of Christianity – seeing Abraham as the spiritual ancestor of Christ – and of Islam – seeing Ishmael as the seed of the Arabic nations with Ibrahim (Abraham) as the true ancestor of the Muslim faith.

CHAPTER 9   Pharaoh Akhenaten – The King who Discovered God

1. Cyril Aldred, *Akhenaten King of Egypt.* Thames & Hudson, 1988; and *Akhenaten and Nefertiti.* The Brooklyn Museum, 1973. Francis Fèvre, *Akhenaton et Néfertiti.* Editions Hazan, 1998.
2. James Henry Breasted, *Ancient Records of Egypt.* Russell & Russell, New York, 1906.
3. James Henry Breasted, *A History of Egypt.* London, 1905.
4. Arthur Weigall, *The Life and Times of Akhnaton.* London, 1923.
5. James Henry Breasted, *The Dawn of Conscience.* Prentice Hall, 1976.
6. Donald A. Mackenzie, *Egyptian Myth and Legend.* The Gresham Publishing Co., London, 1913.
7. *Ibid.*
8. N. de G. Davies, *The Rock Tombs of El Amarna. [I-VI].* The Egypt Exploration Fund, London, 1905.
9. Weigall, *op. cit.*
10. M. Samuel, *Texts From the Time of Akhenaten.* Bibliotheca Aegyptiaca, Brussels, 1938.
11. James Henry Breasted, *Ancient Records of Egypt II.* Russell & Russell, 1906.
12. Siegfried Morenz, *Egyptian Religion.* Cornell University Press, 1994.
13. A. Volten, *Zwei Altagyptische Politische Shriften.* Copenhagen, 1945.
14. In one sense his choice of the sun as a representative of infinite power was more appropriate than any other he could possibly have imagined, and he was 5,000 million years correct. We now know that without the sun, the earth and all the planets in our solar system would not exist – but in about five billion years time the sun itself will die and with it all our planets. 'Sun Storm', *Equinox*, Channel 4, 25 August 1998.
15. 'In the Morning of Man', *The Times Literary Supplement*, 29 November 1947.
16. Breasted, *History of Egypt, op. cit.*
17. Aldred, *Akhenaten King of Eygpt, op. cit.*
18. N. de G. Davies, *The Rock Tombs of El Amarna – Part I.* The Egypt Exploration Fund, London, 1903.
19. A number of the tenets were, subsequently, 'weakened' to a greater or lesser extent, through the influences of traditional Egyptian and local practices.
20. Worship in a Temple has not been possible since the destruction of the Second Temple in Jerusalem in 70 CE, and there is no prospect of a new Temple being built on the old site, as it is today occupied by the Muslim Dome of the Rock.
21. Belief in the hereafter became prominent in post- biblical Judaism. Hell was

referred to as 'Gehonnim', after the valley of Hinnom, south-west of Jerusalem, a place of pagan sacrifice.

22. Kathleen M. Kenyon, *The Bible and Recent Archaeology*. British Museum Publications, 1987; Amnon Ben-Tor, *The Archaeology of Ancient Israel*. The Open University of Israel, 1992.

23. de G. Davies, *The Rock Tombs – Part I, op.cit*

CHAPTER 10   Joseph – Prophet of Destiny

1. The ancient Egyptian 'Tale of Two Brothers' is based on a similar plot of attempted seduction and subsequent false accusation. R.T. Rundle Clark, *Myth and Symbol in Ancient Egypt*. Thames & Hudson, 1978.

2. William Congreve, *The Mourning Bride*, III, vii.

3. Manetho was a third century BCE Egyptian priestly historian, who is believed to have referred to Akhenaten and Joseph in his writings – see Chapter 13.

4. The likelihood of Joseph being 'given' a wife from this pro-monotheistic source fits in well with our historical understanding of conditions at the Temple of On in Heliopolis at the time. As N. de G. Davies notes in a treatise on the Smaller Tombs and Boundary Stelae of El-Amarna: '…it is precisely in Heliopolis that the jurisdiction of the sun-worshipping King [Akhenaten] would be most readily accepted.' N. de G. Davies, *The Rock Tombs of El Amarna – Part V, Smaller Tombs and Boundary Stelae*. The Egypt Exploration Fund, London, 1908.

5. N. de G. Davies, *The Rock Tombs of El Amarna – Part III, The Tombs of Huya and Ahmes*. The Egypt Exploration Fund, London, 1905.

6. N. de G. Davies, *The Rock Tombs of El Amarna – Part II, The Tombs of Panehesy and Meryra II*. The Egypt Exploration Fund, London, 1905.

7. Donald B. Redford, *Akhenaten the Heretic King*. Princeton University Press, 1984.

8. The subsidiary clue to this lavishing of gold collars and associating Joseph with the time of Akhenaten comes from Targum Onkelos – an interpretive commentary on the Pentateuch. In its coverage of Genesis 49:24 we find:

   'And his prophecy was fulfilled for he observed the law in secret and placed his trust in Divine power, then gold was lifted on his arms, he took possession of a kingdom and became stronger.'

   This Targum appears to have been taken from The Book of Jubilees. In the Ethiopian version of this Book, Pharaoh, speaking about Joseph says: '…put a golden chain around his neck, and proclaim before him saying: "El El wa abrir"…And he put a ring upon his hand…'. See Maren Niehoff, The Figure of Joseph in Targums, *Journal of Jewish Studies*, 1987–88; E.J. Goodrich, *The Book of Jubilees*. Oberlin, Ohio, 1888.

9. de G. Davies, *The Rock Tombs – Part V, op. cit*.

10. John Romer, *Romer's Egypt – A New Light on the Civilisation of Ancient Egypt*. Michael Joseph, 1982.

11. Cyril Aldred, *Akhenaten King of Egypt*. Thames & Hudson, 1988.

12. W.H. Murnane, *The Penguin Guide to Ancient Egypt*. Penguin Books, 1983.

13. The memory of the name 'Faiyum' has remained in Hebrew culture and crops up in various forms. Moses Maimonides – one of the greatest Jewish philosophers, for example, writing the 'Iggeret Teman' (Letter to the Jews in

Yemen) or 'Petah-Tikvah' (Opening of Hope), in 1172 CE, was responding to a pleading letter from Rabbi Jacob al-Fayuim of Yemen.

Moses Maimonides, *The Guide for the Perplexed*, trans. M. Friedlander. Dover Publications, New York, 1956.

14. Amy K. Blank, *The Spoken Choice*. Hebrew Union College Press, Cincinnati, Ohio, 1959.

15. The Egyptian concept of 'Maat' started out as meaning straightness in geometric terms, but later came to mean order out of chaos in creational terms – trueness in behaviour, a continual correct human behaviour, an obligation passed from the gods onto the king and then to the people, which gradually included righteous spiritual thinking. A similar parallel exists in Hebrew where the word for straight is 'iasar', which also takes on the meaning of ethical correctness.

Later 'Maat' evolved into guidelines for justice and a legal system, with judges wearing the sign for 'Maat' as they sat in judgement. Here we have the seeds of the divine laws that were to be later developed into detailed instructions and binding laws on the Hebrew people of Canaan.

For those which did not conform to 'Maat' there was, however, the possibility of forgiveness from God, or recourse to magic. We see it in the lessons from Merikare, a Pharaoh of the 21st century BCE, and in the following:

> Though the servant was disposed to do evil,
>
> Yet it is the Lord disposed to be merciful...
>
> Punish me not for my many misdeeds,
>
> I am one who knows not himself.
>
> I am a witless man.

A. Erman, *Denksteine aus der Thebanischen Graberstadt*. Berlin, 1911.

This moral sense is already well developed in the writings of the sage Petosiris of Hermopolis, who lived in the 4th century BCE:

> No-one reaches the saving west unless his heart was righteous by doing 'Maat'.
> There no distinction is made between the inferior and superior person; only that
> one is found faultless when the balances and the two weights stand before the
> Lord of eternity. No-one is free from the reckoning. Thoth as a baboon holds
> [the balances], to count each man according to what he has done upon earth.

E. Otto, *Die Biographischen Inschriften der Agyptischen Spatzeit*. Leyden, 1954.

Here we see the seeds of confession and absolution from sin. Later evolved into the Hebrew Day of Atonement, and the Christian doctrine of Original Sin and redemption through a saviour.

16. Reflections of the divine word's inspirational instruction came out as solecisms of wisdom; the ideas of 'keep reticent', hold the truth within yourself, speak justice and do justice. As such 'Maat', personified as a goddess figure with feather headdress, became the basis of the Egyptian legal system. Judges wore a necklace holding the sign for 'Maat' when they sat in judgement. G. Moller, *Zeitschrift für Agyptische Sprache und Altertumskunde*. Leipzig, 1920.

17. J.B. Pritchard (ed.), *Ancient Near Eastern Texts Relating to the Old Testament*, 2nd edn. Princeton University Press, 1955.

18. William W. Hallo and William Kelly Simpson, *The Ancient Near East, A History*. Harcourt Brace Jovanovich, 1971.

19. Chaim Rabin, Qumran Studies, *Script Judaica II*. Oxford University Press, 1957.
20. Alkaabez, *Menoth ha-Levi*. Venice, 1585.

CHAPTER 11   The Long Trek South

1. Archaeological work, largely carried out by German and French teams, shows that a pseudo-Hebrew Community existed on Elephantine Island until just after 400 BCE. The anomalous existence of the Community is discussed further in Chapter 18. 'Elephantine', *Encyclopaedia Judaica*. Keter Publishing House, Jerusalem, 1992.
2. Dozens of papyri, written in Aramaic, were discovered on the Island of Elephantine at the turn of the 19th century and give us details of the lifestyle of the pseudo-Hebrew Community that lived and worshipped there. A.E. Cowley, *Aramaic Papyri of the Fifth Century BC*. Oxford, 1923.
3. There is the general principle (recognized, for example, by Plato and Leibnitz) that, although every effort can be made to remove all physical reminders of a system or concept, an idea – especially a powerful and plausible one – is the hardest thing to eliminate.
    When terror threatens a valid new idea, the idea tends to retreat to an environment of safety, sympathy or secrecy. Safety was to be found in the remoteness of the Island of Yeb (the Island of Elephantine); sympathy was to be found at On (modern Heliopolis, near Cairo), the traditional centre of sun worship and the site of the first temple to Aten; secrecy was always to be a by-word for the descendants of the priests of Aten.
4. How long the sympathy and loyalty towards monotheism continued at On after Akhenaten's death is difficult to determine. Especially as, if it did continue, it would have done so in secret. There are, however, a few clues to be gained from our knowledge that when Jeremiah fled to Egypt, around 580 BCE, and Onias IV around 175 BCE, the place they sought sanctuary at was On. Onias built a Temple at Leontopolis, north of On, at a place now known as Tell el-Yehudiyeh.

CHAPTER 12   Moses – Prince of Egypt

1. The word 'Moses' meant 'given birth to', and was usually associated with a prefix name relating to a god. But it was not unknown for a short-form name to be used on its own. J.W. Griffiths, The Egyptian Derivation of the Name of Moses, *Journal of Near Eastern Studies*, 1953.
2. Alfred Sendrey, *Music in Ancient Israel*. Philosophical Library, New York, 1969.
3. Philip Hyatt, Yahweh as the God of my Father, *Vetus Testamentum* 5, 1955.
4. Donald B. Redford, *Akhenaten the Heretic King*. Princeton University Press, 1984.
5. E.A. Wallis Budge, *The Mummy*. Outlet Book Co Inc 1989; James Henry Breasted, *Ancient Records of Egypt*. Russell & Russell, 1906.
6. Irving M. Zeitlin, Ancient Judaism. Polity Press, 1991.
7. Sigmund Freud, Moses and Monotheism. The Hogarth Press, 1951.

CHAPTER 13   The Exodus – Moses Does a Schindler

1. Oscar Schindler was a German businessman who, during the Second World War, bribed the Nazis into allowing him to employ over 1,000 Jews in his

Polish factories, thereby effectively saving their lives. His life was featured in Steven Spielberg's 1993 film *Schindler's List*, based on the novel by Thomas Keneally.

2. Ramses II's mummy shows him to have been a tall, distinguished man of lean physique. Usually very little is given away about the personality of pharaohs in surviving texts. The records are invariably of encounters with gods, or exaggerations of military successes and campaigns. We can glean, however, that Ramses II was someone who could be negotiated with and would, under pressure, have seen reason.

   Ramses II's ambitious building programme probably led him to make increasing demands on his construction workers, but it seems unlikely that the work the Hebrews were put to was too distant from their settlement area in the Faiyum. These considerations, however, do not rule out the possibility that teams of Hebrew slaves were drafted into Memphis, which was not too distant, or even to the Theban region.

3. W. Gunther Plaut (ed.), *The Torah – A Modern Commentary.* The Union of American Hebrew Congregations, 1981.

4. *Ibid.*

5. Nina Collins, 'Perspectives', *The Jewish Chronicle*, 30 December 1994.

6. J.H. Hertz (ed.), *The Pentateuch and Haftorahs.* Soncino Press, 1969.

7. Plaut, *op. cit.*

8. Hebrew lettering, from the earliest available inscription (dated at *c.*700 BCE) found on the Siloam conduit at Jerusalem, shows a clear resemblance to Phoenician script of 200 years earlier. The 'Siloam inscription', written in the same script as that on the Moabite stone of the same period (which is now in the Louvre in Paris), was originally acquired by the Museum of Constantinople. The inscription was written on the sidewall of the conduit, and it has been identified with a conduit mentioned in the Second Book of Kings in the Old Testament:

   II Kings 20:20   And the rest of the acts of Hezekiah, and all his might, and how he made a
                      pool, and a conduit, and brought water into the city, are they not written in the
                      book of the chronicles of the kings of Judah?

   During the 6th and 5th centuries BCE Hebrew had fallen out of common use and was replaced by Aramaic. By the 3rd or 2nd century BCE it does not appear to have evolved to more than 20 letters, as can be seen on Palestinian ossuaries (bone caskets) from that period.

   There is other evidence, however, that traces the Hebrew writing to Canaanite origins, influenced by Egyptian. Jonathan Lotan, an Anglo-Israeli scholar, ascribes the origins of Ancient Hebrew to Egyptian rather than Ugarit. He cites a number of examples of Egyptian hieratic words which were adopted into Ancient Canaanite *c.*1500 BCE, in his book *From A to Aleph: 3 Steps to Writing Hebrew* (Qualum Publishing, 1996). See also Jacob de Haas, *The Encyclopaedia of Jewish Knowledge.* Berhman's Jewish Book House, New York, 1946.

9. Immediately after Akhenaten the transient Pharaoh Smenkhkara ruled for a brief period of months.

10. In converting Biblical measurements of length into metric units, the Egyptian standard has been adopted in most descriptions in this book.

The commonly used Biblical measures of length are generally related to the Akkadian or Ugaritic cubit of 44.5cm (17.4 inches), although a 'Royal Cubit' of 53cm was also in use in Israel. The Akkadian and Royal Cubit may have come into use for later references in the Bible, but for earlier Old Testament references I believe that the Egyptian Cubit of 51cm is more appropriate and gives a much more accurate picture of dimension. Almost all generally quoted conversions of cubit measurements for the earlier parts of the Bible are, therefore, probably inaccurate. We can be certain of the accuracy of the Egyptian Cubit at 51cm from the size of the wooden shrine box, designed to hold the metal cubit rod and now in the Cairo Museum's Tutankhamun collection. There is another example in the Liverpool Museum.

11. K. von Sethe, *Die altagyptishen Pyramidentexte, neu herausgegeben und erlautert.* Leipzig, 1908–.

12. The Kohathites were the sons of Levi, who was Jacob's son. Levi's other sons formed the tribes of Gershon and Merari.

13. K. Skorecki, S. Selig, S. Blazer, R. Bradman, N. Bradman, P.J. Waburton, M. Ismajlowicz and M.F. Hammer, 'Y Chromosomes of Jewish Priests', *Nature* Vol. 385, 2 January 1997.

14. For the past 3,000 years it has been the custom of male Jews who considered themselves of the priestly line to marry and to have children only with other Jews also from the priestly line.

15. Geza Vermes, *The Complete Dead Sea Scrolls in English.* The Penguin Press, 1997.

16. Robert Eisenman and Michael Wise, *The Dead Sea Scrolls Uncovered.* Penguin Books, 1993.

17. Vermes, *op. cit.* Letters between [ ] mean likely reconstructions, between ( ) glosses inserted for sense of text.

18. Lucia Raspe, 'Manetho on the Exodus: A Reappraisal', *Jewish Studies Quarterly*, No.2, 1998.

19. *Ibid.*

20. The conventional idea that Ramses II was the Pharaoh of the Exodus is, I believe, wrong. He may well, though, have been the Pharaoh of 'the oppression' who worked the Hebrew slaves to exhaustion fulfilling his building programme.

21. In the Authorized version of the Bible, the rod Moses fashions is referred to as 'a serpent of brass'. As previously mentioned in Chapter 3, brass was unknown until the time of the Romans. In the Hebrew version of the Old Testament the phrase is translated as 'a copper serpent'.

22. John Rogerson, *Atlas of the Bible.* Facts on File, New York, 1991.

CHAPTER 14 Towards Qumran

1. When Moses died, Joshua inherited the task of leading the Hebrews in the conquest and settlement of Canaan – the Promised Land. The conquered Central and Northern areas were divided amongst the tribes descended from Joseph and Jacob, but they continued to sustain attacks from the Philistines, Midianites and Ammonites.

There followed a period of 'Judges', who guided the path of the new 'tribal federation' until *c.*1050 BCE, when Saul was appointed the first King and the beginnings of a dynasty were established. He was followed by King David and his son King Solomon, the latter undertaking wide-ranging social and administrative reforms and building the First Temple at Jerusalem. After King Solomon's death the Kingdom of Israel was split into the Northern Kingdom, ruled by Jeroboam, and the Southern Kingdom, ruled by Rehoboam, Solomon's son. It is in this period that a firm date of 945–924 BCE can be established for the incursion of the Egyptian Pharaoh Shosenq I into Jewish territory. Inscriptions on the Temple of Amum at Thebes list the towns he captured in Judah to the south, and archaeological evidence shows he reached Megiddo in Northern Israel. He is mentioned in the Old Testament as 'Shishak king of Egypt' (I Kings 14:25 and II Chronicles 12:1–9).

Various Hebrew kings continued to rule, albeit with many military setbacks, in the northern and southern kingdoms during the period of the Prophets Elijah and Elisha (from 870–790 BCE). Battles continued with Aramaeans (Syrians), Moabites and Egyptians until, in 722 BCE, the Assyrians conquered the Northern Kingdom and dispersed its ten tribes into its territories further to the north. The Southern Kingdom, now known as Judah, came under the domination of the Assyrians until about 640 BCE, when Assyrian power started to decline and the Babylonians became the force in the region. Nebuchadnezzar II invaded the country and in 586 BCE destroyed the Temple in Jerusalem, carrying the bulk of the population off into captivity in Babylon.

Babylon's control of Judah did not last long and in 539 BCE King Cyrus II of Persia conquered Babylon. According to the Biblical scribe Ezra (Ezra 2:64), 42,360 Jews were then encouraged to return to Israel, which was now part of the Persian Empire. The Persians behaved in a much more benign way towards the Israelites and they were able to commence re-building the Temple at Jerusalem, within a much contracted Judah.

Many Hebrews however, stayed on in Babylonia and, in Biblical terms, they eventually became the dominant literary force. The Babylonian Torah – in the wider sense of Torah as the written and oral Law – differed in many respects from the Palestinian Torah, but it was the former which subsequently established itself as the accepted canon. The Temple was finally re-built in 516 BCE, and when more settled conditions returned in the south, around 450 BCE, both Ezra and Nehemiah returned to Judah from Babylon. Their aim was to shore up a weakening observance of Jewish law and to secure Jerusalem as the religious centre of the country.

Alexander the Great, King of Macedonia, conquered the lands surrounding Jerusalem in 332 BCE and in 198 BCE control over the country came under the Syrian part of the Seleucid Empire (as opposed to the Ptolemaic part, which ruled in Egypt). Attempts by Antiochus IV Epiphanes to Hellenize his inherited Empire and make his subjects worship Greek gods was the last straw for the Jews of Judah, and they revolted under Judah the Maccabee in 167 BCE. As the Hellenic Empire tottered, a free Jewish State was finally re-established in 143 BCE and a line of 'Hasmonaean' Jewish rulers set about re-encompassing the territories – Idumea to the south; Samaria and Galilee to the north; and the Land of Tubius to the east.

The Hasmonaean rule lasted until 63 BCE, when the Romans swept into the Holy Land and Pompey established it as a Protectorate. There was a brief period of interruption by Parthian invaders who set the Hasmonaean

Antigonus on the throne in 40 BCE. Rome responded in 37 BCE by appointing Herod the Great, an Edomite from an Idumean family, as King of the Jews. After three years of fighting he established his title, restored the Temple to its former glory, and ruled the country until 4 BCE and the birth of Jesus.

Just to complete the picture, in 132 CE, 62 years after the Temple had been sacked by the Romans, Bar-Kochba led another Jewish revolt. This episode ended in disaster and brought about the expulsion of Jews from Jerusalem. It was not until the 4th century CE that they were officially able to return. When they were able to return, the reinstated Jews were increasingly marginalized by Rome's growing support of Christianity and the integration of Greek influences and philosophy into its culture – an effect to which Judaism was not immune.

2. The continuity of the Levites is difficult to follow from the Bible, but it is clear that some of them were 'set apart from the community'. In Numbers 16:9 we find: 'the God of Israel hath separated you from the congregation of Israel'. They were thus able to maintain a different form of Judaism from the mainstream, and, I believe, able to keep some of the holy writings secret from the rest of the people.

3. Isaiah 1:11, 13   '"To what purpose is the multitude of your sacrifices unto Me?" saith the Lord: "I am full of the burnt offering of rams, and the fat of fed beasts; and I delight not in the blood of the bullocks, or of lambs, or of the goats"…Bring no more vain oblations; incense is an abomination unto me; the new moons and sabbaths, the calling of assemblies, I cannot away with; it is iniquity even the solemn meeting.'

   Micah 3:9, 11–12   'Hear this, I pray you, ye heads of the house of Jacob, and princes of the house of Israel, that abhor judgement, and pervert all equity…The heads thereof judge for reward, and the priests thereof teach for hire, and the prophets thereof divine for money; yet will they lean upon the Lord, and say, "Is not the Lord among us? none evil can come upon us." Therefore shall Zion for your sake be plowed as a field, and Jerusalem shall become heaps, and the mountain of the house as the high places of the forest.'

4. The new texts discovered at the time of King Josiah are now thought to have formed the basis for the Book of Deuteronomy.

5. The intellectual and upper classes who returned from Babylon were more ready to adopt the language and writing of their Aramaic conquerors and that language superseded Hebrew as the main language of the people until about 200 BCE.

There is clear evidence that the Babylonian 'Haftorah' or prayer texts, developed by the Jews living in what is now Iraq, were markedly different from the Eretz Israel or Palestinian version. For example in the 'Haggadah' (the prayer book used in the Festival of Passover), the Eretz Israel version asks five questions about behaviour at the remembrance feast. In today's 'Haggadah' only four questions are asked. There are also considerable differences in the form of 'Kaddish', the traditional prayer for mourners, and in other standard prayers used in modern Jewish services.

From the prayers in modern-day usage it is apparent that the Babylonian school of Hebrew scholars won out over their Eretz Israel rivals, whose influence was finally overwhelmed with the coming of the Crusaders and the destruction of their places of learning.

6. Habakkuk 2:4.
7. Richard Friedman, *Who Wrote the Bible?* HarperCollins, 1997.
8. The new invaders from Macedonia led by Alexander the Great conquered the country around 330 BCE, and instigated the rule of the Ptolemies in Egypt in 323 BCE.
9. Onias III, the High Priest at the Temple of Jerusalem under the Greek Seleucid rule, resisted Hellenization under the religious persecutions of Antiochus Epiphanes. His brother took advantage of the disagreements and superseded Onias IV to become High Priest. Onias IV fled to Heliopolis, in Egypt, and built a Temple at Leontopolis. He returned to Jerusalem four years later, in *c.*170 BCE, when Menelaus bribed his way into the position of High Priest.
10. Correspondence between Professor George Brooke and the author, 9 July 1997.
11. According to Philo, the Therapeutae were a first century CE studious Jewish community living in lower Egypt. They appeared to share many features with the Essenes of Judaea, and some of their antiphonal singing at Passover may be evident from some of the scrolls found at Qumran.
12. Herr Joerg Frey's affiliations are so long that by the time he has given them to you, you have almost forgotten his name! He comes from the Institut für Antikes Judentum und Hellenistische Religionsgeschichte in Tübingen, Germany.
13. Shlomo Margalit, 'Aelia Capitolina', *Judaica* No.45, Marz, 1989.
14. Geza Vermes, *The Complete Dead Sea Scrolls in English.* Penguin Press, 1997. In Vermes' translation here, letters between [ ] indicate likely reconstructions, and those between ( ) glosses necessary for fluency.

    Although there appeared to be two versions of a cubit in use in Judaea at the time of the Qumran-Essenes, one of 44.6cm and another of 52.1cm, for the purposes of comparison I have taken the cubit to measure 51cm. This latter unit is the one certain length in use in Egypt at the time of Akhenaten. Nicholas Reeves, *The Complete Tutankhamun.* Thames & Hudson, 1990.

    An inscription found inside the Siloam conduit in Jerusalem, built by Hezekiah, King of Judah from 720–692 BCE, gives the length of the tunnel as 1,200 cubits. The tunnel measures 533m and this gives a cubit of 44.4cm. M. Powell ('Weights and Measures', *The Anchor Bible Dictionary*, 1992), gives a best averaged estimate for the cubit of 50cm ± 10 per cent. See also James Henry Breasted, *Ancient Records of Egypt – Vol. II.* Russell & Russell, 1906.
15. N. de G. Davies, *The Rock Tombs of El Amarna – Part II.* The Eygpt Exploration Fund, 1905.
16. Breasted, *op. cit.*
17. W.M. Petrie, *Tell el-Amarna.* London, 1894.
18. Cyril Aldred, *Akhenaten King of Egypt.* Thames & Hudson, 1991.
19. *Ibid.*
20. Michael Chyutin, The New Jerusalem Scroll from Qumran – a Comprehensive Reconstruction. *Journal for the Study of the Pseudepigrapha*, Supplement 25, Sheffield Academic Press, 1997. The New Jerusalem Scroll describes an idealized Holy City envisaged by the Qumran-Essenes. The Scroll was obviously of great importance to the Community as examples of its contents were found in caves 1,2,4, 5 and 11 at Qumran. It describes many City features in a similar manner

to those in the Temple Scroll (*see Chapter 1*), although there are significant differences in dimensions and layout.

21. Ian Shaw and Paul Nicholson, *British Museum Dictionary of Ancient Egypt.* BCA/British Museum Press, 1996.

22. Mark Vidler, *The Star Mirror.* Thorsons, 1998.

23. *Sun Rays Fall Perpendicularly on Abu Simbel.* Egyptian State Tourist Office, London. Press Release No. 225, 5.8.98.

24. Mary Barnett, *Gods and Myths of Ancient Egypt.* Brockhampton Press, 1996.

25. The General Assembly Hall, The Mound, Edinburgh, is the location for the first meetings of Scotland's Parliament, with an official opening ceremony on 1 July 1999. Sometime in the second half of 2001, the Parliament will move to a new building, designed by the Spaniard Enric Miralles, located next to Holyrood Palace in Edinburgh.

26. Roland de Vaux, *Archaeology and the Dead Sea Scrolls.* Oxford University Press, 1959.

27. J. Van de Ploeg, *The Excavations of Qumran.* Longmans, Green & Co, 1958.

28. The Pharisees were the main religious and political opposition to the Temple priests in the Second Temple period. They preached a wider form of Judaism, related not just to the letter of the written text, but also to the Oral Law.

CHAPTER 15 The Lost Treasures of Akhenaten

1. John Marco Allegro, *The Treasure of the Copper Scroll.* Routledge & Kegan Paul, 1960.

2. The body of Akhenaten has never been positively identified. It seems likely that a tomb (WV25) was prepared for him at Thebes before he transferred the seat of his throne to Akhetaten, but it was never occupied. In 1907 a burial chamber, KV55, was discovered at Wadi Biban el-Muluk, in western Thebes, which contained a shrine to Queen Tiyi, Akhenaten's mother, and a coffin and canopic jars. It seems possible that the bodies of both Akhenaten and Tiyi were taken from the Royal tomb prepared for them at Akhetaten and removed to Thebes during the reign of Tutankhamun. The body was a male and carried the same blood group as that of Tutankhamun, Akhenaten's brother (A_2MN), indicating that it may have been Akhenaten. However, its age at death, estimated at 20 to 25, is too low to confirm ownership.

3. The name Faiyum is found in many variations of spelling; I have chosen Faiyum as the preferred variant unless it occurs otherwise in a specific reference.

4. Bezalel Porten, *Archives from Elephantine: the Life of an Ancient Jewish Military Colony.* University of California Press, Los Angeles, 1968.

5. Robert Eisenman and Michael Wise, *The Dead Sea Scrolls Uncovered.* Penguin Books, 1993.

6. Why the 'Admonitions' document should be written in cryptic form is none too clear. In itself it appears fairly innocuous, but it does allude to 'ways of achieving long life' and 'the hidden things of the testimony' which can be understood by examining the past. Perhaps within the text there is an encrypted message.

7. The Old Testament was translated into Greek from Hebrew versions (maintained by Jews settled in Alexandria), in *c.*320 BCE. The New Testament

was copied by the early Christians in Alexandria, *c.*150–200 CE. They added six signs from Demotic Egyptian for sounds not available in Greek.

8. Ian Shaw and Paul Nicholson, *British Museum Dictionary of Ancient Egypt.* BCA/British Museum Press, 1996. R.J. Gillings, *Mathematics in the Time of the Pharaohs.* Harvard University Press, Cambridge MA, 1972.

9. Allegro, *op. cit.*; Florentino Garcia Martinez, *The Dead Sea Scrolls Translated.* E.J. Brill, Leiden, 1994; Geza Vermes, *The Complete Dead Sea Scrolls in English.* The Penguin Press, 1997; Al Wolters, *The Copper Scroll – Overview, Text and Translation.* Sheffield Academic Press, 1996.

10. Vermes, *op. cit.*

11. Recorded interview between Jozef Milik and the author, Paris, 8 November 1998.

12. Henri Gauthier, *Dictionnaire des Noms Géographiques Contenus dans les Textes Hiéroglyphiques.* La Société Royale de Geographie d'Egypte, 1925. Aristide Calderini, *Dizionario dei Nomi Geografici e Topografici dell' Egitto Greco-Romano.* Cisalpino-Goliardica, 1935–1980. Alan H. Gardiner, *Ancient Egyptian Onomastica.* Oxford University Press, 1947. Erich Lüddeckens, *Demotisches Namenbuch.* Auftrage der Akademie der Wissenschaften und der Literatur in Mainz. Wisebaden, Reichert, 1980– . Wolfgan Helck and Eberhard Otto, *Lexikon der Agyptologie.* Wiesbaden, O. Harrassowitz, 1975– . John Baines and Jaromir Malek, *Atlas of Ancient Egypt.* Facts on File, New York, 1985. *Tübinger Atlas des Vorderen Orients.* Univ. Tübingen, Wiesbaden, Reichert, 1977– .

13. This was confirmed by Dr A.R. David, Reader in Egyptology at The Manchester Museum (in correspondance with the author, 18 January 1999), who stated that:

> There is no Greek equivalent of Akhenaten. His previous name, before he changed it to show his allegiance to Aten, was Amenhotep IV. The Greek version of Amenhotep was Amenophis. Also, there is no Greek equivalent of the city, Akhetaten. I am not aware that there is any reference to either Akhenaten or Akhetaten in Greek literature, because the king and the city were obliterated from history until the site of Tell el-Amarna (Akhetaten) was rediscovered in recent times.

14. N. de G. Davies, *The Rock Tombs of El Amarna – Part II.* The Egypt Exploration Fund, 1905.

15. H. Frankfort and J.D.S. Pendlebury, *The City of Akhenaten – Part II.* Oxford University Press, 1933.

16. Allegro, *op. cit.*

17. Shaw and Nicholson, *op. cit.*
    http://touregypt.net/suntempl.htm.

18. Roland de Vaux, *Archaeology and the Dead Sea Scrolls.* Oxford University Press, 1959; Frankfort and Pendlebury, *op. cit.*
    Various designs of jars found at Qumran and nearby Ain Feshkha are illustrated in de Vaux's book. They bear remarkable similarity, in design, size and colouring, to pottery found in the Amarna area of Egypt, dating from the 18th Dynasty and the period of Akhenaten. Particularly good examples of this correlation can be seen in the Petrie Museum of Egyptian Archaeology at University College London – notably Catalogue No. UC 19153, a late 18th-Dynasty storage jar found at Tell el Yahudiyeh, north of Heliopolis.

19. de G. Davies, The *Rock Tombs – Part II*, *op. cit.*

20. *Manos, the Hands of Fate.*
    http:/www.cs.colostate.edu/catlin.

21. de G. Davies, *The Rock Tombs – Part II*, *op.cit.* N. de G. Davies, *The Rock Tombs of El Amarna – Part V.* The Egypt Exploration Fund, 1908.

22. *Ibid.*

23. Paul Fenton, *Genizah Fragments.* Taylor-Schechter Genizah Research Unit, University of Cambridge, 1981–82. http://www.cam.ac.uk/Libraries/Taylor-Schechter.

24. R.H. Charles, *Apocrypha and Pseudepigrapha of the Old Testament II.* Clarendon Press, 1913.

25. J. Pouilly, *La Regle de la Communaute de Qumran: Son Evolution Litteraire.* Gabalda Press, 1913.

26. H.H. Rowley, The Teacher of Righteousness and the Dead Sea Scrolls, *Bulletin of the John Rylands Library* 40, 1957.

27. Shaw and Nicholson, *op. cit.*

28. de Vaux, *op. cit.*

29. de G. Davies, *The Rock Tombs – Part II*, *op. cit.*

30. *Ibid.*

31. There are no obvious queenly candidates who had a tomb built for them associated with either the First or Second Temple in Jerusalem, and certainly not with the Qumran-Essenes. The only remotely possible queens of Israel who could be candidates are Bathsheba – the wife of King David (who had Uriah the Hittite killed in order to marry her); Jezebel – the Baal-worshipping wife of King Ahab *c.*840 BCE; and her daughter, Athaliah, who ruled in her own right and was also a canvasser on behalf of Baal.

32. Geoffrey Thorndike Martin, *The Royal Tomb at El-Amarna – The Objects.* Egypt Exploration Society, 1974.

33. N. de G. Davies, *The Rock Tombs of El Amarna – Part I.* The Egypt Exploration Fund, 1903.

34. Shaw and Nicholson, *op. cit.*

35. de G. Davies, *The Rock Tombs – Part II*, op. cit.

36. W.M.F. Petrie, *Tell el-Amarna.* London, 1894.

37. Frankfort and Pendlebury, op. cit.

38. N. de G. Davies, *The Rock Tombs of El Amarna – Part III.* The Egypt Exploration Fund, 1905.

39. de G. Davies, *The Rock Tombs – Part II*, *op. cit.*

40. S. Goranson, 'Further Reflections on the Copper Scroll', International Symposium on the Copper Scroll, The University of Manchester Institute of Science and Technology, 8–11 September, 1996.

41. Allegro's translation of '...*tithe vessels and figured coins*', is problematic. His translation would certainly exclude 14th century BCE Egypt as a location, and probably the First Temple at Jerusalem too, because the earliest known coins date from 7th century BCE Anatolia (Turkey), and were rather crude blob-like gold or silver units. The use of figured coins spread outward to central Mediterranean areas, but they were not struck in Egypt until Greek influences arrived around 320 BCE. For this reason the translations by Al Wolters ('...*vessels of tribute*'), or Geza Vermes ('...*gold and vessels of offering*'), are preferred.

In general John Allegro uses the term '*tithes*' where other translators use the term '*offerings*' or '*tributes*'. The practice of tithe contributions to the Temple was not unknown in Egypt. Clear examples come from honey, meat and wine, destined as tithe offerings to Aten at Akhetaten. On tithe offerings of wine the formulatory docketed phrasing is 'in the basin of...', a phrasing frequently copied in the Copper Scroll. See J.D.S. Pendlebury, *The City of Akhenaten – Part III*. Egypt Exploration Society, 1951.

42. de G. Davies, *The Rock Tombs – Part I, op. cit.*

43. References to resins and oils in the Copper Scroll indicate that their use was as an offering, whereas in Biblical times unguents were used to anoint a ruler or consecrate holy vessels. This difference in usage can be related to ritual in the Great Temple at Akhetaten rather than the Temple at Jerusalem. There are several inscriptional examples of unguent being offered by Akhenaten – in the 'Jubilee Scene', in the Fitzwilliam Museum at Cambridge, England, and on an alabaster slab excavated at Tel el-Amarna, now in the Cairo Museum. See Cyril Aldred, *Akhenaten and Nefertiti*. The Brooklyn Museum, 1973.

44. Shortly after 1892 the Egyptian Department of Antiquities uncovered a painted pavement in the village of Hawata and removed it to the Cairo Museum. See de. G. Davies, *The Rock Tombs – Part I, op. cit.*

45. Eugene Ulrich, 4QJoshua and Joshua's First Altar in the Promised Land, in G.J. Brooke and F.G. Martinez (eds), *New Qumran Texts and Studies*, E.J.Brill, 1994.

46. Ephraim Stern, 'Gerizim', *The New Encyclopedia of Archaeological Excavation in the Holy Land*. Simon & Schuster, 1993.

CHAPTER 16   The Legacy of Akhenaten

1. Titus Lucretius Carus, 99–55 BCE. From *The Concise Oxford Dictionary of Quotations*, World Books, 1967.

2. Roland de Vaux, *Archaeology and the Dead Sea Scrolls*. Oxford University Press, 1959.

3. Numerous ostraca (pot sherds) and relics have been excavated from the site of Qumran and they all tend to confirm the monastic lifestyle and rituals of the Essene Community described in their scrolls, and by contemporary writers such as Philo, Pliny and Josephus. One such fascinating recent discovery was made in February 1996, by a team of 18 treasure-seeking Americans using a bull-dozer! They literally stumbled upon two 1st-century CE sherds in a wall facing the Qumran Community's cemetery. Whilst the method of 'excavation' is to be deplored, the significance of the find is considerable in that it provides the first non-Dead Sea Scroll tangible evidence that the people at Qumran considered themselves a 'Yahad' – a 'Community'.

The larger piece, written in Hebrew, is part of a 'Deed of Gift' document describing the assets – a house and its surroundings in Jericho, a slave, valuable fruits – that an individual intended to donate to the Community when he joined. There is also a description of the process of entry into the Community involving the giving up of money and worldly goods as a requirement of membership. The phrasing of the Deed is very similar to that used in 5th-century BCE papyri found at Elephantine, in Egypt.

E. Eshel, 'The Newly Discovered Qumran Ostraca', International

Symposium on the Copper Scroll, 8–11 September 1996, Manchester–Sheffield Centre for Dead Sea Scrolls Research.

4. Paul Fenton, *Genizah Fragments*. Taylor–Schechter Genizah Research Unit, University of Cambridge, 1981–82. (http://www.cam.ac.uk/Libraries/Taylor-Schechter). Geza Vermes, *The Complete Dead Sea Scrolls in English – 1QS, 4Q265*. Allen Lane, 1997.

5. In 1898, 140,000 fragments of the 'Genizah' were donated to the University of Cambridge Library to form the Taylor–Schechter Collection; these now constitute 75 per cent of the Genizah fragments known to exist worldwide.

6. Fragments written on paper are post-11th century, those on vellum (leather) are dated between the 8th and 11th centuries, whilst examples on papyrus are from the 6th to the 8th centuries.

7. Elam lay east of Babylonia, in the modern state of Khuzistan. Its capital was Susa, the Shushan of the Book of Esther.

8. O. Eissfeldt, in 'Theologische Literaturzeitung', No.10, 1949; translated by G.R. Driver, *The Hebrew Scrolls from the Neighbourhood of Jericho and the Dead Sea*. Oxford University Press, 1951.

9. Could this ceremony be the forerunner of the 'Barmitzvah', where a Jewish boy, at the age of 13, makes a public commitment to his faith and reads from the Torah in front of a synagogue congregation?

10. The three lower orders of the Masonic movement are known as craft degrees – of which there are about 300,000 members in Great Britain alone, where the modern movement was founded in about 1600 CE. Only a selected few members are 'invited' by a Supreme Council to rise above the 3rd Degree. After that comes the 4th Degree, 'Secret Master', and 5th Degree, 'Perfect Master'. Progress thereafter is through various degrees, many with biblical titles – 13th Degree 'Royal Arch (of Enoch)', 16th Degree 'Prince of Jerusalem', 24th Degree 'Prince of the Tabernacle', 28th Degree 'Knight of the Sun', and up to the 32nd Degree, 'Sublime Prince of the Royal Secret', and the highest 33rd Degree, 'Grand Inspector General'. Stephen King, *The Brotherhood*. Granada Publishing Ltd, 1984.

11. Robert Eisenman and Michael Wise, *The Dead Sea Scrolls Uncovered*. Penguin Books, 1993.

12. The Qumran-Essenes would have had works in their possession whose contents were contrary to their own beliefs. The Dead Sea Scrolls appeared to constitute an archival library of reference material, as well as a place for the Essenes' own works.

13. Yigael Yadin, *The Message of the Scrolls*. Weidenfeld & Nicolson, 1957.

14. Stephen Pfann, 'The Corpus of Manuscripts Written in the Qumran Cryptic Scripts', The Dead Sea Scrolls – Fifty Years After Their Discovery. International Congress, Jerusalem, 20–25 July 1997.

15. Adolfo Roitman, *A Day at Qumran – The Dead Sea Sect and Its Scrolls*. The Israel Museum, Jerusalem, 1997.

16. Ernest A. Wallis Budge, *The Mummy*. Outlet Book Co Inc, 1989.

17. The New Year (Rosh Hashanah) and Chanukah (celebrating the re-dedication of the Second Temple *c.*164 BCE) were festivals developed after the destruction of the First Temple. Other festivals are mentioned in the Temple Scroll, but it is not certain that this scroll was sectarian.

18. The first letter on 'Works Reckoned as Righteous' (4Q394–398), as interpreted by Eisenman and Wise *op. cit.*, gives a detailed exposition on the Essene calendar, and mentions the Passover, Festival of Weeks, Day of Atonement and Festival of Booths (Tabernacles), but not Purim.

Although conventionally associated with the Persian period of the 5th century BCE, Purim has recently been shown to have been based on a much older Assyrian myth dating back at least to the 7th century BCE. Dr Stephanie Dalley, Shikito Research Fellow in Assyriology at the Oriental Institute, Oxford University, at a lecture entitled 'Esther and Purim: The Assyrian Background' given on 24 February 1999, convincingly related the story of Esther and Mordecai to the Assyrian gods Ishtar and Marduk and the name 'Purim' to the Akkadian term for the casting of lots, amongst other commonalities. This attribution to a Mesopotamian rather than Persian source for the Festival of Purim further explains the Qumran-Essenes' essential reluctance to incorporate an 'alien' festival into their calendar.

19. Cyril Aldred, *Akhenaten King of Egypt.* Thames & Hudson, 1988.

20. James Henry Breasted, *Ancient Records of Egypt – Vol II.* Russell & Russell, 1906.

21. Ernest A. Wallis Budge, *The Book of the Dead.* Gramercy Books, 1995; R.T. Rundle Clark, *Myth and Symbol in Ancient Egypt.* Thames & Hudson, 1978.

22. Wallis Budge, *The Mummy, op. cit.*

23. B.-Z. Wacholder, *The Dawn of Qumran.* Hebrew Union College, Cincinnati, 1983; Dwight D. Swanson, '"A Covenant Just Like Jacob's" – The Covenant of 11QT29 and Jeremiah's New Covenant', *New Qumran Texts and Studies.* E.J. Brill, 1994; Philip R. Davies, *Behind the Essenes – History and Ideology in the Dead Sea Scrolls.* Scholars Press, Atlanta, Georgia, 1987.

24. Davies, *op. cit.*

25. Raymonde de Gans, *Toutankhamon.* Editions de L'Erable, Paris, 1968.

26. Fenton, *op. cit.*

27. Davies, *op. cit.*

28. Swanson, *op. cit.*

29. According to a report in the *Jewish Chronicle* of 22 January 1999, the Vatican has now acknowledged the validity of the Jewish Covenant with God.

30. Geza Vermes, *The Complete Dead Sea Scrolls in English – 1QS, 4QS265.* Allen Lane, 1997.

31. Lawrence H. Schiffman, 'The Judean Scrolls and the History of Judaism', The Dead Sea Scrolls – Fifty Years After Their Discovery. International Congress, Jerusalem, 20–25 July 1997.

32. Anthony Tyrrell Hanson, *Jesus Christ in the Old Testament.* SPCK, 1965.

33. This injunction might well be evidence that Tutankhamun was a Prince of the Royal line, but not the blood brother of Akhenaten.

34. Elsewhere animal sacrifice has continued, and still takes place in certain parts of the world amongst particular religious communities. The Incas are even known to have practised child sacrifice up until 500 years ago. A small following of Samaritans still gather at Passover on Mount Gerizim, in Israel, to sacrifice a lamb and keep a midnight vigil. Certain Kali denominated Hindu Temples in, for example, Nepal and Madras still conduct ritual killings, for a monetary offering, of chickens and goats, which are thus made holy and then taken home by individual local congregants to be eaten.

35. N. de G. Davies, *The Rock Tombs of El Amarna – Part II*. The Egypt Exploration Fund, 1905.
36. Florentino Garcia Martinez, *The Dead Sea Scrolls Translated*. E.J. Brill, 1994.
37. Words in [ ] indicates partially preserved text. Words in ( ) are interpolations.
38. George J. Brooke, Exegesis at Qumran – 4QFlorilegium in its Jewish Context, *Journal for the Study of the Old Testament*, Supplement Series 29, 1985.

CHAPTER 17 Physical, Material and Technological Links Between Qumran and Akhetaten

1. Ian Shaw and Paul Nicholson, *British Museum Dictionary of Ancient Egypt*. BCA/British Museum Press, 1995.
2. G.R. Driver, *The Hebrew Scrolls from the Neighbourhood of Jericho and the Dead Sea*. Oxford University Press, 1951.
3. Eugene Ulrich and Frank Moore Cross, *Discoveries in the Judaean Desert, Vol. VII – Qumran Cave 4*. Clarendon Press, 1994.
4. Joseph A Fitzmyer, *Responses to 101 Questions on the Dead Sea Scrolls*. Paulist Press, 1992.
5. Alfred Lucas, *Ancient Egyptian Materials and Industries*. Edward Arnold, 1948; George Posener, Sur l'Emploi de l'Encre Rouge dans les Manuscrits Egyptiens, *Journal of Egyptian Archaeology* 37, 1951.
6. Yoram Nir-El and Magen Broshi of the Soreq Nuclear Research Centre/Israel Museum, Jerusalem, 'The Study of Ink Used at Qumran', The Dead Sea Scrolls – Fifty Years After Their Discovery, International Congress, Jerusalem, 20–25 July, 1997.
7. D. Barthélemy and J.T. Milik, *Discoveries in the Judaean Desert, Vol. I*. Clarendon Press, 1955.
8. *Ibid*.
9. Barry Kemp, Amarna's Textile Industry, *Egyptian Archaeology*, No. 11, Egypt Exploration Society, 1997; Rosalind Hill, *Egyptian Textiles*. Shire Egyptology, 1990.
10. Ronny Reich, 'The Miqwa'ot (Immersion Baths) of Qumran', The Dead Sea Scrolls – Fifty Years After Their Discovery, International Congress, Jerusalem, 20–25 July, 1997.
11. N. de. G. Davies, *The Rock Tombs of El Amarna – Part II*. Egypt Exploration Fund, 1905.
12. E.A. Wallis Budge, *The Mummy*. Outlet Book Co Inc, 1989.

CHAPTER 18 Egypt, Israel and Beyond – The Overlaying Commonalities

1. Today Egypt is mainly Muslim, with small minorities of most types of Christians – especially Coptic. Israel's population is 90 per cent Jewish, with Muslim and Christian minorities. The area once occupied by Assyria is now predominantly Muslim, with Christians and a small number of Jews.
2. E.A. Wallis Budge, *Egyptian Religion*. Gramercy Books, 1995.
3. H. Brugsch, 'Religion und Mythologie', *Thesaurus Inscriptionum Aegyptiacarum*. Leipzig, 1883.
4. Robert Eisenman and Michael Wise, *The Dead Sea Scrolls Uncovered*. Penguin Books, 1993.
5. Theodor H. Gaster, *The Dead Sea Scriptures*. Doubleday, 1976.

6. Irving M. Zeitlin, *Ancient Judaism*. Polity Press, 1991.

7. Siegfried Morenz, *Egyptian Religion*. Cornell University Press, 1994.

8. Wallis Budge, *op. cit.*

9. Brugsch, *op. cit.*

10. John Romer, *Romer's Egypt*. BBC Television Series, 1982. Accompanied by the book, *Romer's Egypt* (Michael Joseph Rainbird, 1982), also by John Romer.

11. From the *Authorized English Bible* of the Church of England, 1870.

12. Egyptian hieroglyphs *c.*1330 BCE. Translated by Professor J.H. Breasted, *Ancient Records of Egypt, Vol. II*. Russell & Russell, 1906.

13. A.Z. Idelsohn, *Jewish Music*. Henry Holt & Co, 1929.

14. *Ibid.*

15. Professor Brooke points out that Psalm 89 is 'probably even datable to the tenth century B.C.' George J. Brooke, Exegesis at Qumran – 4QFlorilegium in its Jewish Context, *Journal for the Study of the Old Testament*, Supplement Series 29, 1985.

16. Alfred Sendrey, *Music in Ancient Israel*. Philosophical Library, New York, 1969.

17. Idelsohn, *op. cit.*

18. Sendrey, *op. cit.*

19. James A. Sanders, The Psalms Scroll of Qumran Cave 11 (11QPsª), *Discoveries in the Judaean Desert, Vol. IV*. Clarendon Press, 1965; James A. Sanders, *The Dead Sea Psalms Scroll*. Cornell University Press, 1967.

   Although the Psalm Scroll is incomplete, it contains 41 psalms of the Biblical canon and eight psalms which are not in the Bible, of which five are known from other Greek and Syriac sources, and three are entirely new. One example of these evocative and beautiful works is the 'Hymn to the Creator' (letters in [ ] are reconstructions):

   > The Lord is great and holy, the Most Holy for generation after generation.
   >
   > Majesty goes before Him, and after Him abundance of many waters.
   >
   > Loving-kindness and truth are about His face; truth and judgement and righteousness are the pedestal of His throne.
   >
   > He divides light from obscurity; He establishes the dawn by the knowledge of His heart.
   >
   > When all His angels saw it, they sang, for He showed them that which they had not known.
   >
   > He crowns the mountains with fruit, with good food for all the living.
   >
   > Blessed be the Master of the earth with His power, who establishes the world by His wisdom.
   >
   > By His understanding He stretched out the heaven, and brought forth [wind] from His st[ores].
   >
   > He made [lightenings for the rai]n, and raised mist from the end [of the earth].

   See also Geza Vermes, *The Complete Dead Sea Scrolls in English*. The Penguin Press, 1997.

20. James B. Pritchard, *Ancient Near Eastern Texts Relating to the Old Testament*. Princeton University Press, 1955.

21. Morenz, *op. cit.*

22. R.N. Whybray, *The Succession Narrative: A Study of II Samuel 9–20 and I Kings 1 and 2*. SCM Press, 1968.

23. F. Griffith, *Stories of the High Priests of Memphis*. Oxford, 1900.

24. Gressmann, *Vom Reichen Mann und Armen Lazarus*. Abhandlungen der (Kgl.) Preussischen Akademie der Wissenschaften zu Leipzig, 1918.

25. O. Weinreich, *Neue Urkunden zur Sarapis-Religion*. Tübingen, 1919.

26. H. Puech, *Revue de l'Histoire des Religions*, 147, 1955.

27. Siegfried Morenz, Amenemope, *Zeitschrift für Ägyptische Sprache und Altertumskunde*, Leipzig, 1953.

28. R.O. Faulkner, *The Ancient Egyptian Book of the Dead*. British Museum Press, 1985.

29. Philippe Derchain, *Chronique d'Egypte*, 30, 1955.

30. Morenz, *Egyptian Religion, op. cit.*

31. W. Baumgartner, *A. Bertholet*. University of Tübingen, 1950.

32. Morenz, *Egyptian Religion, op. cit.*

33. S. Herrmann, II Samuel vii; I Kings iii, *Wissenschaftliche Zeitschrift der Universitat Leipzig*, 1953–4.

34. P. Humbert, *Recherches sur les Sources Egyptiennes de la Litterature Sapientale d'Israel*. 1929.

35. G. Rawlinson, *Histories of Herodotus, II*. London, 1858. Compare Ecclesiastes 8:15:

> to eat, and to drink, and to be merry: for that shall abide with him of his labour the days of his life, which God giveth him under the sun.

Coincidentally many of the wisdom sayings of Solomon in Ecclesiastes are interspersed with the phrase 'under the sun' – quite out of context.

Both Isaiah and St Paul (in I Corinthians 15:32) pick up the concept: 'Let us eat and drink, for tomorrow we die.' See also Isaiah 22:13.

36. Deuteronomy 4:2 – 'Ye shall not add unto the word which I command you, neither shall you diminish ought from it that ye may keep the commandments of the Lord your God which I command you.' Revelation 22:18–19 – 'For I testify unto every man that heareth the words of the prophecy of this book, if any man shall add unto these things, God shall add unto him the plagues that are written in this book: and if any man shall take away from the words of the book of this prophecy, God shall take away his part out of the book of life, and out of the holy city, and from the things that are written in this book.'

37. Morenz, *Egyptian Religion, op. cit.*

38. Miriam Lichtheim, *Ancient Egyptian Literature. Vol. III*. University of California Press, 1980.

CHAPTER 19 Final Clues from the Copper Scroll – Elephantine Island and the Falashas of Ethiopia

1. Martin Gilbert, *Atlas of Jewish History*. J.M. Dent Ltd, 1993.

2. Incidentally, Caesarea has slipped to the north of the Taurus mountains, whereas it should be on the coast of Israel between Tel-Aviv and Haifa!

3. John Rogerson, *Atlas of the Bible*. Andromeda Oxford Ltd, 1985.

4. Bezalel Porten, *Archives from Elephantine*. University of California Press, 1968. Porten, at one time Associate Professor of Hebrew and Bible at the University of California, puts forward the suggestion that the 'Elephantine Colony' originated from Jewish mercenaries brought in to defend Egypt's southern borders around 650 BCE. He has to admit, however, that this proposal has many difficulties, as indicated in the text.

5. G.W. Anderson, *The History and Religion of Israel*. Oxford University Press, 1966.

6. Reuven Yaron, *Introduction to the Law of the Aramaic Papyri*. Clarendon Press, 1961.

7. Astarte was originally the Babylonian goddess Anathbethal, who was adopted into the Egyptian pantheon as the daughter of the god Ra around the time of Pharaoh Amenhotep II. She was the protector of horses and chariots, and became a particular favourite of Ramses II.

8. Yaron, *op. cit.*

9. T. Eric Peet, *Egypt and the Old Testament*. The University Press of Liverpool, 1922.

10. A. Vincent, *La Religion des Judeo-Arameens d'Elephantine*. Paris, 1937.

11. A.E. Cowley, *Aramaic Papyri of the Fifth Century B.C.* Oxford, 1923.

12. 'Elephantine', *Encyclopaedia Judaica*. Keter Publishing House, Jerusalem, 1992. See also Peet, *op cit*.

13. Porten, *op. cit.*

14. *Ibid*. Porten indicates the relative position of the Temple to various adjacent houses. If the Temple was aligned north-west–south-east, the house of Jezaniah ben Uriah and Mibtahiah would be north-west of the Temple, as is indicated in the Aramaic papyri.

15. Michael Chyutin, The New Jerusalem Scroll from Qumran – A Comprehensive Reconstruction, *Journal for the Study of the Pseudepigrapha*, Supplement 25. Sheffield Academic Press, 1997.

16. Despite a modern misconception that Jews are prone to exact punitive interest on money owed to them – a misconception perpetuated by Shylock's antics in *The Merchant of Venice* – the fallacy of this prejudice was brought home to me when I was in the process of buying a property. The Exchange Contract came back from the vendor's solicitors with the usual clause on interest payable should I fail to Complete, struck out. I asked my solicitors, if the vendor had made a mistake, as the exclusion was clearly to the buyer's advantage. They came back with the answer that the vendor was an Orthodox Jew and was not allowed to charge interest on outstanding monies. Jewish law, like Islamic law, does not allow the charging of interest.

17. Yaron, *op. cit.*

18. Porten, *op. cit.*

19. Cowley, *op. cit.*

20. The quotation is from the *New English Bible*. The land of Cush commenced at ancient Syene, in the region of Yeb (Elephantine Island), and extended south into Nubia, modern Ethiopia.

21. Porten, *op. cit.*

22. J.A. Knudtzon, *Deir El-Amarna – Tafeln*. Leipzig, 1915.

23. E.C.B. Maclaurin, Date of the Foundation of the Jewish Colony at Elephantine, *Journal of Near Eastern Studies* Vol. 27, 1968.

24. Amenhotep II's military successes expanded the Egyptian Empire as never before, penetrating south into the Sudan, further than any previous pharaoh, to beyond the barriers of the Southern Cataracts.

25. The area of Lake Tana has changed little in over 2,000 years and one can visualize the scene that must have confronted the weary travellers from Egypt.

    The sound of the Blue Nile Falls, where the waters from Lake Tana pour down, fills the humid air with a deafening roar, like a thousand lions of Judah, and native Amhara tribesman still paddle their flimsy papyrus-reed canoes across the Lake, as they have done for the past millennia.

To the north of the Lake lies the turreted fortress of Castle Gondar, with the immense blue beauty of Lake Tana at its feet. The island would have reminded the refugees of Elephantine, and provided added security from marauders, and a sanctuary – a place where they could carry on their divinely inspired belief in one God and worship him in a cleansed state, washed by the pure, crystal-clear waters of the Lake.

26. Gilbert, *op. cit.* See also 'Elephantine', *Encylopaedia Judaica, op. cit.*

27. Christopher Clapham, The Falasha Fallacy, *The Times Literary Supplement*, 10 September 1993.

28. North American Conference on Ethiopian Jewry, 1996.

29. Graham Hancock, *The Sign and the Seal.* Mandarin, 1993.

30. David Kessler, *The Falashas – A Short History of the Ethiopian Jews.* Frank Cass, 1996.

31. Lionel Bender, *The Non-semitic Languages of Ethiopia.* African Studies Center, Michigan State University, 1976.

32. Wolf Leslau, *Falasha Anthology.* Yale University Press, 1951.

33. Shoshana Ben-Dor, The Religious Background of Beta Israel, *Saga of Aliyah.* Jerusalem, 1993.

34. Roland de Vaux, *Archaeology and the Dead Sea Scrolls.* Oxford University Press, 1959.

35. Joyce Tyldesley, *Nefertiti – Egypt's Sun Queen.* Viking, 1998.

36. de Vaux, *op. cit.*

37. Yemenite Jews on the other side of the Red Sea did celebrate Purim and Chanukah. The Falashas also did not appear to celebrate the Festival of Succot (Tabernacles).

38. This is a somewhat weak excuse, as modern techniques make it relatively simple to detect whether blood carries the HIV virus, and all blood destined for use in transfusions is routinely screened for HIV and other contaminants anyway.

39. Steve Jones, *In the Blood – God, Genes and Destiny.* HarperCollins, 1996.

40. Georges-Pierre Seurat was a 19th century (1859–1891) French artist who developed a style by using a series of dots to create the impression of an image in his painting, which became known as 'pointillism'.

41. Kathleen M. Kenyon (revised by P.R.S. Moorey), *The Bible and Recent Archaeology.* British Museum Publications, 1987.

42. Thomas L. Thompson, *The Bible in History: How Writers Create a Past.* Cape, 1999.

43. N. de. G. Davies, *The Rock Tombs of El Amarna – Part V.* The Egypt Exploration Fund, 1908.

GLOSSARY

Akkadian – A Semitic language originating in the Tigris–Euphrates region in the 3rd millennium BCE. In use at the time of Akhenaten in Egypt, and as the diplomatic language of the Levant, until superseded by *Aramaic*.

Apocrypha – Sacred 'hidden' (from the Greek 'apokryphos') Jewish texts, written during the 2nd Temple period and up to 135 CE, which are additional to the 39 books accepted as part of the Hebrew Old Testament. They are known from the Greek Septuagint version of the Old Testament and were accepted as canon texts by the Catholic Church, but excluded from the canon of the Protestant Churches at the time of the Reformation. They include the Books of Judith, Tobit, the Wisdom of Solomon and Ecclesiasticus – not to be confused with Ecclesiastes, which is part of the Catholic, Protestant and Hebrew Bibles. In the Rabbinic period of the Middle Ages, rabbis tried to suppress Ecclesiastes as it counsels behaviour on the basis that human life is pre-ordained and that oppression and injustice have to be accepted. They nevertheless felt obliged to accept it as part of the holy canon because of its attribution to 'Kohelet, son of David', although modern scholars now think it is probably a 3rd-century BCE text. Other Biblical-related Jewish texts, rejected by the Catholic and Protestant Churches, are called *Pseudepigrapha*.

Aramaic – A Semitic language dating back to 900 BCE. The *lingua franca* of the Persian Empire and used extensively by the Jews after they returned from the Babylonian exile. The cursive script replaced ancient paleo-Hebrew for both secular writings and holy scriptures.

Assyrians – Semitic tribes of ancient west Asia that dominated the Middle East in the 8th century BCE and into the late 7th century. They conquered the Northern Kingdom of Israel around 722 BCE and laid siege to Jerusalem, in the Southern Kingdom, in 701 BCE.

Babylonians – see *Mesopotamia*.

BCE – 'Before the Common Era', taking year 'zero' as the date of Jesus' birth.

Books of the Dead – Egyptian funereal 'incantation' texts, dating back to 2700 BCE found on pyramid and coffin texts, first consolidated as some 200 chapters at the beginning of the New Kingdom period, *c.*1540 BCE. The chapters' spells, hymns, litanies and magical formulae describe rituals and procedures for the dead body in its state of afterlife, and include a description of the last judgement of the deceased. In this procedure, the heart of the deceased is weighed against 'maat' or truth and cosmic order, symbolized by a feather. Judgement on a person's moral behaviour, to decide whether they could enter the land of the dead, was delivered by 42 judges and the god of the underworld, Osiris. Texts were written in Egyptian hieroglyphic, hieratic, or demotic script on papyri, or extracts inscribed on amulets and incorporated into the coffin with the mummified body. One of the best known examples is the *Book of the Dead* prepared for Ani, a royal scribe, dating from the Theban period of 1420 BCE. The 24m-long papyrus is housed in the British Museum, London.

Breasted, James Henry – Born in 1865 at Rockford, Illinois, Breasted studied at Yale, where he first met W.R. Harper, the founder of Chicago University, who promised he would award the first 'Chair of Egyptian' to Breasted. Breasted continued his studies in Germany, where he mastered a number of oriental languages and became interested in archaeology. He spent many years in Egypt and Nubia concentrating his efforts on documenting all known Egyptian inscriptions. In 1919 J.D. Rockefeller Jr. was motivated by Breasted to endow the Oriental Institute of Chicago and they became close friends, with Rockefeller referring to him as 'one of the prophets'. As the 'father' of American Egyptology, Breasted's best known works are his volumes of *Ancient Records of Egypt*, and *The Dawn of Conscience*.

Calendars

Jewish

The Jewish calendar, which is essentially lunar-based, dates the creation of the world as year 'zero', and as being, for example, year 5757 between the autumns of 1996 and 1997.

Prior to about 360 CE, the beginning of the Jewish month was marked by the first visual sighting of the new moon. With the threatened demise of the Sanhedrin (the ruling Jewish religious authority in Palestine) and the need to co-ordinate timings with communities dispersed after the destruction of the Second Temple in Jerusalem, Hillel the Younger introduced a calculated calendar. This Rabbinic Calendar was modified up to about 850 CE, and from then on has remained essentially the same as that used by Jews all over the world today.

Calculations to predict the date of a particular festival or event are extremely complicated and are mainly based on lunar (and partly on solar) movements. The Jewish year comprises 12 lunar months, normally of alternating lengths of 29 or 30 days, but to keep in line with solar-dominated agricultural festivals, the lunar year of 354 days is augmented by adding a full month seven times in a 19-year cycle.

Qumran-Essenes

A purely solar-based calendar, relying exclusively on the sun's movement, giving them a year that contained 364 days. This was divided into 12 periods of 30 days (approximating to months) and one of four extra days was added at the end of each three-monthly period.

Ancient Egyptian

Their year was based on the co-incidence of the helical rising of the Sirius star with the rising of the sun, and made up of 12 periods of 30 days (approximating to months) with five intercalary days added at the end of each year.

Muslim

The Muslim calendar is purely lunar, each month closely following the moon's movements, and as a result it cycles through all four seasons during a period of 33 years.

Christian

Hellenic astronomers of the Ptolemaic Egyptian period, *c.*250 BCE, added the missing ¼ day to the Egyptian calendar (a true year is 365 days, 5 hours, 48 minutes and 46 seconds) by adding an extra (leap) day every four years. This approach was eventually adopted by the Romans, under Julius Caesar, in 46 BCE. The only modification to the 'Roman', or 'Julian Calendar' was made in 1582 CE, by Pope Gregory. His astronomical advisors suggested dropping the leap year whenever the year ended in two zeros – giving us the 'Gregorian Calendar', which is in use throughout the world today.

Carbon Dating – The use of heavy Carbon 14 isotopes for dating materials containing carbon by radioactive decay measurement. The half-life of Carbon 14 is about 5,730 years.

There is a strange coincidence relating to carbon dating, the Jewish Calendar, and life-form creation. The two most momentous dates in the modern history of the State of Israel and the Jewish people almost certainly occurred in 1947 and 1967. The first year had its own 'miracle' related to the finding of the Dead Sea Scrolls. The second, a remarkable coincidence relating to carbon, one of the most useful tools for historical dating and the building block of all organic life – the date Jerusalem was finally unified within the Jewish State after the Six Day War, 29 June 1967, was exactly 5,728 years after the base date from which the Jewish calendar is deemed to have started. It is a lapsed time period also virtually identical to the length of the radioactive half-life of Carbon 14 used in carbon dating!

Scientific creation assigns the beginnings of life to about 3.7 billion years ago, but multicellular life-forms, the real beginning of creatures, burst forth in a very strange event known as the 'Cambrian Explosion' (between the Precambrian and Paleozoic eras) when the first living organisms with hard parts made their sudden prolific appearance on earth. The riddle of this 'explosion' has not yet been resolved and even Charles Darwin had to concede that the event undermined his entire theory of evolution. There was, and still is, no sensible explanation of why multi-cellular lifeforms took so long to appear, nor why these complex creatures have not been

heralded in the Precambrian era by fossil finds that can demonstrate a gradual evolutionary development of their antecedents.

One of the great authorities on early life-forms, Roderick Impey Murchison, described the Cambrian Explosion as: 'God's moment of Creation'. The 'hard' evidence for this explosion of life came from a remarkable find of soft-bodied animals in the Burgess Shale of British Columbia, which revealed an inexplicably enormous range of new arthropod and other lifeform groups, considered to exceed in anatomical range the entire spectrum of invertebrate life in the world's oceans (Stephen Jay Gould, *Wonderful Life – The Burgess Shale and the Nature of History.* Penguin Books, 1991). Here a weird coincidence occurs.

The date of this find, by the famous American paleontologist, Charles Doolittle Walcott, was July 1909, or 5670 in the Biblical calendar. The date of the 'Cambrian Explosion' of lifeforms – 'God's moment of Creation' – is estimated to have been 567,000,000 million years ago, ± 5 per cent. It looks rather like the Bible got its dating right and assumed everyone would obviously know that five extra noughts were always intended to be there!

One of Albert Einstein's favourite expressions was 'Gott wurfelt nicht' – 'God does not play dice'. A strong determinist, he could not easily come to terms with the uncertainties and probabilities of quantum mechanics. However, experimental practice has subsequently verified Quantum Theory. God does indeed appear to play with numbers!

CE – 'Common Era', after the birth of Jesus.

Circumcision – For Jews the ritual circumcision ceremony takes place when a male child is eight days old, or for proselytes at a later age. The practice of circumcision has also been adopted by the Muslims, who follow many of the teachings of Moses (Quran, Surahs 2, 20, 26, 28, etc.) and acknowledge Ishmael (the elder son of Abraham, whose circumcision was taken as a sign of a covenant with God), as the founder of the Arab nations.

Contemporary Movements – Many previously insular modern-day religious institutions are now beginning to look outside their own barricades and are trying to break down the barriers that separate them from other religions. One of the most remarkable of these attempts is currently being pursued by the Catholic Church under the direction of Pope John Paul II. It is the avowed hope of His Holiness to celebrate prayers with representatives of all religions on Mount Sinai at the new Millennium on 1 January 2000 CE.

There are many organizations working for the elimination of prejudice and for increased understanding between religions, including the World Congress of Faiths, the Calamus Foundation and the Maimonides Foundation.

Dead Sea Scrolls – A collection of scrolls and fragments discovered in the caves above Qumran, on the shore of the Dead Sea, generally ascribed to belong to a Community of Essenes who lived there between *c.*250 BCE and 68 CE. (The term is sometimes used to include any ancient scrolls found along the shores of the Dead Sea). The first scroll material was discovered in the Spring of 1947 by Bedouin and, subsequently, up to 1956, ten other caves yielded further examples. The Scrolls include items from every book of the Old Testament, except Esther, *apocryphal* and *pseudepigraphic* material, and other works written, copied or collected by the Qumran-Essenes. To date only some 50 per cent of the material has been translated and published, although this does include all of the major works.

DNA – Each human cell has 46 chromosomes grouped in 23 pairs (except ova and sperm which only have 23 chromosomes). Aligned in single file along each chromosome are thousands of genes. Genes are short strands of DNA. DNA (deoxyribonucleic acid) is a molecule which carries coded heredity details. It is found in the nucleus of almost every cell of all living organisms, except some viruses. It consists of two double helix chains with instructions for the body on how to make the structural proteins or enzymes which control the body's biochemistry – including the production of new copies of DNA.

Essenes – A religious group, centred at Qumran, Judaea, by the Dead Sea at the time of the Second Temple. They practised an abstemious lifestyle with their own versions of ritual washing, *calendar*, religious outlook and philosophy. Those who did not wander the country evangelizing devoted themselves to prayer and writing, including many works now considered as part of the *Dead Sea Scrolls*.

Freud, Sigmund – As well as being the father of psychoanalysis, Freud had an abiding interest in studying ancient religions and archaeology, particularly that of Egypt. In 1931 he wrote a study on the origins of Moses entitled *Moses and Monotheism*, which attracted considerable criticism and reprobation, largely because he portrayed a first Moses as having been murdered by the Hebrews and the arrival of a second Moses. The work was heavily influenced by his own 'angst' in dealing with his Jewish parentage and feelings of guilt over his own non-conformity.

In 1938 the Freuds fled from Vienna to London to avoid the impending Nazi invasion and settled at No.20 Maresfield Gardens, in Hampstead. His passion for collecting ancient artefacts can be seen in the family house, which is open to the public, and still contains many of the personal possessions he lived and worked amongst.

Hellenism – Greek influences in language, literature, philosophy, art and design which spread across the Middle East after the conquests of Alexander the Great in the 4th century BCE.

Hyksos – Semitic invaders from the east who dominated most of Egypt from about 1640 to 1538 BCE. They made their capital at Avaris in the Delta region of the Nile, and worshipped Seth, Anat and Astarte.

Josephus, **Flavius (37–100 CE)** – Jewish historian who became a Roman citizen and wrote, *inter alia*, about the **Essene** community and their settlement on the Dead Sea.

Judaea – Southern region of ancient Israel, including the area of Qumran and surrounding desert region.

Kabbalah – Based on revelations by Shimon bar Yohai, dating from the time of Christ, Kabbalah was codified in the Zohar in the 13th century CE, in Spain. It claims to give the true meaning behind the **Torah** in two forms – one basic and the other secret. Its teaching was prohibited until the 16th century, but parts of its doctrine – of mystical piety and concentration on the presence of God – were absorbed into Hasidism (a branch of Orthodox Jewry) around the 18th century.

Part of the Kabbalah philosophy is that:
- the Torah contains a secret code and that the Zohar can unlock the code
- Judaic astrology can throw light on the meaning of the universe
- meditation can enhance praying, human potential, and elevate consciousness
- the Messiah will come through study of Kabbalah.

There are some similarities in its teachings with Buddhism, Confucianism and Indian religious ideas of inner awareness, and in the ten levels of attainment before one-ness with God can be achieved. There are also overtones of Egyptian mythology in the visible and invisible aspects of God, the judgement of the soul after death and allocation to paradise or hell, or transmigration into animal or other human form where restitution may be sought.

Akhenaten shunned magic and mysticism and it was also strongly resisted in ancient Judaism. Mysticism, magic, divination and sorcery were and are severely frowned on in Rabbinic teaching. Nevertheless, after the Exodus, residual beliefs lingered on in superstition and folklore and eventually found expression in the form of 'Kabbalah' – which can be traced back as far as ancient Egypt.

Maccabees – Jewish priestly family whose head was the High Priest, Mattathias, whose son Judah led a successful revolt against the Greek Seleucids under Antiochus Epiphanes in 167 BCE and re-occupied Jerusalem in 164 BCE. His re-dedication of the Second Temple at Jerusalem is now remembered by celebration of the Festival of Chanukah.

Manetho – 3rd century BCE Egyptian priest from Sebennytus, in the Delta region of the Nile, who wrote a history of Egypt, probably at the behest of Ptolemy II – Philadelphus. His works listed the kings of Egypt and gave two versions of the Exodus from Egypt.

Mesopotamia, Sumeria and Babylonia – Sumeria was composed of city states which emerged about 3400 BCE, in the region of the Tigris and Euphrates rivers, modern Iraq, generally referred to as early Mesopotamia. Babylonia was a kingdom in the southern portion of Mesopotamia formed under Hammurabi around 1790 BCE. Its capital, Babylon, was about 80km to the south of today's city of Baghdad.

Biblical references to these areas, are few and sparse in detail. Abraham sends his servant (probably Eliezer) back to Nahor to find a wife for his son Isaac, but there is little description of the place or its inhabitants. Nineveh is mentioned in the Book of Jonah, as 'an exceeding great city' he is called to try and redeem from its evil ways. Nineveh also features in the Book of Nahum, where it is similarly berated by the Prophet Nahum for its evilness, as he describes its destruction. Apart from these relatively uninformative passages, there is little else.

References to Babylon, where the Jews were carried off to in 597 BCE, are similarly few and far between, and geographic descriptions are vague and generalized.

The City of Ur, located in Mesopotamia, was overwhelmed by a flood in about 4200 BCE, but re-established its importance to become the capital of Sumeria c.3000 BCE. The Temple of Uruk testifies to the wealth and advanced construction techniques, building and craftsmanship of the people at this period. One of Ur's main trading partners was Dilmun, modern Bahrain. Ur was sacked in 2000 BCE, but soon recovered its regional trading position, only to start going into decline around 1800 BCE as Babylon to the north took over the lucrative trade with Persia. By the 14th century BCE Ur was somewhat restored to its former glory.

As part of the region's cultural development numerous mythological stories emerged – one of the best known being that of the King of Uruk, Gilgamesh. In this epic, Gilgamesh sets out on a quest for eternal life – and encounters a Sumerian 'Noah'. Conventional exegesis of the early Old Testament stories relate creation, Noah and the Flood, and the lives of the Patriarchs, to episodes from Babylonian and Assyrian (the Northern portion of modern Iraq) records. This 'tracing' only holds true for limited parts of the early Bible, and soon becomes problematic as the major influence that takes over is Egyptian.

In the Babylonian 'Epic of Atrahasis', written c.1635 BCE, there are a number of clear examples of early 'borrowings'. It tells the story of numerous gods busy digging canals and tilling the land, but they find the work too hard. They complain to the senior god 'Enlil' who decides to kill the strike leader and create man from a mixture of that first unfortunate trade union leader's flesh and blood, and clay.

And God created man in His own image, in the image of God created He him; male and female created He them. (Genesis 1:27)

Then the Lord God formed man of the dust of the ground, and breathed into his nostrils the breath of life; and man became a living soul. (Genesis 2:7)

(The Hebrew word for formed – 'yatzar' has the same sense of a potter moulding clay into a vessel. In the written verse it is recorded with an extra letter (*yod*) for the forming of man but only one *yod* for the forming of animals. One rabbinical interpretation of this is that man alone is endowed with two moral inclinations – one good and one evil. A theme picked up in Buddhism and Taoism.)

Back to 'Atrahasis', where man multiplies and his noise disturbs the gods, who decide to inflict plagues, famines and droughts on man, and finally decide to destroy him altogether by sending a great flood. 'Enki', the creator god, warns his favourite man Atrahasis of the plot to destroy mankind. Atrahasis builds a huge boat to escape the flood and save his family and animals. After the flood he offers sacrifices to the gods who readily accept the offerings. Parallels in the Old Testament can readily be discerned.

And God said unto Noah: 'The end of all flesh is come before Me; for the earth is filled with violence through them; and, behold, I will destroy them with the earth. Make thee an ark of gopher wood; with rooms shalt thou make the ark, and shalt pitch it within and without with pitch. And this is how thou shalt make it; the length of the ark three hundred cubits, the breadth of it fifty cubits, and the height of it thirty cubits.' (Genesis 6:13–15)

And the flood was forty days upon the earth; and the waters increased, and bore up the ark, and it was lifted up above the earth. (Genesis 7:17)

Other Sumerian legends record that as the flood subsided, on the seventh day after the ark came to rest on a mountain (thought to be the Mount Ararat of the Bible) Utnapishtim (the Noah of this version) sent out a dove and a swallow. They both returned to the ark, implying that they had not been able to yet find dry land. Later on he sent out a crow, which did not return. Utnapishtim celebrated his survival by making a sacrifice on the mountain to Enlil, who rewarded him and his family with transportation to a promised land and immortality.

And the waters decreased continually until the tenth month; in the tenth month, on the first day of the month, were the tops of the mountains seen…And he sent forth a raven, and it went forth to and fro, until the waters were dried up from off the earth…And he stayed yet other seven days; and again he sent forth the dove out of the ark. And the dove came into him at eventide; and lo in her mouth an olive-leaf freshly plucked; so that Noah knew that the waters were abated from off the earth.

And Noah builded an altar unto the Lord; and took of every clean beast, and of every clean fowl, and offered burnt-offerings on the altar.

And God blessed Noah and his sons, and said unto them: 'Be fruitful and multiply, and replenish the earth.' (Genesis 8:5, 7, 10–11, 20; 9:1)

All the elements of the flood story in the Old Testament story are here in the Sumerian legends of Mesopotamia. This story of the flood is retold in the 7th century BCE Epic of Gilgamesh, which records much earlier legend. The Epic also has many allusions recognizable in the Biblical story of the Garden of Eden.

This time it is the story of Gilgamesh and his faithful companion, Enkidu. During their adventures they unfortunately fall foul of the goddess Ishtar, who causes Enkidu to die of a plague. Stricken with grief, Gilgamesh sets out to find the secret of immortality. He encounters Utnapishtim who, we have heard from other Sumerian legends, has gained immortality from the god Enlil. Utnapishtim warns Gilgamesh that it is man's providence to eventually die, but Utnapishtim's wife persuades him to reveal the secret of life. Gilgamesh is told of a magical fruit that lies at the bottom of the ocean, which can bring back his youth. He retrieves it from the ocean floor, but whilst bathing in a pool on the way home, the fruit of life is stolen from him by a snake. Gloomily our hero communes with his friend Enkidu, who now resides in the kingdom under the earth, and is told of the inevitability of death.

The story carries the same basic message as that told in the Biblical story of Adam and Eve. There is a world of difference between man and God. If man aspires to be like God he will come to grief.

And the Lord God commanded the man, saying: 'Of every tree of the garden thou mayest freely eat; but of the tree of knowledge of good and evil, thou shalt not eat of it; for in the day that thou eatest thereof thou shalt surely die.'

And the woman [Eve] said unto the serpent: 'Of the fruit of the trees of the garden we may eat; but of the fruit of the tree which is in the midst of the garden, God hath said: "Ye shall not eat of it, neither shall ye touch it, lest ye die".' And the serpent said unto the woman: 'Ye shall not surely die; for God doth know that in the day ye eat thereof, then your eyes shall be opened, and ye shall be as God, knowing good and evil.' And when the woman saw that the tree was good for food, and that it was a delight to the eyes, and that the tree was to be desired to make one wise, she took of the fruit thereof, and did eat; and she gave also unto her husband with her, and he did eat.

And the Lord God said: 'Behold, the man is become as one of us, to know good and evil; and now, lest he put forth his hand, and take also of the tree of life, and eat, and live for ever.' Therefore the Lord God sent him forth from the garden of Eden, to till the ground from whence he was taken. (Genesis 2:16–17; 3:2–6, 22–23)

There are many other creation stories, however, from ancient Babylonia recorded in the languages of Sumerian and Akkadian and from Assyria, which do not easily relate to the Old Testament. In fact, apart from these early correspondences given above, there are surprisingly few Biblical references to Babylonia, but vastly more to Egypt.

Midrash – see *Torah*.

Mishnah – see *Torah*.

Orthography – Form, style and content of words giving an indication of when and where they were composed.

Palaeography – Form, style and shape of the letters and symbols used in writing.

Papyrus – Writing media made from the papyrus plant found growing mainly in the Delta marshes of the Nile, in Egypt. Earliest examples date back to 3035 BCE.

Parchment – Animal skin, usually goat or sheep, specially prepared and used for writing. Used in Egypt from 2000 BCE and in Judaea from about 200 BCE.

Pentateuch – The first five Books of the Old Testament: Genesis, Exodus, Leviticus, Numbers and Deuteronomy.

Persians – People from the area of modern-day Iran who drove out the Babylonians from the Holy Land and conquered Egypt *c.*525 BCE under King Cyrus. They dominated the Middle East for about 200 years. They allowed the Jews exiled by the Babylonians to return to the Holy Land, and generally acted benignly towards them. The Biblical story of Esther is generally thought to have been enacted in Persia.

Philo, Judaeus (*c.*20 BCE–*c.*40 CE) – Jewish-Egyptian philosopher and Greek scholar, born in Alexandria. He worked at Alexandria on Bible commentary and law, and mentions the Qumran-Essenes in his writings.

Pliny the Elder (23–79 CE) – Gaius Plinius Secundus was born in Como, Italy, of an aristocratic Roman family. After a spell in the Roman army he later devoted himself to writing historical treatises on, for example, oration, and the history of Rome. A friend of Emperor Vespasian, he died during the volcanic eruption of Mount Vesuvius in 79 CE. He wrote about the ***Essene*** community by the Dead Sea.

Plutarch (46–120 CE) – Greek historian, philosopher and biographer whose works included 46 portraits of great characters who preceded him.

Pseudepigrapha – Jewish Biblical-related texts, not canonized by the Catholic Church, and those considered to be written under a false name or attributable to biblical characters (see ***Apocrypha***).

Ptolemies – Greek rulers of Egypt who followed the 'Greek Macedonian' period of rule by Alexander the Great, his half-brother and his son, from 332–310 BCE. The Ptolemaic period of Egypt lasted from 305 BCE until the demise of Cleopatra VII in 30 BCE.

Romans – The dominant power in the Middle East and Mediterranean area from the middle of the 1st century BCE to the 4th century CE. The Romans conquered the Holy Land *c.*44 BCE and Octavian Augustus appointed himself ruler of Egypt in 30 BCE.

Talmud – see ***Torah***

Torah – The Torah, in its narrowest sense, comprises the five Books of Moses of the Old Testament. In its wider sense it encompasses all the whole of Jewish teaching. Together with the Ten Commandments given to Moses on Mount Sinai, orthodoxy holds there also came a raft of 603 other Commandments, the basis of the Torah, and an Oral commentary explaining the rest.

The Ten Commandments traditionally given to Moses on Mount Sinai are:

1. I am the Lord your God who brought you out of the Land of Egypt, out of the house of bondage.
2. Thou shalt have no other gods beside Me. Thou shalt not make unto thee a graven image, nor any manner of likeness, of anything that is in heaven above, or that is in the earth beneath, or that is in the water under the earth. Thou shalt not bow down unto them; for I the Lord thy God am a jealous God, visiting the iniquity of the fathers upon the children unto the third

Terminology Relating to Jewish Religious Teachings

1. The Torah* Comprises the Pentateuch of Genesis, Exodus, Leviticus, Numbers and Deuteronomy (according to fundamental tradition given to Moses on Mount Sinai *c.*1200 BCE). Torah contains 613 Commandments, including the Ten Commandments.

2. Oral Laws Made up of *Mishnah* and *Gemarah* to comprise the *Talmud* (a handbook of Jewish observance).

Mishnah	**Mishnah**
(Based on Oral traditions)	(Based on Oral traditions)
Laws, Stories, Moral instruction (*Aggadah*)	Laws, Stories, Moral instruction (*Aggadah*)
(by *Tannaim* – Rabbis pre-200 CE)	(by *Tannaim* – Rabbis pre-200 CE)
+	**+**
Gemarah	**Gemarah**
Discussion of the Mishnah	Discussion of the Mishnah
(by *Amoraim* – Rabbis living from 200–500 CE)	(by *Amoraim* – Rabbis living from 200–500 CE)
Palestinian Talmud	**Babylonian Talmud**
(Written in Hebrew & Western Aramaic)	(Written in Hebrew & Eastern Aramaic)
Compiled from pre-400 CE works	Compiled from pre-500 CE works
(Earliest complete text now in Leyden, Holland, 1st printed version, Venice, 1522 CE)	(Earliest extant text, 14th century codex, now in Munich)

Posekim (codifiers)

The numerous sources of Mishnah were edited by R. Judah Ha-nasi and written down *c.*200 CE. The Palestinian and Babylonian Talmuds both use Ha-nasi's Mishnah, but different Gemarah. The work of codifiers (*Posekim*) of the law (*Hallachah*), such as Maimonides (1135–1204 CE) and Isaac Alfasi (1013–1103 CE) on the Babylonian Talmud, and Asher ben Jehiel (1250–1327 CE), were collated by the Sephardi scholar Joseph Caro (1488–1575 CE) into a work called *Shulhan Arukh*. Moses Isserles (1525–1572 CE) added to this work the views of Ashkenasi scholars, and the supplemented code has become the accepted authority for Orthodox Jewish Law. Where the supplements differ from the main text, the Sephardim Orthodox (Spanish and Portuguese traditions) follow Caro's interpretation and the Ashkenasi (German and French traditions) follow Isserles.

3. Midrash Homilies usually based on Bible texts. One 'Collection' of Midrashim was arranged in Bible order by Yalkut Shimoni in the 13th century, based on 1st–10th century homilies, interpretations and commentaries on the scriptures.

Midrash Rabbah	*Shoher Tov*	*Pesiktot*	*Other Midrash*
Commentaries on the Pentateuch and five Megillot (Song of Songs, Ruth, Lamentations, Ecclesiastes, Esther)	Commentaries on Psalms	Commentaries on Special Sabbaths and Festivals	On Ethics, Morality, Conduct and History

---

* Torah is also used in a wider sense, meaning the whole of Jewish teaching.

and fourth generation of them that hate Me; and showing mercy unto the thousandth generation of them that love Me and keep My commandments.

3. Thou shalt not take the name of thy Lord in vain; for the Lord will not hold a person guiltless that taketh His name in vain.

4. Remember the Sabbath day and keep it holy. Six days shalt thou labour, and do all thy work; but on the seventh day is a sabbath unto the Lord thy God, on it thou shalt not do any manner of work, thou, nor thy son, nor thy daughter, nor thy man-servant, nor thy maid-servant, nor thy cattle, nor the stranger that is within thy gates; for in six days the Lord made heaven and earth, the sea, and all that is in them, and rested on the seventh day; wherefore the Lord blessed the Sabbath day, and hallowed it.

5. Honour thy father and thy mother, that thy days may be long upon the Land which the Lord thy God giveth thee.

6. Thou shalt not murder.

7. Thou shalt not commit adultery.

8. Thou shalt not steal.

9. Thou shalt not bear false witness against thy neighbour.

10. Thou shalt not covet thy neighbour's house; nor his wife, nor his man-servant, nor his maid-servant, nor his ox, nor his ass, nor anything that is thy neighbour's.

Triad – A grouping of three Egyptian gods, often as father, mother and child figures comprising a divine family, who were worshipped on a localized basis. The practice arose during the New Kingdom period of the Amenhotep pharaohs. Examples were the combination of Amun, Mut and Khons at Thebes; Ptah, Sekhmet and Nefertum at Memphis; Horus, Hathor and the child Horus at Edfu; and Khnum, Satet and Anuket at Yeb (Elephantine). A triad worshipped on a national basis was that of Osiris (worshipped locally at Abydos), Isis (worshipped locally at Philae), and Horus (worshipped locally at Edfu).

Ugarit – Ancient city on the Mediterranean coast of Syria, south of the estuary of the river Orontes. Its cultural development made it a leader in language development – producing a compressed alphabet using only 27 letters, which led to the development of paleo-Hebrew.

ILLUSTRATION CREDITS

INDEX